THE FAMILY AMONG THE AUSTRALIAN ABORIGINES

THE FAMILY

AMONG THE

AUSTRALIAN ABORIGINES

A SOCIOLOGICAL STUDY

B. MALINOWSKI

Introduction by
J. A. Barnes

SCHOCKEN BOOKS · NEW YORK

First Schocken Paperback edition, 1963

1913

CONTENTS

CHAPTER I

EXPOSITION OF THE PROBLEM AND METHOD

CHAPTER II

MODES OF OBTAINING WIVES

CHAPTER III

HUSBAND AND WIFE

CHAPTER IV

SEXUAL ASPECT OF MARRIAGE

CHAPTER V

MODE OF LIVING

CHAPTER VI

DISCUSSION OF KINSHIP

CHAPTER VII

PARENTS AND CHILDREN

CHAPTER VIII

ECONOMICS

CHAPTER IX

SUMMARY AND CONCLUSIONS   pp. 292–304

INTRODUCTION

I

MALINOWSKI provoked and enjoyed controversy throughout his life and it is not surprising that even now, some
twenty years after his death, his colleagues and successors
in social anthropology should still be arguing about the
limitations and potentialities of his theoretical ideas, the
extent of the change he may have wrought in the tech-
niques of empirical field research, and his role in develop-
ing social anthropology as a specific specialism with its
own subject-matter and its own pattern of cooperation
with other disciplines. Much incisive and enlightening
comment has been written about Malinowski but to assess
these comments with confidence we have to turn to his own
writings, and to study him as he himself would have recommended, by getting as close to the sources of information as possible. The present volume, his first major work,
has long been out of print and has therefore often been
overlooked by his defenders as well as his critics.

Malinowski is mainly remembered for his books on the
Trobriand Islanders of Papua, for his theory of function-
alism, and for the brilliant group of social anthropologists
that he inspired during his long years of teaching at the
London School of Economics. *The Family Among the
Australian Aborigines* belongs to an earlier phase, before
he had travelled outside Europe, and before he had begun
the direct observation of tribal peoples in their own habi-
tat. It was written at a time when the theoretical arguments of anthropologists were still directed towards, or

against, those ideas of social evolution and universal history that enjoyed such wide-spread interest in the nineteenth century. European scholars were then interested in primitive peoples for what could be inferred about their past rather than what could be learnt about their present way of life. Furthermore the book was written when most of the information available about distant and remote peoples had been collected *en passant* by explorers, missionaries and other travellers, and not by trained ethnographers. Malinowski himself had turned to anthropology after reading Frazer's *Golden Bough*. He had already begun work on his book before he came from Poland to London in 1910. Among the dominant figures in anthropology in Britain at that time were Frazer himself, Westermarck, Seligman and Rivers, and it was under their influence that the book was completed. Yet even in this early work many of the lines of development that were to transform anthropology in Britain during the '20s and '30s can already be traced. We can see here the insistence on real behaviour rather than on the bald statement of 'customs', the interest in breaches of custom as well as in conformity to them, and a clear indication of the thesis that items of social behaviour cannot be studied in isolation but only in their total cultural context. Some of the limitations inherent in these emphases are also already discernible in this book. Thus for an understanding both of the path whereby Malinowski broke away from the outmoded preoccupations of nineteenth-century anthropology, and of the problems that later generations of anthropologists have had to face in building on Malinowski's work, we may well begin by looking at his work on the Australian aborigines.

II

During the nineteenth century many writers had put forward their views on the manner in which human societies had changed from the earliest times up to the present.

Some postulated an initial state of grace from which many groups had degenerated, while other writers argued in favour of multiple acts of creation, each at a different level of social development. In the latter half of the century the most widely held views postulated a common origin for all mankind in the remote past at a low social level, only slightly above that of the animals. From this initial condition of savagery, some branches or races of mankind had advanced faster than others, so that at the present time the various forms of contemporary social life indicated the several stages through which the more advanced peoples had already passed. There were disagreements about the order in which different kinds of marriage — promiscuity, monogamy, polygamy and group marriage—and different forms of government — anarchy, clan organization, monarchy—occurred in the sequence of social evolution, and there were other disagreements about the manner in which changes in various social institutions — marriage, government, economic organization, religion — kept in step with one another and in step with changes in physical characteristics such as skull shape, hair type, and skin colour. But most writers accepted the basic notion of a single sequence which was, by and large, applicable to all mankind. The most important, as well as the most comprehensive, nineteenth-century statement of a theory of unilineal evolution is L. H. Morgan's *Ancient Society,* first published in 1877.

At the lower end of the sequence came the Australian aborigines. They did not cultivate crops and, apart from the dingo, they had no domesticated animals. They had no permanent houses, and they appeared to have no rulers whose authority was accepted beyond the small local group. Furthermore, according to several authorities, they had neither individual marriages nor individual families but were entirely promiscuous. Groups of people living under similar cultural conditions and gaining their food by hunting wild animals and collecting wild plants were known to exist in other parts of the world. But Australia was the only area where hunting and collecting peoples were spread

over a whole continent and where they had clearly remained
for centuries in isolation from peoples with a 'higher' way
of life. The Australian aborigines were therefore the appropriate choice for the living representatives of that
world-wide primaeval culture from which, it was believed,
all other cultures had evolved.

Thus when Malinowski refers in his book to aborigines
as 'low races' and to 'low stages of cultures', we have to
interpret this in terms of nineteenth-century theories of
social and cultural evolution. The attack on these theories
had already been launched before Malinowski began his
book. Boas published his 'Limitations of the Comparative
Method' in 1896, and Westermarck published his *History
of Human Marriage* in 1891 attacking the notion of universal primaeval promiscuity. Yet in England the notion
of unilineal evolution was still an accepted part of orthodox anthropology, and formed part of the background to
those writings of Frazer through which Malinowski had
been attracted to anthropology. W. H. R. Rivers, with
whom Malinowski was also in contact, had begun to move
towards a diffusionist theory that rejected many of the
tenets of evolutionism, but which embodied the same interest in the reconstruction of the remote past. Malinowski, in his Australian book as well as in most of his later
writings, was not so much opposed to theories of social
evolution as uninterested in them. He looked at the Australian aborigines as a living people, whose life was to be
understood not in terms of the past but in the light of its
ecological setting, and of the influence of each social institution on all the others. Only in the last decade has the
tide of professional interest begun to turn again towards
evolutionary problems, due in part to the stimulus of the
centenary of the publication of Darwin's *Origin of Species*
(cf. Steward 1955).

Malinowski was not alone in shifting away from the
interests and controversies of the nineteenth century. His
book was published at a time when other writers were looking at the Australian evidence with new questions to ask,

and in retrospect it seems unfortunate that Malinowski was
unable to comment in this book on several publications
which appeared about the same time. Durkheim's *Les
formes élémentaires de la vie religieuse,* based largely on
material from the Arunta of central Australia, was published in 1912, and was reviewed critically by Malinowski
in 1913 (*Folklore* 24 : 525-531); but in his own book
Malinowski could merely comment sadly on the lack of 'any
attempt to connect the data of folk-lore and the facts of
sociology' in contemporary social science (p. 233). In his
inquiry, he restricted himself to a study of the workings
of the nuclear family and confined his discussion of aboriginal beliefs to those directly concerned with human reproduction and gestation. Presumably if he had ever written
the further study he promised on Australian kinship groups
(p. 303) he would have dealt with those wider problems
tackled by Durkheim: the possible connexions between the
ritual and ceremonial life of aborigines, their metaphysical
beliefs and their forms of social organization. But this
study, like the long announced book on Trobriand kinship,
was never to appear.

In his review, Malinowski was critical of Durkheim's
account of the origin of religion. In the same year, 1913,
Freud published his *Totem und Tabu,* making use of
Australian ethnographic data in a novel way though still
writing within an evolutionary framework. Later on,
Malinowski was to become deeply involved with Freud's
psycho-analytical theories, but the arguments were con-
ducted mainly over Malinowski's Trobriand material, and
again we are denied knowing how Malinowski's understanding of the Australian family might have been modified had Freud published his book a year or so earlier.
Durkheim and Freud were likewise unable to consult
Malinowski's book when they were writing theirs, and we
are left with the tantalizing sight of three scholars, none
of whom had seen an Australian aborigine, making independent use of the same body of ethnographic material
for different purposes; and yet these three were subse-

quently each to exert a decisive influence on the development of social anthropology.

A fourth writer who published in 1913 on aboriginal life was Radcliffe-Brown. He had visited Western Australia in 1911 and began to publish his field results in the following year, but his principal findings were not available in time for Malinowski. Radcliffe-Brown came to exercise a much more potent effect on Australian ethnography than Malinowski, and it is interesting to see even at that date the beginnings of the cleavage between Malinowski and Radcliffe-Brown that was later to assume such importance and which British social anthropology is only now growing out of. Radcliffe-Brown reviewed Malinowski's book in 1914 and after commenting that 'it is by far the best example in English of scientific method in dealing with the descriptions of the customs and institutions of a savage people' went on to argue that Malinowski's statement of the theoretical framework for the study of kinship (Chapter VI) was 'the least successful in the book. The Australian notions relating to kinship cannot be studied without reference to what the author calls "group relationships"; in other words, the relationship systems, classes and clans. As Mr. Malinowski has confined himself, quite justifiably, to a study of the individual family relationships, this part of his work remains imperfect'. Here we have the criticism, often repeated, that Malinowski could not see a descent system existing save as an 'extension' of relationships within the elementary family (cf. Fortes 1957 : 162-3). But the criticism was made by an ethnographer who had the opportunity denied Malinowski of observing the operation of real family life among aborigines in Australia, but whose interests, so far as Australia was concerned, lay precisely in those inter-group relationships that lay beyond Malinowski's immediate terms of reference. Australian ethnography owes much to Radcliffe-Brown's brilliant synthesis of the formal characteristics of its section and clan systems but it has had to wait a long while for the richness of detail on actual family life that Malinowski provided so abundantly from the Trobriand Islands (cf. Stanner 1960).

III

Bronislaw Malinowski was born in 1884 and studied physics and mathematics at the university in Cracow. He became interested in anthropology and in 1909 began work on a study of the Australian aboriginal family (Malinowski 1930 : 21 f.n.). In 1912 he published an article on the *intichiuma* ceremonies of Australia, and the present work = 1913 appeared a year later. In 1914 he went to Australia and thence to Papua, where he worked among the Mailu people. He was awarded his Doctorate of Science in the University of London for his Australian book and his report on the Mailu. He returned to Papua in 1915 to begin work in the Trobriand Islands. Although his published output was prolific, after 1913 there is very little mention of Australia in anything he wrote. One of his students, Ashley Montagu, published a lengthy analysis of aboriginal procreative beliefs to which Malinowski contributed a substantial foreword, but no one closely associated with him carried out in Australia the kind of intensive fieldwork he promoted so successfully elsewhere, particularly in Africa and the South Seas. His Australian inquiry belongs thus to a preparatory phase in his development as a social anthropologist. In one respect, it differs radically from his later work. Malinowski has been criticised for building his universally applicable model of tribal culture on one example alone, that provided by his own work in the Trobriands (cf. Lasswell 1931) and perhaps the fullness of his own field experience made some bias in this direction inevitable; it is always hard for an ethnographer to balance equitably the evidence he gathers at second hand through the writings of others against the information gained personally in the excitement and stress of field inquiry. Malinowski had no first-hand experience of Australia and had instead to sift the often conflicting evidence of a large number of writers with very varied qualifications, who had described aboriginal life as it was at different times over a period of more than a hundred years and at different places scattered over the continent. He discusses at length his procedure for assessing this evidence and gives careful attention to the way in which the theoretical interests of writers may have affected the construction they put upon the events they observed. Thus Malinowski is rightly critical of those writers who assume *ab initio* that Australian aborigines represent the lowest form of human development and therefore cannot possibly live in individual families. In his later writings Malinowski continued to emphasise the importance of separating the facts of empirical observation from the interpretation placed on the facts by the ethnographer, and, though this was not done as formally as some would wish, his writings have passed with flying colours that crucial test, the possibility of re-examination of their ethnographic content from a fresh theoretical standpoint. Malinowski is often regarded, with some justification, as unsympathetic towards historical or diachronic inquiries, and it is noteworthy that, confronted with a mass of ethnographic material, he did not treat it, as some of his evolutionary predecessors would have done, as timeless and of uniform value. Instead he turned to professional historians for guidance on the interpretation of sources (p. 18 f.n.), and endeavoured to evaluate the interests and training of the various writers, their opportunities for direct observation, the internal consistency of their writings, and the like. In fact, he tried to see his sources in the 'context of situation' in the same way as he endeavoured to locate in concrete reality the behaviour these sources describe. Indeed, perhaps the most impressive feature of his Australian book is this constant endeavour to find out what actually happens. This persuasive empirical bias has been regarded by some critics as the greatest limitation in Malinowski's work, and indeed in British social anthropology generally. But though it may be a limitation, Malinowski was surely right in insisting that there must be a solid basis of empirical observation against which theoretical formulations, however abstract, can be tested.

Durkheim had already published his *La division du travail* in 1893, and although Malinowski criticises him for some of his statements, it is probable that he owed much to Durkheim as well as to Wundt, with whom he worked in Leipzig in 1909, in his use of the concepts of collective ideas, knowledge and feelings. Malinowski's treatment of emotion and belief remains firmly based on individual psyches, and he avoids some of the pitfalls of expression that await many a reader of Durkheim. But he stresses the normative force of shared ideas, and the interconnexion of action, knowledge, belief and sentiment. Here we can see the beginnings of Malinowski's later contention that the whole of culture must be regarded as an integrated whole. Carried too far, this can easily come to mean that everything is because it must be, and that nothing in social life can alter or be altered without altering everything else. This is dangerous nonsense; but here in his Australian book we see Malinowski making the valid and pertinent point that the world of the mind cannot be studied in isolation from the world of action, and that men act in the light of their beliefs and values. Coupled with this is a stress on the importance, among aborigines just as in any other on-going community, of the education of children. There is a curious remark that the absence of parental chastisement indicates the insignificance of the education given by parents, 'for it is impossible to conceive of any serious education without coercive treatment, especially at that low stage of culture' (p. 256); this is hardly in accord with the evidence he brings forward for the strong emotional bonds established between parents and children. Here perhaps Malinowski is hampered by the limits of his inquiry. He treats initiation as a tribal matter and therefore lying beyond an inquiry into family life. Furthermore, he says very little about the relations between parents and children when the latter are adults. Had he looked beyond the domestic scene, he would surely have found that inescapable ties of kinship continually determine action in initiation and many other 'tribal' activities, and that obligations towards parents continue throughout life. Initiation may often be a traumatic experience with lasting consequences but it is inseparable from the prolonged process of socialization, the inculcation of values and the transmission of knowledge, begun in the family camp (cf. Hart 1955).

Some of the 'facts of daily life' that Malinowski sought were the ways in which aborigines secured their supply of food. With a hunting and collecting people, there is little to see at first glance; there are no permanent gardens and domesticated herds. It is indicative of Malinowski's early realization of the importance of economic and productive activities in the social life of primitive peoples that, despite the difficulties inherent in the Australian material, he attempted to discriminate between the various rights and obligations attached to tracts of land and associated with different kinds of activity (p. 152). This kind of analysis he was able to carry further and with more success in his Trobriand studies. The economic 'facts of daily life' in aboriginal Australia are the hardest of all to recapture, for since 1788 aborigines have had to compete with white Australians for the comparatively restricted economic resources of the continent; flour and tobacco, sheep and cattle have radically altered the pattern of food acquisition and consumption. Studies of land use and land tenure in agricultural societies have brought refinements of analysis that would probably have come only slowly from inquiries among Australian aborigines. Yet Malinowski's attempt to unravel the complexities of land tenure in Australia remains of methodological importance, despite Radcliffe-Brown's comment that it is 'unsatisfactory, owing to the very scanty information available' (1914 : 32). We still have no satisfactory account.

In this book Malinowski makes one of the first clear

statements that in human society kinship is not the automatic consequence of genetic connexion, but is a set of relationships that arise, at least in part, as a consequence of beliefs about the processes of human reproduction, or as the result of some overt ceremonial act whereby the relationship is validated. As with land tenure, the analysis of the basis of kinship has been carried considerably further by many writers, Malinowski himself being one of the chief contributors. His early formulation of the distinction between what we would now call physical and social kinship seems, in retrospect, more like a first draft than a polished statement. Yet we have to remember that when Malinowski wrote, many scholars were ready to argue that because aborigines were ignorant of the mechanism of human fertilization, there could be no recognition of paternity; and because women copulated with men who were not their husbands, there could be no marriage. Without previous discussions such as Malinowski's, Radcliffe-Brown's bland statement that 'In Australia, fatherhood is a purely social thing' (1930 : 42) would have fallen on deaf ears (cf. Barnes 1961).

His discussion on the limits of sexual licence is illuminating. Here we see him making the crucial observation that when ordinary rules of conduct are set aside in specified contexts, they are replaced not by unbridled licence but by what is, in effect, a new set of rules. He analyses as carefully as the evidence will allow what actually happens during those initiation ceremonies when marital fidelity is temporarily set aside, and shows that there are rules prescribing who may copulate with whom, just as there are rules governing the *pirrauru* institution; and the two sets of rules or laws are different. The subsequent development of Malinowski's approach to law, though sometimes confused in terminology, has stimulated much research into the basis of social control in tribal societies (cf. Schapera 1957), and its roots can be seen in his Australian study. Whereas other writers had interpreted wife-lending and ceremonial licence as evidence that aborigines were lawless savages, Malinowski shows that *pirrauru* relationships, like those of marriage, follow the prescriptions of the class or section system, and that at initiation ceremonies the rules of incest continue to apply. He writes of the sexual features of social life in aboriginal Australia that 'far from bearing any character of indiscriminate promiscuity on the whole, they are, on the contrary, subject to strict regulations, restrictions and rules. Every form of licence must be subject to customary rules' (p. 123). Modern studies of aboriginal life tend to stress the importance of choice and decision- making, but these are choices made in conformity with, or at least in the light of, socially recognized rules. When Malinowski was writing, it was necessary first to stress that there were rules.

While it would be wrong to look upon Malinowski's later work as the inevitable outcome of his Australian inquiry, it is clear that many of the interests and emphases which characterize his later work are already apparent in this his first book. He stresses the social significance of ideas, the force of custom even when customs appeared to be breached, and the interconnexion of all branches of social life with one another. In retrospect it may seem that he overstressed these notions; but when he was writing, these were the notions that direly needed stressing.

IV

The Family Among the Australian Aborigines bears on the problems of present-day anthropology and sociology at many points. Malinowski defines the family in terms of membership, activities and responsibilities. He makes a clear distinction between coitus and conjugal relationships, and looks carefully at the emotional attitudes of husband and wife towards one another and towards their children. Here we have the beginnings of the view of the nuclear family as a primary group embodying persons with specific roles and with specific inter-relationships. We would now make a further distinction in the husband-wife relationship between the husband's uxorial rights over his wife, in her role of wife, and his genetricial rights, those rights in her children that he acquires by marrying her. Malinowski takes a somewhat static view of the family, for indeed he is concerned with the family at only one stage in its cycle of development, and does not look into the social processes whereby every fertile family grows, scatters its members and decays. Thus, while he discusses the relationships between a man and his sister, he leaves out of account the relationship between a man and his brothers, and between a woman and her sisters. A modern analysis of family development would look at these crucial relationships for information about the way in which the sibling group, jointly dependent when young on the care and protection of its parents, later breaks up and by marriage to spouses from other families gives rise to several new families in the next generation. Rivalry between brothers may show itself in the way in which they separate when they marry; the solidarity of sisters in one generation may be perpetuated by the importance given to matrilateral links in the next. For many aboriginal groups in Australia, it is now clear that the keystone of the relationship between a man and his sisters is his ability to determine whom their daughters will marry, and that relationships between brothers are largely coloured by this common interest in their sisters' daughters. Malinowski mentions that in some tribes it is not the father's privilege to give his daughter in marriage (p. 255) but does not follow up this observation.

Malinowski discusses sexual intercourse from two points of view, firstly, as an activity usually taking place between married couples but sometimes between persons not married to each other, and secondly as an activity which we know to be necessary for conception but which is not so regarded by aborigines. Malinowski seems to assume that these two aspects are linked, in that ignorance of the procreative process implies that copulation is given less importance, and hence is less likely to be confined to married couples. His inquiry into the state of knowledge and belief among aborigines about the physiology of human reproduction has been carried much further by Ashley-Montagu (1937) but the correlation between physiological ignorance and tolerated extra-marital copulation remains doubtful. Only recently has Western scientific knowledge about the reproductive process become satisfactory, and European folk-beliefs about conception are sometimes as fanciful as those reported from aboriginal Australia. Present discussions about artificial insemination by donor show that the value of marital fidelity may·be upheld even when there is no insistence on genetic continuity between father and child. Malinowski's discussion would have been enhanced by a consideration of those societies where social continuity between father and son is stressed but where adoption is widespread. Warner, who worked in northern Australia in the 1930s, argued that the aborigines he studied knew about physiological conception, but that for them this was not nearly as important an incident in the reproduction of a child as was its spiritual conception. In answer to a direct question about semen, he was told that 'that was what made babies' (1958 : 24). Unfortunately Warner did not go on to ask, for instance, if some babies were made without semen or if others were made with semen from several different men. Recently Leach has drawn attention to some of the variations in belief from one people to another in the contributions made by the mother and by the father to the different parts of the foetus—blood, bones, flesh, physiognomy, etc. (1961 : 8-20). Malinowski is certainly right in insisting, with Durkheim, that beliefs and forms of social life are interconnected, but unfortunately his painstaking discussion of the aboriginal material on beliefs about human reproduction is seriously limited because he treats physical continuity only in terms of continuity of 'blood', a notion he does not analyse. Our use of the term 'blood relationship' for cognatic kinship, and not for the link between a blood donor and a patient, forcibly reminds us of the complexities of the beliefs underlying kinship.

Throughout his book Malinowski is concerned with the basis of authority in the family and in the tribe. He probably attributes more executive authority to the tribal council in Australia than is justified. The numerous studies of stateless societies in Africa were made long after Malinowski wrote, and hence it is not surprising that he takes at face value statements in the ethnographic literature about headmen and tribal councils operating quite independently, as it were, of the kinship system. Early writers on aborigines in Australia, and indeed on similar peoples in other parts of the world, assumed that public order, where it existed, must be maintained by some kind of traditional centralized authority, embodied either in a king or chief or in a council. This degree of bureaucratic specialization has not been adequately demonstrated for Australia, and recent studies, as well as comparative material from elsewhere, suggest that there was never an external authority, operating independently of the kinship system, which applied sanctions whenever certain norms were transgressed. This reduces the value of Malinowski's attempt to determine to what extent relations within the family are 'legal,' i.e., whether there are norms regulating behaviour in the family 'which enjoy an organized, more or less regulated and active sanction' (p. 11). The lack of a distinction between legal and other forms of publicly imposed sanctions, together with the assumption that a clear division exists between the family and the tribal authorities, leads Malinowski to say that relations between parents and children 'hardly presented any legal aspects' and yet the 'individual family in Australia is legal, in as much as very many aspects of this institution are subject to legal norms' (p. 302). Again we must regret that Malinowski did not go on to make his promised study of Australian 'group relationships', in which the processes by which pressures from a variety of outside sources are brought to bear on members of the family would have been elucidated.

Malinowski argues that the father-child relationship is regulated by the 'spontaneous emotional attitude', that no outer pressures and constraints enter into it, and 'neither social pressure nor economic interest bind the parents to their children' (pp. 186, 191), but leaves unexamined the extent to which this spontaneity is socially conditioned, and how this is achieved. He stresses the necessity for personal contact before people can feel related (p. 133, f.n.) and we are left with the impression that the simple fact of domestic proximity generates the appropriate sentiments in parents and children. This notion lies at the heart of Malinowski's approach to kinship, and indeed Fortes (1957 : 162) argues that this domestic orientation explains why Malinowski was unable ever to complete his long-heralded account of Trobriand kinship. When he does look beyond the nuclear family, Malinowski recognizes the presence of economically-significant obligations between kinsmen, as for example in the gifts of food made by a man to his wife's father (pp. 285, 303), but these are not seen as part of an interlocking network of inter-personal relationships. Malinowski asks the right question, with reference to the limitations in a man's authority over his wife, when he writes that it is 'difficult to say who would interfere with it and what would be the legal form of such an interference' (p. 297); but does not go on to work out the implications of the fact that the woman who is A's wife is also B's daughter and C's sister's daughter.

Malinowski cites with approval Lévy-Bruhl's interpretation of aboriginal thought, and refers to 'the Australian savages, who do not know anything of logic and can neither affirm identity nor perceive contradictions' (p. 214). This view scarcely tallies with Malinowski's later discussions of primitive thinking, nor with the elegance attributed to aboriginal thought by many recent writers who have studied Australian marriage and cosmological systems (cf. Stanner 1956). Indeed, when Malinowski discusses the fact that the Pennefather River tribes believe that a girl's placenta contains part of her spirit which is later put into her brother's daughter, he says that this is a 'complication' and reminds us that 'aborigines do not think in clearly defined ideas, and that there is always a question rather of some broad emotional connection than of a tie logically apprehended' (p. 229). In later years Malinowski referred to the 'emotionally determined value of direct lineage in the male line' in Australia (1937 : xxxi), an evaluation that provides a quite logical and satisfactory explanation of this belief in spiritual continuity between patrilineally related women.

V

Interests in Australian ethnography have shifted away from the domestic relations examined by Malinowski. He notes that a man had the right to dispose of his daughter (or his sister's daughter) in marriage, and regarded this as a legal aspect of the parent-child relationship (p. 191). Yet his thesis is that beliefs about procreation are correlated with family organization; hence his comment that, although the Wiradjuri believe that the foetus is exclusively the product of the father (the mother only nurtures it), 'curiously enough' among them a girl is bestowed in marriage by her mother or mother's brother and not by her father (pp. 230-231). Subsequently writers have paid much less attention to theories of procreation, and have concentrated their analyses on the implications of bestowal in marriage, and on the rules governing these bestowals. The information on the rules of orthodox marriage and on social group organization for Australia as a whole was brilliantly summarized by Radcliffe-Brown in 1930-1931, and the logical properties of these systems have been further examined by Lévi-Strauss (1949). Malinowski comments that in Australia 'the facts of descent do not seem to play a very important role and are not suitable to be chosen as the most important feature of kinship' (p. 184), a remark that might well have been recalled during that long exchange of arguments sometimes known as the

'Murngin controversy' (cf. Berndt 1957 and preceeding papers), arguments which were almost exclusively concerned with rules of prescriptive marriage and descent with minimal reference to the facts of domestic life.

Malinowski says little about the exchange of utilitarian objects and of songs, rites and symbols among aborigines, for in these exchanges the partners are usually members of different domestic families and may indeed live many hundreds of miles apart. The importance of these exchanges in aboriginal life has been well brought out in many studies, particularly in the work of D. F. Thomson. However, after kinship, it is to religion and to totemic beliefs in particular that scholars have given most attention since Malinowski wrote. Lloyd Warner's *Black Civilization* (1937) was perhaps the first full-length monograph on an Australian aboriginal people using modern methods of intensive field work. Since then, the work of Elkin, Berndt, Kaberry, R. and C. Berndt and McConnel has contributed significantly to our knowledge of the rich complexity of aboriginal ritual and ceremonial. Stanner has recently carried further the anlaysis of aboriginal religion. Comparatively little work has been done on aboriginal economic life (cf. McCarthy and McArthur 1960).

Anthropologists have been slow to follow up Malinowski's discussion of aboriginal local organization, and to apply to Australia the detailed method of inquiry into territorial rights that he developed in the Trobriands. Malinowski comes to the conclusion that a tribe had an 'over-right' to a tract of territory, and that non-tribesmen who trespassed were killed. Within this tribal territory, local groups had 'actual' rights to smaller areas (pp. 152-153). This view was perpetuated by Radcliffe-Brown, for whom aboriginal Australia was divided into discrete territories owned by politically autonomous hordes, patrilineally recruited (1930-31 : 35-36). Recent research has challenged this interpretation and it is probable that for much of Australia the notion of discrete permanent local groups each keeping within its own clearly defined territory must be abandoned (cf. Berndt 1959, Falkenberg, Hiatt 1962).

Malinowski was one of the first to see the importance of the disparity of age in marriage (p. 260), and recently the consequences of this disparity have been probed in detail for several groups in northern Australia (cf. Rose, Hart and Pilling). This approach seems likely to give us a much more plausible model of aboriginal marriage systems than emerged from the earlier accounts, which relied almost exclusively on the specification of ideal marriage choices in kinship categories only. Malinowski notes that 'the majority of fights and quarrels are about women' (p. 125), and discusses this fact in connexion with the kind of jealousy found among aborigines. His notion of jealousy has been neglected, but the investigation of how fights start and how they are settled has been carried forward and has become one of the principal keys to an understanding of the dynamics of aboriginal social life. Then as now, most fights are about women (cf. Meggitt, Hiatt 1959). These investigations emphasise the flexibility and range of choice in aboriginal life, despite the operation of apparently complicated and rigid rules of social behaviour.

VI

Meanwhile the Australian aborigines themselves have changed. From the meager information as yet available it seems probable that people like present-day aborigines have been living on the Australian continent for between 10,000 and 20,000 years. When British colonization began in 1788, aborigines were to be found throughout all the habitable areas of the continent, and it has been estimated that they then numbered about 300,000. Their numbers declined as colonization proceeded and probably reached their lowest point in the first quarter of the twentieth century (cf. Elkin 1951, Stanner 1960). There are now about 40,000 aborigines of purely, or mainly, aboriginal ancestry and perhaps 60,000 who are of part-aboriginal descent, some of whom have passed into the white community. In the north and north-west of Australia, where the country is still only sparsely settled, many aborigines live on cattle and sheep stations (ranches) where the men are employed. Others live on settlements run by government and Christian missions. Probably not more than about 2,000 aborigines live without significant direct contacts with white Australians. In the south and south-east many part-aborigines live as migrant and unskilled labourers, and on the outskirts of many country towns there are aboriginal encampments. A few part-aborigines have become preachers, school teachers and contractors, and there are several professional boxers. For the last twenty years or so the official Commonwealth and State policies have aimed at assimilating aborigines to the main stream of Australian life. Progress towards this goal is still slow, but it is likely to increase as more aboriginal and part-aboriginal children attend school alongside their white neighbours.

It is perhaps appropriate at a time when aboriginal life is changing more rapidly than ever before that the Commonwealth government should have announced its intention to found an Australian Institute of Aboriginal Studies, charged with the investigation and recording of the distinctive aboriginal way of life. We may hope that the new Institute will promote further inquiries into aboriginal affairs, a task to which Malinowski would assuredly have given his support.

J. A. Barnes

Australian National University
Canberra, A.C.T.
July 1962

THE FAMILY AMONG THE
AUSTRALIAN ABORIGINES

CHAPTER I

EXPOSITION OF THE PROBLEM AND METHOD

I

THE problem of the social forms of family life still presents some obscurities. What appears to be most urgently needed is a careful investigation of facts in all the different ethnographical areas. I propose in this study to undertake this task for Australia. I shall avoid making any hypothetical assumptions, or discussing general problems which refer to the origin or evolution of the family. I wish only to describe in correct terms and as thoroughly as possible all that refers to actual family life in Australia. In other words I intend to give in outline the social morphology of the Australian family.

It may be well to show briefly the necessity for this task, which to some may appear superfluous, and to indicate the lines on which it will be attempted. In the first place there are some contradictions with regard to the problem of relationship or kinship in Australia, which can be reduced to the question : Is kinship in Australia exclusively individual; or is it exclusively group kinship (or tribal kinship, as it often is called); and, further, do these two forms exclude each other or do they perhaps exist side by side ? When Howitt says : " The social unit is not the individual, but the group; the former

1

merely takes the relationships of his group, which are of group to group," [1] this obviously means that there is no individual relationship, consequently no individual family in Australia. It is important to note that the passage just quoted is placed in the chapter on Relationship in Howitt's chief work on Australia, and that consequently it refers to all the tribes described by the author, *i. e.* to the majority of the known Australian tribes. The same opinion that there is only group relationship and no individual family is supported by another passage, no less important and general, for it is placed at the conclusion of Howitt's article on the organization of the Australian tribes in general : " It has been shown that the fundamental idea in the conception of an Australian community is its division into two groups. The relationships which obtain between the members of them are also those of group to group." [2] And again : " The unit of aboriginal society is, therefore, not the individual, but the group. It is the group which marries the group and which begets the group." [3] There are also a few passages in Spencer and Gillen which deny the existence of the individual family, at least in some tribes.[4]

Thus the impression drawn from the passages just quoted [5] is that there is no individual relationship and, what follows as an immediate consequence, no individual marriage, nor individual family in Australia. Such a conclusion would be absolutely false. For the same author (Howitt) writes : " Individual marriage in Austra-

---

[1] *Nat. Tribes*, p. 157. It is hardly necessary to point out that this phrase is without a precise sense, unless it be evident in what sense the author uses the conception " social unit." One looks in vain for such a definition in Howitt.

[2] Howitt, *Trans. R.S.V.*, *l.c.*, p. 134.

[3] *Trans. R.S.V.*, p. 135.

[4] Compare the passage quoted by A. Lang, just below, and the passage quoted by us, pp. 108 *sqq.*, and p. 243. How far Spencer and Gillen have the right to deny the existence of the individual family among the Urabunna will be discussed in detail below.

[5] I have quoted the best first-hand authorities ; instances could easily be multiplied as well from their works as also from other sources.

lian tribes has been evident to everyone." [1] Curr speaks
in still more positive terms: "No relationship but that
of blood is known amongst Australians." [2] The social
relations which exist amongst the Australian aborigines
are of five sorts; first, those of family; second, those of
the tribe; third, those between associated tribes; fourth,
those of neighbours who belong to different associations;
fifth, all other persons. [3] We see that in Curr's statements
there is again no room for any kind of group relationship.
Obviously Curr's information contradicts in plain terms
the foregoing set of statements, and such a contradiction
among our best informants is truly puzzling. There
seems to be some misunderstanding in the present
problem.

This is not only my own opinion. Mr. A. Lang discusses the same question and finds it necessary to prove
in a short article that individual relationship exists in
Australia. He says: "It is certain that 'blood' or
'own' relations are perfectly recognized. Messrs. Spencer
and Gillen inadvertently deny this, saying: 'The savage
Australian, it may be said with truth, has no idea of
relationships as we understand them.'" This example
is not the only one, as has been shown above, and indeed
their number could be easily multiplied. Mr. Lang proves
by several instances that this opinion of Spencer and Gillen
is erroneous, and concludes: "The savage Australian
does discriminate between his actual and his tribal relations. It was necessary to make this fact clear and
certain, as it has been denied." [4] The same contradiction
has also been pointed out by Dr. Westermarck: "As to
the South Australians, Mr. Fison's statements have caused
not a little confusion. On his authority several writers
assert that among the Australian savages groups of males
are actually found united to groups of females." [5] And

---

[1] *Trans. R.S.V.*, p. 115.
[2] Curr, *A.R.*, i. p. iii.
[3] Curr, *A.R.*, i. p. 60.
[4] *Procs. B. Academy*, vol. iii. 1908, May report, p. 4.
[5] Westermarck Ed. *The History of Human Marriage*, p. 56.

in a footnote Dr. Westermarck quotes Lubbock, Morgan, Kohler, Kovalevsky. With such views Dr. Westermarck contrasts Curr's [1] opinion that strict monogamy obtains, and that of the Rev. J. Mathew,[2] " who fails to see that group marriage ' has been proven to exist in the past and certainly does not occur in Australia now.' "

Again E. Grosse in his well-known book, speaking of Howitt's work on the Kurnai says that this author " . . . hat sich so gründlich in seine Hypothese einer Gruppenehe . . . der prähistorischen Australier vertieft, dass er darüber ganz vergisst, seine Leser darauf aufmerksam zu machen, dass die historischen Australier in Einzelnehe leben." [3] This is quite true, especially the remark that one of the chief sources of error in sociology is speculating on the origins and prehistory of an institution before this institution is thoroughly known in the present state.

And it seems as if in the present case a good many of the difficulties may be solved by understanding some of the statements made as referring to hypothetical earlier stages. As a matter of fact the passage quoted above, where the existence of group relationship is affirmed, is continued thus : " The idea of the relation of individual to individual, and of individual parentage, without reference to the group, is of later origin, and is the result of a number of social forces acting in the same general direction and producing change." [4] It is evident therefore that group relationship is supposed by Howitt to be the former state, and individual relationship a kind of innovation. But there is such a lack of clearness, such a confusion of the past and present tenses, that we are here again at a loss. Take for example the following passage : " The latest advance which has been made in the subject of Australian marriage was the conception of marriage in the group, and of group to group, and of the filial relation

[1] Curr, *A.R.*, i. p. 126.
[2] Mathew, *J.R.S.N.S.W.*, xxiii. p. 404, quoted from Westermarck, *H.H.M.*, p. 57.
[3] E. Grosse, p. 6.   [4] *Trans. R.S.V.*, p. 135.

of one group to another." [1] This last phrase should be, in all probability, understood in the past tense, as referring to prehistoric times. But the author gives absolutely no hint whether this be so or otherwise. And when he on the next page refers to Mr. Curr's assertion, that there is actually no group relationship in Australia, and criticizes this assertion, a suspicion is aroused that this view of the existence of marital and filial groups is meant to express the actual status. This is enough to show how vague and puzzling the question of the individual family and individual relationship still is.

It is unnecessary to insist on the bewilderment, but the polemical mood in which our informants always approached the problem of relationship and family has had its unfortunate consequences. In the first place it is easy to see that these two groups of facts—individual relationship and group relationship—are treated by the writers as if they excluded each other, or at least as if one of them were gradually encroaching upon the other. Whereas it is quite possible that both individual and group relationship might exist side by side, originating from different sources, and expressing two different sets of social relationships. In the second place, the polemical attitude of our best informants (Howitt, and Spencer and Gillen) against individual relationship resulted in their giving very meagre information about the individual family. As a matter of fact, in all theoretical passages of works devoted to the social organization of the Australian tribes, the individual family is passed over in absolute silence.[2] As this unit obviously plays a foremost part in the social life of Australian tribes, I submit it is quite justifiable that in these pages some information about this unit should be gathered and its importance brought out. Special attention has been devoted to the facts of actual family life.

[1] *Trans. R.S.V.*, p. 113.
[2] As *e. g.* in the general treatises of Spencer and Gillen, *Nat. Tr., Nor. Tr.,* Howitt's *Nat. Tr.,* Howitt and Fison, *K.K. Idem* in *J.A.J.,* xii. p. 33. Howitt in *Trans. R.S.V.,* p. 100, and in *Smithsonian Reports,* p. 79.

To sum up, it may be said that the defects in our information as to the individual family, and the contradiction and confusion surrounding it, do of themselves justify an examination of this institution. These contradictions are due probably not to any intrinsic reasons, but to certain theoretical postulates and axioms adopted by some of our informants. And as the exact description of actual facts seems to suffer therefrom, a revision of the theoretical side of the problem, as well as a collection of evidence from a somewhat extensive number of sources appears advisable.

But over and above clearing up some contradictions, solving some difficulties, and filling up a gap in the information concerning Australian kinship organization, there is a much deeper justification for a detailed collection and classification of facts referring to the individual family in Australia. I mean, it is only such a proceeding that can give us a scientific, correct and useful definition of the Australian individual family (or any other social unit in general). *A priori* only a vague meaning can be attached to the term " individual family," when it refers to a society different from ours. For the essential features of the individual family, as of all other social institutions, depend upon the general structure of a given society and upon the conditions of life therein. A careful and detailed analysis of the family life and of the different aspects of the family unit in connection with other social phenomena is therefore necessary. Such an analysis enables us to describe the said unit in a complete and exact way.

It is Dr. Rivers to whom we are indebted for emphasizing the methodological standpoint in this connection. In his article [1] he points out that we cannot *a priori* assert the existence of even such an apparently unquestionable fact as individual motherhood in every human society whether actual or hypothetical. To affirm that in a given society motherhood is individual and not communal (group motherhood), a strict analysis

[1] *Anthrop. Essays*, pp. 309 *sqq.*

of a whole series of circumstances is necessary. Applying
Dr. Rivers' argument to the other family relationships,
we may say that all the circumstances referring to the
relation between man and wife, parents and children,
brothers and sisters, must be submitted to a careful and
detailed analysis; and that only such an examination can
give us the right idea of what may be called the individual
family in a given society—in this case the Australian
individual family.[1]

As mentioned above, many authors, who have contributed so much in other respects to our knowledge of
Australian kinship organization, have not entered into
details as to the family life, or actual relationship. Even
Mr. Thomas, although he quite acknowledges the existence
of individual relationship, confines himself to the remark
that in Australia exists "the family in the European sense."
But this expression is not adequate. We cannot possibly
find in Australia any social unit that would exactly fit
the forms of our individual family; for this is intimately
connected with the structure of our society, and none of
the social conditions it requires are found in Australia.
We can only say a unit which is *analogous* to our individual
family, and even then we would be more metaphorical
than exact. Mr. Lang, on the other hand, is not exhaustive enough for our purpose—which is a description of the
family unit that will define it fully for sociological use.
Nevertheless as he writes in reply to Dr. Rivers he has
accepted the latter's methodological standpoint, and he
gives a series of apposite remarks and examples. But he
concludes: "It is needless to give more examples; the
savage Australian does discriminate between his actual
and his tribal relations." This conclusion is quite correct,
but it is not sufficient. The mere affirmation that the
actual relationship exists and is recognized by the natives
is not enough. This has been obvious to every careful,
unprejudiced reader of the first-hand ethnographical
material.

[1] Comp. below, p. 206, the second paragraph of footnote 1.

The aim of the present study is to *define what* this individual relationship is; to describe its different aspects and features; how it manifests itself in its different social functions and, as far as can be ascertained, how it must impress itself upon the native mind. And here lies the important methodological point on which some stress must be laid. It is not *the* actual relationship, or *the* individual family, or " family in the European sense " which we have to look for in Australia. It is the aboriginal Australian individual family, with all its peculiarities and characteristic features, which must be reconstructed from the evidence. It will be necessary to describe minutely all the relationships generally embraced by the term Family,[1] and to describe them in terms taken from the native social life. In other words we have to look for the connection between the facts of family life and the general structure of society and forms of native life; and to take into account all psychological data available, such as ideas on procreation and reincarnation,.

Only by such a description can we reach a correct and scientific definition of a given institution in a given society. It is essential that the elements of this definition should be taken from the conditions of social life in the given society. As an example we may take the legal side of marriage. Amongst us marriage is a legal act enforced on the one hand by the authority of the law with all its complicated social working and the power of the State at its back; on the other hand by the authority of the Church, which exercises a profound moral pressure in relation to this institution. These or even analogous factors will be sought in the Australian tribes in vain. And yet marriage there is not deprived of its legal validity and of its social sanction. It is not an act of mere fancy, brutal force or accident, but the legal factors have there quite a specific character, and can be found and understood only in connection with the general tribal structure and government.

Besides all that has been said above against a general

---

[1] Defining that term only broadly at the outset.

offhand affirmation, that the individual family exists in Australia, it may be added here that such an assertion is practically quite useless. No further conclusions or inferences can be drawn from such a vague statement. Only by knowing exactly and minutely all the features and characters of the said unit can the different questions attached to this problem be answered; only so can it be judged whether the individual family or certain features of it are survivals or innovations; or whether they are so deeply rooted and connected with the social life and the whole organization of the tribes, that neither of these suppositions is justifiable. Such special and concrete definitions of a given social phenomenon in a given ethnic area, as the one which it is intended to give here for the Australian individual family, can serve also as a basis to form by induction a general conception of the individual family; and only from a rich collection of such material from different peoples can any sociological laws be constructed. As said above, a general working definition of the word individual family may be accepted at the outset of our investigations. After a careful analysis of all particular relationships concerned; and further, of the economic unity of the family, division of labour within it, legal sanction, etc., content can be given to the rough definition laid down at the beginning, and scientific exactness can be given to our conception of the individual family in Australia.

It seems desirable in this place to make a digression in order to consider the problem of law and the legal side of social phenomena in the Australian aboriginal society, as we shall often have to use these concepts. A more detailed and exhaustive discussion of it would involve a treatise on primitive law, but as I am unable to indicate any place where the concepts in question are defined in a way satisfactory for the present purpose, I define them here briefly.[1]

---

[1] In the treatises on primitive law and on family law such general concepts as "legal" or "law" are never explicitly defined.

All social organization implies a series of norms, which extend over the whole social life and regulate more or less strictly all the social relations. We find such norms and rules in the Australian aboriginal society, different kinds being enforced by different forms of social sanction. The validity of some is due to the evil results which are intrinsically connected with their violation. So *e. g.* we know that the breaking of certain food taboos has as an inevitable consequence premature grey hair, eruptions on the skin, or some other mishap. There are other rules, which are observed because any departure from them would bring general contempt and ridicule upon the culprit; a form of chastisement to which the natives are said to be extremely sensitive. There are still other types of social norms, sanctioned by a more direct collective action. In some cases the magicians of the tribe will use the dreaded method of " pointing the bone," thus bringing about the illness and death of the culprit; or a regulated fight ensues; or a man has to undergo a definite ordeal. Occasionally a group of people organize an armed party

---

Perhaps such a definition is superfluous for a specialist, but I think that especially in the ethnology of primitive peoples precise concepts and explicit definitions are necessary. I may, however, mention the following places where there are some attempts at definition—

Post, l.c., i. sec. 3, pp. 8–10. The author gives a few remarks about the beginnings of law. He maintains it existed as *Rechts-gefühl,* feeling of legality, and was evolved through a system of juridical verdicts, given according to this sentiment. There were no legal norms at the beginning.—This passage is unsatisfactory, both because it does not give any strict definition and because it does not seem to be in agreement with the facts.

Kohler, l.c., p. 323. No strict definition given. Besides the author says that there is no organization (*staatliche Organisation*), no tribunal, and no executive among the Australian aborigines. This assertion may be questioned; compare below.

Durkheim, D.T.S., pp. 28 *sqq.* and 108 *sqq.* There are some interesting remarks bearing upon our subject; but there are no sufficiently clear definitions, especially none to suit the laws of quite primitive peoples.

Lord Avebury, l.c., chap. xi. pp. 464 *sqq.* No definition of what " law," " legal," should mean in very low societies, attempted. Law and custom are not discriminated. Some interesting remarks on punishment (pp. 495 *sqq.*) are not utilized in order to afford strict concepts.

on their own account, but with the consent of the community; and so on.

Briefly it may be said that different types of social norms have different kinds of collective sanction and that we may suitably classify the norms and regulations according to the kind of sanction they enjoy. Here seems the proper place to introduce the concept of Law, Legal. We can agree to call such norms Legal, which enjoy an organized, more or less regulated and active social sanction. To make this definition plausible, we may remark that it makes the Australian legal institutions correspond to what we call law and legal in higher societies. Further it would be necessary, in order fully to justify our definition, to show : (1) that among the Australian blacks there exist such modes of regulated, organized and direct social sanction; (2) that they differ from other modes of sanction and that the collective mind is quite aware which norms enjoy just this form of sanction.

In answer to the first problem we may generally point to the existence of tribal government. That a kind of centralized authority exists in Australia and that it has well-determined functions has been shown at full length by Howitt.[1]

[1] *Trans. R.S.V.*, pp. 103 *sqq*; *J.A.I.* xii, p. 35; *J.A.I.* xiii, p. 282. And especially *Nat. Tr.*, chap. vi. pp. 295–354. The elucidation of the problem of authority and justice in Australia is one of Howitt's chief merits. In the passages quoted, there will be found ample material to exemplify all that is said in the text. I shall give, however, a few more detailed references on some special points. Howitt does not classify the facts according to the principle just enunciated. But all he says fits perfectly well into our scheme, and he puts stress on some essential points; viz. that there is a tribal as well as a supernatural punishment; that there is a central authority, and that it had means to enforce and execute its decrees. Curr (*A.R.*, vol. i. pp. 53 *sqq*.) emphatically denies the existence of any kind of government; but his polemic is due to the misunderstanding of the word *government* as it should be applied to the Australian aboriginal society. For general discussion of this problem compare also G. C. Wheeler, pp. 46–52. Interesting details, corroborating Howitt's opinion may be found also in the following places : Spencer and Gillen, *Nat. Tr.*, pp. 12 *sqq*., p. 324, p. 477, pp. 491 *sqq*. *Nor. Tr.*, pp. 26 *sqq*. R. Dawson, pp. 64–65. Hodgson, p. 204. J. D. Lang, p. 331. G. S. Lang, pp. 9–10. Grey, ii. p. 222. Eyre, ii.

This government consists roughly speaking of headmen and a tribal council, composed in the first place of old men of the tribe, skilled magicians and experienced warriors. This camp council seems as a rule the more influential factor, and only in few cases are we informed of chiefs with extensive powers.[1] What is important for us is that one of the main functions—if not the chief one—of those central authorities is to decide in case of difficulties

---

pp. 214, 318, 385. Woods, p. 8. L. Schultze, p. 225. J. B. Gribble, p. 114. J. Mathew, p. 129. Compare also the following extracts, where I shortly indicate what is to be found—
Ch. Wilkes, ii. 204. Obedience to elders. *Idem*, i. 222. Regulated fights. Wilson, 144. Reverence towards old men. Bennett, pp. 177–178. Chiefs chosen for personal qualities. Turnbull, p. 91. Ordeals as punishment for crime. p. 101. Respect for and authority of old men and magicians. Barrington, 81. Pacific settlement of differences. Henderson, pp. 107, 158. No chiefs: only "doctors" wield some authority; p. 160, Duel as redress of injuries. Macgillivray, i. 151. Power and authority of old and experienced men; p. 152, Important instances of justice. *Idem*, ii. p. 27. Authority wielded by some important and privileged men. G. W. Earl, p. 275. Alleged powerful chiefs (unreliable). Campbell, 171. Instances of important and influential men. B. Field, 67. Description of two regulated fights. Krichauff, p. 77. Old men and doctors in council: they carry out the resolutions arrived at, or see that these are carried out; p. 78, Laws, which the warriors or old men uphold. Penalties: reprimand, exit, and ordeal. Sutton, p. 18. Hereditary "kingship." Wilhelmi, p. 183. No chiefs. Respect for old men and their magical powers. D. Mathews, p. 49. Council of old men. S. Newland. *Proc. R.G.S.S.A.*, iii. p. 40 *sqq.* Examples of important and powerful men. Mrs. Bates, p. 52. Regulation of offences by ordeals.
All these references bear indiscriminately on one or the other of the important features of government and of legal or other norms discussed in the text.
[1] Chiefs are reported by Taplin (Woods, p. 32); J. Dawson, pp. 5 *sqq.* But these statements, especially the latter, seem subject to doubt. Compare Curr, *A.R.*, i. pp. 55 and 58. Howitt and his correspondents report chiefs among the Dieri, Tongaranka, Wiimbaio, Theddora, Yuin, Wiradjuri, Gurnditch Mara, Kulin, etc., *Nat. Tr.*, pp. 297-320. Compare also Waitz Gerland, p. 790. But the term "Chief" appears somewhat vague; probably it is usually applied to influential individuals, whose importance is due to their personal qualities and not to their social position. The influence of old men, magicians and "doctors," is almost universally reported, and the council made up of them seems to wield the real power in the tribe. Compare Howitt, *Nat. Tr.*, pp. 320-326, for some of the above references.

in tribal affairs and to give sentence, a function which is that both of a legislator and of a judge.[1] The old men are the only depositories of tribal lore; they also know the rules and norms and how to apply them. We are informed in many places that they discuss important matters and decide vital questions; and especially in cases where any law has been transgressed. They possess also executive power; they can organize an armed party; they arrange and control the regulated fights; and they have also in their hands the personal power of punishment by magic.[2] It may therefore be said in general that the rudimentary form of central authority, as found in Australia, possesses quite clearly traceable features of juridical functions and executive power; it forms a kind of tribunal, and it has its organs to carry out the sentence. It is hardly necessary to add, that those institutions exist only in a rudimentary form; but they appear to be quite

[1] See Wheeler, p. 122, where it is said that offences like murder by magic, breaches of the marriage regulations, and the revealing of ceremonial secrets are dealt with by the elders and headmen. The legislative powers of old and influential men is mentioned : Howitt, *Nat. Tr.*, pp. 89 *sqq.* (new norms introduced by individuals under alleged supernatural command or vision). Spencer and Gillen, *Nat. Tr.*, pp. 12 *sqq.* (important changes in custom, law, organization by individual initiative), *idem*, *Nat. Tr.*, p. 324. *Nor. Tr.*, pp. 26 *sqq.* (a kind of tribunal formed by old and influential men). Spencer and Gillen, *Nat. Tr.*, p. 477 (old men in council assembled decide); p. 490 (Atninga, avenging party, despatched by old men, whenever vengeance is to be taken); pp. 491 (old men discuss and settle matters with an Atninga party). Howitt, *Nat. Tr.*, pp. 297, 298 (Council of Pinnaru described); pp. 320 *sqq.* (deliberating in all important matters).

[2] For the methods of carrying out justice, *i. e.* for the executive organs, see Wheeler, pp. 131–139, where the " authorized agents " (avenging parties, etc.), regulated fights, expiatory ordeals and blood revenge, methods which, as different forms of carrying out justice, are more or less executions of a sentence and have the character of legal proceedings.

See also under the heading " Executive power of tribal councils of old men," in Howitt's *Nat. Tr.*, chap. vi. pp. 295 *sqq.*—The Pinya party of the Dieri tribe. *Ibid.*, pp. 297, 321 and 326.—An atonement of the offence by barter, p. 329. Direct action of magicians, *ibid.* p. 343. Compare also the Kurdaitcha, Illapurinja, and Atninga parties of the Arunta. Spencer and Gillen, *Nat. Tr.*, chap. xiii. p. 475. All these parties are more or less under the control of the tribal council of old men.

unmistakable. Besides this central authority, which sometimes takes the juridical functions upon itself, there are other forms of organized action, carried out by groups of individuals, personally interested in the case. Here the legal character, *i. e.* the feature that distinguishes such action and the underlying norm from mere violence, fancy or custom—lies in the fact that such an action is regulated by strict rules and prescriptions. And it is in just such a mutual connection of a norm and social enforcement that the fundamental feature of legality may be seen. So *e. g.* in the Central Tribes a man who has by magic charmed away a woman can reckon upon the actual support of a definite group of his kindred. The legality of his act is based upon the existence of a certain norm and the existence of a form of active and regulated social support which enforces this norm. Without the norm the social action would be mere violence. Without the social enforcement the norm would be a moral or customary rule; so enforced, it may properly be called a law.[1] It is impossible, for want of space, to deal here more in detail with this question, which could correctly be answered only by collecting all the evidence available, and bringing the results into connection with the general features of Australian society, such as age grades and tribal secret societies. I only indicate here the point of view, and I shall in what follows refer to it and exemplify it by concrete instances.

The second problem, viz. whether the distinction between the customary and religious rules and legal norms may be considered as well defined in Australia, is still more difficult to answer. The small differentiation of that society hardly allows any very clear and definite sociological distinctions. But, broadly speaking, it seems that the distinction between (1) a trespass, whose

---

[1] Compare Spencer and Gillen, *Nat. Tr.*, p. 554 : " . . . a man's right to woman secured by means " of magic " is supported by the men of his own local group." Compare also the description of this method of charming away a woman in *Proc. R. Geogr. Soc. S. Australia*, vol. iv. p. 26, by F. Gillen.

punishment is supernaturally entailed by its very com-
mittal; (2) a trespass, punished by ridicule and public
contempt; and (3) a crime, punished by the decision of
the community, acting as a whole, or by its central organs,
or certain groups of it—that this distinction between sin,
improper conduct and crime (as we can call those three
categories) is quite well marked in different features of
aboriginal social life. What might fully elucidate this
question, would be a collection of facts, classified
according to these categories.[1]

These few remarks are merely made to settle the
terminology. By definition a given norm or rule is Legal
if it is enforced by a direct, organized, and definite social
action. And by the word legal will be designated this
side or aspect of a given social relation which is regulated
by laws, as just defined.

[1] So *e. g.* there could be placed in the *first category* different
kinds of food taboos. In the Arunta, food procured or handled
by certain relatives may not be eaten by a man; nor may be
eaten any food in their immediate presence. Such food would
disagree with the man. Spencer and Gillen, *Nat. Tr.*, p. 469.—If
certain food taboos were transgressed during initiation by the
boys, their wounds would inflame. *Ibid.* p. 470.—Certain taboos
must be observed during pregnancy both by the woman and her
husband; if they were transgressed the sickness of the woman
would be worse and the man would lose his skill in hunting.
Ibid. p. 471.—Compare also Mitchell, ii. p. 29, and Wilhelmi,
p. 176. If the man should transgress the mother-in-law taboo,
his hair would prematurely grow grey, or he would soon become
bald. This belief is very widespread. Howitt, *Nat. Tr.*, p. 296.
D. Mathews, p. 49. Mrs. Bates, p. 50. Compare also Waitz
Gerland, p. 795, where different norms, enforced by supernatural
punishment, are mentioned, and also MacGillivray, ii. 10, Eyre
ii. 339, Stanbridge, p. 289. Different ceremonies and ordeals at
mourning and burial are regulated by *custom;* the same thing
may probably be said of some of the initiatory ordeals. Non-
compliance would involve the general ridicule or contempt of the
tribesmen : Spencer and Gillen, *Nat. Tr.*, p. 510. As *crimes* may
be mentioned : transgression of the class rule as well in marriage
as in sexual intercourse. Spencer and Gillen, *Nat. Tr.*, p. 495, say
that the usual punishment is death. Killing by magic : Spencer
and Gillen, p. 476; Waitz Gerland, p. 794. In some cases the transgression of the mother-in-law taboo seems to be punished by
expulsion from the local group : Howitt, *Nat. Tr.*, p. 296.—
Salvado says that marriage under thirty years is punished by
death (p. 267). Such examples could be indefinitely multiplied.

Our considerations indicate also in what direction an analysis of the social conditions in Australia would be interesting from the point of view of primitive jurisprudence. In the first place, there is a great variety of modes in which the different legal norms are preserved, impressed upon the social mind, and taught to different members of the society. Here the connection of different norms with religion, myth, totemic cultus, organization of the secret society, etc., might be discussed. In the second place a careful investigation of the different forms of social sanction, based partly on belief, partly on collective ideas and feelings, partly on actual institutions and direct enforcement, might be carried out. In connection with it there might be a classification of the norms; and the domain of the purely legal norms, or rather the properly legal aspect of norms and different social phenomena could be exactly traced. In other words each norm should be studied in connection with the way in which it is " codified " (*i. e.* preserved for and imparted to social knowledge); and in connection with its sanction. In the case of a legal norm the tribunal and the executive organs should be indicated as far as possible. Undoubtedly we find in such a primitive society as the Australian many institutions still in a state of confusion, which on a higher level are quite well determined and differentiated. But the more confused the phenomena, the clearer our conceptions must be in order exactly to follow the different ways in which the elements are interwoven and combined. What is an isolated and defined institution in a higher society, may be merely a side or aspect of social phenomena in a lower one. But it is highly important to use definite concepts to denote such aspects or sides in undifferentiated societies, because it often widens our horizon and puts our ideas to a crucial test.

I wish to add that in the present case it is only the necessity for clearness and convenience that makes a definition necessary. The domain of primitive jurisprudence cannot be considered fully explored yet; the chief aim of a good definition is to state the proper problems and to show the groups of facts that must be inquired into in order to give right answers to the problems proposed.

II

Having thus justified the scope of the present book and indicated the general lines on which its task should be carried out, a few words must be devoted to the method of dealing with the evidence. We start our investigations with (1) the Australian first-hand information, and (2) a general idea of the object of our research, that is a general idea of the individual family. This implies that during the process of research these two sets of data must be checked against each other. On the one hand we must continually extract from the evidence all that corresponds to our general idea of the individual family; on the other hand this idea must be specialized and determined according to the evidence.

It is clear enough what, broadly speaking, is meant by the Individual Family. But what exactly will be the features of this institution in Australia, that must be extracted from the evidence. This evidence is, on the other hand, given in the majority of cases in a very crude state, without reference to any theoretical points of view. The facts are often given in a purely casual and colloquial way. It is part of the task to sift out each one of them, and to ask if it can have any bearing on the present subject. Many facts that seemed not to bear immediately on it, yet furnished some very useful inferences. In short, the first duty of such a work as the present is to ask from the evidence right questions in the right way.

But even if a certain point has been settled upon as essentially important to be inquired into, and information referring to it has been gathered, the task is not yet finished. The statements collected on this point will as a rule present more or less radical discrepancies. After we have heard twenty opinions on the same subject which by no means agree with each other, to which shall we adhere ? A method of dealing with evidence must be fixed upon. In the first place the statements are of the most heterogeneous character and value. They must be submitted to some criticism before use can be made of them.

After the degree of their reliability has been settled, and after, by a criticism of each statement, some of the contradictions have been removed, it must be considered how far the differences between the statements may be regarded as due to irreducible, local variations of the given institution; in other words, the problem must be discussed from the geographical standpoint.

Finally a certain system of weighing the evidence must be chosen, so as to draw from it the most correct conclusions, and never to prove too much or too little. So there are three different processes : criticism, localization of differences, and drawing of conclusions; all of which must be done according to a careful and conscientious method.

A few remarks about the latter must be given here without any attempt at completeness. That preliminary criticism is necessary seems hardly to need justification; to look at the irreducible inconsistencies and contradictions of a series of statements concerning any given point is enough. But such criticism must not be arbitrary; it must conform to strict rules.[1]

The first point to which attention must be paid, is to ascertain the exact meaning of a given statement. As many of our informants do not use exact terminology

[1] The ethnographic sources do not differ essentially from the historical ones. The purpose of a descriptive ethnography (such as is adopted in this monograph) is also nearly identical with the historian's task so far as positive statement of an actual state of things is the aim of both. The rules of criticism of sources apply therefore to our subject as well as to any other historic science. This will become obvious to every ethnographer who reads the excellent manual of MM. Langlois et Seignobos. The proof of the indispensability of such a criticism is to be found there, too. The method of criticism of sources adopted in this paper was accepted after a careful study of this useful book.

but write in a colloquial language, often spoilt by literary pretensions, we occasionally run the risk of being misled by a word or by a turn of expression.[1]   In other words, it never seems advisable to cling blindly to the verbal meaning of a statement before having put it to the test. So, for instance, in the problem whether the natives live in families or tribes—the *family* and *tribe* having been exactly defined, a phrase like " the aborigines live in families " may not be accepted as argument, for by the word " family " the author may possibly have understood what we have designated by the word tribe.[2]   I shall, as a rule, quote each statement *in extenso*, and give, if necessary, an interpretation or correction.[3]   The sense in which a word is used may be, in the majority of cases, easily settled from the context, examples given by the author, and other instances where he uses the same word.   When a phrase is hopelessly ambiguous, it is wrong to make any use of it.

After the sense of a statement has been settled more or less reliably, two cases must be discriminated.   If the statement is purely a record of facts, and, still better, if it is exemplified by concrete instances, there is generally no reason to disbelieve it, especially if in the general character of the author there is a guarantee of his trustworthiness; and if he actually has had good opportunities of observing the natives.   But if the statement involves a judgment, a generalization, or abstraction, we must be much more careful.   Broadly speaking, statements of this latter kind are generally much more contradictory than mere statements of fact.   It will be seen that the

[1] We obviously do not speak here of such writers as Howitt, W. E. Roth, Spencer and Gillen, authors who had a theoretical training.   But, as may be pointed out here, in the present work no writer is excluded, provided that he has had opportunities of first-hand observation, or opportunities of private information from first-hand observers.

[2] See below the discussion of this topic, Chap. V., I.

[3] Much weight has been attached to a very extensive reproduction of the original text.   More important statements are always adduced verbatim; less important, or too cumbersome ones, are abridged, but keeping as closely to the original words as possible.

information concerning the treatment of women by their husbands, concerning sexual matters, and concerning the authority of husbands, will present many more discrepancies than the information concerning the modes of obtaining wives, economics, and other concrete questions. The first category implies much more abstraction and qualifying judgment than the second. It must be borne in mind that statements of the first category are the result of a long and complicated series of mental processes, and that their quality and value is dependent upon many conditions. All these conditions must be mentally analyzed and each of them must be taken into account in order to ascertain its bearing upon the final form in which we find the statement. The conditions in question may be shortly set forth as follows : Did the author possess all the qualities necessary for a good ethnographer ? Had he good opportunities to observe the natives and a good method of doing so ? Were the latter still in a primitive condition, or in an advanced state of decay ? A few words may be said in the first place about this last point.

Only in exceptional cases is it possible to say anything definite on the state of the natives the author had under observation.[1] In general, it may be taken as a rule that all writers who were in any close contact with aborigines, had to do with fairly degenerated specimens. They were usually squatters or missionaries, and had to do with blacks hanging round farms or with remnants of tribes gathered in missions.[2] Their immediate observa-

---

[1] For instance, we can judge this from Curr's *Recollections ;* we know pretty well the state of the different tribes investigated by Howitt, Spencer and Gillen, and by Roth. In many other cases a general idea may be formed from different hints.

[2] The aborigines in their natural uncorrupted state appear to have been extremely shy, and great difficulties would undoubtedly have arisen had any one attempted to come into more intimate contact with them. But in the early days of the settlement of Australia there was nobody with such intentions. It is sufficient to read very early accounts, such as the voyages of Gov. Phillip, Barrington; as also accounts of explorers like Grey, Eyre, Leichardt, Mitchell, Sturt, etc., to see how shy and inaccessible were the blacks in their really savage state.

tions, especially in sociological matters, which are at once affected, when conditions of life change, and when blacks become degenerate, could be of little value. But there was still the possibility of gathering information from the natives themselves, who could, properly questioned, give their recollections of the bygone times. This was the way in which probably A. W. Howitt got so much of the most valuable information on the Kurnai tribe, which he never saw in its primitive state. But only few writers had the mental training and the opportunities of the writer just mentioned. And the majority probably communicated to us simply what they saw—not even considering the problem how far the conditions then present tallied with the primitive normal state of things in the aboriginal society. Allowance must therefore be always made for the degeneration of the blacks as a possible factor affecting ethnographical evidence. In many cases there will be no room for doubt. For instance, in sexual matters it is obvious that contact with the white man invariably fosters a great deal of depravity. An improvement in sexual morality may, on the other hand, take place ·if the natives are gathered in a mission station.[1] But this cannot have any connection with aboriginal custom.

If, therefore, it is found, as is in fact the case, that all writers, who either inquired into the matter with really scientific precautions, or had to do with pure, primitive material, inform us that, speaking broadly, the sexual relations were strictly regulated; and on the other hand, all settlers, casual observers, and people who obviously had already corrupted blacks under observation, speak of unrestricted immorality and even of incest,[2] it may be safely said that the second type of statements refer to degenerate blacks. Here the general *a priori* suppositions quite

---

[1] For examples how natives on mission stations may be forced into morality, legal and Christian marriages, etc., the reader may be referred to the personal diaries of missionaries. Compare *e. g.* the article by the missionary D. Mathews, *l.c.* pp. 48 *sqq.*
[2] See below, the statements, pp. 92 *sqq.*

harmonize with what is to be found in the evidence; the second type of statements may be therefore fittingly discarded. In the same way it may be assumed that with a general dissolution and corruption in the aboriginal society, and with all kinds of vices engrafted upon it the general level of conjugal affection and the standard of treatment of the wife by her husband went down. The contrary cannot possibly be assumed.

So it appears that, even from the quality of the material the observer had at his disposal, some useful hints may be obtained as to the direction in which our statements need correction. Furthermore it was said above that useful indications can be gathered from the way in which the observer was in contact with the natives; whether the observer was a long time in contact with the natives or only a short time; whether he made his observations with deliberate scientific aim, or whether they were made casually and recollected afterwards; whether he had good opportunities for observation, and under what conditions this was carried on, and so forth.

All these questions may throw much light upon the relation between the writer's statement in its final form and the actual state of things to which it refers. These questions are also in close connection with the point mentioned below, touching the profession of an observer. For it is usually the privilege of the missionaries to be in a long and intimate contact with the natives, to have their confidence, and sometimes to understand even their language, while it is the ethnographer's privilege to understand the aim of his inquiries. In some cases there are fairly detailed data about these points, and such information about the conditions and circumstances under which the writer got his evidence greatly increases its value. In all cases where the evidence is contained in memoirs, diaries, descriptions of travels, expeditions, etc., it is possible to form an idea as to what kind of relation existed between the respective author and the material of his observation. So it appears that Curr and Salvado had especially good opportunities; it is possible to picture the way in which authors like Collins, Taplin, Grey, Eyre, Lumholtz, Angas, Strehlow and others, came into contact with the natives. This is much more difficult to say in the case of writers who wrote only short articles (Oldfield, Stanbridge, Bonney, Palmer, Cameron and others), which merely give information without any details as to how it was gathered. In the case of ethnographers, observing themselves or collecting the observations of others—like Howitt, Spencer and Gillen, Roth, and some others—we might expect to be informed minutely about the way in which they obtained their information. Unfortunately this is only partly the case.

The questions how the condition of the natives, and how the method of observation can affect the final statements have been discussed at length. It was done in order to exemplify how from such considerations may be gathered useful hints, nay even positive indications, as to the direction along which the given statement may be corrected, if corrected at all. There are, besides these points, several other important points referring to the qualifications of the ethnographer that cannot be omitted when any correction of statement is made. There is no room to discuss them in detail; they would lead us too far into the domains of methodology, of ethnographic research. They must be enumerated briefly. So it is quite clear, that not only the personal character but also the profession or occupation of the writer influences very considerably the value and trustworthiness and the character of the information given. The personal character of the ethnographer is a rather delicate matter, but nobody could deny that some authors inspire us with the belief that everything they say is their real conviction, based on solid foundations of facts, while other authors fail to produce the same impression on the reader. It is also clear that a missionary, a police trooper, or an ethnologist, will each look with different eyes upon the same facts; each of them will group the essential features and generalize quite differently, and will express himself in terms which are by no means of the same degree of exactness and clearness. Ultimately each man will have his professional bias : the missionary will be influenced by his creeds and his moral ideas, the ethnologist by his theories, and the squatter or police trooper will sometimes, where there is room for it, allow play to his feelings,which usually are not ones of pure sympathy for the natives. As a matter of fact, it is allowable to speak without exaggeration of professional types of information. That the utmost caution is necessary, and that thus only are to be found indications of the directions in which it is possible to interpret some possible error, is an almost superfluous statement. Of course a careful and complete study of the whole work of an author enables one to judge much better how far his profession or personality may have affected his statements. And this is also the reason why an ethnologist confining himself to a small ethnic area is in a better position than the general one. For he is able to know his sources better, having a much more restricted number to deal with.

Not less important as regards our attitude towards a given writer's statements is the purpose with which his book is written. The greatest confidence of course is inspired by books written with a purely scientific aim. Even the articles of observers who are not men of science are apparently much more carefully written if they are intended for purely scientific use in serious scientific journals (as some articles in the *Journal of the Ethnological Society*, *Jour. Anthrop. Inst.*, etc.). Memoirs, descriptions of travel, and so on, give—*ceteris paribus*—less guarantee; often much more room is left to phantasy, to a tendency to amuse, perhaps puzzle or interest. Concrete instances of this could be easily adduced.

At the end of all his mental operations, each observer had to generalize his observations, to express their common features, and formulate these in abstract and exact language. Here the most important points are personal intelligence and some mental training. The first is to be found even among the casual writers; for only people of a somewhat higher level of mentality would care to observe and write down their observations. But mental training in a scientific direction is exclusively to be found among the ethnographers; some of them stand far above all our other informants in matters of rather theoretical aspect, especially if social phenomena are concerned. And we may usually, in case of contradiction, take this information as the firm basis from which to start the operation of criticism. But on the other hand, there are reasons to mistrust general opinions laid down by professional ethnologists, for they are very often not simple generalizations, but theoretical inferences. Cases will be often met with where a general remark, which could be taken as a statement of fact—and often is given in such a form—appears after a more careful analysis to be quite a conjectural deduction from purely hypothetical premisses, or from incorrect definition. In all cases—*e. g.* where actual existence of group marriage is alleged—it will appear that this statement is a deduction from certain phenomena, which allow of quite a different interpretation, and that the term " marriage " is defined somewhat loosely.[1]

To sum up briefly : criticism of statements has in the first place to ascertain the exact and correct verbal meaning of each of them. In the second place many general but sure hints are afforded by a detailed analysis of the conditions under which the evidence was obtained and set forth by the author. The important points here are : quality of the material under observation; modes in which evidence was obtained (by inquiries from natives, by immediate observation, etc.) ; character, profession, and training of the informant, including possible bias, theoretical, moral, and personal. All these points appear at first sight rather impalpable, but as shown above they may afford good hints, especially if taken into account simultaneously.

[1] Compare also above, pp. 2–5.

Now we pass to the second point indicated above on page 18, namely, the discussion of the local differences which may introduce some apparent contradictions into the statements. Assuming the possession of a series of statements, the correctness of which we accept within certain limits, there may still be some contradictions between them, due to the differences between the tribes, to which these statements refer. The task will be consequently to indicate these differences and to give certain reasons why some of the contradictions may be dealt with in this way and why others cannot be reduced to local differences. In the first place, in order to facilitate the application of the geographical point of view, the survey of the statements will always be made in the same geographical order. I begin with the south-east end of the continent and proceed then westwards and north-wards, enumerating first the tribes of Victoria, then the tribes of the South territory of South Australia. I proceed over New South Wales to the Central and Northern tribes; then to Queensland, ending with West Australia. The order is kept only roughly without pedantic accuracy, which cannot be achieved, as many writers do not even trouble to localize their statements with anything approaching exactitude.

It may now be laid down in which cases it is possible to point with certainty to local differences between the different tribes and reduce to these factors the contradictions which are found. If the same author, who is known to be well-informed concerning the whole area (either personally or through reliable informants), points expressly to such differences, there is no reason to disbelieve him. Many such local differences are indicated in the extensive works of Spencer and Gillen, and Howitt. As an example may be quoted the differences in sexual matters, pointed out by Howitt in *Reports of the Smithsonian Institution* (compare below, pp. 100 and 101). But even in the case of such reliable authors as the ones just mentioned it should always be carefully considered whether they knew with the same degree of exactness all the tribes they compare. Further, when there is independent information about geographically-separated tribes from reliable authors of the same degree of exactness, to whose information we have reason to ascribe the same weight, we may also safely point, if there are any contradictions, to local differences. But if quite contradictory statements about some tribe or tribes living in close neighbourhood are given, we hardly feel inclined to attribute these contradictions to local differences. A very important indication of the advisability of introducing the element of geographical differences is further the question whether the tribes in question are in general different from each other, and whether they belong to different types of culture. Although very little can be said on that point, still on quite broad lines we must, *e. g.* acknowledge that the Kurnai were a tribe with many singularities, that the Arunta and other Central tribes clearly differ from the S.E. tribes, etc. As we shall make very little use of the geographical factor, what is said above may be considered sufficient on that point.[1]

Passing now to the third and perhaps most important methodological point, we may say a few words as to what method should be adopted for the drawing of conclusions from evidence considered as reliable. This is neither a logical proceeding, nor is it a kind of induction. Properly speaking, a witness's statement may be either accepted

[1] As far as I see, in the present state of our knowledge, it is only admissible to speak with greatest care and in very broad lines of the Australian types of culture. Interesting attempts have been made in this direction by Dr. Graebner, Mr. N. W. Thomas, and Father Schmidt. The two latter especially base their work on a profound and extensive knowledge, and formulate their results with the utmost reserve and carefulness. Fr. W. Schmidt has at his disposal the powerful instrument of linguistic knowledge. Mr. W. N. Thomas knows the Australian facts as nobody else does. Their conclusions are therefore of much weight. The present investigations afford little opportunity to point out geographic differences. Compare Fr. W. Schmidt, "Die Stellung, d. Aranda," etc., *Z. f. E.*, 1908, pp. 866 *sqq.*; F. Graebner, *Ibid.*, 1905, pp. 28 *sqq.*; *Globus*, xc. Consult also N. W. Thomas, *Kinship*, and the same, *Z. f. E.*, 1905.

or rejected. But in this book importance has been laid on presenting the evidence in a quite definite way. Evidence is not used in order to exemplify or to prove a given assertion on a special point. Such a proceeding appears to be rather dogmatic, for usually in such cases the author gives preference to an *a priori* opinion, and looks afterwards for its confirmation in the ethnographic first-hand literature. Owing to the contradictory character of the latter, practically anything can be proved from it. In the present book the author merely sets forth the problem; for instance, such quite general questions are asked, as: How are wives obtained in Australia? What is the treatment of the wife by her husband? What are the sexual relations in general? and so forth. On each of those general topics evidence is afterwards collected, without prejudice or preference given to any type of opinion. There is, therefore, much less risk of bias or one-sidedness; the whole care is to make the best of the evidence thus collected; and a series of statements upon a given subject is presented. Each of them gives information on several points at once; at any rate each of them may usually be analyzed into a series of simpler statements. And this analytical operation will be our first task. There is always one or more assertion sufficiently general, or simple, which will be contained in all or in the majority of our statements and will be contradicted by none. These may be considered as established by our evidence. On other points there will be contradictions. Often these contradictions will be only apparent, due to a confusion in terminology, or to the defective way in which the writers have expressed themselves. Here recourse must be had to our first form of criticism, to the ascertainment of the exact meaning of each statement (verbal criticism). If that fails, the contradictions must be recognized as real ones. In case they cannot be attributed to any local differences, we must try to eliminate them. And on this point recourse must be had to the criticism of the statements from the point of view laid down above (p. 25). Some of the statements may be discarded as untrustworthy; the correct interpretation of others may be determined; and thus the contradictions will vanish. Sometimes this is impossible; the contradictions remain irreducible. Then they must be simply pointed out, and there is nothing further to be done. Undoubtedly much greater service is rendered to science by pointing out really irresolvable contradictions and obscurities than by establishing fallacious certitude.

Especially if on the part of the field ethnographers there could be expected some interest in the results of theoretical research, such indications of contradictions on points, the theoretical importance of which should be proved, would be of real value.[1] Only such a co-operation between theoretical writers and observers can give us satisfactory results. To make indifferent observation is easy. To note essential things and give useful observations is impossible without theoretical knowledge and an insight into the laws of sociology. It would be better if field ethnographers would consider the questions of theoretical writers, and take into account in their scheme of investigations the utilization subsequently to be made of their work.

Returning, after this digression, to our theme, it may be observed that the method of dealing with evidence is very simple : there is the analytical operation, of finding the essential points contained in a series of statements; in other words, the operation of analyzing these statements into simple factors and stating which are common to all the statements and may be accepted as well established. A further task consists in pointing out the irreducible contradictions. This operation obviously contains all the others—criticism of the text and contents of the statement, and reduction of contradictions

[1] Mr. Thomas in his work on Australian kinship suggests at every step questions which apparently are quite within the scope of investigation, and upon which our present evidence gives no answer. But unhappily I have not been able to trace any influence of this important work in the recent ethnographic publications.

to local differences. It is evident also that, although theoretically the criticism of statements was dealt with first, then the question of geographical differences, and in the third place the problem of handling a series of statements, as a matter of fact, the first step is to make a survey of all our evidence, resolving it into a set of problems, and then to take each problem separately; in this way we shall find contradictions and endeavour to eliminate them, and we shall be compelled to exercise criticism on the statements.

I would like to add here that to help us in the decision between several contradictory opinions, there is still one criterion beside the hints enunciated above (which refer to the character of each individual statement). I mean the criterion whether the final opinion drawn from the evidence is compatible or not with the other well-established features of Australian sociology. When deciding to adhere to some view, which is not established by a unanimous and categoric opinion of all our informers, it is always necessary to put this view to the test of other well-established facts. There are some views which are quite incompatible with the general conditions of life in the Australian aboriginal society and with the resulting mode of living. As a good example of such deductive demonstrations we may quote the passage in Curr, where he arithmetically proves that the statement of Dawson about the Australian chiefs and their court cannot be true.[1] Another example is afforded by the interesting passage of Howitt quoted below *in extenso* (pp. 113 and 114), which relates how the author thinks that our ideas on group marriage should be modified by what we know about the aboriginal mode of living and about the natural character of men. As a rule it is well always to try to ascertain whether our conclusion does not stand in contradiction with some part of our well-founded knowledge. Thus in practice it is always necessary to start with a crude series of facts, and in any

[1] Curr, *A.R.*, i. pp. 53 *sqq.*

attempt at criticism to be guided by the contradictions found in them. If then criticism and corrections, made according to our rules, remove the contradictions, we have another guarantee that our corrections were good. For if a series of statements, which at first sight seemed to present irreconcilable contradictions, do agree after we have applied to such of them as were either in a minority or appeared vague or came from uncertain sources, corrections or interpretations (the latter based on principles laid down quite independently), it may be concluded that our reason for applying the correction and the way in which we have done it, were sufficiently correct and justified.

To use a series of statements as they are given would be in the majority of cases quite impossible. All the contradictions imaginable would be present, and we should either helplessly drop any attempt at forming an opinion, or we should get out of the difficulty by a purely arbitrary act. We could by an act of faith believe in some of our writers and accept only what they say or what confirms their opinion, and completely ignore any contradictory information. That would even enable us to form a much more certain and detailed view on many points. Our way of proceeding compels us often to relinquish a very precise, definite opinion, which we could hold if we accepted one statement to be ultimately true, and neglected the others; but it gives us at least the conviction that any more precise conclusion would be unfounded. That all the corrections must be carried out on grounds of ample justification and in the most discreet way is quite clear. It will be seen that in the subsequent pages only rarely have statements been amended, and then the reasons are always given. But it is important that even these few corrections should be done systematically. The above indications will, I trust, help to a certain degree to justify the method adopted in dealing with evidence.

Our methodological considerations were necessarily

taken on broad lines. To give a detailed and precise description of the method of treating the Australian material would require a whole volume, for there are in all individual cases so many influences and possibilities that may be considered as sources of error, and so many elements to take into consideration, that it would be nearly impossible to trace all the mental processes that have to be followed here. I found it also impossible to give explicitly all my reasons in each place where I ventured to correct a statement. Nevertheless, I have not thought it superfluous to give in outline the chief points adopted in this criticism. In the first place even these general hints will be quite sufficient to indicate the writer's motives to every one who has had to deal in an analogous way with ethnographical materials. And then they will serve as a proof that these questions, doubts, and precautions, were present to his mind while weighing the evidence. In the last place, as science is essentially based on mutual help and mutual agreement, if we had a whole series of workers on a given ethnographic material, a certain general assent, if such could be obtained, would undoubtedly be the best criterion of reliability of sources. But matters should be openly and explicitly discussed.

To sum up, the chief methodological principle which we have striven to keep always before us, is a thorough clearness about every step of our reasoning. In the first place, therefore, care has been taken to give an explicit and a perfectly clear survey of the statements; and to draw conclusions in such a way that all our reasons for drawing them shall be as clear as possible to the reader, so as to enable every one to apply his own criticism as easily as possible at any stage of our reasoning. Necessarily in a study such as the present one, some allowance must be made for a subjective element in the final judgments on the value of the evidence. But just as the writer must ask for a certain amount of trust in his scientific judgment, so he is bound to give every means to the reader to enable him always fully to judge and exercise his criticism on the use the author is making of this liberty.

In order to achieve this as far as in us lies, the methodological principles set forth above have been adopted. They are in short, as follows : We accept as facts those points in which all statements agree. On controversial points we try to eliminate the contradictions by applying textual criticism to the statements, or by pointing out the possible sources of error, or by showing that these contradictions must be set down to local differences between the tribes. In drawing conclusions, we shall point out those facts which are well established, and also point out those which are more or less uncertain or contradictory. The sources used are not very numerous, but it is hoped that they will be found sufficient. They have been impartially chosen and include each of the various types of Australian evidence.

CHAPTER II

MODES OF OBTAINING WIVES

KEEPING to these general methodological principles, the aim of this study will be merely an objective, unprejudiced description of the different forms of the Australian family organization.

In accordance with what has been said above, let us accept at the outset a general definition, along the lines of which our investigations will be carried out. My choice for this purpose is the well-known definition of Dr. Westermarck : " Marriage is a more or less durable connection between male and female, lasting beyond the mere act of propagation till after the birth of the offspring." In another place (*Moral Ideas*, ii. p. 364) Dr. Westermarck completes this definition : " As a social institution, on the other hand, it has a somewhat different meaning : it is a union regulated by custom and law. Society lays down the rules relating to the selection of partners, to the mode of contracting marriage, to its form, and to its duration." We may also remember that Dr. Westermarck first pointed out that " marriage is rooted in family, rather than family in marriage "[1]; and that he insists on the importance of economic elements in family life, and especially

---

[1] (*Hist. H. Marr.*, chap. iii.) Dr. Westermarck's work was written on much more general lines. He did not aim at a purely morphological reconstruction of family life in any ethnographical province. 1 did not, therefore, refer to his researches in the methodological sketch ; here, however, they must serve as a starting point. It is the most exhaustive treatise on the individual family ; all the essential parts of the problem are sketched in a masterly manner in this fundamental work, and the outlines of more special investigation indicated.

on the facts of the rearing of children and the mode of living.

These remarks of Dr. Westermarck, corroborating what has been said in the introduction, direct our analysis to the relationship between parents and children as well as between the conjugal parties; resolving thus the marriage problem into the more general family problem. On the other hand, Dr. Westermarck, in these short passages quoted, as well as throughout his work, insists on the general and sociological aspect of family life. We shall try to apply his points of view systematically to our Australian material, keeping in mind the addition of the legal side of the question.

As each relationship is intended to be separately treated, let us begin with that of man and wife, and especially with its " legal " aspect. The first point for discussion will be the modes of obtaining wives. In this the search will be for elements, that enforce *ipso facto* the validity of marriage; there will probably be found in them the expression of some collective ideas, referring to the validity, moral or customary sanction, that marital union enjoys in the eyes of the native. It is also highly important for the whole question of marriage and family to ascertain whether the modes of obtaining wives are subject to any norm, compliance with which was enforced by an active intervention of society in some form. Such norms, according to the definition given above, would be legal ones, and they, necessarily, involve and presuppose a series of collective ideas, the knowledge of which would afford a deep insight into the primitive social mechanism.

Betrothal or marriage ceremonies that would express a sanction of purely social or even *mystic* or moral character are few, although not quite absent. Nevertheless the widespread practice of allotting young girls even in infancy, or before birth sometimes, shows *ipso facto* how deeply rooted the idea of the individual right of a man to a woman is in the native mind. Also in the case when wives are obtained by elopement or capture, there are certain ordeals, formalities or duties, that give to such a marriage its social sanction.

The following statements it will be seen present but little field for correction. What we are asking for in this place are merely facts which are evident and palpable enough not to escape the attention of even ordinary observers. Only the betrothal ceremonies and acts seem to have been more esoteric, and therefore they are reported in only a few cases, where the authors were more intimately acquainted with native customs and ideas.

Statements.—Amongst the Kurnai marriage was brought about generally by elopement; sometimes by capture; and less frequently by exchange or by gift.[1] In cases of elopement " the male relatives searched for her (the fugitive), sometimes with success, sometimes without success. If the couple could remain away till the girl was with child . . . she would be forgiven." [2] Otherwise, if found, she was badly chastised, and the man had to fight her relatives. If they should persevere in their plans and elope two or three times . . . they would be forgiven.[3] The Kurnai are the only people among whom elopement was the general rule. The punishment was there accordingly not very severe, and the marriage legalized in case of perseverance, or if the couple were skilful enough not to allow themselves to be soon caught.

J. Bulmer, Lake Tyers, Gippsland, says that among the Gournditch-Mara the majority of wives were obtained by exchanging a sister or a near relative. Elopement was always followed by bloodshed.[4] " Marriage was by betrothal of children by their respective parents, therefore by exchange of sisters," says Howitt [5] of the same tribe.

Exchange of sisters (own or tribal) was practised by the Youin; the marriage being arranged by the fathers; there was a mutual public agreement between them. " The two being thus promised to each other, the girl is looked upon as the future wife of the boy." In cases of elopement, if there was a baby the marriage was legalized, especially if a sister (tribal or own) could be given in exchange.[6] Here we may note that the arrangement was made publicly, during one of the tribal gatherings. The future brothers-in-law exchange gifts, and on the day of the arrangement

---

[1] Howitt, *Kamilaroi and Kurnai*, p. 343. See also their modes of getting females by capture. Compare pp. 200 *sq.* and pp. 348 *sq.*   [2] p. 202.   [3] *Ibid.*

[4] In Brough Smyth, i. p. 77. Compare also Howitt, *Kamilaroi and Kurnai*, p. 350.   [5] *Nat. Tr.*, p. 249.

[6] Howitt, *Nat. Tr.*, p. 263 264. Compare also *Trans. R.S.V.*, p. 117.

keep ostentatiously the whole time together. Thus the whole affair was known to everybody and had a sort of tribal approval.

Among the Woeworung girls were promised in infancy. The arrangement was entered into by the respective fathers, then made public. The old men of the tribe had to decide when the girl was to be handed over to her husband. There was a kind of betrothal ceremony consisting in a public giving up of the bride to the bridegroom.[1]

In the Bangerang tribe " wives were obtained by the exchange of females with any other tribe; so that a man who had a daughter, exchanged her for a wife, for himself or his son, as he thought proper." The custom of exchange of females was a check on abusive cruelty and ill-treatment by the husband. A Black said once to Curr, " If he beats my sister, I'll beat my wife." [2]

In the Victorian tribes described by Beveridge, girls were usually exchanged. It was the father who had to dispose of his girl; there was no betrothal ceremony. Only the woman was bound by the marriage; the man could always send her away.[3]

Amongst the South-west Victorian tribes " parents betroth their children when just able to walk." [4] The arrangement was carried out by the respective fathers. As a sign the boy's father gives the girl an opossum rug, shows her attention, and gives her " nice things to eat." The girl's father visits sometimes her intended husband. " No marriage or betrothal is permitted without the approval of the chief of each party." [5] The girl's mother and aunts must not look at her intended husband from the moment of betrothal.[6] In cases of elopement against the wishes of parents fights take place. A second elopement makes the marriage lawful.[7] Exchange of sisters exists also, with consent of chiefs. The ceremony of betrothal is described at length by the same author.[8] The bride and the bridegroom are painted and specially dressed. Food is stored for the purpose, as feasting and amusement accompany the ceremony. The chief is present and gives his consent. Two months after the betrothal the two do not sleep alone, but with the bridemaid and brideman. The alleged approval of the chief in this statement would be interesting, but here we may mistrust our author, for the general information about the chiefs, their power, etc., seems to be not quite correct (see Curr, *A.R.*, i. p. 53). Besides, the whole style of the book is not strictly scientific, and shows signs of literary embellishments. We must also attach some caution to the detailed description of the betrothal ceremony. It is the only account of a detailed and elaborate ceremony of this kind, with feasting, chief, abstinency, etc. Interesting and important as it is, we may attribute it to local exception, but we cannot consider it as established beyond doubt.

Amongst the Wotjobaluk (S. Victoria) girls were exchanged in infancy by the elder brother. The father's consent was essential :

---

[1] Howitt in *Trans. R.S.V.*, p. 116.
[2] Curr, *Recollections*, p. 248.
[3] Beveridge, p. 22.
[4] J. Dawson, p. 28.
[5] *Ibid.*, p. 28.
[6] *Ibid.*, p. 29.
[7] *Ibid.*, p. 34.
[8] *Loc. cit.*, p. 31.

he could also dispose otherwise of his daughter.   The marriage arrangements and agreements were publicly made at large tribal gatherings.[1]

Stanbridge says that " females are generally betrothed in early infancy," either to friends, or to those whose friendship is solicited. Although the father decides when she has to be given away, " the bridegroom is sure of obtaining his bride, as the honour of the family and of the tribe is considered to be involved in the fulfilment of the betrothal."   In case of subsequent elopement it is the duty of the family to chastise the guilty pair.[2]   This statement is not quite clear, inasmuch as we scarcely understand how the mediæval idea of honour is to be applied to Australian Blacks. Probably it means that the family and local group of the girl have some reason to keep the promise; whether this reason be of magical, legal, or customary character is an open question.   But inferring by analogy we may say that all these factors are coercive here, as in the other tribes.   The family must also support the husband in case of elopement.

" Whenever a female child was promised in marriage to any man, from that very hour neither he nor the child's mother were permitted to look upon or hear each other speak, nor hear their names mentioned by others; for, if they did, they would immediately grow prematurely old and die."   This statement refers to the Jajaurung tribe of Victoria.[3]

" Female children are betrothed usually from early infancy, and such arrangements are usually adhered to," with rare exceptions.   Exchange of sisters is commonly practised, but the parents' consent is essential.   " If a wife be stolen, war is always continued until she is given up, or another female exchanged." These statements refer to the Lower Murray and Adelaide tribes.[4]

There is a very plain and primitive orm of betrothal, performed by the " principal old man in the c amp " amongst the Lower Darling natives.   They usually exchange sisters, and girls are promised in infancy.

Among the Parkengee tribe of the Darling River, " A brother had the right of giving away his sister, which he usually did with a view to his own matrimonial interests.   They were in this way promised when quite children, and in the event of the death of the claimant, his nearest of kin became possessed of his rights."[6] This means that levirate was valid in case of betrothal.

Exchange was the chief feature of the Narrinyeri marriage. Sometimes the father, usually the brother, disposed of the girl.

---

[1] Howitt, *Nat. Tr.*, p. 241.   Also *Trans. R.S.V.*, p. 116.

[2] *Loc. cit.*, p. 288.   (Mount Gambier tribes.)

[3] Brough Smyth, ii. p. 156, on the authority of some first-hand observer.   Brough Smyth gives also (i. pp. 83, 84) a detailed account of courtship and betrothal.   But according to our criterion we do not accept it as a first-hand evidence; nevertheless, it may be useful as illustration.

[4] Eyre, ii. p. 319.

[5] F. Bonney, *J.A.I.*, xiii. p. 129.

[6] S. Newland, *loc. cit.*, p. 21.

There is a simple ceremony, consisting in a formal handing over of the bride, who seems usually to be rather unwilling.[1] It is a social disgrace for a girl not to be given away; if she goes by herself and lives by her own choice with a man, she is "regarded as very little better than a prostitute."[2] A woman is supposed to signify her consent to the marriage by carrying fire to her husband's wurley and making his fire for him.[3]

Among the natives of Yorke's Peninsula, "Betrothal took place in infancy, and the marriage ceremony after circumcision and other rites performed on the male."[4]

"In the Geawe Gal tribe marriage was ordinarily by the gift[5] of the woman and by consent of both fathers . . . and would be arranged years before the time of marriage." In cases of elopement the offender had to fight the female's relatives; he retained her only if victor. In cases of capture, only a woman of the right class could be retained.[6]

In New South Wales marriage was arranged by the parents. If two people fell in love, they eloped, but if the family applied to the camp council, the latter would interfere and punish the culprit.[7]

Henderson says that among the Blacks of New South Wales abduction always arouses fights.[8] Using legal terms, this means that abduction of a woman, whether married or not, was considered a crime.

Of the courtship in some of the New South Wales tribes we have an account by J. Turnbull: "When a young man sees a female to his fancy, he informs her she must accompany him home; the lady refuses; he not only enforces compliance with threats, but blows: thus the gallant, according to the custom, never fails to gain the victory, and bears off the willing though struggling pugilist."[9] In the following context the author asserts that violence is here a mere formality. It is difficult to say anything definite about this statement. If it refers merely to the final marriage "ceremony" it might be accepted. But if it is to be accepted as describing all that refers to marriage, it is obviously false. The author was a "circumnavigator," and in his voyage round the world, about the year 1800, had probably little opportunities for observing the Australian aborigines. Such statements as this, uncritically accepted (as this is, e. g. in Waitz-Gerland), are usual sources of error in ethnology and hence in sociology.

---

[1] H. E. A. Meyer, quoted by Rev. Taplin, loc. cit., p. 10.

[2] Ibid., p. 11.

[3] Ibid., p. 12. Taplin's own remark. See also Kamilaroi and Kurnai, p. 350, where it is added that in cases of unsuccessful elopement against the parents' will, the couple were severely punished; the offender being even put to death.

[4] Sutton, p. 17.   [5] I think it means not by exchange.

[6] Howitt, N.T.S.E.A., p. 216. Geawe Gal, Hunter River, New South Wales; possessing the Kamilaroi sub-class. See also Kam. and Kurn., p. 250.

[7] G. S. Lang, p. 11.   [8] Loc. cit., p. 110.

[9] Turnbull, pp. 98, 99.

In some other New South Wales tribes " the ceremony of marriage is peculiar. In most cases the parties are betrothed at an early age, and as soon as they arrive at the proper age, the young man claims his ' gin ' or wife." [1] " The women are considered as an article of property, and are sold or given away by the parents or relatives without the least regard to their own wishes." [2] The well-known elements of infant betrothal, and a kind of purchase of a female from her family, are contained in this statement.

According to another author, who has written about the New South Wales tribes, the girls are given away at a corroboree. Sometimes they are " stolen," but then fights always ensue. [3] This statement contains the feature of publicity of marriage. It does not say anything about the conditions preceding such a public allotment.

According to Tench, capture was the prevalent form in which marriage was brought about in the Port Jackson tribes. [4] Tench was in very early times at the settlement, but being a military man and making only a short stay, he hardly had very good opportunities of observing the natives. His statement cannot outweigh all the contrary ones.

The statement of Barrington, who says that among the Port Jackson natives blows are the usual mode of courtship and that they are well accepted as a token of tenderness, [5] can only be understood if we accept these facts as a kind of pretended marriage by capture. But much importance cannot be attached to it.

Amongst some tribes in the neighbourhood of Sydney [6] small children are betrothed, and as a sign of that the girl wears a necklace. In another place [7] the same author says that marriage by capture occurs.

Among the tribes of the South-east coast of New South Wales (Hawkesbury River to Cape Howe) the " marriages are regulated by a system of betrothal." " The old men assemble in council," and establish the relation of *Nanarree* between a boy and a girl or woman. The boy then marries eventually the woman's daughter. The *Nanarree* couple " theoretically occupy the position of son-in-law and mother-in-law." They are tabooed to each other. A man and woman may be *Nanarree* to several individuals. [8]

We read of an instance of a formal betrothal (called *Bahumul*), although meagre in its ceremonial, among the Euahlayi tribe. A baby girl is destined by her parents to be " given to a man." She is brought to him, some feathers are taken off the baby's head and put on the man's. Her grandmother says, " Look at him and remember him, because you are promised to him." " That makes it a formal betrothal, binding to both sides." " I have heard great camp rows, because girls made a struggle for independence, having found out they had only been promised, not formally betrothed, to some old chap whom they did not wish to

---

[1] Wilkes (smaller edition), i. p. 225.   [2] *Ibid.*
[3] Hodgkinson, *loc. cit.*, pp. 229, 230.   [4] *Loc. cit.*, p. 199.
[5] *Loc. cit.*, p. 168.   [6] C. P. Hodgson, p. 220.
[7] *Ibid.*, p. 243.
[8] R. H. Mathews in *J.R.S.N.S.W.*, xxxiv. pp. 263, 264.

marry." Here we meet with an instance of a formality, which has in itself much more than a simple promise, that is " binding for both sides." [1]

Amongst the Wiradjuri the girl was promised in infancy and sisters were exchanged.[2]

Amongst the Dieri the individual or *Tippa Malku* marriage was established when girls were quite young, and upon the basis of exchange, the decision lying in the hands of the mother's brother. In another place we read that the *Tippa Malku* marriage was brought about sometimes also by the council of old men.[3] *Pirrauru* " wives" were allotted by the council of old men.[4] In cases of elopement the offender was pursued by the kindred.[5]

The German missionary, L. Schultze, informs us about the Central tribes that " the betrothal is solely and absolutely arranged by the father of the girl. He promises and contracts his daughter, within the limits of the class, to whomsoever he pleases." " A youth cannot select a bride for himself, or a girl a bridegroom." " The betrothal is often made by the father, soon after the girl is born, from mercenary motives," for the future son-in-law is obliged to hunt and provide his father-in-law with food.[6]

We are informed about the Central tribes that " girl-stealing is not a trifling matter." Fights always ensue as the result of it.[7]

By the detailed data given by Spencer and Gillen [8] we get a good insight into the legal and customary side of the modes of obtaining wives amongst the Central tribes of the Arunta nation. Methods of securing a woman are (*a*) charming by means of magic, (*b*) capture, (*c*) elopement, (*d*) the custom of *Tualcha-Mura*, by means of which a man secures a wife for his son by making an arrangement with some other man, with regard to the latter's daughter. The legal side of the first method is shown by the fact that a man's right to a woman, secured by means " of magic, is supported by the men of his own local group." [9] Capture is the " very rarest way in which a Central Australian secures a wife." If captured by an avenging party, the woman must be lawfully allotted to one of the men (who has exclusive right to her afterwards).[10] There is an accompanying ceremony, and the decision lies in the hand of an old man, the leader of the party.[11] In cases of elopement there was always a fight, sometimes between the two parties only, sometimes their local groups taking part.

---

[1] Mrs. Parker, *loc. cit.*, p. 55.   [2] Howitt, *Nat. Tr.*, p. 211.

[3] Howitt, *J.A.I.*, xx. p. 55, and Frazer, *ibid.*, xxiv. p. 169.

[4] Howitt, *N.T.S.E.A.*, p. 177, and *J.A.I.*, xx. pp. 57 *sq.*

[5] *Kam. and Kurn.*, p. 350.   [6] *Loc. cit.*, p. 236.

[7] W. H. Willshire, *loc. cit.*, p. 27.

[8] Spencer and Gillen, *Nat. Tr.*, chap. xvii, *Methods of obtaining Wives*, pp. 554 *sqq.* Compare also *Nor. Tr.*, pp. 32 and 33.

[9] Compare also the detailed description of charming by magic (different methods) given by J. Gillen in *Proc. R.G.S.S.A.*, iv. pp. 25 *sqq.*

[10] No other man of the party having any access to her. *Nat. Tr.*, p. 556.

[11] *Nat. Tr.*, p. 555. The story related in this place is given by the author as an illustration of a general custom.

There were some (tribal) relatives having a special duty of supporting the eloper. Sometimes the aggrieved husband will consent
to hand over the wife; the offender has then an ordeal to undergo.[1]
" The fourth and most usual method of obtaining a wife is that
which is connected with the well-established custom " of *Tualcha-Mura*.[2] This is a relation between a man and his mother-in-
law [3] established by a simple ceremony,[4] and it signifies that the
man has the right to take as wife the daughter of the woman. In
this way " practically every man in the tribe is provided with at
least one woman to whom he is lawfully entitled."[5] He has a
definite right over her; he may waive it or exchange it for another
right over his mother-in-law's son.[6] He stands in a definite
relation to his *Tualcha-Mura* (mother-in-law); receives her hair to
make his hair girdle,[7] and may not speak to her. He has the
duty of providing his father-in-law with food, which is a condition
for the obligations to be kept.[8] It is seldom that these obligations
are broken; and if the parents give the girl to someone else,
the latter is sure to have to undergo a struggle with the former
fiancé.[9] All this holds good also in respect to the Northern
Central tribes.[10] There, too, " as a general rule women are
obtained quite peacefully by the system of betrothal."[11]

Among all the tribes, described by Spencer and Gillen, there
seem to be some marriage ceremonies.[12] In their first work
(*Nat. Tr.*) these authors describe such ceremonies among nine
tribes.[13] In the main these ceremonies consisted of a ritual
defloration of the girl by men standing to her in a definite relationship. In each case the girl had to submit to sexual intercourse
with a series of men standing to her also in a definite relationship.
Men of forbidden degrees have on these occasions access to
women. The girl was afterwards painted and decorated and
handed over to her husband, to whom she was allotted.[14] In
the *Northern Tribes* there is also a detailed description of
this ceremony among the Warramunga,[15] where the husband
keeps abstinence for three days after marriage. Among the
Binbinga, Anula and Mara tribes the ritual defloration seems not
to be a marriage ceremony, *i. e.* seems not to be connected with
the handing over of the girl to her allotted husband.[16] Messrs.

---

[1] *Nat. Tr.*, pp. 556, 557. The story told, pp. 557, 558, where
both the eloped woman and her actual husband have an ordeal to
submit to from the former husband. After having renounced
her in this way she became the property of the man with whom
she had eloped.   [2] *Ibid.*, p. 558.

[3] Who is often of the very same age as he, pp. 558, 559.

[4] *Ibid.*, p. 559.   [5] *Ibid.*, 554. As also *Nor. Tr.*, p. 33.
[6] *Ibid.*, p. 559.   [7] *Nat. Tr.*, p. 559.   [8] *Ibid.*, p. 555.
[9] *Ibid.*, p. 560.   [10] *Nor. Tr.*, p. 77.   [11] *Ibid.*, p. 33.
[12] Compare *Nat. Tr.*, chap. iii., pp. 92 *sqq.*, and *Nor. Tr.*, chap.
iv., pp. 133 *sqq.*   [13] *Nat. Tr.*, pp. 92 *sqq.*
[14] For detailed description see *Nat. Tr.*, pp. 92, 93 (Arunta
and Ilpirra), p. 94 (S. Arunta), pp. 94, 95 (Kaitish), p. 95 (the
remaining six tribes). These ceremonies differ only in details
from each other in different tribes.
[15] *Nor. Tr.*, p. 135.   [16] *Ibid.*, p. 135.

Spencer and Gillen state the existence of this ceremony among sixteen tribes. It is to be noted that these ceremonies do not seem to express any special sanction of the marriage to which they lead, unless they are viewed as " expiation for marriage." [1] Then they might be interpreted as the renouncement of all men's rights and claims to a woman for the benefit of her future owner. The ceremonial handing over of a woman may be also regarded as expressing the public sanction of marriage. We must still notice an interesting ceremony amongst the Warramunga, Tjinjilli, Gnanji, Binbinga, Mara, which consists of some hair being given by the maternal uncle of the girl to her future husband. This hair is worn by him under his arm-band; " it is a simple plan of publicly announcing the fact " of the betrothal.[2] Amongst the Binbinga there is a form of betrothal. The future husband must present his father-in-law with boomerangs, etc., and must avoid him, but goes on giving him presents.[3]

Among some tribes of South Queensland (Bunya-Bunya country) marriage was arranged without any consent of the contracting parties. Sometimes it was arranged when the girl was an infant, and she was then promised to some man of importance or influence. Sometimes exchange of females took place at large tribal gatherings. Elopement was known in these tribes, and a fight decided whether it was legalized or not.[4]

We find a ceremony of betrothal among the Kuinmurbura. " The parents having painted the girl and dressed her hair with feathers, her male cousin takes her to where her future husband is sitting cross-legged in silence, and seats her at his back and close to him. He who has brought the girl after a time removes the feathers from her hair and places them in the hair of her future husband, and then leads the girl back to her parents." The future son-in-law must give presents of game to the father of his promised wife.[5]

We read about the natives of Moreton Bay, that marriage is generally contracted with the consent of the relatives of both parties and the approval of the tribe. As a form of betrothal they join their hands. The stealing of women from neighbouring tribes ends usually in war.[6]

Among the Herbert River natives, exchange of sisters or daughters is the commonest way of obtaining wives.[7] Girls are promised to their respective husbands [8] in infancy and delivered at the age of nine or ten years.

We find in Brough Smyth an account of a betrothal ceremony, as practised by the natives on Fraser Island (Queensland). This description is given by a correspondent of the Rev. L. Fison: " The bride makes a fire, and the other natives come and place white feathers on her head; then the bride places feathers on the head of the bridegroom; the bridegroom makes a fire, and every one

---

[1] According to Lord Avebury; see *Nat. Tr.*, p. 96.
[2] *Nor. Tr.*, pp. 603, 604.   [3] *Ibid.*, p. 77, footnote.
[4] Tom Petrie, *loc. cit.*, pp. 59, 60.
[5] Howitt, *Trans. R.S.V.*, p. 118.
[6] J. D. Lang, *loc. cit.*, p. 337.   [7] Lumholtz, *loc. cit.*, p. 154.
[8] *Ibid., loc. cit.*, p. 165.

of the blacks present on the occasion brings a firestick and throws it down at the bridegroom's fire." [1]

Girls were betrothed in infancy by their mothers amongst the Wakelbura. It was supposed that a girl would be given in exchange for her.[2] In case of elopement, there was a severe fight, and only after a victory over many adversaries could the man keep his wife.

Among the North-West Central Queensland tribes [3] " each male can have an official wife " supplied him by the camp in general council assembled,[4] and an unofficial one of his own choice. " Both share equal rights and responsibilities." The consent of the girl's family is in both cases essential.[5] The ceremony of betrothal consisted in exchange of firesticks, and " is binding on both sides." [6] Exchange of sisters is practised, too.[7] If eloping, " both have to run the gauntlet of the outraged community," which gives them a rather harsh reception. After which " the couple is now recognized as husband and wife." [8] In cases of elopement of a married woman there is a fight, or compensation is granted to the injured husband. In another place Roth says that taking a girl against the wishes of parents was punished by death.[9]

According to Macgillivray's information, infant betrothal even before birth was prevalent in the Port Essington tribes.[10]

The following account is reported by a Lascar who spent several years among the tribes of the North-East coast (Raffles Bay) : " Their marriage ceremony is performed in the following way : The father and mother of a female child lead in one hand between them the intended bride (whilst in the other they each carry a piece of burning wood) towards the intended husband, he standing with his back towards them. When they arrive at the appointed place, the parents lay down the burning pieces of wood, beside which the child sits down, and the parents retire, on which the husband turns round to his wife and takes her home." [11]

We are informed about the natives of the Cape of York Peninsula and Prince of Wales Islands : " In most cases females are betrothed in infancy, according to the will of the father, and without regard to disparity of age. Thus the future husband may be, and often is, an old man with several wives." [12]

J. Forrest, speaking of the natives of Central and Western Australia, says : " Betrothal is very general. A cnild a year old will sometimes be betrothed to an old man, and it will be his duty to feed and protect her, and (unless she is stolen by someone else) when she is old enough she becomes his wife." [13]

" The girls are not the exclusive property of the father until he thinks fit to give them in marriage to some of his friends ; by the

---

[1] *Loc. cit.*, i. p. 89.

[2] Howitt, *Nat. Tr.*, p. 222, and *Trans. R.S.V.*, p. 117.

[3] W. E. Roth, *Ethnol. Stud.*, pp. 180, 181, sec. 323.

[4] See *Ibid.*, sec. 238.   [5] *Ibid.*, p. 181, under *a*.   [6] *Ibid.*

[7] *Ibid.*, p. 181, under *b*.   [8] *Ibid.*, p. 181, under *c*.

[9] W. E. Roth, *N.Q. Ethnog.*, Bull 8, p. 5.

[10] *Loc. cit.*, i. p. 151.   [11] Wilson, p. 144.

[12] Macgillivray, *loc. cit.*, ii. p. 8.   [13] *Loc. cit.*, p. 317.

law of these people the females, from the time of their birth, are appropriated to certain males of the tribe, and not even the parents have the right to set aside these obligations." If this man dies, the mother may dispose of her daughter.—This refers to the Watchandee tribe of West Australia.[1] The same author writes that elopement is punished in these tribes by the death of the female, and a severe ordeal is imposed on the male; an instance is adduced to illustrate this.[2] The statement is quite unique in this, that it asserts no right of the family to betroth their daughter. On the other hand, we are by no other author informed of such a thing as a man having an *a priori* right to a girl. We are led to the supposition that these male individuals are simply men belonging to the right marriage class. For undoubtedly in an exogamous tribe, having four or eight classes and being not too numerous, the number of marriage-able individuals must have been very limited, and one of them might have had some special prerogatives. This supposition would also account for the severe punishment inflicted in case of elopement with a man to whom " she did not lawfully belong," viz. with an individual of the improper class. Otherwise this statement would be contradictory with all the others, and we could hardly harmonize it with the general view we form of the aboriginal marriage rules.

Among the tribes observed by Salvado " Le sauvage demande la personne qu'il veut épouser au père de celle-ci, et si celui-ci ne l'a promise à aucun autre, et n'y voit pas d'empêchement, il la lui accorde. Dès ce moment, la jeune personne appartient au sauvage qui l'a demandée, quoiqu'elle reste en compagnie de sa famille, jusqu' à l'age de la puberté. Cet engagement est inviol-able, et si jamais un pére y manquait, ce serait la cause de beau-coup de sang répandu. Le sauvage pourtant quand il demande une jeune personne en mariage, s'il ne se fie pas à la parole du père, l'emmène avec lui et lui tient lieu de frère, jusqu' à ce qu 'elle ait atteint l'âge convenable Dans aucun cas on ne demande à la jeune personne son consentement. Neanmoins j'ai entendu dire à des fiancés : ' Je l'aime et elle m'aime aussi.' "[3] " L'au-tre manière de prendre femme est de la ravir à son père, ou à son mari, soit à cause de sa rare beauté, soit parceque son mari la maltraite. Mais ensuite si celui-ci la trouve, il la tue sans pitié, aussi le ravisseur l'emmène-t-il au loin, et tâche de se soustraire à tout jamais à la présence de l'offensé." [4]

In West Australia " female children are always betrothed within a few days after their birth; and from the moment they are betrothed the parents cease to have any control over the future settlement of their child." The woman is kept by her husband as his exclusive property. " Stealing a wife is generally punished with death." It means that elopement was punished by death, but we are not told if both parties or only one, and which one. This statement agrees with our last one. It might be, therefore, that in West Australia the rules were in this regard more stringent. But it seems more probable that death was

---

[1] Oldfield, p. 249.   [2] *Ibid.*, pp. 249, 250.
[3] Salvado, *loc. cit.*, p. 278.   [4] *Ibid.*, pp. 278, 279.

the extreme punishment only, and that usually an ordeal was sufficient.[1]

We are informed in G. F. Moore's vocabulary of West Australian languages that the word meaning " firm," " fixed " is " applied to a man and wife as firmly united together." [2]   It shows that this idea must have been strongly inculcated in the aboriginal society, if the expression for firmness and marriage were associated in their language.   By itself, such a linguistic argument might be justly designated as futile; but it is a valuable addition to the other evidence in our possession.   The same author mentions three modes of obtaining wives : infant betrothal, inheritance from a brother or relative (levirate), and elopement.[3]

We read in Scott Nind's description of the aborigines of King George's Sound : " The girls appear to be at the disposal of their father and are generally bespoke in their infancy; even before they are born we have been told to whom they were betrothed, if they prove to be females."   Sometimes exchange of relatives is practised.   In some cases boys are adopted as sons-in-law—a custom called *cotertie*.[4] This seems to be analogous to the customs reported from Central Australia and New South Wales. " Attentions and presents are paid more to her (the bride's) father than to herself, and indeed the trifles she receives are generally transferred to him.   These chiefly consist of game or other articles of food; the father, perhaps, receives a cloak, spears or other implements." [5]   The author says : " I do not think they have any nuptial ceremony." [6]   Another mode of procuring a wife is to carry her off; sometimes against her will, generally by mutual agreement.   In both cases the couple must beware of the husband's revenge.   If the female become pregnant and presents are given to the husband, she is released from her first engagement.[7]   A woman may be also betrothed during her husband's lifetime to a man, to whom she passes when widowed.[8]

Browne relates that girls were often promised in infancy; elopement also often took place.[9]

We have also six statements in the answers given to Professor Frazer's *Questions* (*J.A.I.*, xxiv., pp. 157 *sq.*).   I have not ranged them with the foregoing, for they seem not to be of equal accuracy [10] except perhaps that of Police Inspector Foelsche, Port Darwin, North Territory, South Australia.   And this agrees with the majority of our data : girls are promised in infancy to men of different ages, and go to live with them when arrived at puberty. It is noteworthy that all these six statements deny the existence of any betrothal ceremony.   Five of them inform us that wives were obtained by " purchase " from their parents.   The word purchase covers, probably, the fact that the girl's parents obtained,

[1] Geo. Grey, ii. pp. 229, 230.   [2] *Loc. cit.*, p. 5.
[3] *Loc. cit.*, p. 41.   [4] *Loc. cit.*, p. 38.   [5] *Ibid.*
[6] p. 38.   [7] *Ibid.*   [8] p. 39.   [9] *Loc. cit.*, p. 450.
[10] They are given by police troopers, stationmasters, etc. One of them is Sam Gason, whose information about the Dieri we know from another place.   It is crude, but not quite useless; here he does not teach us anything new.

at the marriage contract, and probably ever after, gifts from their future son-in-law. We have such statements already in our collection, and it seems that wherever there was no exchange of females the girl's family received some compensation for her in another form.

According to our already described methodological plan, the area or range of the facts covered by all this evidence must be divided into smaller fields. Or, in other words, it is needful to bring our information under several headings, show the points upon which there is complete agreement, and discuss the other points in greater detail.

There are forty-nine statements (including one of the six just summarily mentioned). Not all of them give us full information concerning the whole of our subject; some mention only one or other of the methods of obtaining wives, without asserting or denying the existence of the other forms. But roughly speaking, we may say that in all tribes there are on the one hand some normal, pacific modes of obtaining wives (exchange of relatives, promise in infancy, betrothal), and on the other hand some more or less violent forms (elopement, capture). About twenty-three of the forty-nine statements, all which are explicit and reliable, assert the existence of both these forms amongst the tribes they deal with. The violent forms, elopement and capture, seem to have been rather the exception than the rule, but there seems to have been not a single tribe in which elopement was completely absent.[1] Among the Kurnai elopement was a prevalent form of marriage. In all other tribes the methods, called here normal or pacific, were prevalent. The main features of these forms are : betrothal in infancy, exchange of sisters or relatives, and a series of obligations and mutual duties which both contracting

[1] Compare *Trans. R.S.V.*, p. 118. Howitt says that in all South-Eastern tribes elopement was in use; especially if there was any difficulty in finding a relative for exchange, or if two people fell in love with each other. It was considered a breach of custom and law, but it was a valid, recognized form of marriage if legalized subsequently. Practically the same may be said of all tribes of the continent.

parties undertake. All these features may be briefly discussed.

The custom of *betrothing* females *in infancy* seems to be very widespread. That this custom was known in all tribes appears in all the statements explicitly or implicitly (with the exception of those statements only which were discarded as unreliable, *e. g.* those which assert marriage by capture as the most usual form). So in the tribes described by Howitt and his correspondents (chiefly referring to Victoria, New South Wales, and South territory of South Australia) girls were as a rule promised in infancy, and these engagements were kept. This appears the most usual way of obtaining wives amongst the Central tribes, in Queensland, and in West Australia (J. Dawson, Curr, Stanbridge, Howitt, Eyre, F. Bonney, R. H. Mathews, Spencer and Gillen, T. Petrie, Grey, Browne); whereas according to Oldfield, girls belonged by birth to a certain man. In Roth's statement we are not informed whether women were allotted by camp council in infancy or when grown up.

This widespread custom of infant betrothal had its important consequences, some apparent at first sight. So it is evident, that not only had the woman no voice as to her husband, but even the latter had scarcely a choice in the proper sense of the word. For when he entered into the engagement, although he was often of a mature age, he could not have any idea how his bride would look when grown up. The legal importance of this form of marriage and all the mutual obligations connected therewith will be discussed below.

Another point of importance is that this form of marriage contract was in many tribes combined with the *exchange* of sisters or relatives. Fifteen statements mention this explicitly as the most usual condition under which a female could be obtained. It must have been prevalent in the South-Eastern tribes.[1] In the case of

---

[1] Speaking of the South-Eastern tribes in general, Howitt says : " It may be safely laid down as a broad and general pro-

exchange it was usually the sister who was given in exchange for a wife,[1] but sometimes also a father secured a wife in exchange for his daughter (Curr, Taplin, Beveridge), which is in perfect accord with the fact that disparity of age was very frequent in Australian marriages. At any rate the father's consent was always essential (Stanbridge, Beveridge, Schultze, Taplin on the Narrinyeri, Rusden on the Geawe Gal, Howitt on the Wotjobaluk). In general when a girl was promised in infancy it was always done by her family; or at least with the consent of her family. As, for instance, in N. Central Queensland, where, according to Roth, girls were disposed of sometimes by the camp council, but by agreement with the family. By the word family must be here understood in the first place the girl's father, whose consent, as just said, was essential, then her brothers and nearest relatives, who would eventually have profit from exchanging her. But also other members of the female's family are interested in the transaction and possibly benefit by it.

The important *part* played by the *family* appears in all our statements; the only contradictory one is that of Oldfield, who says that the parents had no right over their daughter from her birth (but see above our critical remark). From the moment of the " betrothal " the man or boy enters into a certain relation to his future wife's nearest relatives; he has certain duties to perform, certain obligations to fulfil, and certain restrictions to observe. In the case where it is the male's family which makes the contract for him, the two families have certain duties towards each other and stand in a certain mutual

---

position that among these savages a wife was obtained by the exchange of a female relative, with the alternative possibility of obtaining one by inheritance (Levirate), by elopement, or by capture."—*Trans. R.S.V.*, p. 115.

[1] " It seems to me that the most common practice is the exchange of girls by their respective parents, as wives for each other's sons, or in some tribes the exchange of sisters, or of some female relatives by the young men themselves."—*Trans. R.S.V.*, p. 116.

relationship. They exchange gifts (Yuin, Woljabaluk, S.W. Victoria and others); the boy's father has to give presents to the girl, and the boy is visited from time to time by his future father-in-law (W. Victoria); the future mother-in-law is tabooed (Jajaurung, New South Wales, according to R. H. Mathews; Central tribes); in the Central tribes there is the relation of Tualcha Mara and the duty of hunting for the future father-in-law. In the Binbinga there is a present at the betrothal and sometimes duties afterwards.

It seems that in all cases, even when exchange does not take place, it is the father who disposes of his daughter (compare just above). This privilege is important : in this way, as we saw above, an old man may procure a young wife for himself. In other cases by these means the friendship of an influential man may be gained. It is therefore probable that the father, who wields all the authority in the family, enjoys this privilege of disposing of his daughter.

We may view the facts of exchange of females on the one hand, and the various duties of the husband towards his (future or actual) wife's family on the other, also in another light; they show distinctly the features of *marriage by purchase*. In the first place let us remark that the two forms—exchange of females and exchange of gifts or duties for a female—seem to be localized in different areas. We saw that Howitt affirms that exchange is the prominent feature in the South-eastern tribes with the exception of the Kurnai. In those of our statements which refer to this area we found with very few exceptions (J. Dawson, Stanbridge, G. S. Lang, Mrs. Parker) confirmation of his views. The above exceptions do not deny this fact. They are not very explicit, so that we can hardly insist on them as negative evidence. On the other hand, in the Central and Northern area, exchange of females seems not to take place. Here we have some detailed statements, such as those about the Dieri by Gason and Howitt, about the Arunta by

Spencer and Gillen, about the other Northern tribes by the same authors, about the N.W. Queensland tribes by W. E. Roth. In all these explicit statements there is not a single remark about exchange. Nor is the latter mentioned in any statement referring to the Central and Northern area, nor in the four statements which refer to West Australia. We may therefore conclude with a high degree of probability that we have here to do with a real geographical difference between the tribes indicated. As to Queensland, exchange was probably known in the Central and Southern tribes (Tom Petrie and Lumholtz mention it), whereas, as we saw, it was absent in the Western part of that colony. But in nearly all these tribes, where exchange of females is apparently not in use, there is evidence of the existence of duties and obligations on the part of the future husband towards his parents-in-law. We may remember the five statements in which the word purchase was used, and the statement of Wilkes. Schultze says explicitly that the father often gave his daughter away from mercenary motives. The same is confirmed by the more exact and detailed statement of Spencer and Gillen, where the duties of providing the father-in-law with game are reported to be a necessary condition for the obligations to be kept. Among some of the Northern tribes (Binbinga, Anula, Mara) the man has to present his father-in-law with boomerangs and weapons at the contract, and then to supply him with game. There is no information about purchase-marriage either from Queensland or from West Australia. But such a negative evidence is not convincing. Again among the Kurnai, where exchange of females happened very seldom, there were duties of supplying the parents-in-law with game (compare below, pp. 283 *sqq.*). So that if we leave on one side the Western part of Australia and Queensland, and take into consideration only the Northern, Central and South-Eastern tribes, we may say that exchange of females and obligations, of gifts and hunting duties were geographically exclusive. Now it appears to me that exchange of females was a kind of marriage by purchase. If we regard as the chief feature of the latter the fact that the bridegroom has to contribute for his wife something of more or less equal value, we must agree that exchange of females was such a kind of contribution, and even a very fair one.[1] Besides, it appears that the exchange of females was often accompanied by exchange of gifts (compare p. 50, Yuin, Wotjobaluk). That the façts reported from the Central and Northern area show a form of marriage by purchase appears quite clear.

As a further characteristic feature we are told in several instances that such mutual agreements are made *publicly*, during great tribal gatherings, so that all the tribe knows about it (Yuin, Woeworung, New South Wales according to Mathews, New South Wales according to Hodgkinson). Or else the bride is publicly handed to the bridegroom (Narrinyeri, Lower Darling, Kuinmurbura, Fraser Island). In the Central and North Central tribes there are outward signs : the maternal uncle's hair worn under the arm-band; or hair is procured from the future mother-in-law. In some New South Wales tribes a necklace is worn as a sign of engagement (Hodgson).

In some statements we are directly told that there is no *betrothal or marriage ceremony* (in the six notes in *J.A.I.*, xxiv.). But this negative evidence seems on one side to result from the slight and superficial acquaintance these observers had with the aborigines; on the other side from the fact that even in cases where we have such ceremonies described by very reliable informants and their binding power asserted, they are described as being so simple and insignificant, that it is easy to conceive they might readily escape the notice of even a good observer, or at least their nature and importance might be misunderstood. We possess nine statements about betrothal or marriage ceremonies. We

[1] With reference to the Australian facts Dr. Westermarck makes the same remark. " The simplest way of purchasing a wife is no doubt to give a kinswoman in exchange for her." —*H.H.M.*, p. 390.

have Dawson's detailed statement, which seems, never-theless, not to be absolutely trustworthy. But we are also informed of the existence of some simple and appar-ently insignificant ceremonies by J. Bonney, Taplin, R. H. Mathew, Mrs. Langloh Parker, Spencer and Gillen, Roth, Fison's anonymous correspondent, Howitt on the Kuin-murburu, Wilson.[1] Some of these are our best sources.

Turning now to the other, the *violent form* of obtaining wives, we may distinguish the *elopement*, when both sides are consenting, and *capture* where the woman is secured by a mere act of brutal force. These latter forms occur, but they are by no means frequent. They are mentioned by several writers (Hodgson, Rusden, Turnbull, Tench, Barrington and Collins); and by the two latter as the only form of marriage. That this is obviously incorrect was mentioned above in connection with their statements. It is characteristic that all statements reporting the prevalence of marriage by capture refer to New South Wales, and more especially to the neighbourhood of Sydney. But I think that it would be inadvisable to attribute this to a local peculiarity of those tribes. It appears more probable that as all those reports date from the early days of the settlement, and were written nearly at the same time, their opinions cannot be considered as independent, and they are pro-bably repetitions of the same erroneous view which may be assumed to have been held by the general public in the settlement.

This is confirmed by the following comparison of two statements. The first, that of Collins, stating the exist-ence of a crude form of marriage by capture runs thus : " These unfortunate victims [the wives] of lust and cruelty . . . are, it is believed, always selected from the women of a different tribe from that of the males (for they ought not to be dignified with the title of men), and with whom they are at enmity . . . The poor wretch

---

[1] Curr, *A.R.*, i. p. 107, says also that in some tribes there are some insignificant marriage ceremonies.

is stolen upon in the absence of her protectors. Being
first stupefied with blows, inflicted with clubs or wooden
swords, on the head, back and shoulders, every one of
which is followed by a stream of blood, she is then dragged
away through the woods by one arm, with a perseverance
and violence that it might be supposed would displace
it from its sockets."   In this manner the woman is said
to be dragged to the man's camp, where " a scene ensues
too shocking to relate." [1]   The second statement made
by one of Howitt's reliable correspondents, depicts the
state of things with quite different colours : " When a
young man has passed a certain number of Boras (initiations) he has a right to choose a wife from among the
unmarried and otherwise unappropriated women of the
tribe who are of the class permitted to him by the native
laws.   He claims the girl in the presence of her parents
by saying ' I will come and take you by and by,' and
they cannot refuse her to him unless he be specially
disqualified—as, for instance, if his ' hands are stained
with the blood of any of her kin.'   And even in that
case he may carry her off by force if he can in spite of
their refusal.   For this purpose he generally comes by
stealth and alone.   But if he be a very bold warrior,
he sometimes goes openly to the girl's camp and carries
her off, defying the bravest of her friends to meet him
in single combat if they dare to stay him." [2]   In this
second statement it may be noted that only the unappropriated girls of the tribe and those who are lawfully
marriageable may be obtained in this way.   Besides,
this proceeding appears much more in the light of elopement than capture.

Important it is to note that in utter contradiction with
those few statements, made by some early observers in
New South Wales, *capture* is usually reported to be merely
an exceptional form of contracting marriage.   That it
was in existence in nearly all tribes seems beyond doubt.

[1] Howitt in *Smiths. Rep.*, p. 79⁸
[2] *Ibid.*

Spencer and Gillen, Howitt,[1] Curr [2] mention that marriage
by capture occurred.   But all these authors add emphatically that this was the most exceptional mode of acquiring
a wife.[3] And it appears from Spencer and Gillen's
account that capture is effected rather by an avenging
party than by an individual enterprise. And even in
the case of capture, possession does not mean right.
The woman must belong in the first place to the right
class (Rusden, Spencer and Gillen), and in the case related
by Spencer and Gillen she had to be especially allotted
to one of the men by the leader of the party.

Elopement on the other hand is, as we mentioned above,
to be found in nearly all tribes. In all cases it is considered
as an encroachment on the rights of the family or of
the husband over the girl, and it is punished. But the
severity of punishment seems to vary according to
the tribe; in the Kurnai elopement was probably the
most usual way of getting married; it was therefore not
so severely punished. The latter seems to apply to all
Victorian and New South Wales tribes. In the Central
tribes charming by magic and subsequent elopement
led to a fight or ordeal, but the matter was apparently
not very serious. Whereas, we read in Roth, Grey,
Salvado and Oldfield that the punishment was death.[4]
Nevertheless, as we have come to the conclusion that
these three statements are not quite clear on this point,
we may not take this for granted as a geographical distinction between the South-Eastern and North-Western
(including W. Queensland) regions. It may be also
that abduction of a woman was punished by death or

[1] *Kam. and Kurn.*, p. 343.   [2] *A.R.*, i. p. 108.
[3] That capture of females occurs only very seldom is affirmed
by Palmer, *loc. cit.*, p. 301, and by Taplin, p. 10. J. Mathew,
J.R.S.N.S.W., xxiii. p. 407, states that marriage by capture
takes place between members of hostile communities. Quoted
from Dr. Westermarck, *H.H.M.*, p. 389.
[4] Also Curr, *A.R.*, i. p. 108, affirms that elopement was usually
severely punished and only very seldom legalized. He knew
only three cases where eloped couples were allowed to live together permanently.

at any rate more severely in case she belonged to a forbidden class.

In general it may be said that elopement was always punished, and in the majority of cases afterwards, under certain conditions, legalized and acknowledged. These conditions are : in the first place that bride and bridegroom belong to the right class; and then, pregnancy of the woman or the birth of a child (Kurnai, Yuin); or a victory in the fight which ensues after the offender has been caught (Kurnai, Yuin, Davis, Central tribes); or subsequent exchange of a relative (Yuin, L. Murray, Wakelbura); or a second or third elopement (Kurnai, W. Victoria). Victory in a combat did not mean that it was by pure force that the offender kept the woman. For these combats were regulated and often assumed the form of an ordeal to be undergone (Central and Northern tribes). It is well to notice that the majority of our informants when speaking of elopements never observe the point whether the woman was already married or not.

A few theoretical conclusions from all the facts just enumerated may now be drawn. We have asked at the outset for all the actual circumstances, as well as legal factors connected with the modes of obtaining wives, which express and enforce the validity of marriage. We asked also how does the mental attitude of the native express itself in these facts, as far as individual marriage is concerned. Must we admit that the aborigines have an idea of individual conjugal rights ?

In the first place it is quite obvious that according to our definitions of the word *legal*, the ideas of legal and illegal may be applied quite legitimately to the Australian marriage. For there exist different norms, the compliance with which assures to a match its recognition by society, and actual protection at its hands. Whereas, if a marriage was brought about outside these legal norms it had either to be legalized afterwards, whereupon it enjoyed the same privileges, or it was considered illegal and was interfered with. It appears, moreover, from all the facts reviewed that it was always a difficult matter to secure a wife outside the usual forms. The legal norms for marriage consisted in the bringing about the marriage in one of the forms discussed above, and consequently in the fulfilment of the series of conditions, obligations and duties connected therewith. In all these forms there is involved some kind of control of the social group concerned, which enforces the mutual obligations, and which in case of breach of contract had the privilege or the duty of amending the wrong. In the most frequent form, *i.e.* when a female child is promised in infancy, her family is under an obligation to keep the arrangement. Her relatives have not the right to dispose of her otherwise after they have once promised her (Curr, i. 107), and they must also watch over her and prevent any attempt at capture or elopement, as they would have the duty of rescuing her (Curr, Stanbridge). In this case we are also told that the respective local group would interfere. The fact that the engagement was made publicly, and so was known and acknowledged by all the members of the local group and perhaps even of the whole tribe, emphasized its legal aspect. The cases where the tribal authority disposed of the girls or had to give consent itself shows this in a still stronger degree. We see therefore that two social factors were involved in the legal side of the marriage : the family, which was responsible for the carrying out of marriage and often for its maintenance,[1] and the community,[2] which gives its consent and often controls the right performance of expiatory ordeals. It may also be remarked that the mere moral sanction, which stamps one act as right and another as wrong, gives a strong support to the offended party and paralysed the help that the friends would perhaps like to give to the offender. Although it is difficult to adduce sufficient evidence in order to show

[1] Family means here in the first place the father, who disposed of his daughter; or in some cases the brother or near relative, who got or will get a wife in exchange for her.

[2] Or better, what was called above the tribal government.

in detail what were the obligations of the family and where the tribal supervision began—and it seems that these matters were possibly settled only roughly and on broad lines in the Australian society—one thing appears quite clearly from the whole evidence, viz. that in all tribes only those couples were secure from any interference who had married according to the legal form or whose marriage was subsequently legalized. We are informed by Spencer and Gillen that in some cases (when elopement was brought about by magic) there were some relatives who were lawfully entitled to help the eloper. This shows also clearly how little the settlement of these affairs was arbitrary. Elopement was in this case, and in all others, considered as a trespass; when it was a girl it was an encroachment on the rights of the family; when it was a married woman it was an offence against her husband and also perhaps against her family. According to circumstances and varying with the tribe, it was considered as a more or less serious trespass and punished accordingly. In order that an elopement might result in an acknowledged union, it had to be followed always and invariably by certain expiatory acts. Even in the case of capture, we saw in the example given by Spencer and Gillen that the woman was lawfully allotted to one of the party. Individual capture seems to occur very seldom; in its legal aspect it would not differ essentially from the elopement, but it would have had probably less chances of being made valid.

After the legal aspect of marriage has thus been established, it may be pointed out that several of the features of Australian marriage and betrothal set up, besides these legal bonds, other ties which in themselves lead to the carrying out of marriage, and afterwards keep husband and wife together.

In the first place, exchange of women. When a man was to receive a wife in exchange for his relative, it is clear that he felt himself strongly bound to keep his promise; for he lost as much as his partner in case he broke the agreement. We saw also that betrothal established a certain status between the families of the male and the female respectively. This status, the main feature of which was exchange of gifts, with a preponderance of the male's gifts and duties, such as providing food, created certain obligations which further enforced the validity of the contract.

As pointed out above, we can even find, at least in the Central and Northern tribes, clear features of marriage by purchase. Equally important in this light is the fact of exchange of females. This has its theoretical consequences. The two main facts of collective psychology, expressed by marriage by purchase, are (1) that there is a certain value attached to the woman and expressed by the conventional price; (2) that there is the idea of right of property or at least of the individual personal right of the husband over his wife, acquired by him through the fact of purchase. These two facts are very important. For both these sets of ideas can only have been evolved in a society where individual marriage was a well-known, well-recognized and fundamental institution. There would have been no reason to pay for a wife if the possession of her would confer no positive rights on the owner.

The following point may also be adduced here, viz. that generally the old men and other men of influence and power secured the young females of the tribes. It was easier for influential and important men to maintain their right over their wives before as well as after actual possession. Besides, we are informed by all (with the exception of R. H. Mathews) that the rules of exogamy were very strong, excluding in the majority of tribes a good number of females from all attempts by the males of forbidden classes. This undoubtedly contributed also to increase the security and validity of the marital union, by reducing to very few the number of the men who were in a position to interfere with the rights of the husband.

If we now look behind the facts of all these customs, rules and practices to the underlying social psychology, we see that the idea of the individual rights of a man to a woman must have been deeply impressed upon the aboriginal mind. The female, when promised in infancy, belonged to a certain man, who afterwards took possession of her. Neither he nor she had a choice; she belonged to him by the title of obligation; he had no choice, for all the other females were already distributed. Thus, as infant betrothal was prevalent in the majority of the tribes, there was a status in which everybody belonged to somebody or other. At least there were no free females. That such a state of things is indicative of a deeply-rooted idea of personal, individual rights over a woman seems clear. If the value of such rights were not known, nobody would care to secure them so eagerly and so early, especially as the acquirement of these rights was apparently never gratuitous. On the other hand, this complete allotment of all the females of the tribe must have in turn impressed upon the native mind the idea that marriage is a question of regulated rule, of a well-established order, and not a question of private initiation and enterprise. If a man chooses the other way, *i. e.* tries to conquer a wife, he must be prepared to undergo the consequences of it and thus expiate for having broken the custom and rule. It must also be borne in mind that legal norms presuppose the existence, in the society in which they are in force, of quite clear and definite ideas of the rights which they involve. It is impossible that in a given society there would be norms concerning the legality of individual marital rights without the idea of such individual right being known to the social mind. In Australia there are such legal norms, as has been shown above. And *a fortiori* there must be not only a clear idea of the individual rights of a man to his wife, but these rights must be highly valued.

Marriage contract in nearly all societies is accompanied

by some ceremonies, which possess in themselves some
binding force, generally of a magical and religious character. This seems to be the case in Australia too. We
are in no place told what in a given ceremony would have
magical power, and how the natives imagine the working
of this power. Nevertheless, we read that in North
Central West Queensland the exchange of fire-sticks is
binding, and that among the Euahlayi the simple promise
of a girl does not create any obligation unless it is strengthened by the act of formal betrothal. It can mean only
that to such acts was attributed some magical power,
and that this was coercive.[1] From whatever form of
superstition it may be derived, it seems beyond doubt
that the rudimentary ceremonies described above, such
as exchange of fire-sticks, placing of feathers, joining of
hands publicly, etc., had some inherent force and an
importance as sanctions. They were a form of sacrament. Now I would like to point out that whenever
it happens that a certain legal or social fact is transformed
into a sacrament, *i. e.* is supposed to be accomplished
by the performance of some formality endowed with a
supernatural sanction, we have every reason to suppose
that this legal or social fact is very deeply rooted in the
collective mind, that it corresponds to very inveterate
ideas.[2] This seems to be, therefore, also the case in
Australia, where individual marriage has also its kind of
sacrament. This is another fact, another social institution,
in which the collective ideas of the community find their
expression. And everywhere we find not only that the

[1] Reasons have been already advanced to support our belief
that such betrothal ceremonies were in fact more frequent than
our informants report. Considering now the force attached by the
natives to what is called infant betrothal, we perhaps have
another reason to justify this supposition.

[2] There is no room here to discuss this general assertion at
length. But it may be made plausible by pointing out that a
certain status must be quite fundamental in a society to get the
religious sanction (for instance monogamy in our country), and
that it requires undoubtedly a long process in order to transform
this sanction into a formal act and put into a material form the
accumulated action of many social forces.

idea of individual marriage exists, but that it by
no means bears the features of anything like recent
innovation, or a subordinate form subservient to the idea
of group marriage. As well in the betrothal ceremonies
as in infant engagements, in the ideas of legality of marriage, exchange of females and purchase of the wife—in
all these facts we find that the aborigines have a deeply-
rooted idea and high appreciation of the individual
rights of the husband to his wife.[1] It is also to be noted
that, as Spencer and Gillen inform us, when a man wished
to persuade a woman to elope with him, he resorted to
magic; in this presence of a magical element lay a certain
degree of justification that ensured him the help of some
of his relatives.

In short the modes of obtaining wives enforced and
expressed of themselves a good deal of the validity of
marriage. We have still to ask if the marriage was
binding for both sides or only for the female. This is
an important question and closely connected with the
legal aspect of marriage. For marriage being a kind of
obligation, the question presents itself, whether only
one party was bound by it or both. There is but little
direct evidence upon this point in the statements.
Beveridge asserts stoutly the latter; from Dawson's
statement we conclude that the former was the case,
as he says that a man could only under certain conditions
repudiate his wife and had to ask the permission of the
Chief. But it must be borne in mind that marriage
had by no means the features of a contract into which
both consorts would enter with mutual agreement.
Marriage in Australia must be much more viewed in the
light of a privilege acquired by the man, and for which,
as we saw, he usually has to pay in one way or the other.
It was always a great advantage to a man, both for
sexual and economic reasons, as will be clearly evident
in the respective chapters. The economic advantages

[1] In what these individual rights consist will be discussed in
detail below. Evidently it is erroneous, though a frequent error,
to understand here exclusively the sexual rights.

persisted even when she grew old (compare Lumholtz, p. 207). It was therefore scarcely necessary to compel an individual to fulfil an obligation that was advantageous to him. It may be therefore said that marriage, being an advantage for a man—usually acquired by exchange, gifts, or an act of bravery, sometimes inherited (Levirate) —was an obligation binding on the woman in the first place. There are practically no reasons to suppose that a man would ever repudiate a wife. As long as the woman was young, her husband tried obviously by all means to keep her, and would display all his personal force and social influence to frustrate any attempt at abduction. When his wife grew old he would, perhaps, secure a new one if possible; in two of the few authentic anecdotes told of the natives a man is represented as possessing one old wife and another quite young (see Grey, loc. cit., ii. pp. 350–361, and Curr, Recollections, pp. 141– 145); there was no reason to repudiate the old one, as she would go on working and providing food for her husband.

In the statements referring to treatment of women, there will be some which show that husbands sometimes displayed a great affection towards their old wives. Moreover, Mr. Mathew's statement (on p. 73) mentions explicitly that marriage bonds lasted usually for life; Roth and Lumholtz inform us that great respect was often paid to old women, consequently it can hardly be supposed that they were cast off by their husbands as useless. We must also remember that usually there was a great disparity of age between the husband and wife. As infant children were often betrothed to mature men, when they reached puberty their husbands were quite old already. Such a woman was kept until the death of her husband, when she fell to the lot of his younger brother or the nearest relative (tribal brother) who wished to keep her.

The practice of the Levirate seems to be very widespread.[1] To us it seems to be in the first place the

[1] Howitt, S.E. Tr., pp. 193, 224, 227, 236, 248, Kulin tribe, p. 255; Yuin tribe, p. 266; Kurnai tribe, Kam. and Kurn., p. 204;

expression of the idea of complete right of a man over his wife. With his death this right was not extinguished, but only passed to his nearest relative. If she were elderly she would probably become the property of a young boy, as these were usually deprived of wives. Such couples—of which one was quite young and the other more than mature—seem to be very frequent. In these cases marriage lasted till the death of the older party. From this it may be concluded that it was the husband's interest to keep his wife. As to the latter, the only way in which she could have dissolved the marriage bonds appears to be by finding a protector with whom to elope. This undoubtedly occurred from time to time. But then it was not a simple pacific dissolution of marriage, only an act of violence, always pursued with varying vehemence, as shown above.

From all this we may conclude that marriage was not as a rule an ephemeric occurrence among the Australian natives. In the majority of cases it lasted for life; anyhow, for a long period. To supply here the *experimentum crucis*, let us quote some contradictory instances. Lumholtz says that the women usually change their husbands so often that the children do not generally know their fathers and never grow very attached to them (*loc. cit.*, p. 193; comp. below, p. 245). Salvado, speaking of the unhappy lot of an aboriginal beauty, mentions that she has very often to pass from hand to hand, being continually coveted and captured by some new lover who is stronger than her actual possessor. The same is related by Grey. Lumholtz's cursory statement is not explicit enough to enable us to judge whether it were not formed from observations of " civilized blacks." He was only a short time in personal contact with the natives, and what he gathered from the settlers applied

---

Trans. R.S.V., p. 118; Wotjobaluk, Wakelbura, Turribul, *Trans. R.S.V.*, p. 118; J. Dawson, p. 27; *J.A.I.*, xxiv. p. 170 (Gason on the Dieri); *Ibid.*, p. 194 (Inspector Foelsche on the Pt. Darwin tribes); Lumholtz, pp. 160, 161; Salvado, p. 278.

probably in the main to blacks corrupted by contact with civilization. Salvado's and Grey's information applies only to exceptional cases when the belle excited special passions by her personal charms. Besides, from all we know, elopement, and still more capture, were not every-day occurrences which would follow each other in the case of the same woman. On the contrary, if an exceptionally desirable woman were taken away by some strong and influential aggressor from her lawful husband, the former would have power enough, personal and social, to retain her, if he had enough to secure her. That elopements occurred and that they were more frequent in the case of a beautiful and useful woman is beyond doubt. Still the picture that we would form from these three statements does not seem to fit the framework of the other facts.

The question as to the length of the normal duration of the Australian marriage is a very important one. And, unhappily, the scanty evidence does not allow of a sufficiently clear and detailed answer. Nevertheless, the few statements that say anything about this matter point to a lifelong duration, or at least to a long period of marriage. At any rate the view often expressed that the primitive pairing family is a highly unstable unit, formed and dissolved very frequently, according to the whim of the moment, without any serious obligation for a longer duration of the common life—this view appears absolutely denied by the Australian evidences. It is impossible to find a direct answer in the evidence to the question whether the general rule was duration for life, or whether, after the wife became useless both sexually and economically, she was repudiated. But our short discussion pointed rather to the first view. Moreover, if marriage were not a serious matter and if it were possible to form and dissolve it without further ado, all its features set forth in this chapter (legality, actual obligations, purchase, etc.) would be absolutely unnecessary; in fact they would be quite unintelligible.

In such a low society as the Australian especially, when an institution (here individual marriage) shows so many aspects, even in a rudimentary state, it proves that this institution has a very firm basis. As the act that brought about marriage was usually one of importance and subject to many conditions, so also an attempt to dissolve it was grave in itself and in its consequences.

Now let us summarize our results in a few words. Marriage was brought about as a rule in the form of infant betrothal, which was binding on both parties; it was accompanied by the exchange of relatives; always there were certain mutual obligations. In cases when a man secured a wife without her family's approval (but usually with her own consent), this act was considered a trespass, both in the cases of a girl and of a married woman. The couple was pursued, and unless the elopement was in some way expiated and legalized, both were punished. The idea of legality may be safely applied to Australian marriage in all its forms. For in all there was the necessity of a previous or subsequent sanction of society, and if this were absent society used actually to interfere with the union. The idea of the individuality of marriage was also quite clear to the aboriginal mind and expressed itself in many of the facts connected with the marriage contract. It may be added that it was only in marriage by elopement that the man and woman had a free choice. In all the normal cases neither of them had any voice in the matter at the time of actual marriage.

CHAPTER III

HUSBAND AND WIFE

It may be said that marriage in either of its forms makes the woman the property of her husband. We must, of course, carefully define the word " property." This we shall do by analyzing the economic duties of the woman, the sexual rights of the husband, and in general, the limits of marital authority, and the features of the treatment applied by a native to his wife. As the economic aspect will be better described below, in connection with the family life in general (including relations of parents to children), I shall here pass briefly over this point, remarking that the economic function of a wife is most important in the aboriginal life. She has to provide the regular food supply, to undertake the drudgery of camp life, the care of the children and all household implements, especially on marches. There remains the sexual aspect of marital life and the authority of the husband, including the treatment of the wife.

Let us turn to the latter question and pass in review some statements illustrating the general character of the marital relations; the limits of the husband's authority and power; the actual use he makes of his authority, *i. e.* the treatment of the family; and last, but not least, what idea may be deduced from our evidence as to the feelings of the two consorts towards each other. On this subject few reliable statements will be found, and even these will be rather contradictory. And it would be unreasonable to expect anything else. We are asking here not for a report of plain facts, but for a judgment on more or less complicated and hidden phenomena; this refers especially to the psychical side of the question, *i. e.* to the problem of conjugal affection. But even the other aspects of the problem—authority and treatment—although they are but a sum of facts, are always given in the form of vague general assertions and in that of qualified judgments.

Very few writers trouble at all about the deeper, underlying phenomena. What they see is the way in which a woman is treated by her husband; they often judge this way according to their own moral principles and sensitiveness. They forget that, using the words of Messrs. Spencer and Gillen, "what would cause very serious pain to a civilized woman only results in trifling discomfort to a savage." For all these reasons there will be more scope for corrections in these statements than in the series given above.

Statements.—Amongst the Kurnai there were certain limits to the husband's authority: "Although a man might kill his wife under certain circumstances, and his act would be then approved by custom and by public opinion, yet, under other circumstances, he might not do so without incurring blood feud." [1] All the duties of the family were "shared equally" by man and woman.[2] This statement, as to the limits of authority, is in agreement with all we shall find afterwards: nobody and nothing could interfere with the husband if he ill-treated his wife, unless her life was threatened. Then her relatives intervened. What the expression of "sharing the duties" means, is not quite clear. If it refers to economic functions, we shall have a better picture later; but it stands as a contrast to such expressions as "slave" or "drudge," used in connection with the wife's rôle by so many writers. In another place Howitt says: "I have known many instances . . . including several cases among the Kurnai, of men carrying their wives about the country when too old or too sick to walk." [3] This would point to a great affection, not only resulting from erotic motives, but from real attachment, such as unites human beings who have lived and suffered much together.

---

[1] Howitt, *Kam. and Kurn.*, p. 206.
[2] See below on economic side of family life.
[3] *Nat. Tr.*, p. 766.

Among the Bangerang " community of interests between man and wife is much less than amongst civilized people. The husband gorges himself before he gives the rest of his food to his wife. He is a constant check on her free will and inclinations. She regards him more as her master and enemy than as her mate. But as she is not very sensitive, and educated to her lot, she bears it patiently, and after a year or two she is happy on the whole." [1]

Speaking of the Australian aborigines in general, Curr says : [2] " The husband is almost an autocrat. His wife he may ill-treat as he chooses. In rare instances he will exchange her for another, repudiate, or give her away." He may not kill her; her relatives would kill the first of his blood. " Otherwise the husband may treat his wife as he likes." " The husband is the absolute owner of his wife. He may do as he pleases with her, treat her well or brutally, ill-use her at his pleasure; keep her to himself, prostitute her, exchange her for another, or give her away." But he adds, " Yet . . . they are, on the whole, fairly happy, merry and contented."

Amongst some West Victorian tribes, " notwithstanding this drudgery and the apparent hard usage to which the women are subjected, there is no want of affection amongst the members of a family." [3] The author speaks even of " persistent disrespect and unkindness " of a wife towards her husband; [4] he speaks also of women being " legally separated " [5] from their husbands; and of magic charms worked by husbands for punishment of their wives; [6] all this would point rather to a regulated and less brutal treatment. Here we have the usual concurrence of " hard usage " and affection. Characteristic is the addition of " apparent " to " hard usage." It is, perhaps, the whole style of treatment which appears to be hard to a European observer : the scale is shifted, but undoubtedly the nervous system of the natives is less responsive, too. What Dawson says about separation and husbands recurring to magic to influence their wives, seems to speak still more in favour of the good position of women. But we must remember, that in his whole book, Dawson

---

[1] Curr, *Recollections*, p. 259.

[2] *A.R.*, i. pp. 60, 110. Curr knew personally only the Bangerang tribe, and some others in North Victoria (Glenbourn and Murray tribes), and his general observations must be taken as framed on this material, as he does not seem to be sufficiently aware of how many and deep differences there might be between different tribes.

[3] Dawson, p. 37.   [4] *Ibid.*, p. 36.
[5] *Ibid.*, pp. 35, 36.   [6] *Ibid.*, p. 36.

uses rather bright colours to picture the native character, and tries never to say anything that could shock a European reader.

Bonney asserts that " quarrels between husband and wife are rare, and they show much affection for each other in their own way." Apparent coolness in their relations is required by custom. He gives an example of a couple who "loved each other," and did not even greet after a long absence.[1] According to the statement the treatment of women was fairly good, and there was also no want of mutual affection.

Angas writes that among the aborigines, whom he had under observation (Lower Murray tribes), the man walks proudly in front, the woman following him; she is treated like a slave, and during meals receives bones and fragments like a dog.[2]

About some of the Lower Murray natives we are told by Eyre, " But little real affection exists between husbands and wives." " Women are often sadly ill-treated by their husbands," " beaten about the head with waddies," " speared in the limbs," etc. Here we have bad treatment based on absolute authority and complete want of affection. Besides, we are told, " each father of a family rules absolutely over his own circle." [3]

A statement of Mitchell (quoted by B. Smyth, i. p. 85), suggests that there could not be much affection between husband and wife. " . . . After a battle they (the women) do not always follow the fugitives from the field, but not infrequently go over, as a matter of course, to the victors, even with young children on their backs." [4] This statement sounds not very trustworthy. We never hear of open battles, in which fugitives would leave the camp unprotected. Besides, even if affection would not bind them to the " fugitives," would fear of the stranger and enemy not act in this direction ? Little weight must be, therefore, attached to this evidence.

Taplin, about the Narrinyeri, says that sometimes the treatment of women by their husbands is very bad ; but this is not always the case. " I have known as well-matched and loving couples amongst the aborigines as I have amongst Europeans." [5] This last comparison shows that the ill-treatment was not a clearly distinctive feature of the aboriginal married life.

The Encounter Bay tribe (Narrinyeri) regarded the wives

---

[1] *Loc. cit.*, p. 130.
[2] *Loc. cit.*, i. pp. 82, 83.
[3] *Loc. cit.*, ii. pp. 321, 322.
[4] This statement refers, probably, to the Murray and Darling River tribes, without any exact localization. [5] *Loc. cit.*, p. 12.

" more as slaves than in any other light." [1]   This statement implies lack of affection, absolute authority, and probably bad treatment.   Nevertheless, we cannot be content with such a metaphorical and peremptory phrase on such an important subject.   It is, therefore, useless, and adduced only as an example of how different and contradictory the statement of even good informants may be.

We are told of a case, where a black woman of the Murrumbidgee River tribe, who lived in marital relations with a white bushranger, evinced for him the greatest affection and attachment, and even several times helped him to escape justice with great self-sacrifice.   Although she was ill-treated by him in the most brutal and revolting way, nothing could alter her feelings.[2]   This example may serve as an illustration of how attached a black woman may be to her husband, even if he ill-treats her.

An account of the brutality of a woman's treatment is given by Tench (referring to the Port Jackson blacks).   " But, indeed, the women are in all respects treated with savage barbarity; condemned not only to carry the children, but all other burthens, they meet in return for submission only with blows, kicks, and every other mark of brutality." [3]   But Tench's statements do not appear to go very deeply below the surface of superficial observations.

The same author in another place adduces the wounds and scars of women as examples of " ill-treatment." [4]   How much weight is to be attached to such an inference is well known, after the explanation given by Spencer and Gillen.[5]   I adduce this statement as one which is obviously unreliable, at the same time being typical of a whole class of statements based upon insufficient and superficial observations.

Interesting is what Turnbull says in his old account : " The women appear to attach themselves faithfully to their husbands thus chosen : they are exceedingly jealous of them." [6]

C. P. Hodgson,[7] speaking of some New South Wales tribes, says that *gins* were slaves of their men and had all the drudgery of camp.   The misleading term " slave " is of little use to us.

According to Collins, in the Port Jackson tribes the father enjoyed absolute authority over his family.[8]

---

[1] H. E. A. Meyer in Woods, p. 191.
[2] Bennett, pp. 248, 249.   [3] *Loc. cit.*, pp. 199, 200.
[4] *Loc. cit.*, p. 181.   [5] Compare their statement below.
[6] Turnbull, J., p. 99 (concerning some tribes of New South Wales, probably of the neighbourhood of Port Jackson).
[7] *Loc. cit.*, p. 217; compare p. 208.   [8] Collins, i. p. 544.

Dr. John Fraser [1] speaks of the bad treatment of the woman by her husband amongst the natives of New South Wales. Further he says: "In spite of the hardness of their mode of life, married couples often live happily and affectionately together. . . ." [2]

G. W. Rusden writes: [3] " . . . a man had power of life and death over his wife." This asserts absolute authority; we know, that as a rule, the man had not the power of death over his wife unless she proved especially guilty.

Rob. Dawson relates of the Port Stephens blacks, that they treated their wives very badly—with club and spear. [4]

Hodgkinson remarks that the women are better treated in the River MacLeay tribes than among the other tribes he had under observation. [5] This may point to a real difference in the treatment of women among different tribes, or to the fact that the other tribes which Hodgkinson might have observed were nearer the settlements, and therefore more degenerate.

As to the Euahlayi, Mrs. Parker remarks only : "In books about blacks, you always read of the subjection of the women, but I have seen henpecked black husbands." [6] This statement, which implies that bad treatment was not universal, is inexact and therefore of little use.

We read about the Central Australian tribes of Finke River : "Some married couples agree very well, live frequently quite alone in solitude, and together provide for their wants." [7] The wives are only ill-treated in case they elope.

"The women are certainly not treated usually with anything which could be called excessive harshness" among the Aruntas. [8] Only in cases of infidelity "the treatment of the woman is marked by brutal and often revolting severity." [9] The same is repeated of the Northern tribes of Central Australia. [10] We are also told that the scars that the majority of women possess are due, not to the barbarity of their husbands, but to the mourning ceremonies, during which the women beat and wound themselves severely. And the authors

---

[1] *Abor. N.S.W.*, p. 2. This work is not written by a first-hand observer; I quote his opinion because the writer seems to have got sometimes good personal information, and to be an able compiler.

[2] *Ibid.*, p. 35.

[3] *Loc. cit.*, p. 283. The tribes in question are the Geawe Gal, New South Wales, Hunter River.

[4] *Loc. cit.*, pp. 66, 67.   [5] *Loc. cit.*, p. 229.

[6] *Loc. cit.*, p. 58.   [7] L. Schultze, p. 237.

[8] Spencer & Gillen, *Nat. Tr.*, p. 50.   [9] *Ibid.*

[10] *Nor. Tr.*, pp. 32, 33.

conclude: "Taking everything into account, however, the life of one of these savage women, judged from the point of view of her requirements . . . is far from being the miserable one that it is so often pictured."[1]   For what would be a severe pain to a white woman is for them merely a trifling discomfort.

We read in Barron Field, on the authority of two ship-wrecked men, who spent some time among the natives of Moreton Bay, that the women are there usually well treated by their husbands.[2]

Another analogous statement is given on the Moreton Bay tribes: "The wife is rather the drudge or slave, than the companion of her husband." This (although badly formu-lated) means bad treatment and lack of affection as well.   But we read further on that cruelty is perpetrated usually under the effect of rum; this corroborates our supposition made in connection with Lumholtz's statement.   And we learn yet: "but instances also of warm and deep affection are not infrequent."[3]   And the author confirms it by an example.

Among the Kabi and Wakka: "Husbands were usually affectionate to their wives, but when angered they were often brutal, thrashing them unmercifully with waddies, sometimes breaking their limbs and cracking their skulls.   Still the conjugal bond generally held out for a lifetime."[4]

Lumholtz says: "The women are the humble servants or rather slaves of the native."[5]   The women are ill-treated in the most cruel manner; he gives an example of a wife being awfully maltreated for a trifle.[6]   But this happened among "civilized blacks."   If she elopes she may be even killed. But sometimes they are examples of loving couples.[7]   In another place we read of love and jealousy and of the great affection they are capable of;[8] and an example thereof is given.   This statement suggests to us that much of the ill-treatment was due perhaps to the "civilization" of the blacks.

An analogous statement in this regard is given by Palmer, concerning the tribes of Upper Flinders and Cloncurry River. The lot of the women is hard and they are often treated with club and spear.   There are, nevertheless, happy and mutually regardful couples.[9]

Roth says[10] that among the North-West Queensland tribes the man has absolute authority over his wife.   In another place we are informed, that "in the case of a man killing his

[1] *Nor. Tr.*, p. 33.   [2] *Loc. cit.*, p. 66.
[3] J. D. Lang, p. 337.   [4] J. Mathew, p. 153.
[5] Lumholtz, p. 100.   [6] *Ibid.*, p. 161.
[7] *Ibid.*, p. 163.   [8] *Ibid.*, p. 213.
[9] Palmer, p. 28   [10] Bull. 8, p. 6.

own gin, he has to deliver one of his own sisters " to be put to death. And " . . . a wife has always her ' brothers ' to look after her interests." Thus, in some extreme cases, the husband's authority seems to be limited by his wife's kindred, who protect her.

The women among the Cape York natives are reported to have a very hard life, but occasionally there exists a strong attachment between a married couple.[1]

In West Australia the man is said to possess a full and inheritable right over his wife.[2] Grey says that they have very much to suffer, especially from the jealousy of their masters.[3] The authority of the husband appears also in the story, told in Chapter XVII, where the husband inflicts a severe beating on his two wives; nevertheless, he seems to display also a certain affection for them and great care, protecting them as far as possible.[4]

We learn from Bishop Salvado that : " La méthode qu'il [the husband] emploie pour la [his wife] corriger est si barbare, qu'il arrive bien souvent que . . . il lui traverse une jambe de son Ghici, il lui casse la tête de son Danac et lui prodigue mainte autre tendresse de ce genre," [5] in cases of jealousy. In general " L'état d'esclavage dans lequel toutes sont retenues est vraiment déplorable. La seule présence de leurs maris les fait trembler, et la mauvais humeur de ceux-ci se décharge souvent sur elles par des coups et des blessures." [6] The barbarous modes of treatment are well known to us; what is more important is the great fear they are said to have of their husbands. But, in another place, the same author speaks of tender and affectionate couples: " I love her and she loves me " [7] as a native said to him. So this statement seems not so contradictory after all with all the others, although it contradicts itself.

Among the natives of King George's Sound the women are generally very ill-treated by their husbands. But in spite of that they do not lack affection and often quarrel among themselves, taking the part of their respective husbands.[8]

Here we have a great diversity of statements and much contradiction. We read of barbarous ill-treatment and

---

[1] Macgillivray, ii. pp. 8, 9.
[2] Grey, ii. p. 230.   [3] *Ibid.*, pp. 248, 249.
[4] Compare Grey, ii. chap. xvii. p. 350, especially pp. 353, 354; point 3, p. 359.
[5] *Loc. cit.*, p. 279.   (Tribes of South-west Australia, New Nurcia, Melbourne and Swan districts.)
[6] *Ibid.*   [7] *Ibid.*, p. 278.   [8] Browne, p. 450.

of deep affection; of drudgery and slavery imposed on
wives, and of henpecked husbands; of fugitive men
having recourse to magic, and of women mercilessly
chastised, prostituted, and so on. Some statements
contradict themselves. All this shows, in the first place,
that our authors were lost in the diversity of facts and
could not give an adequate generalization, which should
picture for us the characteristic features of this relation (between husband and wife) as they distinguish
it from the same relation in other societies. In fact, a
good characterization of a given phenomena can be
obtained only by comparing it with other phenomena of
the same kind found under different conditions. Otherwise the observer will invariably note that aspect of the
phenomenon which struck him most strongly, and not
the one that is objectively the most characteristic, as is
found in the present case. This is the more evident in
that we do find a few statements (Howitt on Kurnai,
Spencer and Gillen's remark on the Central tribes,
J. Mathew), which contain all the apparently contradictory elements found in the other statements, but
harmonized with one another. From these few consistent
statements it appears that, although the husband had
a nearly unlimited authority, and in some cases, when he
had special reasons (and undoubtedly deemed himself to
be within his rights), he might use his authority for a very
brutal and severe chastisement, nevertheless, there was
usually a mutual fondness and kindness. Taking this
picture as a standard, it is possible to understand and
make consistent all the other statements if we assume
that they exaggerate some of the traits of the general
picture.[1]

[1] Illustrating this point is a passage in Nieboer's *Slavery*
(pp. 9 *sqq.*) bearing very closely on our subject. His aim is to
discuss whether the position of the wife in Australia may be
characterized as slavery. He arranges the evidence in two
contrasting sets : in the first he gathers all shadows of the picture,
in the second the bright spots. So he adduces several instances
which show that the girl has no voice in the choice of her husband;
and, on the other hand, he shows that from a series of other

But we can make still better use of our evidence by asking some definite questions and seeing how far we get a clear answer to them. And we shall see that if, in this way, the whole picture be analytically divided into sections, the evidence will yield a quite unambiguous answer on some important points concerning the relation between man and wife in the Australian aboriginal society.

The first inquiry is into the legal aspect of the husband's authority. In accordance with our definition of " legal," we shall try to ascertain to what extent the relationship of man and wife was left to follow its natural course; at what point society interfered; and what form this intervention assumed.

After the question of authority has been answered, that of treatment will be dealt with. The legal authority gives us only a knowledge of the limits which society set to the husband's ill-treatment. But even if his freedom went very far, and if he was not compelled from outside to a certain standard of good treatment, he might feel compelled to it by his own affection.

Therefore we are led, in the third place, to ask the psychological question concerning mutual feelings be-

statements it may be inferred that the girl often marries according to her feelings. (In our discussion of the modes of obtaining wives, we saw that when betrothed normally, by engagement in infancy, neither the girl nor, practically, her husband choose in the true sense of the word. Whereas marriage by elopement is brought about by mutual consent. These two forms of marriage would correspond therefore to Nieboer's two contradictory series.) Under the second heading, Nieboer gathers statements as to barbarous treatment and want of affection on one hand, and of affection and rights of the woman on the other. Under the third heading the economic duties and the importance of the woman are discussed, one set of information exaggerating it, the other reducing it to small proportions (we shall treat this subject beneath). Nieboer's computation is very interesting as an illustration of how one can prove *pro* and *contra* from ethnographical material, even while confining oneself to a limited area and subject. All the series of statements collected in this book are further examples of the same fact. As a result of his discussion, Nieboer dismisses of course the term " slave " used by many writers to designate the woman's position in Australia.

tween husband and wife. Affection is, of course, the most important, fundamental characteristic of any intimate personal relationship between two people. But it is, at the same time, rather difficult to give any more detailed answer on that point, when it is a question of savages whom no one has intimately studied from this point of view, and of whose psychology we have only a very slight idea. More cannot be expected than to get an answer to the quite general question : Is there anything like affection between the consorts, or is their relation based only on the fear of the woman of her husband ? I would also remark that these three points—affection, treatment, and authority—although closely related, may be separately analysed, as each of them is of a different character : affection is a psychological, authority is a social factor; the treatment, being a result of them both, must be investigated separately, as we cannot foretell from either of its components the form it will assume; on the other hand, it is precisely from the treatment that we can best judge of the affection.

1. *Authority.*—It seems beyond doubt that in the aboriginal society the husband exercised almost complete authority over his wife; she was entirely in his hands and he might ill-treat her, provided he did not kill her. Out of our thirty statements, in six cases (Kurnai, Bangerang, Lower Murray tribes, according to Bonney, Geawe-Gal, Port Jackson tribes, North-west Central Queenslanders) the absolute authority of the husband is explicitly affirmed. We read in them either the bare statement that the husband had an absolute power over his family; or, in the better of them, we are more exactly informed that he had only to abstain from inflicting death on his wife. It was the latter's kinsman who would avenge her (Kurnai, Bangerang, North-west Central Queenslanders). It is difficult to ascertain in what form society would interfere with the husband if he transgressed the limits of his legal authority, *i. e.* killed his wife. Curr informs us that the

woman's relatives would avenge her death. Howitt
says that there would ensue a blood feud, which comes
nearly to the same. It is very probable that the woman's
kin retained some rights of protection.[1] The remaining statements implicitly declare that the husband's
authority was very extensive. (Encounter Bay tribes
according to Meyer; New South Wales tribes according to
Hodgson; Port Stephens tribes according to R. Dawson;
Arunta; Herbert River tribes; Queenslanders according
to Palmer; Moreton Bay tribes according to J. D. Lang;
South-Western tribes according to Salvado; West
Australians according to Grey.) It is clear that wherever
we read of excessive harshness and bad treatment,
wounds, blows inflicted on women, the husband must
possess the authority to do it; in other words, he does
not find any social barrier preventing him from ill-treatment. Especially as, in these statements, such ill-treatment is mentioned to be the rule and not an exception.
In two statements we can gather no information on this
point. According to the statement of J. Dawson on the
West Victoria tribes, the husband's authority appears
strictly limited by the potential intervention of the chief,
who could even divorce the woman if she complained.
But Curr warns us against Dawson's information concerning the chief and his power.[2] Curr's arguments
appear to be very conclusive. Too much weight cannot
be attached, therefore, to Dawson's exceptional statement.
Discarding it, we see that we have on this point fairly
clear information. We may assume that society interfered but seldom with the husband, in fact, only in the
extreme case of his killing his wife. Six statements are
directly, and the remainder indirectly, in favour of this
view, and the only one contradictory is not very trustworthy.

But is there nothing in this assumption that would
appear to contradict other well-established features of

[1] Compare N. W. Thomas, p. 19.
[2] Curr, *A.R.*, i. p. 53 *sqq.*

Australian social life ?   Against the husband's authority
there could only be the intervention of the Central Tribal
Authority or of the woman's kin.   But the former was
not strong enough to enter into questions concerning the
private life of a married couple.   The Tribal Government
probably had to deal only with grave offences against the
welfare of the whole tribe.   And we never hear that it
interfered with any household questions.   The woman's
kin, on the other hand, seems to have waived nearly all
its rights over the woman (compare also above what had
been said about the betrothal).   Nevertheless, as mentioned above, it was the woman's kin who eventually
intervened.   It must also be borne in mind that as
marriages were, without exception, patrilocal,[1] the wife
was far away from her family, and, therefore, much less
likely to be protected by her relatives.   And, as we shall
see below, when discussing the aboriginal mode of living,
the single families live in considerable isolation, so that
it would appear rather difficult to assume any intervention
from outside in matters of family life.   It appears, therefore, that all the circumstances on which family life
depends point very clearly to, and are in complete agreement with, our assumption of a very extensive authority
of the husband over his wife (or wives), limited only in
some extreme cases by the kin of the woman.

2. Passing now to the other point : how far does the
husband make use of his power ? in other words, how
does he usually *treat* his wife ?   Without entering more
in detail into the motives that regulate his conduct, it
is clear that even if we know his authority, we by no
means know how he usually used or misused it.   Here
our impression when reading the evidence is undoubtedly
that the general way in which wives are treated in aboriginal Australia is a very barbarous one.   In fact, out of
our thirty statements, fourteen speak more or less explicitly of barbarism, slavery, wounds and scars, etc.
Only seven assert that the average treatment is a fairly

[1] See N. W. Thomas, p. 16.

good one and that bad treatment is only a consequence
of certain trespasses, which are considered punishable and
consequently punished. The remaining nine statements
say that treatment is sometimes good, sometimes bad, or
do not say anything about the subject. But in this case
it is apparently needful to give a more careful consideration of the quality of the information than of its quantity.
In fact, four [1] out of the seven of the authorities who
affirm good treatment are very clear and explicit, and
their statements are consequently quite consistent with
themselves; two of them are, besides, our best authorities.
Schultze and Bonney seem also in general to be quite
trustworthy. From the other part of our evidence (that
which asserts barbarous ill-treatment) only three are
fairly reliable (Curr, Salvado, and, to a certain extent,
Eyre). But even these are not so consistent with themselves : they affirm, that in spite of the barbarous ill-
treatment, the women seem to be rather happy. If they
were happy as a rule, it means that this ill-treatment did
not appear to them cruel, and that they did not suffer
under its atrocity. Consequently that it was only
apparently bad (the same expression is used by Dawson,
loc. cit.) in the eyes of the observers, and was not bad as
measured by the standard of native sensitiveness. The
statement of Spencer and Gillen confirms this view explicitly. The statements affirming bad treatment (Curr,
Salvado, Eyre, etc.) do not distinguish the important
point whether this ill-treatment was a punishment or
not ; whether it was inflicted only in definite cases where,
according to the unwritten tribal law, the wife was guilty
of an offence, or whether it was inflicted in fits of bad
temper and ungracious mood. This distinction is very
important ; in the first case the husband would have only,
so to say, an executive power of the collective, customary
will, and his bad treatment would be only an act of
justice ; in the second case he would have been a real
tyrant and his ill-treatment a mere act of brutality.

[1] Spencer and Gillen, Howitt, F. Bonney, and L. Schultze.

This remark has also an important connection with the problem of authority discussed above. Howitt's statement, as well as Spencer and Gillen's, points very clearly to the fact that the ill-treatment was only an act of justice (from the aboriginal point of view). Mathew, on the other hand, explicitly says that the ill-treatment was caused by fits of anger. The other statements keep silence on the point. Some of them speak, indeed, of a purely arbitrary harshness without any reason, but this refers to " civilized blacks," especially under the influence of rum and other white man's vices.

There is a point that must not be forgotten in dealing with this question. The majority of observations were made on degenerated blacks (such as were in missions, raised on farms, in the service of white men, etc.). These blacks may have had quite different manners and customs from those of the aborigines in their primitive state. And their manners were not changed in the direction of amelioration, but the reverse. This conclusion is corroborated by an interesting passage in Howitt.[1] This author says that examples of alleged contempt and discourtesy of a man to his wife, as e. g. a man gorging himself with meat and throwing only a bone to his wife, may be partly " the consequence of the ' new rule ' under the influence of civilization." They sometimes express customary rules of magic origin and are no sign of contempt at all. And the author adds that when he had the opportunity of observing the blacks for a week in more primitive conditions, " this week passed without a single quarrel or dispute." This all shows that, in case of contradiction, we may suppose that the statements affirming unusual ill-treatment are affected by errors due to bad material, insufficient observation, and false inference, rather than that the statements of kindness are exaggerated.

It would be interesting to note what effect the widespread practice of exchange of relatives (see above) had

[1] *Nat. Tr.*, p. 777.

on the treatment of wives. Naturally it might be supposed that for his own sisters' (or relatives') sake every man would probably be more lenient towards his wife. But as Mr. Thomas justly pointed out, the exchange of females may be conceived also in the light of a certain family giving up its rights to a female, and receiving another one in exchange.[1] It would be, therefore, difficult to say anything *a priori* on this influence. A phrase quoted by Curr suggests that the former assumption would be nearer to truth. A black said once to him, speaking about his sister given in exchange for his wife : " If he beats my sister I shall beat my wife." Whether this common-sense idea of justice prevailed in general in the aboriginal mind it would be difficult to decide without further knowledge. But possibly exchange of females was also a cause of the amelioration of the woman's lot.

To sum up shortly, we have ten against four statements in favour of indiscriminate ill-treatment of wives. But, if we reduce both these figures by using only reliable ones, we have four against three in favour of good treatment. By closer analysis we find that ill-treatment is—in the primitive state of the aboriginal society—in most cases probably a form of regulated intra-family justice; and that although the methods of treatment in general are very harsh, still they are applied to much more resistant natures and should not be measured by the standard of our ideas and our nerves. For otherwise we should not understand how the feature of happiness, which is reported by nearly all our informants, could be present.

3. These considerations directly lead us up to an answer to our last question, viz. whether there is a kind of *mutual affection* or whether there is only the power of the man, and the legal factors, that bind the consorts together. In the first place, it is well to bear in mind that in this respect there must have been a great variety of cases corresponding to the characters of the individuals concerned. We only ask here, therefore, the quite general

[1] *Loc. cit.*, p. 20.

question whether, as implied in some statements, there was an absolute absence of any kind of personal feeling in all Australian families and the wife considered her husband as her master only and her natural enemy, she being merely his slave. But here we find also that the few statements (Curr, Eyre, Meyer, Mitchell) that imply such an opinion are not very clear and explicit (in this category we include all the statements as to slavery and drudgery which can possibly embrace not only the treatment itself but the underlying feelings) ; whereas there are ten statements (Howitt, Bonney, Dawson, Lumholtz, J. D. Lang, Salvado, Turnbull, Grey, Mathew, Macgillivray) [1] which affirm that there is real affection between husband and wife. Some of them come from our most reliable writers and are very explicit (Howitt, Bonney, Lumholtz, Salvado). As what has been said of the treatment refers indirectly to this point (for treatment is regulated by personal feelings and not by tribal authority), we may say that the assumption of a complete lack of any feelings of affection or attachment does not seem very plausible. That these feelings would show themselves in another way than in our society seems beyond doubt. But that they would be completely absent and their places taken only by fear and awe—that is not in agreement with our evidence. Even judging on this question *a priori*, we could hardly suppose that there would be a complete absence of all factors that tend to create mutual affection between consorts. In the first place we may remember that in many cases the motive of sexual love was not absent from the aboriginal marriages. This was apparently always the case in marriages by elopement, which occurred in all tribes and was, under certain conditions, a legal and recognized form of contracting marriage. In the cases when, following infant betrothal and other circumstances, the husband was much older

[1] For examples of conjugal affection see also an article written by a " bushman " and one of the members of Leichhard's Expedition. *Science of Man*, 1904, p. 47.

than his wife, the motive of sexual love was probably not reciprocal, but it would operate as a cause for more tender feelings on the part of the males. In the second place, it must be remembered that there are no reasons why the blacks should be completely alien to the feelings of attachment. Husband and wife lived more or less completely separated from the community, forming a more or less isolated unit (see below, on the mode of living). They had many interests in common, and, this being the strongest bond, they had common children to whom they were usually much attached.

To sum up this chapter, it may be said that the husband had a well-nigh complete authority over his wife; that he treated her in harmony with the low standard of culture, harshly, but not excessively harshly; that apparently the more tender feelings of love, affection and attachment were not entirely absent from the aboriginal household. But it must be added that, on these two last points, the information is contradictory and insufficient.

MOURNING AND BURIAL CEREMONIES

Among the duties and obligations which determine the relationship of husband and wife, there are some which may be mentioned in this place. I mean the customs and rites connected with mourning. Mourning expresses a whole complex of feelings and ideas, of which two sets are important here, inasmuch as they throw light upon the relationship of the mourner and the mourned. Firstly, mourning always expresses sorrow and grief (real or feigned) for the deceased; secondly, the various mourning ceremonies imply the idea that there was a strong tie between the two persons involved, a tie which persists after death and which must be broken by the magical virtue of rites.[1] Both these interpretations of mourning (sorrow

[1] Compare Levy Bruhl, p. 389.

for the deceased and the necessity of breaking the bond)
involve the idea that the relationship between husband
and wife was acknowledged by society as an individual
and strong personal tie.   As the modes of obtaining wives
have shown us that to bring about a marriage it was
necessary to get the sanction of society; so the long
mourning of the widow and the different formalities she
has to perform, before she becomes the property of the
dead man's heir or is allowed to remarry, show that
marriage was not dissolved at once, even by the death
of the man. It shows, therefore, that the tie between
husband and wife was not a loose one, and not merely
established by the fact of possession or cohabitation;
and that the appropriation was based not only on legal
ideas, but deeply rooted in magico-religious feelings and
representations.

The idea that mourning is performed in order to express
sorrow, apart from its being obvious in the ceremonies
themselves, is realized and formulated by the natives.
When a very old and decrepit woman dies, or an old man
who has lost his memory and is useless in tribal matters,
the natives do not perform any elaborate ceremonies.
They allege as a reason that they " do not feel enough
sorrow for them." [1]

Ceremonies involving the motive of sorrow are mentioned in several places by Spencer and Gillen. Among
the Arunta, " when a man dies his special *Unawa* or
Unawas smear their hair, faces and breasts with white
pipeclay and remain silent for a certain time until a
ceremony called *Aralkililima* has been performed." [2]
The widow has a special name.   In some of the northern
tribes she has to keep silence.   *E. g.* " Among the Warramunga . . . the widows are not allowed to speak for
sometimes as long a period as twelve months, during the
whole of which time they communicate only by means

[1] Spencer and Gillen, on the Central and North Central tribes
(more especially the Kaitish and Unmatjera), *Nor. Tr.*, p. 506.
[2] *Nat. Tr.*, p. 500.

of gesture language." [1]   Among the Arunta the widow
has to live in the woman's camp and suspend, to a large
extent, her usual occupations.[2]   When she wishes the
ban of silence to be removed, she has to perform a ceremony in public, which consists in the main in an offering
of vegetable food to the younger brother and sons of the
deceased.   "The meaning of this ceremony, as sym-
bolized by the gathering of the tubers or grass seed, is
that the widow is about to resume the ordinary occupations of a woman's life, which have been to a large extent
suspended, while she remained in camp in what we may
call deep mourning." [3]   Analogous ceremonies of nearly the
same duration and involving similar ordeals and privations, are in use in some other tribes : among the Kaitish
and Unmatjera the widow has her hair cut off, she has
to smear her body over with ashes, during the whole time
that mourning lasts, *i. e.* several months, she has also to
keep silence.[4]   Amongst all these tribes the women
inflict upon themselves the most cruel wounds.   "The
women seem to work themselves up into a perfect frenzy,
and to become quite careless as to the way in which they
cut and hack themselves about, with, however, this
restriction notable on all such occasions, that however
frenzied they apparently become, no vital part is injured,
the cutting being confined to such parts as the shoulders,
scalp, and legs." [5]   The authors give a detailed description
of such ordeals undergone by two widows of deceased
men in the Warramunga tribe.   "The actual widow
scores her scalp with a red-hot firestick." [6]

Taking mourning customs as a measure of the intensity
of sorrow and grief, it may be seen that here these feelings
are supposed to be very strong, as the hardship and ordeals
are very great.   Of course, there is no question of individual feelings.   The widow may be in some cases really
glad that her husband has died, as well in Australia as

[1] *Nat. Tr.*, p. 500.   Compare also *Nor. Tr.*, p. 525.
[2] *Nat. Tr.*, pp. 501, 502.   [3] *Ibid.*, p. 502.
[4] *Nor. Tr.*, p. 507.   [5] *Nat. Tr.*, p. 510.
[6] *Nor. Tr.*, pp. 521 *sqq.*

in any of our modern societies. What is shown at any
rate is, that society supposes and requires such feelings,
and that they are duties according to the social moral
code; in fact, that sorrow and grief for the deceased are
required by the collective ideas and feelings. Whether
these feelings are displayed in order to appease the spirit
of the deceased, whether there is real sorrow as a basis
for these customs, these are questions irrelevant in this
place.

Probably many different motives contributed to form
the mourning rites and duties, as they are now in existence. These duties have in Australia apparently not
merely a customary, but also a legal character. For we
read in Spencer and Gillen: " a younger brother meeting
the wife of a dead elder brother out in the bush, performing
the ordinary duties of a woman, such as hunting for
' yams,' within a short time of her husband's death,
would be quite justified in spearing her." [1] And, again,
it is said in another place, that if a woman would not
comply with the severe ordeal which is her duty, " she
is liable to be severely chastised or even killed by her
brother." [2]

Whatever more special explanation might be attempted
of all these laws and customs it is certain that they
express the fact that the marital bonds are very lasting. The obligations last after the death of the husband, and expiation must be made for the eventual
new union. For Spencer and Gillen give a detailed
account of all the complex formalities and duties to be
performed before the widow can remarry, or rather is
given up to the younger brother of the deceased, to whom
she belongs by law.[3] After the performance of several
ceremonies and a long lapse of time, she may still, if she
likes, paint a narrow white band on her forehead, which
is regarded as an intimation that she is not anxious to
marry at present, as she still mourns, though to a less

[1] *Nat. Tr.*, p. 502.　　　[2] *Nor. Tr.*, p. 522.
[3] Levirate; see above, p. 63.

degree than before, for the dead man.[1] " The spirit of
the dead man was supposed to have been watching
all these proceedings as he lay at the bottom of the
grave." [2]

Unfortunately the other authors do not give anything
approaching Spencer and Gillen's full account of burial
and mourning. In particular, if there is any description,
the actual and tribal relatives are not differentiated. All
that I have adduced here from Spencer and Gillen refers
to the actual widow. A short remark of Roth may be
quoted : " In the Boulia district when a man dies, his
nearer relatives have special mourning performances.
These nearer relatives, in the case of an adult male, are
considered to be the *wife* and his brother and sisters by
the same mother, not his father or mother; with an
adult woman, only the brothers and sisters by the same
mother." [3] Amongst the Dieri, " a widow is not permitted to speak until the whole of the white clay which
forms her ' mourning ' has come off without assistance "
(perhaps some months).[4] There is also a statement about
the husband's mourning. Amongst the Victorian tribes,
" when a married woman dies and her body is burned,
the husband puts her pounded calcined bones into a little
opossum skin bag, which he carries in front of his chest
until he marries again, or until the bag is worn out."

To sum up, it may be said, that as far as Spencer and
Gillen's evidence may be taken as typical of what burial
and mourning is in Australia, the legal and customary
aspects of the marriage bonds is not less strongly expressed
in the way in which they are dissolved, than it is in the
way in which they are brought about.

[1] *Nat. Tr.*, p. 507.   [2] *Ibid.*
[3] Roth, p. 164.   [4] Howitt, p. 724.

CHAPTER IV

SEXUAL ASPECT OF MARRIAGE

THE next point in our investigation is the sexual aspect of the Australian marriage. Unfortunately it will not be much easier to draw a decisive inference from the evidence in this case than it was in the foregoing one. There is perhaps less patent contradiction between the statements; and we are able here to reduce many of the incongruities to geographical differences. But the whole question is very complicated by the fact that the sexual features of marital life in Australia have caused much discussion in connection with the hypothesis of primitive promiscuity and group marriage. They have been very often interpreted according to this hypothesis. Different customs have been pointed out as unmistakable survivals of previous states of marital communism or group marriage. Group marriage has even been said to be in actual existence amongst some tribes.

In accordance with our opening statement, polemics will be strictly avoided here, particularly in reference to questions of prehistory; and, therefore, we need not concern ourselves with the problem whether certain facts point to the previous existence of group marriage or promiscuity; nor with the problem whether certain features are survivals of a similar state of things.[1] Highly

[1] The solution of this problem would, in the first place, require a revision of the concept of *survival*, in order to avoid arbitrariness when classifying one custom as a survival, another as an innovation. I venture to say such classifications have been made too carelessly. I think it will be clear from the whole of this book, that the individual family should not be considered as a mere innovation, and that, accordingly, there is hardly any justi-

objectionable from our point of view, however, is the fact
that our best informants (especially Howitt and Spencer
and Gillen) describe the facts of sexual life of to-day in
terms of their hypothetical assumptions. To gain, therefore, a clear picture of the actual state of things we shall
have to disintegrate all that is hypothetic in the statements from the actual facts.

That is the first reason why it will be necessary to
submit here and there the statements to some discussion.
But there is another reason. Being concerned with the
problem of the individual family and individual relationship, we must keep in mind that although the sexual aspect
of family life is very important, nevertheless, it is only
one side of the picture, and that to outline this picture
correctly, we may not exaggerate one side of it. Now, by
a quite illegitimate silent assumption, the sexual features
are often treated as the most important—in some cases
as the exclusive factors of marriage. But marriage, as
we saw and shall have the opportunity to see still more
clearly, is rooted in all the manifold facts that constitute
the family life : mode of living, economics of the household, and above all the relation of the parents to their
children. Unless it is proved, therefore, that the unity of
family life and the individuality of the family break down
on all these points, no general inference as to group
marriage can be drawn from the mere facts of sexual
communism. In other words, sexual licence is nothing
like group marriage. How far we have the right to infer
the *actual* existence of group marriage (*ergo* group family)
from sexual facts in Australia, must therefore be discussed now, while we are concerned with the sexual aspect
of the Australian family.

I wish to make it quite clear that any discussion upon
our evidence will be carried out merely with the aim of

fication for treating the customs in question as survivals. But
this is only by way of parenthesis; these problems lie outside
our task. They must be treated on a broader basis than that
of the Australian ethnographic area only.

getting a clear picture of the actual state of things. It is not our task to polemize with the general theories as to the previous state of things, origin of family, etc., set forth by our authors. For a criticism of Howitt's, and Spencer and Gillen's speculations on the origin of marriage, the reader may be referred to the excellent chapter in Mr. Thomas's work. This criticism seems to me to leave no doubts that the general views expounded by the ethnographers mentioned above are hardly founded on any of the Australian facts. These views are mere hypotheses, drawn theoretically from facts. Personal knowledge of these latter could hardly have enabled the ethnologists to theorize more correctly on them. From Mr. Thomas's criticism it results also, that it is no exaggeration to say that the continual application of these hypotheses to the actual state of things considerably obscures the clearness and value of their evidence. It is necessary to add, nevertheless, that Howitt especially always gives very first-rate information concerning family life, the institution of marriage, etc.; and, according to my view, his theories are contradicted by the excellent and admirably rich information he himself gives on social matters. If we can seldom agree with him as speculative sociologist, we always admire him in his ethnographic research.

The following statements are intended to give an account of all the features of sexual life in Australia, especially as far as they bear upon family life. We shall, therefore, in the first place pay attention to the way in which sexual intercourse is limited and determined by marriage. Are the marital relations the exclusive right and privilege of the husband? Or has he only a certain over-right, modified by some other factors (which we must endeavour to determine). Or is there (at least in some tribes) really a sort of group marriage (using the word " marriage " to designate mainly the sexual side of it) ? In the second place we must also pay some attention to the more general questions of chastity, licence before marriage, and so on. And finally, the features of the interesting and important forms of ceremonial and regulated licence must be traced more in detail.

Statements.—Amongst the Kurnai " the husband expected strict fidelity from his wife, but he did not admit any reciprocal obligation on his part towards her."[1]. . . " The expected fidelity towards the husband was enforced by severe penalties. In cases of elopement her life was in his hands. . . . Each man not only expected his wife to be faithful to himself, but he, on his part, never lent her to a friend or to a guest." [2] In another place,[3] Howitt says, about the same tribe, that sometimes wives were exchanged " by order of the old men " to avert some impending danger to the tribe. We see that with these rare exceptions, the husband had quite exclusive sexual rights over a woman. Even the general practice of wife-lending seems to have been entirely absent. Now, as Howitt is a strong adherent of the theory of group marriage, we may accept his statements asserting individuality of " marriage " as especially trustworthy.

Amongst the Murring [4] " the only occurrence of licence is when a visitor from a distance is provided with a temporary wife by the hosts. . . . In cases of elopement, when the woman is captured, she becomes for a time the common property of the pursuers. With these exceptions, marriage seems to me strictly individual." [5] (We see that here again Howitt speaks of individual marriage where there are only, in fact, individual sexual rights.) The only exceptions were here, wife-lending to visitors and the characteristic form of punishment.

Curr says : [6] " Amongst Australians there is no community of women. The husband is the absolute owner of his wife (or wives)." He is very jealous and " usually assumes that his wife has been unfaithful to him, whenever there has been an opportunity for criminality ; hence the laws with respect to women are very stringent." A woman is completely isolated.[7] The husband will, nevertheless, often " prostitute his wife to his brothers " or visitors.[8] Here we see the same : the man

---

[1] Howitt, *Kam. and Kurn.*, p. 205.

[2] *Ibid.*, p. 202, Latin footnote ; p. 205.

[3] *Smith. Rep.*, 1883, p. 810.

[4] *Ibid.*

[5] As Howitt uses the term " marriage " to denote only its sexual side, we must understand that sexual rights are strictly individual.

[6] *A.R.*, i. p. 109. This may be considered as trustworthy only in reference to the North Victorian tribes, especially the Bangerang, whom Curr had under personal observation.

[7] See below, Chap. V.   [8] *A.R.*, i. p. 110.

can dispose of his wife (the term prostitute is here probably used rather in rhetoric sense, for it does not seem that the man would receive any direct contribution for wife-lending); but he is very jealous in all cases where anything might happen behind his back.

On the West Victorian aborigines Dawson writes [1] that illegitimate children were rare, and the mother was severely beaten, sometimes even put to death, by the relatives. " The father of the child is also punished with the greatest severity and occasionally killed." The woman's relatives do not even accept his presents as expiation. " Exchange [2] of wives is permitted only after the death of their parents and, of course, with the consent of the chiefs, but is not allowed if either of the women has children." What is said about illegitimate children, would point to sexual morality before marriage. But we can hardly conceive how in a society, where females are handed over to their husbands, often before, and at the latest at reaching puberty, there could be illegitimate children at all. The whole statement is not clear.

Beveridge [3] says of the aborigines of Victoria and Riverina: " Chastity is quite unknown amongst them." "In their sexual intercourse . . . they are not in the least bit particular, consequently incest of every grade is continually being perpetrated." [4]

" Among the Wotjobaluk it was not usual for men to have more than one wife, and they were very strict in requiring fidelity from her, and did not lend a wife to a friend or to a visitor from a distance." Death was the punishment for both the wife and her accomplice in case of adultery.[5] According to this statement not only fidelity is required in this tribe, but even chastity is known as a virtue. This seems rather exaggerated, and as it is given only by a correspondent of Howitt, we shall not attach to it too much weight. Nevertheless, this, in agreement with all our other statements on Victoria, shows that the standard of sexual morality could not be very low there, as we might infer from the foregoing statement.

" Marriage is not looked upon as any pledge of chastity

---

[1] *Loc. cit.*, p. 28.

[2] He doesn't say if temporary or permanent exchange. Probably the first, as he speaks below of divorce.

[3] *Loc. cit.*, p. 23.

[4] This assertion of incest is quite in contradiction with all we know about Australians and undoubtedly false; it may be true in the case of quite "civilized" blacks, perhaps. I quote it as an instance of how, from one statement only, one might draw absolutely false conclusions.

[5] Howitt, *Nat. Tr.*, p. 245.

indeed, no such virtue is recognized." And in a Latin foot-note the author enumerates the proofs: promiscuity of un-married people; wife-lending and exchange; general cere-monial licence.[1] But the Adelaide tribes were much degener-ated, and possibly some customs relate to the Lake Eyre tribes, with whom the author was also acquainted.

J. Moore Davis [2] speaks in a Latin passage of the licence at corroborees and of the rights of access enjoyed by old men at the initiation of the girls. The statement is not localized.

Among the Narrinyeri, youths during initiation are allowed unrestricted sexual licence.[3]

In the Turra tribe : " Women were bound to be faithful to their husbands, also the husbands to their wives. Whoever was guilty of unfaithfulness was liable to be punished by death at the hands of the class of the offender." [4] This statement is very clear; but if it is equally correct it reports quite an exceptional state of things.

Schürmann writes about the Port Lincoln tribes: " Although the men are capable of fierce jealousy, if their wives trans-gress unknown to them, yet they frequently send them out to other parties, or exchange with a friend for a night; and as for near relatives, such as brothers, it may almost be said that they have their wives in common." [5] But does this community of wives refer merely to sexual matters ? It is probably so, as the author mentions it in connection with the general description of this side of aboriginal life.

C. Wilhelmi writes about the same tribes : " Although the men are apt to become passionately jealous if they detect their wives transgressing without their consent, yet of their own accord they offer them and send them to other men, or make an exchange for a night with some one of their friends. Of relatives, brothers in particular, it may be said that they possess their wives jointly." [6] This statement and the fore-going can hardly be looked upon as independent; for Wilhelmi knew the missionary Schürmann personally, and had from him a good deal of his information; the two statements are almost literally identical.

Amongst the Yerkla Mining tribes : " A wife is bound to be faithful to her husband." She is severely punished; if

[1] Eyre, ii. p. 320, about the Lower Murray River tribes.
[2] Brough Smyth, ii. p. 319. This statement (and the whole article) does not refer to any single tribe; there are mentioned tribes from all over the continent.
[3] Taplin, loc. cit., p. 18.
[4] Yorke Peninsula, Kühn, loc. cit., p. 286.
[5] Loc. cit., pp. 222, 223.
[6] Ch. Wilhelmi, p. 180.

successively guilty, killed.[1] Women are lent, but very
seldom.[2]

A. L. P. Cameron reports some cases of sexual licence among
the Darling River tribes. They used to exchange wives
" either at some grand assembly of the tribe, or in order to
avert some threatened calamity." But the author adds,
" This custom is, I think, rare at present." [3] At any rate, we
may bracket this statement with that of Howitt, who also
speaks of wife exchange, in order to avert impending calamity.

Charles Wilkes writes, that jealousy is very strongly
developed among the New South Wales blacks. From it
originate occasional quarrels, and the women suffer especially
from jealousy and suspicions. There are also regulated fights
and ordeals in order to settle quarrels and enmities ensuing
from sexual matters.[4]

Tench mentions the sexual licence of unmarried girls among
the Port Jackson tribes.[5]

We read about the natives of Botany Bay, that the men
were very jealous.[6]

Turnbull says, that quarrels arise usually from jealousy
in sexual matters. The affair usually becomes more general
and involves the whole tribe.[7]

Amongst the Geawe Gal there were probably occasions
on which " promiscuous intercourse (subject to the class rules)
took place." [8]

Amongst the Kamilaroi " the punishment for adultery was,
that when a woman was *taramu*, that is, shifty, wanton,
adulterous, the husband complained to his kindred, who
carried the matter before the headman, and if the charge was
found to be true, her punishment was to be taken without the
camp and to be handed over to all comers for that night, and
her cries were not heeded." [9] Women were lent to friends,
visitors, but with their own consent.[10] This statement
confirms again the majority of those relating to the South-east
tribes. The husband did not tolerate any trespass in these
matters; and the community intervened. On the other hand,
he had (with her consent) the right to dispose of her.

Amongst the Euahlayi : " There are two codes of morals,
one for men and one for women. Old Testament morality for

---

[1] Howitt, *Nat. Tr.*, p. 258.   [2] *Ibid.*
[3] *Loc. cit.*, p. 353.   [4] *Loc. cit.* (smaller edition), i., p. 226.
[5] *Loc. cit.*, p. 199.   [6] Phillip, pp. 34, 35.
[7] *Loc. cit.*, pp. 90, 99. Tribes of New South Wales, probably
from the neighbourhood of Sydney.
[8] Rusden, *loc. cit.*, p. 281.
[9] C. E. Doyle in Howitt's *Nat. Tr.*, pp. 207, 208.
[10] *Ibid.*

men, New Testament for women." [1] This applies, probably,
chiefly to sexual matters, for we read in another place,[2]
" Unchaste men were punished terribly. . . . The death penalty
for wantonness was enforced." Also a girl " found guilty of
frailty " is severely punished by her relatives.[3] An " absolute wanton " is ignominiously treated, the result being
almost inevitably death.[4] This statement is incomplete, as
we are not told if adultery and wantonness are punished
only when they are perpetrated without knowledge of the
husband; in other words, we are not informed if the widespread custom of wife-lending was absent or not among the
Euahlayi.

Amongst the Dieri there was besides the regular Tippa
Malku marriage, the occasional *Pirrauru* relation. The
sexual intercourse of the latter was confined to some festival
or to the case when the Tippa Malku husband was absent.
The number of *Pirraurus* of each man was limited, and they
were strictly assigned to each other. There was sexual
jealousy amongst the *Pirraurus*. The husband had, apparently, the right to decline the use of his wife to any *Pirrauru*.
The *Pirrauru* relation will be discussed more in detail below.
The custom of wife-lending is prevalent : " continually their
wives are lent for prostitution, the husband receiving
presents." [5] It may be noted, that this is the only place
where wife-lending is stated to take this form. Besides, we
are informed by Howitt that the unmarried girls and widows
were allowed a considerable amount of sexual freedom, this
custom being called *Ngura-mundu.*[6]

The Urabunna, living in the neighbourhood of the Dieri,
had an institution analogous to the *Pirrauru* custom. Besides
his *Nupa* or individual wives, of whom he might possess one
or two, who were " specially attached to him and lived with
him in his own camp," he could have several *Piraungarus*
to whom he had " access under certain conditions." [7] (But
we are not informed what these conditions are ; we may infer,
however, that they are analogous to those existing among the
Dieri, which we know in detail : see below.) Our authors inform us further that the *Piraungarus* " are to be found
living grouped together." [8] We shall discuss below this
Piraungaru relation more in detail.

---

[1] Mrs. Parker, p. 58.   [2] *Ibid.*, p. 59.
[3] *Ibid.*, p. 60.   [4] *Ibid.*
[5] *J.A.I.*, xxiv. p. 170. Gason in answer to Prof. Frazer's
"Questions."
[6] *Nat. Tr.*, p. 187.
[7] Spencer and Gillen, *Nat. Tr.*, p. 109.
[8] *Idem.*, *Nor. Tr.*, pp. 72, 73.

Amongst the Arunta nation, there are different occasions on which men besides the husband have sexual access to the woman. There are the customs at the " initiation " of the girls.[1] And there are many cases in which the husband is compelled by custom to waive his rights on behalf of some one else; such instances generally happen in connection with ceremonial gatherings.[2] It is important to note that on these occasions men have access to women with whom it would be most criminal for them to have intercourse under normal conditions; and a man may cohabit even with his mother-in-law, from whom he is under normal conditions absolutely isolated.[3]

The ceremonies of initiation of girls in Central Australia, and sexual promiscuity connected with them, are also mentioned by W. H. Willshire. Women after initiation are sexually " at the mercy of all who may get hold of them." [4] The same author mentions also the sexual " immorality " of the natives in question.[5] This raw statement, although inadequately formulated, corroborates Spencer and Gillen's exact data.

Analogously in the Northern tribes there are several exceptions from the individuality of sexual relations. The man may lend his wife to his friends or to people whose favour he wishes to gain. There are customs at the initiation of girls, when several men, standing to the girl in a certain group (tribal) relationship, have access to her. In the third place there is the sexual licence connected with certain ceremonies, when men are obliged to cede their wives to some of their tribesmen.[6] And we read the description of the most horrid atrocities which men inflict as punishments upon their unfaithful wives.[7] We read in the same place that the charming away of women by magic was one of the chief sources of fights and quarrels. About sexual jealousy in the Central and Northern tribes, we read : " Now and again if a husband thinks that his wife has been unfaithful to him, she will certainly meet with exceedingly cruel treatment." [8]

We are informed about the existence of the practice of

---

[1] Spencer and Gillen, *Nat. Tr.*, chap. iii. pp. 92–96; and *Nor. Tr.*, chap. iv., pp. 133 *sqq.* About these ceremonies, some words were said above, pp. 42, 43, in connection with marriage ceremonies.

[2] *Nat. Tr.*, pp. 96, 97.

[3] *Ibid.*, p. 97, and *Nor. Tr.*, p. 137. The features of these ceremonial licences will be discussed more in detail below.

[4] *Loc. cit.*, p. 30. [5] *Loc. cit.*, p. 36.

[6] Spencer and Gillen, *Nor. Tr.*, chap. iv. pp. 133 *sqq.*

[7] *Idem.*, *Nor. Tr.*, p. 474. [8] *Ibid.*, p. 33.

exchange of wives among the Northern tribes (Port Darwin, Powell's Creek) in the answers to Prof. Frazer's "Questions." [1]

J. D. Lang says about the aborigines of Queensland, that the "conjugal relations are maintained with great decency." But he mentions the custom of wife-lending.[2]

Amongst the Maryborough tribes, sexual licence is allowed before marriage and there is a camp of unmarried girls.[3] Many, however, "remain perfectly virtuous until their promised husband fetches them." [4] Women who were wanton after their marriage "are looked down upon as the prostitutes of the tribe, and are lent to visitors as temporary wives." [5] Here chastity seems to be not so strongly required. But the statement is somewhat odd as regards the camp of unmarried girls.

Amongst the Kabi and Wakka tribes (Queensland, near Maryborough), there are cases where the "seniors of the camp" have some rights over a woman. In general none but the husband had any matrimonial "rights over the wife, and the jealousy made him take good care she was not interfered with, unless he was a consenting party." [6] Here we have again the characteristic feature: the husband had exclusive sexual rights over his wife; but he might dispose of her, and used to do so.

Amongst the North-west Central Queensland aborigines [7] there is a certain licence before marriage "unless they should happen to be betrothed"; in that case the husband does not like it. "Morality in its broadest sense is recognized a virtue." And in another place we are informed that "if an aboriginal requires a woman temporarily, he either borrows a wife from her husband for a night or two in exchange for boomerangs, a shield, food, etc., or else violates the female when unprotected, when away from the camp, out in the bush." In the latter case, if the woman is unmarried "no one troubles himself about the matter." If married, a quarrel would ensue if the husband came to know anything.[8] Roth gives also an account of the initiation ceremonies, in which females, arrived at puberty, are ceremonially deflorated by old men. It is important to note that the exogamous class rule is disregarded on such occasions, when several men of forbidden degrees have access to the woman, but blood relations are strictly excluded. A girl acquires a new designation, corre-

---

[1] *J.A.I.*, xxiv. p. 178.   [2] *Loc. cit.*, p. 237.
[3] Howitt, *Nat. Tr.*, p. 232.
[4] *Ibid.*, p. 233.   [5] *Ibid.*
[6] J. Mathew, pp. 161, 162.
[7] Roth, Bull. 8, p. 7, § 3.
[8] *Idem, Ethnol. Stud.*, p. 182, § 327.

sponding to the new age grade; she becomes marriageable and enters altogether into a new status.[1]

Among the natives of Cape York the unmarried girls are allowed to have free intercourse, but a female once married is required to be absolutely faithful to her husband, and this requirement is enforced by severe punishments.[2]

Amongst the tribes of West Australia : " The crime of adultery is punished severely — often by death." [3] Grey speaks also of the " stern and vigilant jealousy." [4] " . . . the bare suspicion of infidelity upon their part is enough to ensure to them the most cruel and brutal treatment." [5] But he mentions also the continuous rows and plots that issue round a beautiful woman,[6] who knows sometimes how to evade the precautions of her husband. Grey speaks emphatically of the " horror of incest." [7] Fidelity seems, therefore, to be severely enforced in these tribes. Grey says nothing about wife-lending. Chastity does not seem to have obtained there, nevertheless.

We read in Oldfield, about the West Australian tribes, that there was an " initiation " ceremony before a female was considered fit for marriage ; in it " all the males of the tribe " partook. Women sometimes betray their husbands.[8]

Mrs. D. M. Bates reports, that among the tribes of West Australia she had under observation, there exists a " certain tribal morality " and " bad or loose living women (according to their ideas) occupied much the same status in a certain degree as our unfortunate sisters do amongst us." There were even contemptuous names for women of bad conduct.[9] Unfortunately, this statement says absolutely nothing of what would be the most interesting thing to know, viz. the ideas of the natives about sexual matters, in other words, the code of the " tribal morality." Here, besides the fidelity which was strictly required, a complete chastity is affirmed. On the whole it seems to agree roughly with Grey's and Salvado's statements ; he also does not mention any regulated licence. As our information on West Australia is so scanty, we can hardly decide whether sex morality stands there much higher than in the Central and North-eastern peoples ; but as we have reason to regard both the information of Grey and of Salvado as trustworthy and accurate, we may assume that this difference actually existed.

---

[1] *Ethnol. Stud.*, pp. 174 *sqq.*   [2] Macgillivray, ii. p. 8.
[3] Grey, ii. p. 242.   [4] *Ibid.*, p. 252 ; also see p. 248.
[5] *Ibid.*, p. 249.   [6] *Ibid.*, pp. 248, 249.   [7] *Ibid.*, p. 242.
[8] *Loc. cit.*, p. 251. The tribes in question are those of the Murchison district.
[9] *Loc. cit.*, p. 51.

Similarly Bishop Salvado speaks of the great jealousy of the natives of South-west Australia and of their morality. "Le sauvage ne pardonne jamais l'insulte faite à la pudeur des femmes qui lui appartiennent; c'est un outrage qui se paye cher et le plus souvent par la mort." [1] ". . . je n'ai jamais observé autour de nous un seul acte tant que ce soit peu indécent ou déshonnête parmi eux . . . au contraire j'ai trouvé les mœurs louable au plus haut point." [2]

Scott Nind informs us about the natives of King George's Sound, that "infidelity is by no means uncommon. The husband keeps a jealous eye on his wife, and on the least excuse for suspicion she is severely punished." [3]

In reviewing this material, the first thing to be noted is a considerable geographical variety of custom and law in sexual matters. There are clear and radical differences between the South-eastern tribes, the South Central, North Central, and Northern Queensland tribes. The views on sexual morality apparently differ as much as the actual practices. Whereas in Victoria, South-eastern New South Wales, and the Southern territory of South Australia there are no traces of regulated licence, or at least not in a very conspicuous form—in the South Central tribes the features of *Pirrauru* relations; in the Central and North Central different forms of ceremonial licence are highly developed, and play an important part in tribal life. In Queensland there does not seem to exist such a very strict sexual morality, as far as we can gather from our statements. Our five statements from West Australia do not give a very clear picture. Undoubtedly these geographical differences, as here indicated, must be conceived as merely rough approximations. There are too many contradictions between the statements concerning the South-eastern area; the data as to Queensland and West Australia are too few and vague to allow anything beyond mere generalities. But broadly, as is indicated above, these local differences undoubtedly exist.

Besides the data contained in the statements there

---

[1] *Loc. cit.*, p. 279.   [2] *Loc. cit.*, p. 280.   [3] *Loc. cit.*, p. 39.

is, to confirm this view, the opinion of A. W. Howitt.
In his article on the tribal and social organization in
Australia, this writer directly points out the radical
differences existing between the South Central and the
South-eastern tribes in sexual matters; and as he knew
from personal acquaintance or from reliable informants
the whole area, we may consider this geographical
difference as thoroughly established.[1]

Let us now draw some general conclusions from the
evidence. The points selected at the outset for special
attention were : first, the problem of the rights, privileges,
and restrictions of the husband in sexual matters; second,
the question how is chastity in general, considered and
valued ? third, a survey of the cases of ceremonial or
regulated licence.

1. The first question may be broadly answered by saying
that the husband had in general a definite sexual " over-
right " over his wife, which secured to him the privilege
of disposing of his wife, or at least of exercising a certain
control over her conduct in sexual matters. In some cases
this over-right amounted to quite an exclusive right, which
even in some exceptional ·tribes was never waived.
We read of cases where the husband was not only never
compelled by custom, or any other social force, to dispose
of his wife, but apparently never did it on his own impulse.
In these cases we may say that the absolute faithfulness
of a married woman was enforced, and that her chastity
was recognized as a virtue. (Wotjobaluk, Turra, and the
South-western tribes according to Salvado.) Besides there
are several other statements, from which it appears that
the sexual rights of the husband were nearly exclusive,
and that he was not inclined to waive these rights in
order to derive therefrom any personal profit. So among
the Kurnai there was no wife-lending nor any other similar
custom, and wives were exchanged only in quite exceptional cases in order to avert impending evil. The same

---

[1] See *Smith. Rep.* for 1883, pp. 804 *sqq.* Chap. iv. on " Marital
groups," p. 810, and *Trans. R.S.V.*, pp. 115 *sqq.*

is asserted in Cameron's statement. Among the Yerkla Mining women are but seldom lent. Mrs. Parker writes that wantonness was considered a crime among the Euahlayi, and nearly the same has been said by Mrs. Bates about the West Australians. Roth speaks of morality in a broad sense. Grey and Macgillivray write that women were expected to be strictly faithful to their husbands. But in these two last cases we do not know whether lending or exchange of wives was entirely absent, or is only not mentioned by the authors. All the statements which affirm strict and vigilant jealousy, without further analysis, leave the question open as to whether the husband ever allowed adultery to his wife, or whether he punished it only when perpetrated without his consent. But interpreting these statements according to the other more detailed ones, it may be said that in general, such exclusiveness of marital rights and appreciation of chastity seem rather to be an exception; and some caution must be used in accepting the above-mentioned cases of absolute faithfulness and chastity required from married women. As a rule, even where there is not regulated licence, wife lending and exchange, hospitality, etc., seem to be more or less practised.

In the majority of statements these customs are found in one form or the other; in these cases we cannot speak of an absolute fidelity or exclusive individual sexual right of the husband. We read in fifteen of our thirty-eight statements of the customs of wife-lending or exchange; and in twelve some form of sexual licence is mentioned. But in all these cases, where the woman is given away, this is done with the consent and generally on the initiative of her husband, who in the majority of cases derived some benefit from the transaction.[1] Exchange of wives obviously implies an advantage to the husbands. The same must

---

[1] It is to be mentioned that we find an indication in a few statements that fidelity was binding only on the female, the males considering themselves free from any obligation (Howitt's statement on the Kurnai, and Mrs. Parker's statement on the Euahlayi.) This holds good, probably, in all the tribes.

be assumed in the case of hospitality and wife-lending when the courtesy of the husband presupposes a reward in one form or another. In the case of ceremonial licence as related by Spencer and Gillen, wife-lending is always a kind of retribution for religious services. Payment of this nature occurs also for other services, and may be used as bribery towards an avenging party.[1] The husband always disposes of his wife, who is never allowed to take the first step in this matter, and it is consequently he who benefits from her conduct. This conduct does not seem punishable or wrong in any sense to the native mind. Quite otherwise is it with the woman who trespasses without the sanction of custom or without her husband's approval. In all such cases she is considered culpable and more or less severely punished. This is directly stated by Shürmann and Wilhelmi, and appears in nearly all the other statements.

The punishment dealt out in cases of elopement was discussed above in connection with the mode of obtaining wives. We saw that as a rule the punishment is severe. Sometimes the kindred of the offended party (*i. e.* the husband) help him to punish the offender; sometimes the whole local group takes his side. Several of our statements assert that in cases of elopement, the woman when caught becomes the common property of all her pursuers, and that afterwards she has to undergo severe punishment (Kurnai, Murray tribes). In some statements we read that adultery is punished with death (Wotjobaluk, Turra, Kamilaroi, Euahlayi, South-western tribes); in others, that the punishment for adultery or even a suspicion of it is very cruel (Curr, Spencer and Gillen, J. Mathew, Grey). It appears, therefore, that the husband is very careful about maintaining his over-right over the sexual life of his spouse. He very often has to submit to some customary practices, and often subordinates his wife to some private aim; but he must always give the initiative, or at least have the sexual life of his wife under his control.

[1] See below, page 107.

2. In the second place a word about the chastity of the unmarried women is necessary. Here we may remark at the outset that this question seems relatively unimportant, as we know that girls are handed over to their promised husbands on arriving at puberty, or even before.[1] On the other hand, it seems hardly probable that girls would have sexual intercourse in their extreme youth (that is, before being married); during this period, girls are continually under the control of both parents, and especially of the mother, and as it will appear from the statements referring to the "bachelors' camp," it is probable that males and females are kept apart from each other before reaching puberty.

That girls had no sexual intercourse before marriage is also suggested by the custom of "initiating" girls by the old men, which takes place immediately before they are handed over to their husbands. From the detailed descriptions of Spencer and Gillen and W. E. Roth it appears that at this initiation girls are deflowered (Central, North Central and Central Queensland tribes).[2] On the other hand, the custom of levirate—i. e. of handing over the widow to the deceased's brother or nearest relative— seems to be very widespread (compare above, page 63); so that there are hardly any marriageable and unmarried widows in the aboriginal society. Accordingly we find but little indication of any misconduct in the case of unmarried females, and the few instances we meet with are so little detailed that they do not throw much light upon this question; it is especially uncertain whether they are exceptional innovations, or whether they have any more serious social *raison d'être*. It is mentioned that there exists an unmarried girls' camp with sexual licence (Maryborough tribes, see below, p. 266). Roth mentions that unmarried girls are free in their conduct as long as they are not promised in marriage.

---

[1] Comp. Chap. II., and Chap. VII. p. 257.
[2] Spencer and Gillen, *Nat. Tr.*, chap. iii., and *Nor. Tr.*, chap. iv. Roth, *Ethnol. Stud.*, p. 174, § 305.

We read of a similar freedom in the Dieri tribe, as also in the statements of Tench and Macgillivray. The most important form of licence before marriage seems to be, therefore, the practice of initiation just mentioned.

Speaking now of chastity in general, and summing up both what was said under the first and the second heading, it may be affirmed that it is not considered in the light of a necessary virtue. Before marriage the girl has to submit to a general sexual intercourse, and after it the woman becomes on many occasions the property of another man. This refers more especially to the tribes described by Spencer and Gillen and Roth. It was said at the outset that a much stricter morality seems to have prevailed in the South-eastern tribes, although there, too, we read of sexual licence (during initiation among the Narrinyeri, and in general, according to Beveridge and Moore Davis). But as it was there possibly much more rarely practised —we are informed by our very best source, Howitt, about several tribes, that they knew and practised chastity (Kurnai, Turra, Wotjobaluk, etc.)—we may keep to the geographical distinction.

3. Let us in the third place speak more in detail about customary and ceremonial licence, as it merits for many reasons our special attention. Here belong, besides the ceremonial defloration of girls by old men (just spoken of), the different forms of licence practised at large tribal gatherings, and especially the *Pirrauru* relationship, found in several of the South Central tribes.

Besides the exact and detailed data about ceremonial (or ritual) defloration that are given by Spencer and Gillen and Roth, these ceremonies are mentioned also by Willshire, Beveridge, Moore Davis, Mathew, and Oldfield. But the short notes of those latter authors are hardly sufficient to allow any further discussion ; they may be considered as a confirmation of the more exact evidence, but the latter, and especially Spencer and Gillen's data, must serve as material for all analyses. These ceremonies, on the one hand, seem to correspond to the initiation ceremonies of

the males.   It is only in this light that they are represented
by Roth, who does not mention any close connection between these ceremonies and marriage, but represents them
as the condition of marriageability.   The said ceremonies
possess, as a matter of fact, many points of analogy with
the male initiation ceremonies.   They are performed on
arrival at puberty; Roth states that the girl then acquires
a new name and new status.   The operation performed
then upon the initiated is also to some extent analogous
in both cases.[1]   On the other hand Spencer and Gillen
represent these ceremonies as directly connected with
marriage.   What the underlying ideas in this connection
are, it is difficult to say.   It has been suggested that such
ceremonies express a kind of expiation for marriage.[2]
But as this idea is not directly embodied in this institution,
and as it is not necessarily a condition of its existence,
and, moreover, as it has not been directly affirmed by the
natives, it may be treated merely as an assumption.

A very important and striking feature of ceremonial
licence in general, is that the sexual intercourse, which
takes place on that occasion, is not subject to class rules.
We are indebted to Messrs. Spencer and Gillen for a
very minute account of customary licence, which takes
place as a rule during corroborees and other ceremonies.
" In the Eastern and North-eastern parts of the Arunta,
and in the Kaitish, Iliaura and Warramunga tribes, considerable licence is allowed on certain occasions, when a
large number of men and women are gathered together
to perform certain corroborees.   When an important
one of these is held, it occupies perhaps ten days or a
fortnight, and during that time the men, and especially
the elder ones, but by no means exclusively these, spend
the day in camp preparing decorations to be used during

---

[1] See Spencer and Gillen, *Nor. Tr.*, p. 133, where this is explicitly mentioned.   The names of both ceremonies in the Arunta
seem to indicate this analogy; *atna—ariltha—kuma* and *pura—
ariltha—kuma* (for their meaning see the place just quoted).

[2] *Idem*, p. 96, apply this concept, due to Lord Avebury, to
this special case.

the evening. Every day two or three women are told
off to attend at the corroboree ground, and with the
exception of men who stand in the relation to them of
actual father, brother, or sons, they are, for the time being,
common property to all the men present on the corroboree ground." [1] On all such occasions the class rules are
disregarded, they are even broken, so to say, in the most
radical way : a man may have, in connection with certain performances, access to his mother-in-law, who under
normal conditions is most strictly tabooed to him.[2]
And again, in the Warramunga tribe an example is
quoted when a tribal father has access to his tribal
daughter on ceremonial occasions.[3] This example refers
to a case where the woman was offered by her husband as
a kind of retribution for some services rendered in performance of ceremonial functions. In the same tribe
there are other occasions (in connection with burial) on
which a man is bound by custom to offer his wife to a man
who was useful to him.[4] The class rule is disregarded in
such cases, too. This holds good also in the case when a
man receives this form of reward for having been useful
to the community as a messenger.[5] When an armed
avenging party is sent to carry out a sentence on some
other local group, the latter may attempt to bribe the
members of the avenging party by offering them some
women. If these are accepted, the sentence is not carried
out, and the avenging party returns peacefully home.
Sexual intercourse under this condition is also not subject
to the class rule.[6] It may be said, therefore, that on all
occasions [7] when ceremonial licence takes place, the strict
class exogamy does not hold good ; whereas incest, as regards blood relationship, is always strictly forbidden. This
refers both to the initiation rites and to ceremonial licence
in the tribes described by Roth and by Spencer and Gillen.

---

[1] Spencer and Gillen, *Nat. Tr.*, pp. 96, 97.
[2] See *ibid.*, pp. 96–99 (for the Arunta tribe).
[3] *Nor. Tr.*, p. 138.   [4] *Ibid.*, p. 139.
[5] *Ibid.*   [6] *Ibid.*, p. 140.
[7] The *Pirrauru* custom excepted.

In this place a somewhat extensive digression concerning the *Pirrauru* custom must be made. This question plays such an important part in all speculations about a former state of group marriage, and it is undoubtedly such an interesting fact by itself, that it would be impossible not to give here an account at least of its most essential features. The custom in question consists in the fact, that in certain of the South-east Central tribes a man and a woman are put into a relationship which involves occasional sexual connection and some other mutual rights and obligations, to be discussed in detail below. This custom is found in the tribes living North, South and East of the Lake Eyre, the Urabunna, the Dieri, Yantruwunta,[1] and other kindred tribes. We know the most about the Dieri, whom Howitt chooses and represents as a typical example of all these tribes, and whose *Pirrauru* practices in his opinion differ only slightly from those of the neighbouring tribes. This is important, for our knowledge about the Dieri practices is much more ample than in the case of any other tribe; and it does not agree in all particulars with what we are told about the Urabunna by Spencer and Gillen.[2] We shall, therefore,

[1] For a detailed enumeration and description of all tribes among whom practices of the *Pirrauru* type exist, see Howitt, *J.A.I.*, xx. pp. 31-34. In this article, which is nearly exactly reproduced in Howitt's last work (*Nat. Tr.*), we possess, undoubtedly, the best information about the *Pirrauru* custom. In another place (*Folk-Lore*, xviii. p. 184), Howitt assigns a still wider area to the *Pirrauru* practice. "Altogether, Dr. Howitt reckons that the tribes which practised a form of group marriage like the *Pirrauru* of the Dieri must have occupied an area of some 500,000 square miles, extending for a distance of 850 miles from Oodnadatta, the northern boundary of the Urabunna, to the eastern frontier of the Dieri, or of the Mardala tribe between the Flinders Range and the Barrier Range."—Frazer, *Tot. and Exog.*, i. p. 371.

[2] We have reasons to doubt whether these authors were as well informed about the Urabunna tribe as about the Arunta nation. Anyhow, the information they give about the *Piraungaru* custom is much inferior as well in respect of quantity as quality (the inconsistency of their statement is shown above) than that about the Arunta, and the conclusions they draw therefrom are not quite in accord with the facts as they relate them (see below, p. 118).

rely in the first place upon the information given about
the Dieri by Howitt, Gason, and Siebert, and in our
general view of the *Pirrauru* we shall be guided by this
information.

It is first to be noted that the custom in question exists
side by side with individual marriage. We find this
expressly stated in three places by Howitt.[1] But besides
these merely verbal assertions of authorities, we have
much better proofs of the assertion in the facts related
by them concerning the *Pirrauru* customs. From these
facts it clearly appears that individual marriage existed
quite independently of the *Pirrauru* relation, and that it
was even only slightly affected by this relation. We shall
enumerate the most important features of the *Pirrauru*
custom of which we are informed, occasionally remarking
under each heading what is the difference between
marriage and the *Pirrauru* relation. It will appear that
many of the factors that constitute marriage are completely absent in that relation, and that others play in
each quite a different rôle.

1. In the first place, let us ask how was the *Pirrauru*
relation brought about. We are informed that on the
occasion of large tribal gatherings such as corroborees,
invitation gatherings, etc., when the whole tribe was
present, the old men and the heads of the totems, assembled in camp council, decide which men and women

---

[1] *J.A.I.*, xx. p. 53, *Smith. Rep.*, p. 807, *Trans. R.S.V.*,
p. 100. In *J.A.I.*, xx. p. 53, Howitt says that among all these
tribes there are two forms of marriage. " There is a marriage . . .
which may be spoken of as ' individual marriage.' " " There is
also a marital relation existing between a man and a number of
women, or between a woman and number of men. This latter
connection may be spoken of as group marriage." We see that
Howitt uses here the word " marriage " only to design the
individual union, and speaking about the *Pirrauru*, correctly
employs the words " marital relations." This sounds quite
differently from the repeated denial that the " individual marriage does not exist in the tribes " made by Spencer and Gillen
(*Nat. Tr.*, pp. 63, 109; *Nor. Tr.*, p. 140). And again Howitt says
(*Trans. R.S.V.*, p. 115), " Individual marriage in Australian tribes
has been evident to every one, but beside it exist also group
marriages."

should be allotted to each other. The result of this decision is then publicly announced.[1]   Now we know[2] that the individual or Tippa Malku marriage is brought about in quite a different way: the girl is promised as an infant to her future husband.   Such an infant betrothal is usually accompanied by exchange of females; and the decision lies in the hands of the girl's family (her mother's brother).   We see that the mode of obtaining the individual Tippa Malku wife is quite different from the way in which the *Pirrauru* relationship is established; and we see also that the latter does not show any of the characteristics which enforce and express the individual character of marriage.

Undoubtedly it has its legal aspect, for it rests on the authority of the camp council of old men, which seems to be the only form of tribal authority known in these tribes. The old men seem also to keep an eye on the *Pirrauru* connections in their subsequent course (see below under 5). These relations, therefore, bear, thanks to this sanction of the tribal elders, the character of validity and legality, and are to a certain degree compulsory. (How far they are compulsory in the case of the husband of the allotted woman, see below under 6); but they involve neither the mutual obligation of two families, nor a period of long engagement, nor any factors expressing collective ideas of the individuality of mutual appropriation of a man and a woman.[3]

There are still two points connected with this heading which emphasize the difference between the individual marriage and the *Pirrauru* relation,[4] namely that individual marriage must precede *Pirrauru* relations;   in

---

[1] Howitt, *J.A.I.*, xx. p. 56.   *Smith. Rep.*, p. 807.

[2] See above, p. 41.

[3] Collective ideas which closely correspond to our ideas of monogamy, of monopolization of the marital rights and relationship in the widest sense of the word; special stress being laid on the point, that by the word " marital " relations I do not mean sexual relations, either exclusively or even in the first place.

[4] Points to which attention was drawn by Mr. N. W. Thomas, *loc. cit.*, p. 129.

other words, that only married women may be made
Pirraurus. Secondly, that although any woman may
have only one Tippa Malku husband (men may have
several Tippa Malku wives), she may have several *Pirraurus*. This very point induced many writers to consider
the *Pirrauru* as a form of group marriage.[1] That this
relation bears a group-character is beyond doubt. That
it must be clearly distinguished from marriage is just what
we try to show here.[2]

2. Another interesting point about the *Pirrauru*, is
that no consent of the parties is asked.[3] But this appears,
according to other data, to hold strictly good only as far
as the woman is concerned. For we are told [4] in another
place that a woman's wishes are not taken into account
unless through the mediation of her husband. Hence
it seems that on one side a man's wishes may be taken into
account, and on the other side a man may even dispose
of his own wife. This points to the fact that a husband's
consent or mediation when his wife is concerned may be of
some weight. The same conclusion results from the fact
(already noticed by Mr. Thomas in this connection) that
two men may eventually exchange their wives in connection with the *Pirrauru* custom.[5] All this appears quite
plausible if we bear in mind that [6] the old men keep the
greatest number of females for themselves—at least all
the most comely ones. And that these very men have
afterwards the right of disposing of their wives. They
will, on the one hand, exchange some of the females with
each other; on the other hand, they will allot perhaps some of their wives to one or another of the
young men living in celibacy. In fact, we read that very
often old and renowned warriors give their wives to some

---

[1] Howitt, *Nat. Tr.*, p. 187. *J.A.I.*, xx. p. 56. Spencer and
Gillen, *Nor. Tr.*, p. 73 ; *Nat. Tr.*, p. 64. Howitt, *Smith. Rep.*,
p. 197.

[2] The same was argued from a different point of view by
Mr. N. W. Thomas, *loc. cit.*, pp. 127 *sqq.*

[3] *J.A.I.*, xx. p. 56.　　　[4] Howitt, *Nat. Tr.*, pp. 181, 187.

[5] *Ibid.*, pp. 181, 182, 187.

[6] See below, pp. 255 *sqq.*

youngster, who regards it as a great honour.[1] In conclusion it appears probable that the man had a voice in the choice of his *Pirrauru* or had not, according to his personal influence. As to the woman, it was her husband's part to decide, or at least to influence the opinion of the camp council. But statements are not clear on this point, and we are left here to a great extent to our own conjectures.

3. From the foregoing, it results that the husband still retains some over-right and control over his wife. And that is a very important point. For in the light of this fact, the waiving of sexual privileges connected with the *Pirrauru* custom does not appear to encroach any more on the husband's right to his wife than the custom of wife-exchange or wife-lending. This fact of the necessity of the husband's consent is confirmed by Howitt's explicit statement. We read[2] that a man has right of access to his *Pirrauru* only during the absence of her husband or, if the latter were present in camp, only with his consent. It is evident, therefore, that the husband's rights are by no means annihilated or superseded by the *Pirrauru's* rights. He waives his rights voluntarily, and his consent is essential.

4. Another point of importance is that this relationship does not constitute a permanent status, and that it may be actualized only at intervals. In the first place, the sexual licence involved in this custom is exercised during the tribal gathering, for the night in which the assignation of *Pirraurus* took place; the licence lasts for about four hours.[3] This relation is probably renewed during some of the next gatherings; during the husband's absence; when a man is sent on an embassy with his

[1] Howitt says, explicitly (*Nat. Tr.*, p. 184), that " the leading men in the tribe have usually more Tippa Malku and *Pirrauru* wives than other men." The Pinnaru, Jalina Piramurana had over a dozen wives, and to get one of them as *Pirrauru* was a great honour for a man.

[2] *J.A.I.*, xx. p. 56; *Nat. Tr.*, p. 184; *Smith. Rep.*, p. 807, under 5.

[3] *J.A.I.*, xx. p. 56.

Pirraurus; in some cases where the husband gives his consent. But although none of our sources say so expressly, we may safely deny the assertion that the *Pirrauru* relation had a permanent status. For, if it were actually valid and exercised permanently, we would not be informed, as we are, as to the special occasions on which it takes place, and of the conditions under which it may be exercised. Again, if the *Pirrauru* involved a permanent status or, more explicitly, if groups of men and women who are *Pirraurus* to each other respectively, normally and permanently live in marital relations, no one of our authorities, who plead so strongly for the character of group marriage in the relation in question, would omit to emphasize such an important feature, which would support their views in the highest degree. For this is a crucial question indeed : if the *Pirrauru* right entitles, in the first place, only to a short licence and establishes permanently merely a facultative right, then, even in its sexual aspect, it does not approach the rights established by Tippa Malku marriage in these tribes. And, although the evidence on this point is not quite decisive, we are, as we saw, entitled to suppose that the sexual licence connected with the *Pirrauru* is only an occasional one.

Besides the facts and reasons enumerated above, I may adduce a very important passage from Howitt's last work, which may be considered the ultimate opinion of this eminent ethnographer concerning the problem of group marriage in Australia—a hypothesis of which he always has been a most ardent supporter. " A study of the evidence which has been detailed in the last chapter has led me to the conclusion that the state of society among the early Australians was that of an Undivided Commune. Taking this as a postulate, the influence on marriage and descent of the class division, the sub-classes and the totems may be considered on the assumption that there was once an Undivided Commune. It is, however, well to guard this expression. I do not desire to imply necessarily the existence of complete and continuous communism between the sexes. The character of the country, the necessity of moving from one spot to another in search of game and vegetable food, would cause any Undivided Commune, when it assumed dimensions greater than the immediate locality could provide with food, to break up into two or more communes of the same character. In addition to this it is clear, after a long acquaintance with the Australian savage, that in the past, as now, individual likes and dislikes must have existed; so that, admitting the existence of common rights between the members of the Commune, these rights would remain in abeyance, so far as the separated parts of the Commune were concerned. But at certain gatherings, such as Bunya-bunya harvest in Queensland, or on great ceremonial occasions, all the segments of the original community would reunite. In short, so far as the evidence goes at present, I think that the probable condition of the Undivided Commune may be considered to be represented by what occurs on certain occasions when the modified Communes of the Lake Eyre tribes reunite." [1]

This shows that after a long and mature consideration of the problems in question, Howitt came to the conclusion that " group marriage " never could have existed as a permanent status, and that it could have been established only in connection with large tribal gatherings. In such a light the hypothesis of former or even actual " group marriage " becomes very plausible, or rather it ceases to be a hypothesis and it becomes one of the best established facts of the Australian ethnology.

But at the same time, although we may accord the term "group marriage" (if any one wishes at any price to retain it), we must note that such a state of things is radically different from marriage in the usual sense of the word, and in particular from marriage as found in actual existence in the Australian aboriginal society, and described in this study. It will be sufficient to point out that such

[1] Howitt, *Nat. Tr.*, pp. 173, 174, beginning of chap. v.

an occasional sexual licence lasting several hours during an initiation gathering could not create any bonds of family, such as may result from community of daily life and community of interests, common inhabiting of the same dwelling, common eating, especially common rearing of children—all factors which, as will be shown below, act only in the individual family and tend to make out of the individual family a well-established and well-defined unit.

We must adduce one fact which stands in opposition to what is just said. I mean the statement of Spencer and Gillen, that amongst the Urabunna the Piraungarus are " generally found living grouped together." This statement might possibly point first to a permanent state of marital relations, secondly to a common mode of living. Now it may be remarked that such an off-hand statement on such a crucial point shows undoubtedly that the authors were insufficiently informed themselves on this point, and that, therefore, we must accept this statement with the utmost caution.[1]

The problem of the mode of living of the *Pirrauru* groups involves two questions—first, what persons constituted the local group (temporary or permanent) ; and second, how the members of a *Pirrauru* group lived within it. The statement of Spencer and Gillen may mean that a group of *Pirraurus* constituted a given temporary local group. But within this group husband and wife must have formed a distinct unit. Now as to the question of how far such a grouping of *Pirraurus* (if we accept the above statement as correct) would imply a permanent marital status between the *Pirraurus*, it is impossible to answer. On this point, too, the information about the Urabunna is vague and defective, and it is safer to base our conclusions on the more explicit and reliable material given by Howitt in the case of the Dieri.

5. Did the *Pirrauru* union last for the whole life, or could it be dissolved ? In one place we read that the relation in question lasts for life; in another place we are

[1] Compare above, p. 108, note 2.

told [1] that the old men watch over the *Pirraurus* in order that there may result no trouble from mutual jealousy; and if a man has too many *Pirraurus* they compel or advise him to limit himself to one or two. No answer can be given, therefore, to this question.

6. We mentioned above that if the *Pirrauru* relation, according to Howitt's supposition there quoted, only involved sexual licence during big tribal gatherings, this relation would be absolutely deprived of any of the characters that are the chief constituents of marriage and family. But here we must indicate that such an assumption is not quite justifiable. In fact, in some of the facts related about the *Pirraurus*, there are hints pointing to the existence of economic bonds and of community in daily life between *Pirraurus*. We read [2] that if in the absence of her husband a woman lives with one or two of her *Pirraurus*, she occupies with them one hut and shares with them the food. Therefore, in the absence of her husband, a *Pirrauru* actually took his place, and in this case the *Pirrauru* relationship is not merely a sexual connection, but it assumes the real form of marriage. In another place [3] we read that a man possessing several *Pirraurus* may lend one of them to some one who is deprived of this advantage. Thus it seems that the *Pirraurus* acquire a kind of real right over their *Pirrauru* wives; and that it goes as far as the faculty of disposing of them. And again we are informed that if a woman has a young man for a *Pirrauru*, she is often jealous of him and looks strictly after him, and if he does not obey her readily enough, tries even to compel him by punishment.[4] All these instances, which could perhaps be further multiplied, show that under certain circumstances, which we unfortunately do not know with sufficient precision, the *Pirrauru* relationship assumes a much more serious character than a mere sexual licence exercised during a few hours.

---

[1] Howitt, *Nat. Tr.*, p. 182.   [2] *Idem, J.A.I.*, xx. p. 57.
[3] *Ibid.*, p. 58.   [4] Howitt, *Nat. Tr.*, p. 183.

7. There remains still to examine what form the relationship of children to parents assumes in the tribes where the *Pirrauru* relationship exists. Here we are quite well informed that the individual relation between the children of a woman and both their parents (their mother and her Tippa Malku husband) is fully recognized by the aborigines. It is true that Spencer and Gillen say that there is only a " closer tie " between the married couple and their children, and that the children acknowledge the *Pirraurus* of their parents as parents.[1] But this statement is very unsatisfactory ; such a complicated question cannot be answered by a short phrase; for we are by no means aware what the words "closer tie" mean. As unsatisfactory is Howitt's remark, that owing to the promiscuous sexual intercourse, no woman can know if the children are the offspring of her husband or of the *Pirraurus*, and, therefore, the children must be considered as possessing group fathers and not individual fathers.[2] Apart from the objection that this applies merely to paternity and not to motherhood, which would remain at any rate individual, we must point to our subsequent investigations, which will show that the physiological question of actual procreation does not play a very important part in the determination of relationship. Probably it does not play in these tribes any part at all, as they (at least the Urabunna) seem not to have any knowledge of the actual physiological process of procreation. So we see that although both Howitt and Spencer and Gillen try to prove the existence of group relationship between the *Pirraurus* and their children, their conclusions appear to be ill founded in facts, and to be rather the fruits of speculation than of observation. Our suspicions are strengthened by the unsophisticated remark of Gason, to which we must ascribe much weight, as he knows the Dieri tribe better than any one else, and as he has no theory of his own to prove or to demolish. He says : " The offspring of the *pirraoora*

---

[1] See below, p. 243.   [2] *J.A.I.*, xx. p. 58.

are affectionately looked after and recognized as if they
were the natural offspring of the real husband and wife."
Although this phrase is not very happily formulated, its
meaning appears to be that the married couple recognize
all the children of the woman and treat them with kindness and affection, without making any distinction. If,
according to the views just mentioned, the children were
accepted by all the men cohabiting with a given woman,
i.e. by her husband and all the *Pirraurus*, the phrase
quoted above would be obviously quite meaningless ; for
why should the offspring be recognized as if they were the
husband's own children in order to be treated well ? It
may also be pointed out that the Dieri father is very
affectionate to his children.[1] And in all the statements
referring to this subject we clearly see that it is a question
merely of the individual father and by no means of a
group of fathers.

After this survey of what appear to me to be the most
important points referring to the *Pirrauru* custom, we
see that nearly each one of them is involved in contradictions and obscurities. To draw any general conclusion
we must proceed with the utmost care and precaution.
Our information about *Piraungaru* of the Urabunna is
nearly worthless. And we may safely repeat with
Mr. Thomas, that if the authors knew more facts and
knew them better than we can do from their description,
then perhaps their conclusions, drawn from these unknown facts, may be correct; but if they draw their
general conclusions only from the facts they communicate
to us, then we are justified in rejecting them.

Our chief aim in discussing the features of the *Pirrauru*
relationship was to ascertain how far this relation possesses
the character of marriage. That it is a " group relation "
is beyond doubt.[2] That it is a form of marriage has been

---

[1] See below, pp. 195, 238 and 243.
[2] Compare, however, the definition given by N. W. Thomas,
loc. cit., p. 128, who shows also how misleading an indiscriminate
use of such terms may be.

accepted by Howitt, Fison, and Spencer and Gillen without much discussion.[1]   Mr. Thomas has shown already how unsatisfactory the reasons are, on the strength of which *Pirrauru* is considered to be a form of group marriage, or even a survival of the previous stage of group marriage. He has shown how insufficient, in the light of an exact definition, the information is, how many essential points we still want to know to be able to make any more conclusive assertion.   Mr. Thomas' criticism bears especially on the lack of a strict use of the term " group marriage." He gives a correct definition (page 128 of the work quoted) of this term, and consistently puts to its test the views propounded by the previously mentioned writers.   From this discussion he concludes that in the *Pirrauru* relationship we can find neither the features of an actual group marriage nor the traces of such a previous state of things.[2] This criticism and conclusion appear to me so convincing and final, that I would have simply referred to them without entering again upon this rather perplexing question, were it not a good opportunity for pointing out again by means of this example, that the sexual aspects of marriage and the family cannot be discussed separately, detached from each other ; and for showing how incorrect it is to represent the sexual side of marital life as the complete and unique content of marriage.   On the contrary marriage may not be, as so often repeated here, detached' from family life ; it is defined in all its aspects by the problems of the economic unity of the family, of the bonds created by common life in one wurley, through the common rearing of, and affection towards, the offspring. In the above points I tried to show that in nearly all these respects the *Pirrauru* relationship essentially differs from marriage and cannot, therefore, seriously encroach upon the individual family.   This will appear

---

[1] And some others.   For instance, Prof. Frazer in his new work, *loc. cit.*, i. pp. 363 *sqq.*, where the theories and views of these authorities on *Pirrauru* are accepted without any criticism.

[2] *Loc. cit.*, p. 136.

still more clearly when all these points are exhaustively discussed in their bearing upon the individual family.

Now I would like to show that Howitt, as well as Spencer and Gillen, based his assertions as to the group marriage character of the *Pirrauru* relation upon a misleading exaggeration of the importance of the sexual side of marriage. Spencer and Gillen say that every man has one or two individual wives or *Nupa* " allotted to him as wives, and to whom he has the first but not the exclusive right of access." [1] But besides these there is the *Pirrauru* institution in which " a group of women actually have marital relations with a group of men." And as a conclusion, it follows simply, that in Australia there exists a group marriage, and that not a " pretended " one (Spencer and Gillen criticize here Dr. Westermarck's expression), but a " real " one. This reasoning would inspire some mistrust by its summary and laconic character alone.[2] But it is also evident that in the passage quoted the authors speak exclusively of the sexual side of marriage, and that they actually mean to imply that this sexual side is everything which requires attention, if marriage in a given case should be described. And this is obviously false. The incorrect reasoning is repeated by the same authors in their later work.[3] From the fact that sexual access is open to the *Pirraurus*, and that there are no special names for the individual parents and children (which does not seem to hold good for the Dieri, however), the inference is drawn that group marriage exists instead of individual marriage. Not even the

---

[1] *Nat. Tr.*, p. 109.

[2] Mr. Thomas has also remarked (*loc. cit.*, p.128) that Spencer and Gillen, who speak on page 109 of the real and not pretended group marriage among the Urabunna, say on the next page, that in the same tribe group marriage preceded the present state of things—and so contradict themselves. Such a carelessness is remarkable in a work, which in all other respects is a masterpiece; and all these reasons induce us to suspect that the subject in question must have been in theory as well as in facts not very familiar to our authors.

[3] *Nor. Tr.*, p. 140.

conditions under which a man has access to his *Pirrauru* are discussed ! Our discussion (from Howitt's detailed data) has shown that even in sexual matters the *Pirrauru* are far behind the Tippa Malku; indeed, that there is no comparison between the sexual rights of an individual husband and of a *Pirrauru*.

The same insufficiency of reasoning is shown by Howitt. He says in one place[1] that there is individual as well as group marriage among the Australian aborigines. But under the word marriage he understands the right of sexual access. And on this ground he asserts that among the Kurnai there existed individual marriages exclusively; and among the Dieri there was also group marriage. It is characteristic that no one of these writers tried to give any explicit definition of marriage; but from what I have quoted it appears quite clearly how one-sidedly and narrowly they conceived marriage.[2] And this conception was not only fatal to the theories and views held by them on the question, but it vitiated to a certain extent also the information they gave us about these facts. For they did not try to ascertain and to inform us about the most important particulars, which were perhaps not quite out of the reach of their investigation.[3]

We have based our discussion of the *Pirrauru* relation

[1] *Trans. R.S.V.*, p. 115.

[2] In order to appreciate my argument, the reader is requested to peruse the passages referred to from the works of Howitt, and from Spencer and Gillen, and judge from their full text whether I am not right. The full quotations of these passages would have encumbered the present work. As polemics are always rather barren, I preferred to abstain from them.

[3] This is an instance of the general truth that descriptive ethnography is highly dependent on the theories known and accepted by the investigator, and that information may be useful or useless according to whether the theoretical principles are correct or not. It is impossible for an observer to go below the surface if he does not discuss the phenomena and theorize on them. On the other hand such speculations, if carried on by the untrained faculties and unaided efforts of the writers, or under the influence of a theoretical prepossession, may be entirely misleading.

on a broad conception of marriage, determined by factors of the daily life, the household, the relation to children, etc. In our systematic and objective description of facts relating to the *Pirrauru* relation we found in the first place that individual marriage exists besides the custom in question; that it has its radically distinctive features —a different form of betrothal or allotment of a wife to a man; an entirely different kind of sexual rights and privileges; and, what is perhaps the most important fact, an absolutely different aspect of the child question, connected with the fact that only a man and his wife form a real household, live in the same wurley, and share their food supply together and in common with their children. All these points constitute a real and radical difference between the individual marriage connected with the individual family, and the purely sexual connections involved in the *Pirrauru* relation in its usual form, *i. e.* when the husband is present in camp. It is only during the latter's absence or during diplomatic missions that the *Pirrauru* relation assumes at all the character of marriage: then both *Pirraurus* occupy the same camp, the woman provides food for her *Pirrauru*, etc. But these occasions are only temporary and exceptional ones, and we are, unfortunately, not informed, even with the smallest degree of approximation, how often they may on the average occur, whether they are very rarely realized exceptions, or whether they are facts that take place fairly often. At any rate, it is certain that these essential features of the *Pirrauru* relationship never take place simultaneously with the individual marriage. In other words, the individual marital relations are in force when the real husband is in camp and all rights (even the sexual ones) of the *Pirraurus* cease. So that although the *Pirrauru* relation, on exceptional and probably rarely recurring occasions, assumes a few more of the characteristics of marriage, it never becomes anything like actual marriage. And this is to be noted, too: the full actuality of *Pirrauru* relations may come into force only under the condition that the husband be absent. It is only by an incorrect and superficial exaggeration of the sexual side of marriage, that the custom in question has been baptized group marriage.[1] And still less acceptable is the assertion that this " group marriage " is " the only form of marriage in existence " among the South Central tribes.

We may remark about the sexual features of social life in Australia in general, that far from bearing any character of indiscriminate promiscuity on the whole, they are, on the contrary, subject to strict regulations, restrictions, and rules. Every form of licence must be subject to customary rules. The principle of class exogamy is maintained in the majority of cases : so the *Pirrauru* relation is subject to class rule, as is also wife-lending, wife-exchange, and the rare cases of licence among unmarried girls and widows. But the licence occurring during religious, totemic, and other ceremonies is, as we have seen above, not subject to the class rule. Even the most prohibited and tabooed degree—that between a man and his mother-in-law—is violated by custom.

This fact is also noteworthy for the criticism of theories which see both in class exogamy and in sexual licence survivals of former group marriage. At some ceremonies of a magical and religious character sexual licence occurs, in agreement with the principle that survivals are always connected with religious facts. But if class exogamy is also a survival of group marriage, why should *this* fall in abeyance on such occasions ? For if these two principles were so deeply connected, why should one of them (class exogamy) be entirely neglected on the very occasion when the other (ceremonial licence) is most conspicuous ? Is that not again one of the serious difficulties in the way of the hypothesis of a previous group marriage, a difficulty which at least must be accounted for, and which is always completely ignored by the authors concerned ?

[1] Unless we give to the word marriage a new meaning, which would be hardly useful.

There is justification for saying that the notion of adultery and the reprobation thereof is well known to the aborigines, and that they punish and condemn unlawful unions of all kinds. As W. E. Roth says, " morality in a broad sense " is well known to the Australian aborigines. It could be even said that sexual morality does exist, only according to a special code, which is obviously different from ours, if we understand by " morality " the fact that there exists a series of determined norms and that these norms are followed.

Closely connected with this question is the more psychological problem of sexual jealousy. The existence of sexual jealousy, especially on the part of the males, has been often referred to by various authors in order to criticize the theories of primitive promiscuity and group marriage. On the other hand, it was pointed out that motives of jealousy are much less strong among some primitive peoples; and many instances have been adduced to prove this assumption. So *e. g.* about the Australians, Spencer and Gillen say : " Amongst the Australian natives with whom we have come in contact, the feeling of sexual jealousy is not developed to anything like the extent to which it would appear to be in many other savage tribes." . . . " It is indeed a factor which need not be taken into serious account in regard to the question of sexual relations amongst the Central Australian tribes." [1]

It seems to be beyond any doubt that sexual jealousy, as *we* conceive it, is completely absent from the aboriginal mind. It has always been a serious defect in ethnological reasoning that such ideas and feelings as those connected with our meaning of " jealousy " have usually not been analyzed, nor the question asked whether they had any meaning and place in a given society, or whether we must assume other corresponding elements to give a new content to the word. Our sexual jealousy— the ideas as well as the feelings involved therein—is

[1] *Nat. Tr.*, pp. 99, 100.

moulded by innumerable social factors; it is connected with the notion of honour; it is the result of ideals of pure love, individual sexual rights, sacredness of monogamy, etc. One of the strongest motives is the care for the certainty of physiological fatherhood : paternal affection is strongly enhanced by the idea of blood connection between a man and his offspring. All these factors are obviously either absent or deeply modified in the Australian aboriginal society. It is, therefore, quite wrong to use the word jealousy and ask if it is present among them, without trying to give to it its proper content.

In the first place, we may assume in this society, as in the whole of mankind and in the majority of higher animals, a physiological basis for jealousy in the form of an innate instinct;[1] a natural aversion of an individual towards an encroachment on his sexual rights and a natural tendency to expand these rights as far as possible —within certain variable limits. That among the Australian aborigines such instincts of jealousy are not absent, that they are, on the contrary, very strongly developed, is evident from nearly all the facts quoted and all general considerations. It is proved by the high esteem in which in some tribes chastity is held; by the fact that fidelity is required in all other tribes, and that it yields only to custom. The demand for fidelity in all tribes has been discussed above. There is a whole series of statements that emphatically affirm a very strong feeling of jealousy; and connected with it is the fact that the majority of fights and quarrels are about women (Curr,

---

[1] This expression is perhaps inexact. But this is not the place for psychological and biological analyses. The reader may be referred to Dr. Westermarck's conclusion that there is a strong instinct of sexual jealousy among primitive races of men, both in males (*H.H.M.*, pp. 117-132) and in females (*ibid.*, pp. 495-500). This instinct is inherited from our animal ancestors (compare Darwin, *Descent of Man*, ii. p. 395). Important for us are the examples of female jealousy, quoted by Westermarck from the Australian material; Narrinyeri, Taplin, p. 11; Palmer, p. 282; Lumholtz, p. 213; Waitz Gerland, pp. 758, 781.

Dawson, Mrs. Parker, Schürmann, Wilhelmi, Wilkes, Turnbull, Phillipps, Tench, Spencer and Gillen). Now, that these instincts of jealousy do not assume the delicate and refined form they possess in our society, results merely from the difference in the corresponding collective ideas which influence and mould the elementary instinct.

With our few data available we can attempt only a sketch of the psychology of the feelings of jealousy among the aborigines. It may be observed that although the sentiment of sexual love might be postulated in all human hearts, it seems to be, to a certain extent, banished from the majority of the Australian matrimonial matches by the very way in which they were brought about.[1]

This must also to a great extent deprive jealousy of its violent character. On the other hand, social opinion, which in our society works through ideas of honour and ridicule, strengthening the feelings of jealousy and giving to them a certain outer prestige, even in cases when they may not be actually felt—in the Australian Aboriginal Society uses these factors with a directly contrary effect. As a matter of fact, in many cases, public opinion compels a man to give his wife away; it is considered an incident of hospitality, a virtue. In other cases it is an honourable duty, as e. g. in cases of wife offering during a ceremony in order to express gratitude. We read that in cases where a man begrudges his wife to a *Pirrauru* he is regarded as churlish. Obviously, these social factors act here to modify and moderate the feeling of sexual jealousy. We find no instance or statement which would point to a contrary influence of these factors in the Australian aboriginal society.[2] But, as pointed out above, the idea

---

[1] Compare above, p. 83.

[2] Custom referring to a certain point—here e. g. to the question whether it is honourable or ignominious to waive one's marital rights—stands in the relation of correspondence to the collective ideas and collective feelings on this point. The expression of Spencer and Gillen that the feeling of jealousy is "subservient to that of the influence of tribal custom" is therefore incorrect (*Nat. Tr.*, p. 99). It would be obviously quite erroneous to assert that there is any collective feeling which

of individual sexual over-right and control over his wife is strongly present in the aboriginal mind. This right is undoubtedly realized as a privilege, and the natural tendency to keep his privileges for himself, or dispose of them according to his wish or interest, must create a strong opposition to any encroachment. In other words, the sexual act has its intrinsic value, and it is considered as an unquestionable advantage. And the right to this advantage constitutes a kind of private property. The feeling of jealousy exists here in its economic sense : the proprietor of a certain object begrudges the use of it to any one whom he does not invite to it, or who is not otherwise entitled to the privilege. And this seems to me one of the strongest probable sources of jealousy, besides the natural physiological impulse of aversion, mentioned above. I think it is corroborated by the facts enumerated, which show that the husband vigilantly watches over and keeps his over-right.

In regard to the motive of jealousy as connected with

---

would not be subservient to the tribal custom. It is consequently meaningless to affirm that the given feeling here is subservient. We may, therefore, discard also the logical conclusion at which Messrs. Spencer and Gillen arrive from these premisses : viz. that jealousy is a matter of no importance when dealing with the Central Australians (*ibid.*, p. 100). A certain tribal or national custom expresses or formulates public feelings, and, on the other hand, if there is a certain type of collective feelings or ideas, they must have their legal or customary forms wherein to express themselves. We should say : the Australian customs show that there is no such collective feeling as jealousy in our sense, which would obviously object to such customs as theirs. The collective feelings in Australia which correspond to our jealousy do not imply, therefore, the idea of absolute exclusiveness; the idea of inviolable personal access of a man to a woman does not exist there; that is proved by the custom in question. But outside the limits prescribed by tribal custom there is little adultery ; jealousy seems to be exceedingly strong, and the same tribal law, which in some cases compels the man to give up his marital rights, in other cases justifies him in the utmost brutalities, and allows him even to inflict death with impunity upon his wife. Owing to the scantiness of our information we can hardly say whether sexual jealousy is stronger or weaker in Australian than in other societies; we can safely affirm that it is different.

the question of progeny—the care to be sure of a man's own real paternity of his children, we may remark that this motive must be absent in many tribes, viz. in those tribes where the physiological rôle of the father in procreation is not known. We know with all certainty that this is the case in the Central and North Central tribes, as well as in the North-east part of the continent.[1] But it appears to be the case in the South Central tribes. It is stated that the Urabunna have quite analogous beliefs in reincarnation of ancestors, in their dwelling-places, and other totemic matters.[2] Spencer and Gillen do not say anything definite about the appreciation or want of knowledge of physiological paternity, but that is perhaps because they were less well acquainted with the Urabunna, who were also probably in a more advanced stage of decay. By analogy it may be inferred that the Urabunna, like all the other neighbouring tribes, had with the whole apparatus of analogous beliefs, also the lack of the knowledge in question. We might infer the same about the Dieri and kindred tribes, who seem to be almost identical in all respects with the Urabunna, but of whose religious and totemic ideas we are by no means so well informed as of their social organization; in fact, for these psychological data it is undoubtedly to Spencer and Gillen that we owe the major part of our knowledge about Australia.

Certainly the ignorance of physiological fatherhood in the South Central tribes is of a hypothetical character. But provided it is a fact, we see that the area occupied by tribes which believe in the supernatural begetting of children extends over the whole Central and North-east area. There is no evidence on this point in the case of the Western tribes. We find only in the South-eastern tribes a knowledge of the real process of procreation. It is interesting to note that thus the area of greater sexual promiscuity and less pronounced

---

[1] See below, pp. 209 sqq. and 226.
[2] Spencer and Gillen, Nor. Tr., pp. 146 sqq.

jealousy is conterminous with the area where natural paternity is unknown. Whether there be any real dependence between these two series of facts it is impossible to assert, as our knowledge of the natives' psychology is too scanty. But if our information on this point be reliable, and if these limits be correct, then the coincidence just noted is rather suggestive.

To return to the question of jealousy, we have, after having stated the general problems, discussed the influence exercised on it by social pressure or custom and other psychical factors. Finally we have shown that the sexual act is not in all tribes conceived as leading to childbirth, and that this bears upon the problem of jealousy. But it must be remembered that they have ideas of the sexual act which are entirely foreign to us, and which may account also for some differences in their views of, and feelings about, jealousy. Here come in ideas of the magic influences and virtues attributed to the sexual act. In Australia there are unmistakable signs of it.

The ceremonial act of defloration, in connection with the initiation of females, is undoubtedly connected with some mystic ideas of its magical character. This is shown especially clearly in the fact that this ceremonial act is employed for medicinal or hygienic purposes, as stated in Roth and in Beveridge.[1] We saw that the only instance of the exchange of wives in the Kurnai tribe was when it was ordered by the old men, to avert impending evil. The same is reported by Cameron of some of the Darling River tribes. This shows clearly how feelings of jealousy, which seem to have been fairly strong in this tribe, may be subservient to a belief in the magical, beneficial influence of sexual intercourse, performed in a certain prescribed way. The many instances in which sexual intercourse, usually not between husband and wife, takes place during certain religious ceremonies, as well as the fact of sexual abstinence, which is often to be observed on such occasions, shows that it has its magical

[1] Roth, *Ethnol. Stud.*, p. 174. Beveridge, p. 53, Latin note.

side. From this conception of the sexual act as endowed
with some magic properties, there would result differences
in the ideas and feelings connected with jealousy. On the
one hand, such magic properties would require in some
cases the waiving of individual sexual rights, as we saw
in some of the instances just mentioned. And in these
cases the instincts of jealousy would be suppressed by the
more powerful feelings inspired by supernatural apprehensions. On the other hand, it is possible—although
there are no examples of it—that the very magical aspect
of the sexual act would make it especially subject to
jealous watchfulness and exclusiveness. Apart from
any speculations, it appears certain that all these different
ideas and conceptions are in intimate interdependence,
and that we can only safely speak about jealousy (or any
other such compounded psychical complex) in a given
society, when we know all such connections.[1]

To sum up our results in this survey of jealousy in the
Australian aboriginal society. *Negatively : A priori* it
may be said that nothing like sexual jealousy in our sense
of this word—save the broad and uncertain physiological
instinct—can exist. As a matter of fact, a whole series
of customs, duties, and tribal regulations absolutely contradict the existence of jealousy in our sense. *Positively :*
The existence of strong instincts of jealousy in many cases
must be acknowledged. To understand the more definite
forms which these instincts assume, it is necessary to
note the presence or absence of motives which would
influence, check, or develop these instincts. The unquestionable physiological instinct of jealousy and the
natural tendency to keep up one's private exclusive rights,
are two sources from which jealousy seems to be derived.
It is deeply influenced by the ideas on the magical character of the sexual act which the Australian aborigines

[1] The idea of a radical difference in the psychological aspect of
jealousy among lower races of men is set forth by Dr. Westermarck : " Jealousy . . . is far from being the same feeling in
the mind of a savage as in that of a civilized man."—*H.H.M.*,
p. 30.

undoubtedly possess; and in the majority of tribes by the absence of the knowledge of physical paternity. The tribal customs show that it does not amount to the idea of exclusive inviolable personal rights which essentially characterize our conception and feelings of jealousy. But within its narrower limits it seems to be very strong and important.

CHAPTER V

MODE OF LIVING

I

THE three points hitherto discussed refer more exclusively to the relationship between husband and wife, and do not involve that between parents and children. They bear more on marriage than on the family. But, as so often repeated, the full description of marriage can be made only in connection with, and on the basis of, a knowledge of the family life in its larger sense. We proceed now to this more general discussion, and in order to carry it out on broad foundations it will be well in the first place to consider the family unit [1] in connection with the territorial and tribal organization; that is to consider the mode of living of the family in connection with the higher territorial and tribal units. It has been repeatedly said that each social unit should be discussed in connection with the general structure of society and the general conditions of life in a given area. When theoretically stated this appears a commonplace; in practice it is seldom carried out by ethnologists.

That the facts of aggregation are of the highest importance in sociology appears also to be quite clear.[2] These

[1] Under the term " family unit " I understand in this study only the group constituted by husband, wife and their children.

[2] " In the study of population . . . the facts of aggregation or grouping are the first to claim our attention." (F. H. Giddings, *Princ. of Sociology*, p. 79). In fact all the social phenomena of higher order corresponding to differentiation and constitution depend upon the facts of grouping. In the lowest societies, as the Australian, the mode of living in very small groups pre-

facts have been described by Mr. Wheeler for the Australian aboriginal society, and we shall in several places refer to his work. It will serve us as a basis in the following discussion, which nevertheless does not appear superfluous as it is connected more exclusively with the problem of family. In this connection the main question to be asked is : Do the natives usually live scattered, in single families, or in larger groups ? All the features of family life—the husband's authority, the sexual marital relation, the economics of the household, the relation of children to parents—would appear in a different light, and our ideas thereon might in many respects be modified according to the answer we obtained to the above question. This point (*i. e.* the mode of living) would also be decisive in the problem of group relationship : if the natives live normally in single families, which assemble only occasionally, then the individuality of the family relationship is placed beyond any doubt. And if there are, besides, any group relations, they must radically and absolutely differ from the individual one; for the latter, and it only, is constituted by the most powerfully binding element— continuous daily contact. If, however, the aborigines live in more or less numerous groups, our question is still open, and we have to inquire : Do the families, which (permanently or temporarily) form one body, live in a state of social communism and promiscuity ? Or are

---

cludes *a priori* the possibility of any higher social formations. We may say that the social horizon of a community extends as far as the contact of its members. In higher societies this contact need not necessarily be an actual one; as a rule in more developed communities members of a social unit (nation, town, association) only come exceptionally and in a diminutive degree into immediate contact. But there are innumerable ways of mental contact. On the contrary there is no other form of contact but the personal one among the Australian blacks, and it is the first condition for the formation of any social bonds amongst them. In the discussion of all kinship bonds we should never lose sight of the fact that it is highly improbable that people who never were in personal contact could feel more closely related than people who usually live together.

they more or less isolated from each other ? That will form the second part of our task.[1]

Let us now gather information about the first point, *i. e.* the size of the groups in which the natives live.   Our statements are at first sight contradictory on this point; but this is largely due to the total lack of fixed terminology.   It will be well to settle the latter beforehand and determine more exactly what we are to look for in the statements.   For that purpose we must forestall the results of our research and broadly outline the state of things; it will give us a guiding thread through the statements.   Roughly speaking, in Australia the tribe as a social unit is characterized by name, common speech, custom and territory.[2]   It is divided (and sometimes subdivided again) into smaller groups; these consist of individuals closely related, possess a sort of government, and are connected with a portion of the tribal territory which they practically use in common.[3]   For the social division of the tribes is connected with and complicated by a parallel territorial partition.   And there is always a certain territory allotted to the exclusive possession of a certain group.   The tribe (as defined above) cannot be considered as proprietor[4] of the territory, for its different

---

[1] The importance of the aboriginal mode of living in the study of family life and kinship bonds has been well brought out by Dr. Westermarck (*H.H.M.*, pp. 42 *sqq.*, especially pp. 43–47). His general inference—that in low societies the scattered mode of living brings into prominence individual kinship bonds, and isolates the family unit—will be corroborated by our conclusions drawn from the Australian material. The few Australian examples—quoted and interpreted by Dr. Westermarck—have been vehemently disputed by Herr Cunow (*loc. cit.*, p. 122, footnote).   His criticism, if compared with the data presented in this chapter, will appear quite unfounded.   Herr Cunow's book does not, by the way, deserve its good reputation.   There are many statements in it, given without references, which I have been unable to verify in the first hand evidence.

[2] See Wheeler, *loc. cit.*, pp. 15 *sqq.*, and the references given there.

[3] *Ibid.*, pp. 45, 46.

[4] To guard against misunderstanding I wish to emphasize that such words and expressions as " proprietor," " ownership," " landed property," " rights to a tract of country," etc., are not

divisions may not encroach upon each other's grounds. We shall call (by way of definition) a *Local Group*, such a division of the tribe as possesses the exclusive right to use a given territory and to dwell within its limits. In the following statements we will give a series of examples of these local units, and the different forms they assume in different tribes. It will be possible, too, to give a more precise meaning to the word " proprietorship "; and to see in what sense land may be possessed or claimed by the Australian blacks. The authors seldom try to give to these terms any clear meaning, or to discern all the existing differences; but these will be evident enough from the facts contained in the statements. The problem of territorial division is only the basis for our main question, viz. the mode of living. The Local Group, which is the joint owner of its territory, is, so to say, only the upper limit of aggregation; *i. e.* the body of persons actually and normally living together cannot be larger than that group, for only its members are (in normal conditions) admitted to its grounds. But this Local Group may also live scattered over its district. There will be several data in our information which would rather confirm us in this supposition.

Now let us review the statements, bearing in mind the exact meaning given to the words Tribe, Local Group and Family. We have agreed to call Local Group a unit owning in common a portion of country, and we are asking how big this unit is in different tribes; if it lives scattered or in a body; finally, what idea can we form of " land ownership " in Australia.

---

to be taken in the sense which they possess in application to higher societies, to our own society in particular. Their correct meaning will be gathered from the following discussion. For the sake of clearness and brevity it was sometimes needful, in the text, to use the above expressions, instead of the more correct ones like " possession," " claims to a country," etc. The term " property " has a definite legal meaning, which makes it impossible to apply it in its full sense to the low society with which we are concerned.

Statements.—The Kurnai were divided into five exogamous " clans." [1] These were divided and subdivided several times, " each subdivision having its own tract of hunting and food ground, until the unit was a small group of kindred, frequently an old man, his sons, married or unmarried, with their respective wives and children." The author gives an instance of a family claiming a certain island and the swans' eggs laid on it, as its property,[2] and living under the authority of the oldest male in the family." " Taking such a family [3] as the tribal unit of the Kurnai, it was the aggregation of such families that formed what may be called a division, inhabiting a large area, and the aggregate of the divisions formed the clan." [4] This, and the expression family as " tribal unit," shows that probably its members lived actually together. It is a pity that Howitt does not give even approximately the numbers. Again, in another place, he writes of a " natural spread of families over a tract of country," and of " elders as heads of families." [5] These " families " unite in cases of mutual need for aid and protection [6] and in cases of corroborees, initiations, etc.[7]—Here the local group was a small unit of related persons. It claimed a certain territory and exclusively used its products, and vested authority in its oldest male. These local groups usually must have lived isolated from each other, because of the exclusive right in using the given area. Howitt mentions also the beginnings of individual claims to some products (swan's eggs) being even transmitted by inheritance.[8]

The statements of Howitt concerning the Murring tribes are not quite clear. " Claims to a particular tract of country arose in certain of these tribes by birth." [9] He does not say if these claims consisted in actual right to live, roam and hunt over the said tract of country. It is probable, however, that just this is the meaning, as he speaks immediately afterwards of an hereditary principle as to the grounds determining the habitation where one lives—a father pointing out the bounds of his child's country—" where his father lived, or himself was

---

[1] According to Howitt's terminology.
[2] Howitt, *Nat. Tr.*, pp. 73, 74.
[3] We would say *local group*, as we reserve the term *family* for an undivided group living in the closest unity, and consisting of a man, his wife and his children.
[4] Howitt, *Nat. Tr.*, p. 74.
[5] *Idem, Kam. and Kurn.*, p. 215.   [6] *Ibid.*
[7] Compare chapter on initiations in Howitt's *Nat. Tr.*, and *Kam. and Kurn., passim.*
[8] *Kam. and Kurn.*, p. 232 footnote.
[9] *Nat. Tr.*, p. 82.

born and had lived." [1]   If we can assume that each " family "
(= local group) had its hunting-grounds so designated this
would point to a far-going subdivision of country and consequently of the tribe ; we can hardly infer anything conclusive
from this statement alone.   But it appears clearer in the
light of the following remark : " The local group has in all
cases been perpetuated in the same place from father to son
by occupation, I may almost say by inheritance, of the
hunting-grounds." [2]   It seems, therefore, that generally in
the tribes studied by Howitt, the local group (he calls it
the " family," speaking of the Kurnai) was a very well-defined
unit.   And that, in the tribes in question the people who
inherit a certain territory from father to son are just members
of the local group.   Its rights to the hunting-grounds were
based on some—perhaps magic or religious—ideas of heredity.

An analogous state of things is reported to have obtained
among the Wurunjerri (Victoria) : " The right to hunt and
to procure food in any particular tract of the country belonged
to the group of people born there, and could not be infringed
by others without permission." [3]   In the territory of the same
tribe there was a stone-quarry, the material of which was very
valuable to the natives.   The quarry was the property of a
group of people living on the spot ; the head of this group had
special rights in connection with it.   " It was Billi-billeri,
the head of the family, whose country included the quarry,
who lived on it, and took care of it for the whole of the
Wurunjerri community." [4]   This statement appears to me
very important, as it shows how rights of possession might
belong to a local group and centre in the headman of this
group.   This statement suffices to reconcile the apparent
contradiction between individual claims to a country and
group claims.

The local groups amongst the Bangerang, who lived at the
junction of the Murray and Goulburn Rivers, seem to have been
more numerous, owing, perhaps, to the easiness of food supply
on the banks of two fishy rivers.[5]   The tribe was divided in
two exogamous moieties,[6] and the land " was parcelled out
between these two sub-tribes." [7]   Each respectively lived in
a body, although moving sometimes from place to place.
Curr speaks of their head-quarters in places abounding with
fish.[8]   One of the sections numbered about 150, the other some-

---

[1] *Nat. Tr.*, p. 83.   [2] Howitt, *Smith. Rep.* 83, p. 816.
[3] Howitt, *Nat. Tr.*, p. 311.   [4] *Ibid.*
[5] Curr, *Recollections*, pp. 231, 240.
[6] Local exogamous moieties, not phratries !
[7] Curr, *Recollections*, p. 243.   [8] *Ibid.*, p. 231.

what less. These two " sub-tribes " or moieties constituted, therefore, rather numerous local groups. The "sub-tribes" of the kindred tribes mentioned by Curr seem also to have been numerous,[1] and to have lived each in a body,[2] so that they would be, according to our terminology, numerous local groups. Curr speaks also of individual property in land, but this seems to have had only a purely fictitious meaning, having nothing to do with any real right.[3] Private property in other things (*e.g.* fishing weirs, etc.) was known.[4]

Curr uses the term *tribe* in place of our *local group*. In his general work on Australia he gives a definition of tribe which quite agrees with what we called local group.[5] " By the word tribe I mean a number of men closely allied by blood, and living in the strictest alliance, offensive and defensive, who, with their wives and children, occupy, practically in common, and in exclusion of others, a tract of country. . . ." Everybody must respect the customs of his tribe; and as no one may live apart from the tribal community, " there is no alternative between compliance with tribal custom and death."[6] " Although the lands of a tribe are *nominally* parcelled out amongst its members, it is the fact that they are used in common, and for several reasons must have always been used so." First, because for mutual protection the tribesmen must have often associated. Secondly, because of the economic conditions the tribe often was compelled to feed on a given spot.[7]

Angas, describing his travels in the Murray River district, tells that he met several times with native encampments; from the passage in question [8] we may infer that they were small groups. He says [9] that on the seaside (Encounter Bay), on the lakes, and on the Murray banks, where means of subsistence were fairly easy, the local groups were numerous. But this information is very loose.

Amongst the tribes of the Lower Murray River " particular districts having a radius of from ten to twenty miles, or in other cases varying according to local circumstances, are considered generally as being the property and hunting-grounds

---

[1] *Ibid.*, p. 234.
[2] It is never said clearly; but compare the story told in XIII, of the meeting of two tribes, and *passim* through the work, p. 174 and others.
[3] *Ibid.*, pp. 243, 244.   [4] *Ibid.*, p. 243.
[5] It is used here in agreement with G. C. Wheeler, Spencer and Gillen, Howitt, etc.
[6] Curr, *A.R.*, i. pp. 61, 62.   [7] *Ibid.*, pp. 64, 65.
[8] *Loc. cit.*, i. p. 74.
[9] *Loc. cit.*, i. p. 81.

of the tribes who frequent them." [1]   Eyre speaks of a further
division of land amongst single individuals; it is handed down
hereditarily in the male line. " A man can dispose of or barter
his land to others." [2]   At any rate, all members of a " tribe "
(= local group) may roam over the common territory.   It
seems, nevertheless, to be rather a formal than actual, exclusive
right.[3]   The local groups may not trespass on their respective territories without permission.[4]   The whole local group
congregates only " if there is any particular variety more
abundant than another, or procurable only in certain localities.
Should this not be the case, then they are probably scattered
over their district in detached groups, or separate families." [5]
Here we are well informed on our principal points : the local
group is the exclusive joint landowner; the individual has
some claims which are not quite clearly defined, but surely
do not mean exclusive economic *usum fructum*. They live
scattered in small parties over their area.   There is another
passage in Eyre's book that confirms this latter point.   He
says that each family is independent and governed by the
father; but that, " as a matter of policy, he always informs
his fellows where he is going."   So that " although a tribe
may be dispersed all over their own district in single groups . . .
yet if you meet with any one family, they can at once tell you
where you will find any other. . . .   In cases of sudden
danger or emergency, the scattered groups are rapidly
warned or collected " by messenger or smoke signals.[6]

Mitchell's expedition, when exploring the interior of South-
East Australia, met a party of blacks on the banks of the
Murray, whom they had seen before on the Darling a few
hundred miles distant.[7] This would apparently contradict
the assumption of fixed boundaries.   But the general evidence
shows that, in exceptional cases, and with the leave of the
neighbouring tribes—especially if these were friendly—a local
group or any party of natives were allowed to travel even
considerable distances for purposes of warfare, barter or
ceremonial gatherings.

Amongst the Aborigines of Encounter Bay and Lower
Murray River (the Narrinyeri) the local groups (H. E. A.
Meyer calls them " tribes," [8] or " large families " of connected
people) seem to be numerous (the country abounds with fish
and birds).   These local groups have their head-quarters,
from which their name is derived.   But only in cases of great

---

[1] Eyre, ii. p. 297.   [2] *Ibid.*, pp. 218, 297.   [3] *Ibid.*, p. 297.
[4] *Ibid.*, ii. p. 297.   [5] *Ibid.*, p. 218.   [6] *Ibid.*, ii. p. 317.
[7] Mitchell, *loc. cit.*, ii. p. 92.
[8] H. E. A. Meyer, *loc. cit.*, p. 198.

abundance of food does the local group live and move together.
Usually single families roam in parties; the sick and aged
remain in the head-quarters, and suffer often from want of food.
Not only in search of food, but for the sake of performing
corroborees, initiations, etc., and visiting each other, do these
local groups roam about the country.[1]

From a passage in Taplin [2] we may infer that the local
group of the Narrinyeri near Lake Alexandrina numbered
about 200 natives.[3] The local groups of this tribe were, besides,
exogamous, totemic, and had a regular form of government.
We have not even a hint as to their mode of living; but
if plentiful food supply was the chief condition of larger
aggregations, then these latter would naturally have developed
better in the lake country.

Among the natives of Yorke's Peninsula there are local
divisions; each with a certain totem and with headmen.[4]
This seems analogous to the conditions among the Narrinyeri
and Central tribes; but the information is not detailed
enough to be considered quite reliable.

The Port Lincoln tribes seem to roam about in small parties
of several families.[5] This statement is not sufficiently clear;
probably a number of such parties constituted a local group.

We read, again, about the Port Lincoln tribes: " Each
family has its distinct place, where they live together." [6] The
uncertainty as to the sense in which the word *family* is used
here makes this statement nearly useless. The same author
says in another place: " It has been remarked that the
population and general condition of the natives of Australia
greatly depend on the nature of the locality they occupy;
where the country is sterile and unproductive the natives
are found to congregate in small numbers. In fertile districts
they are comparatively numerous." [7] This opinion is in
agreement with the fact that the population round Lake
Alexandrina, where food supply was plentiful, was extremely
dense.[8]

An author who has made his observations on the blacks
of the Murrumbidgee River (New South Wales) and Moreton
Bay (Queensland) writes: Each " tribe " (= local group)
occupies a definite tract of country; a trespass of its boundaries by a stranger is punished with death.[9] This common

[1] H. E. A. Meyer, *loc. cit.*, pp. 191, 192.
[2] Taplin, *loc. cit.*, p. 35.   [3] *Ibid.*, p. 36.
[4] T. M. Sutton, *loc. cit.*, p. 17.   [5] Schürmann, *loc. cit.*, p. 221.
[6] Chas. Wilhelmi, p. 178.   [7] *Ibid.*, p. 165.
[8] Compare T. Gill, *loc. cit.*, p. 223, on the authority of Dr.
Moorhouse.   [9] G. S. Lang, *loc. cit.*, p. 5.

district is subdivided among families of the local group. " During seasons when all the members of the tribe are not congregated together, each family hunts on its own grounds." The author quotes, also, instances where trees were marked and belonged to individuals.[1] This statement answers both our questions as to land ownership and modes of living; in both respects the " family " is the unit : it owns its area and it lives on and uses it normally in isolation from the others; proprietorship means here exclusive use. But we must bear in mind that what is called here family may as well be a small local group of closely related people, like those among the Kurnai. At any rate it certainly means that the blacks live in very small groups, perhaps in individual families, and that this scattered mode of living rests on a territorial basis. (In general the authority of G. S. Lang cannot be said to be of the best.)

We read in the travels of Gerstaecker that natives carefully keep to the boundaries of their own district. So that a traveller, to be quite safe, should always change his guide when entering upon a new territory.[2]

We read about the tribes of New South Wales in general : " Though they are constantly wandering about, yet they usually confine themselves to a radius of fifty or sixty miles from the place they consider their residence. If they venture beyond this, which they sometimes do with a party of whites, they always betray the greatest fear of falling in with some Myall or stranger blacks, who they say would put them to death immediately."[3] We find here again the local group owning its territory and having head-quarters; as well as the sacrosanctity of boundaries.

Turnbull remarks about the New South Wales tribes that the best food supply, and consequently the largest gatherings, were possible on the sea-shore and on the banks of fishy rivers.[4]

An example of family proprietorship in land is mentioned by Collins.[5] From it, it appears that this sort of proprietorship meant rather some mystic claim than any exclusive right of economic character.

We are informed that among the natives of New South Wales there is a great number of small tribes, each containing from forty to fifty individuals. " Each tribe has a certain beat, or hunting-ground, frequently of not more than twenty miles in

---

[1] G. S. Lang, *loc. cit.*, p. 14.
[2] Refers probably to the Murrumbidgee tribes. *Op. cit.*, iii. p. 9.
[3] Chas. Wilkes (larger edition), ii. p. 187.
[4] *Loc. cit.*, p. 89　　　　　[5] *Loc. cit.*, i. p. 599.

diameter, from which they never move, unless on certain occasions when they visit the territory of a neighbouring tribe for the purpose of a fight, or a ceremony. Sometimes, the tribe will wander about in parties of five or ten; at other times all the members will encamp together." [1] In substituting the word *local group* for *tribe*, we get here again a fairly good statement.

In the statements of Fraser we find again the local group; he calls it "sub-tribe." It derives its name from a certain locality, owns a tract of country, which is guarded jealously against any infringement from any of the neighbouring sub-tribes.[2] This statement is illustrated by an example, and therefore appears rather trustworthy.[3]

" Each tribe is divided into independent families, which acknowledge no chief, and which inhabit in common a district within certain limits, generally not exceeding above ten or twelve miles on any side." The tribes number from 100 to 300.[4] " The families belonging to a tribe meet together upon occasions of festivals at certain seasons, and also to consult upon all important occasions." [5] The first phrase is not clear : we are not told whether what he calls the tribe owns its area in common, or whether the divisions called " independent families " possess each its own district. From the context, however, we see that we must assume the latter. Three hundred people occupy in Australia usually more than a hundred square miles.

Hodgkinson, speaking of the tribes between Port Macquarie and Moreton Bay, says that the tribes (local groups) keep each within very narrow limits. The district of each of them measures about 150 square miles; usually some ten to twelve miles of a river bank and the adjoining hinterland. " The whole body of a tribe is never united on the same spot, unless on some important occasion. They are more generally divided into small parties of eight or ten men, with their women and children, for the greater convenience of hunting, etc., and these detached companies roam over any part of the country within the prescribed limits of the main tribe to which they belong." [6] This statement agrees with the general type of information.

Of the Coombangree tribe, New South Wales, it is said : " Each tribe kept its own belt of country and separated into

[1] Henderson, *loc. cit.*, p. 108.
[2] *Loc. cit.*, p. 36.   [3] *Loc. cit.*, p. 37.
[4] Port Stephens tribe.   R. Dawson, pp. 326, 327.
[5] *Ibid.*, compare also p. 63.
[6] Hodgkinson, *loc. cit.*, p. 222.

small camps, and only collected on special occasions." [1]   In this statement the words " local group " should be substituted for " tribe."

The Dieri, divided into five local hordes, are still subdivided into smaller " local groups, each having a definite tract of hunting and food ground." [2]   These local groups cannot be very numerous.   The whole tribe numbers about 250. There are at least ten local groups, since they include about twenty persons each.   But we do not know whether such a local group lived in a body or scattered over its territory.[3]

We owe one of our best statements as to the nature of the local group to Spencer and Gillen.   Its totemic character, its organization with the *alatunja* at its head, the different functions of magico-religious character and many other social functions and characteristics define it perfectly well.[4]   The territorial division seems to be much the same in all the tribes studied by Messrs. Spencer and Gillen.   " In all the tribes there is a division into local groups, which occupy certain well-defined areas within the tribal territory." [5]   The possession of land is vested in them. " There is no such thing as one man being regarded as the owner of any tract of country.   In every case the unit of division is the local totemic group." [6]   This statement is quite clear.   The local group owns a certain area, and all the individuals have the right to hunt and roam over it.   They do not do it in one body, they live scattered in much smaller parties of one or two families.   " The members of this (local group) wander, perhaps in small parties of one or two families, often, for example, two or more brothers with their wives and children, over the land which they own, camping at favourite spots, where the presence of water-holes, with their accompaniment of vegetable and animal food, enables them to supply their wants." [7]   Here the picture is perfectly clear : the territorial unit is the local group; within its grounds all members have the right to hunt and roam; no other people may trespass over the boundaries.   Such trespasses do not in reality frequently happen.[8]   The area is not only economically the property of the local group, there are much stronger ties between the land, once the hunting and ceremonial ground of the Alcheringa ancestors, and their actual

---

[1] *Science of Man*, 1900, p. 116, article by A. C. McDougall.
[2] Howitt, *Nat. Tr.*, p. 46.   [3] Gason, *loc. cit.*, p. 258.
[4] *Nat. Tr.*, pp. 9, 16 and *passim* throughout both works, especially in connection with the description of totemism and totemic cult.
[5] *Nor. Tr.*, p. 27.   [6] *Ibid.*
[7] *Nat. Tr.*, p. 16.   [8] *Nor. Tr.*, p. 31.

descendants.[1] But the local group does not form one body; division into single families seems to be, under ordinary circumstances, the normal status. We get here a good insight into the inner structure of a local group, the chief feature of which is the isolation of families. The local group acts as a body chiefly on ceremonial occasions. To sum up : the local group is the joint land-owner; proprietorship means exclusive rights to hunt and roam over the country; but in the native's mind it has much deeper roots, and the connection between the local group and its hunting-grounds is based upon all their traditions and creeds. Their mode of living is scattered; they hang usually round favourite spots (see below).

Speaking of the totemic myths of the Northern tribes Mr. Mathews says : " In those olden days, as at present, the totemic ancestors consisted of families or groups of families, who had their recognized grounds in some part of the tribal territory." [2]

Among the natives of Queensland [3] the territory is parcelled out completely amongst the different local groups; the boundaries are well known and mutually respected. This district is again subdivided amongst the members of the local group; the proprietor " has the exclusive right to direct when it should be hunted over, and the grass burned and the wild animals destroyed." If other men aggregate and use the products of his land he is regarded as the master of ceremonies. This statement gives us at least a clear and consistent definition of private proprietorship, which seems to be of a formal, ceremonial character. But it is not complete. We do not know if normally each family enjoys its district alone, with the head of the family always master of ceremonies, or whether the whole local group, or parts of it, hunt and roam usually in bodies. This statement is, therefore, not very useful.

We read about the Kabi and Wakka tribes of Queensland : " A few families claiming the same territory usually camped and travelled together, sometimes in smaller, sometimes in larger numbers. I characterize such family groups as communities." [4] And again : " Such communities were con-

---

[1] The ties between a totemic local group and its hunting-grounds are based on the whole cycle of totemic ideas on re-incarnation, supernatural conception; on the Oknanikilla and Ertnatulunga. The reader must be referred to the works of Messrs. Spencer and Gillen and Strehlow and to what is said about these points below in connection with the native ideas on conception (Chap. VI.).

[2] *J. and Pr. R.S.N.S.W.*, xl. p. 108.

[3] Moreton Bay. J. D. Lang, p. 335, 336.

[4] J. Mathew, i. p. 128.

stituted by a few families occupying the same small area in common." [1] This is a clear definition of what we called local group, and agrees perfectly well with the general picture already outlined.

E. Palmer says that the game and other products of a certain country belonged to the tribe (= local group) there residing ; the boundaries were respected and trespassers punished by death. [2]

In North-West Central Queensland the " tribe " (our local group) has its head-quarters. [3] This group has also an over-right over its territory, " over which the community as a whole has the right to hunt and roam." [4] There is still a further subdivision ; each family possesses hunting-grounds of its own, and no other has the right to any product thereof without the family's permission. In the case of tribesmen, transgression is a trifle ; in that of strangers, a very serious offence. [5] The statements of Roth do not, however, say anything about their mode of living. The mention of " head-quarters " points to a subdivision of land amongst families and to a scattered mode of living. In all probability we may assume here the following form : the local group as joint owner of its land ; and single families having special rights to certain parts of it, and camping as a rule separately or in small groups, and aggregating in cases of emergency at the head-quarters. This is the only statement which attributes to families and individuals respectively a virtually exclusive right over a certain ground. We read in another place of the mode or rather the principle according to which individual proprietorship is determined in the North Queensland tribes : " The child's own country, its ' home ' where it will in the future have the right to hunt and roam, is determined not by the place of actual birth, but by the locality where his *choi* had been held apart." *Choi* is the spirit part of the child's father, embodied in the father's afterbirth. The place of this *choi* is carefully determined after the child's birth, according to a customary ceremonial. [6] The extent of a local group is determined in the following statement : " there were from twelve to twenty heads of families constituting the group, each with its particular division, who together made the tribe." [7] Here again the land seems to be allotted to the local group, though, according to the foregoing passages, there was a further subdivision according to families.

---

[1] J. Mathew, i. p. 129.   [2] E. Palmer, *J.A.I.*, xiii. pp. 278, 279.
[3] Roth, *Eth. Stud.*, p. 133, § 226.   [4] *Idem*, Bull. viii. p. 8.
[5] *Ibid.* and *Proc. R.S.Q.*, pp. 50, 51.
[6] Bull. v. pp. 18, 23.   [7] *Idem, Proc. R.S.Q.*, p. 69.

As an instance showing that there were sometimes territorial changes and shifting of tribes may be quoted the statement of G. W. Earl, who says that a big tribe came from the
interior and established itself at the base of Coburg Peninsula.[1] How far this statement is reliable it is difficult to say.
Anyhow it is in opposition to the numerous and reliable
statements which affirm that tribal boundaries were strictly
kept and never changed.

The natives of Melville Island seem to have lived in more
numerous groups. Major Campbell says that their "tribes"
number from thirty to fifty persons each. On visiting an
encampment he found about thirty wigwams, which would
point to about fifty persons at least. "They lead a wandering life, though I think each tribe confines itself to a limited
district." [2]

A clear statement concerning the scattered mode of life is
given of the North-Western aborigines by J. G. Withnell,
who lived amongst them for twenty years. "The natives
generally live in families at various intervals of a few miles
down the course of each river and its creeks." [3] "In fact they
are small families constantly moving camp a few miles in any
direction they please." [4] In another place we read : "The
natives are divided into many tribes, having their boundaries
defined." These tribes are obviously our local group. The
members thereof live scattered in small parties, called by
Withnell "families." Very interesting is Withnell's information concerning totemic local centres quite analogous [5] to those
described by Messrs. Spencer and Gillen. It is important in
our present discussion because it throws light upon the
problem of the connection between an individual or a family
and a certain tract of country. From Withnell's information [6]
it results that among the North-Western tribes there were also
totemic centres, allotted each to a "family" (local group or
part thereof?) at which ceremonies for the multiplication of
the totem were performed. The claim to such centres is
hereditary.

We read in Grey about the tribes of West Australia.
"They appear to live in tribes (= local groups), subject,
perhaps, to some individual authority; and each tribe has a
sort of capital, or head-quarters, where the women and children
remain whilst the men, divided into small parties, hunt and
shoot in different directions. The largest number we saw
together amounted nearly to 200, women and children

---

[1] *Loc. cit.*, pp. 241, 242.   [2] *Loc. cit.*, pp. 156, 157.
[3] J. G. Withnell, *loc. cit.*, p. 8.   [4] *Ibid.*
[5] *Idem*, p. 31.   [6] *Loc. cit.*, pp. 5, 6.

included." [1] This directly asserts that the local group lived
in one body; for of course the men were bound to return
always to the head-quarters. Now if we had to assume that
the local group numbered about 200 individuals we could
hardly allow the possibility of obtaining food. Especially
as in another place Grey says : " Landed property does not
belong to a tribe, or to several families, but to a single
male; and the limits of his property are so accurately defined
that every native knows those of his own land, and can
point out the various objects which mark his boundaries."
This land is divided by the father amongst his several sons.
But Grey does not define what proprietorship means. These
two statements are quite inconsistent with each other; if
every man of a big local group had to go to hunt on his own
grounds (and we know that the food area for an Australian
family is not small) they would have to spend their life in
making journeys between their hunting-grounds and head-
quarters. We must either suppose that Grey's tribes were
quite small local groups which lived each on its own territory, and that when he speaks of from 100 to 200 persons
assembled he refers only to exceptional meetings, or that the
individual ownership of land had no real economic meaning,
and that the natives actually lived in these tribes in more
numerous bodies (perhaps the coastal tribes at least). This
statement is, therefore, not very useful.

Bishop Salvado asserts a subdivision of land among single
families (although he calls " family " a small party of related
natives, see p. 257) acquired by right of birth.[2] Neighbouring
families, small local groups, may enjoy their land in common.[3]
Such small parties are quite independent, and governed by
the oldest male.[4] They lead, as we may infer from that,
normally a solitary, isolated existence. This statement of
Bishop Salvado is also in agreement with the generality of
our evidence. His " family " is evidently a small local
group. (It reminds us of a similar unit amongst the Kurnai,
also interrelated, owning a portion of land, governed by the
oldest male). He says such small groups have been often
incorrectly called tribes by other authors.

Mrs. Bates says the South-West Australians were divided
into tribes or families; " these tribes appear to have been
aggregated into geographical groups . . . each occupied a
definite tract of country." [5] But in another place she says that
" each (family) occupied a definite tract of country " with well-

[1] Loc. cit., i. p. 252.   [2] Loc. cit., p. 265.
[3] Loc. cit., p. 266.   [4] Loc. cit., p. 267.
          [5] Loc. cit., p. 53.

marked boundaries.[1] This statement is marred by the lack of precision in using words like tribes, families, etc. The only thing that can be made out of it is that there was some local unit owning a definite tract of country. The right of ownership is defined by the right of hunting. A man is allowed to hunt merely his own district. But he has access to his wife's district too.[2]

In King George Sound each " tribe " (= local group) owns a certain district ; this is further subdivided among individual families ; each of these portions being hereditary in a certain family, which is proud of the extensiveness of its grounds. But all the members of the local group may roam and hunt over the whole territory. " Under normal conditions and in its own district the tribe (= local group) is divided into small parties or families ; each party forming a camp of six or eight wurleys." [3] Only on special and important occasions does the local group aggregate. Strangers are not admitted to the territory. We see here, again, the actual proprietor of the land is the local group ; families have some merely formal (or magical) claim to portions of it. The local group roams in parties, which are nevertheless not so very small. In from six to eight huts there may live from three to four families (we must count besides the married couples also the old people and grown-up children).

Scott-Nind says about the natives of King George Sound, " An encampment rarely consists of more than seven or eight huts ; for, except the fishing and burning seasons, at which times large parties assemble together, their numbers are generally small, and two or three huts suffice. The number of individuals, however, seldom exceeds fifty." [4] " These encampments generally consist of near relatives, and deserve the name of families rather than of tribes." [5] Natives who live together have the exclusive right of fishing or hunting upon the neighbouring grounds, which are, in fact, divided into individual properties ; the quantity of land owned by each individual being very considerable. Yet it is not exclusively his, but others of his family have certain rights over it ; so that it may be considered as partly belonging to the tribe. The individual owner must be present on his grounds when the members of his group fire the country for game.[6] We have here again the local group as real and exclusive landowner, the individual having only mere formal rights over the land. Scott-Nind describes with details how in connec-

---

[1] *Loc. cit.*, p. 52.   [2] *Loc. cit.*, p. 53.
[3] Browne, *loc. cit.*, pp. 476, 478.   [4] *Loc. cit.*, p. 28.
[5] *Ibid.*   [6] *Ibid.* ; compare also p. 44.

tion with and dependence on plentiful food supply, the natives gather in larger numbers at appropriate seasons.[1] He says in several places that the parties in which the natives live and roam about number only a few individuals.

Out of the thirty-nine statements collected, thirty-one describe a certain group or family as owning a definite tract of country in common; this group is, by definition, what we called above the local group. But there are some complications as to its rights of possession over the given area. On the one hand there is some kind of "over-right" of the tribe over the district inhabited by all the local groups of which it is composed.[2] On the other hand there is a further complication arising from the alleged individual claims to landed property. As to the tribal over-right, it presents itself chiefly in the fact that, first, tribesmen (members of related and friendly local groups) are often invited and allowed on the territory of the local group; secondly, in cases of trespass, while strangers are punished severely (often by death), tribes-men are only considered slightly culpable. The tribe may probably sometimes congregate as a whole on a part of its grounds with the consent of the local group con-cerned. We must imagine the local groups of the same tribe as living in amicable relations and voluntarily exercising hospitality towards each other, especially in cases when food is plentiful on their territory.[3] But as a general rule the whole tribe neither uses its whole district, nor has a local group, forming a division of the tribe, the right to use any but its own territory without

---

[1] *Loc. cit.*, p. 36.

[2] Compare G. C. Wheeler, *loc. cit.*, pp. 62–67. In the above statements I did not include explicitly all the contexts referring to this point, as it lies outside our proper field of investigation. It may be found, more or less explicitly, in some of them (J. D. Lang, *e. g.*). I mentioned it here only to give a fuller account of all aspects under which possession of land presents itself in Australia.

[3] Compare Wheeler, *loc. cit.*, where this question is thoroughly discussed, and also Curr, pp. 244 *sqq.*, Roth, Bull. 8, p. 9; Salvado, p. 265; Grey, ii. p. 272; Browne, *loc. cit.*, p. 445; G. S. Lang, p. 5.

asking permission. The tribal over-right seems therefore of little importance.

The rights of a local group over its territory are, on the other hand, the most important form of ownership, and the only one which possesses economic features. These rights mean that all members of a local group may roam over its territory and use all the products, hunt and collect food and useful objects. In the case of the Central and North Central tribes we are expressly told that no individual or family claims may interfere with the rights that every member of the local group has to the whole local area. In twenty-one of our thirty-one statements referring to the right of the local group, we are not told of any family or individual proprietorship. In the remaining eight cases single families or male individuals seem to have some vague claims to special tracts of country. In three cases the information is ambiguous on this point. In the case of the Bangerang, Moreton Bay tribes (J. D. Lang), King George's Sound natives (Nind and Browne), this right is either of a merely mystic, intangible character,[1] or it is a formal right which gives to the individual the priority in decisions as to hunting, burning of grass, etc., and makes him " master of ceremony " in cases of an assembly on the given spot. In two instances this individual " land ownership " is stated to assume a more economic aspect (G. S. Lang and W. E. Roth). There are, besides, two statements on family " ownership " which do not mention the local group. According to one of them (Collins) individual claims to land have a mystic, fictional character; according to Grey's statement, individual property in land was the only positive one; but this latter statement is inconsistent and does not define the sense of the word " property," [2]

[1] This mystic character of some individual claims to a particular tract of country appears also from Roth's statement, and from a passage of Oldfield (*loc. cit.*, p. 252). " Every male is bound to visit the place of his nativity three times a year." But this writer could not ascertain the purpose of it.

[2] Compare Grey, ii. p. 233, and the letter of G. S. Lang quoted by him therein. It appears that both these writers were to a

and is therefore of little weight.   So on the whole we have
three statements asserting that landed property of an
economic character was vested in individuals or in single
families respectively.   On closer examination, one of
them appears to be quite ambiguous (G. S. Lang), and
another one inconsistent with its context (Grey).   Roth's
statement seems to be an exception.   He says : " For
one family or individual to obtain, without permission,
vegetable, fowl or meat upon the land belonging to
another family " constitutes a trespass; but then he
adds that owing to their great hospitality each family
readily invites its neighbours and friends to partake of
the products of its land.   Roth's statement, although an
exception, deserves to be noted, owing to its explicitness
and to the reliability of the author.   It is only regret-
table he does not inform us concerning one point
more, whether these families or individuals respectively
resided usually on their territories and used them exclusively, or whether they usually aggregated and lived
on each other's domains, every one being only the host
on his own territory.   It is only in the first case that
individual proprietorship would have an actual importance; accepting the second hypothesis, we revert to the
case where the local group (a number of aggregated
families) possesses the actual right of use of the land, the
individuals being only formal landlords of their parcels.
If we accept, on the other hand, the view that single
families were in a purely economic and legal sense owner
of their own tract of land, *i. e.* that they enjoyed the *usum*

---

certain extent inspired by a humanitarian tendency, namely to
show that the Australian aborigines were not quite without ideas
of property in land, and that they were wronged by the white
settlers, and thus deserved compensation for the loss of their
hunting-grounds.   The letter mentioned was written to some
humanitarian society.   We may, therefore, still more distrust
these statements.   We have seen that the idea of possession of
land, of an exclusive right to use a certain tract of country, was
well known to our aborigines, but that they conceived of it as
vested in a group, not in individuals.

fructum of the latter for themselves, and that exclusively,[1] then we must also believe that the families lived scattered, and assembled only in exceptional cases. This consequence is important. But we see easily that although it is inevitable, supposing actual land ownership in single families, still the latter state of thing is not a necessary condition of it. Even when land is invested in the group, single families may live scattered (compare below). Claims to land by individuals and families in the North-Western Central Queensland tribes were also based on ideas of a magico-religious character, being probably a mere magical connection of an individual or family with a portion of the country. (Compare the statement from *North Queensland Ethnography*.)

Summing up, there are three different kinds of " proprietorship " in the aboriginal society; or more correctly three kinds of claims to, and connections with, a certain territory. First, actual rights of roaming, hunting, fishing and digging; these rights belong usually to the local group (exceptionally, perhaps, to single families or individuals). Secondly, the customary right of local groups forming a tribe, mutually to use their hunting-ground; these forms of proprietorship have been designated " tribal over-right." [2] Third, the immaterial claim of individuals or families to a portion of the local district; this special right seems to be rather exceptional, and it appears problematic whether it has any economic character. In the light of this distinction it can easily be understood how the actual right of the local group was modified in two directions. The tribesman was tolerated on or invited to the ground, whereas the non-tribesman

[1] It is well to remember that there cannot be drawn a sharp line of distinction between a " family " and a " local group "; moreover, in the use of these terms our authorities are mostly careless and indiscriminate. As to the individual possession of land, it has been pointed out in connection with Howitt's statement on the Wurunjerri, that the individual rights of some influential man (headman) might be the expression of the rights of his local group.

[2] In agreement with Mr. Wheeler.

was killed. On the other hand, individuals or single families had possibly some claims of an unimportant character to particular spots. In general, we find it expressed in nearly all the statements more or less explicitly that the natives had a very clear idea of the rights of the local group to its territory, and that the boundaries of it were respected without exception.[1]

We pointed out that the rights of individuals to a certain tract of country had in general some vague magical character, and that they were probably always derived from some mystical relation of the individual to his birthplace or to another special spot. Now it may be added that there are hints pointing to the fact that possession of land in its real form, *i. e.* as invested in the local group, was probably based to a considerable degree on ideas of religious or magical kind. The information is unambiguous and detailed on this point as regards the Central and North-Central tribes. We know of a whole series of ideas of totemic character that bind a group of men to a given locality. How far this was valid in the other parts of the continent it is difficult to decide on the basis of the information available. But putting side by side the facts we know about the extremely large area investigated by Spencer and Gillen, with what we know of mystic individual rights in other tribes, we are justified in supposing that everywhere the rights of the local group (the only ones that present a real economic character) were the sum or resultant of such individual rights of magical or religious character, or that the group as a whole was attached by such ties to its area.[2]

[1] Compare nearly all of our statements, especially those of Spencer and Gillen, Howitt, Curr. Mr. Wheeler writes in his conclusions (*loc. cit.*, p. 161). " Territorial conquest is never sought, for the absolute right of the local group to its district is fully recognized." The respect for boundaries is also stated : in *Science of Man*, xi. (1910), p. 197 (" tribal " area sharply marked; death is the punishment for trespass). *Ibid.* (1900), p. 85. *Ibid.* (1901), p. 9.

[2] It is impossible to enlarge here upon this interesting subject, which would require a separate study to itself. The two volumes of Messrs. Spencer and Gillen especially are full of facts, showing

Now to pass on to the main problem : to the mode of living. From the previous discussion we may infer that when the local groups are very small in themselves, then *ipso facto* the natives live scattered in very small groups (Kurnai, probably Murring, Dieri, New South Wales tribes according to Rob. Dawson, and tribes described by Salvado).

The same applies to the cases where we are told that the families own exclusively a certain area (Roth, G. S. Lang, Grey). But these cases were found to be not quite beyond question. In some instances when the local group is a larger unit, and there is no subdivision of land amongst families, several statements mention that the natives lived scattered in small groups, varying from two to four families perhaps. (Murray tribes according to Eyre ; the Central and North-Central tribes according to Spencer and Gillen ; the Moreton Bay tribes according to J. D. Lang ; New South Wales tribes according to McDougall, Henderson and Hodgkinson ; the Kabi and Wakka, West Australians according to Withnell, Browne, Scott-Nind.)

In some cases there are reasons for supposing that the local group was larger (Bangerang, Western Victoria, at Encounter Bay, on the lakes ; perhaps on the sea-shores in West Australia according to Grey). The remainder of our information (fifteen statements) does not give any clear answer to this question. From these approximately exact data we come to the conclusion that the majority of tribes lived in small groups of two or three families

---

that the tribal traditions, the totemic cult, the initiation ceremonies, and all other magical (or religious) functions were intimately bound up with the locality in which a local group lived.
The local group itself was, so to say, an offshoot of the local
totem centre, the *Oknanikilla*; the " spiritual parts " of its
member, closely associated each with its *Churinga*, are enshrined
in the *Ertnatulunga*. That the local group is intimately connected with its territory is no wonder. Such a form of possession,
although it involves an extremely strong bond of union between man and land, is evidently something quite different
from more developed forms of proprietorship.

of six to nine individuals each, and only in a few tribes were there larger bodies living in actual daily contact.

To get a more reliable answer on this point it is better to drop the less clear evidence and to take into consideration only such as is better and more reliable. If only the fully reliable and unambiguous statements be used, there are twelve affirming that aborigines live in small parties, which in some cases shrink to one family only (Howitt on the Kurnai; Eyre; R. Dawson; G. S. Lang; McDougall; Spencer and Gillen in the Central and North-Central tribes; Henderson; Hodgkinson; Rev. Matthew on the Kabi and Wakka; Withnell; Salvado). It should be noted that (1) some of these authorities are our best informants (Howitt Spencer and Gillen, Salvado); (2) that the area covered by these peoples is very extensive, and that the tribes in question are scattered over the whole continent. The statements which assert the mode of living in larger bodies are much less reliable. But it appears undoubted that the statements of Curr and Dawson, perhaps also those of Meyer, Schurman and Taplin (confirmed by Angas), are of quite unquestionable reliability. It is therefore clear that there were local differences in that respect. And such a geographical difference in the mode of living appears quite plausible, from general considerations. The reasons which must have determined the degree of aggregation in the Australian tribes were peculiarly economic ones : the scarcity of food supply was conditioned partly by the aridity of the soil, partly by the primitiveness of the means of procuring subsistence. Where the means of subsistence were plentiful and not easily exhausted, there larger groups could permanently aggregate. This was, in the first place, the case where fishing was at all possible. The Bangerang tribe resided in two large bodies at the junction of the Glenelg and Murray rivers; the large group of the Narrinyeri on Lake Alexandrina; probably the coastal tribes in general were larger and more sedentary. This seems corroborated by the fact that they had usually larger and better-built huts (see below). The same factors would also tend to produce a more sedentary mode of living (the Bangerang, the Kurnai (partly at least), and possibly other coastal tribes). The view that density of population was directly dependent upon the nature of soil is strengthened by the direct statements of Wilhelmi, Turnbull, Moorhouse and Angas.[1]

It may be mentioned that in places where, and times when, plenty of food was available, large numbers of natives gathered, but only temporarily, *e. g.* when a whale was stranded, or the Bunya-Bunya nuts were ripe, etc.[2] But as the major part of the continent is arid, we must suppose that the usual mode of living was in very small groups of one to three families; these groups being in exceptional cases regular local groups, in the majority of cases merely portions of them.

Let us briefly examine whether this general assumption contradicts any other features of Australian tribal

[1] The difference in physical geography between the coastal regions and the Central parts, the greater variety in the South-East region in general, and the relations of these physiographical features to the social features of the Australian aboriginal society, are well brought out by Prof. Frazer in his beautifully written chapter on Physical Geography (*Tot. and Exeg.*, chap. v. § 1, pp. 314–339). Prof. Frazer's conclusion that the coastal and South-Eastern tribes are more advanced involves the assertion set forth here that coastal tribes,' and in general tribes living in more fertile regions, live in more numerous, stable and permanent aggregations. Many of the instances and quotations of Prof. Frazer's chapter directly confirm our results, and the reader is referred to this chapter, which reviews nearly all the geographical differences that can be traced in Australia. That I do not agree with Prof. Frazer's views as to group marriage, etc., and with all his conclusions referring to prehistoric times, hardly needs to be pointed out, and does not affect the importance for my argument of his splendid collection and exposition of facts. Especially the two passages from Grey, quoted by Prof. Frazer *in extenso*, which had escaped my attention, are very valuable. They show that on the coast, where the soil is more fertile, the natives lived in larger bodies.

[2] Tom Petrie, *Reminiscences*, chap. i. Besides, compare gatherings at initiation. R. H. Mathews, *Proc. R.S.N.S.W.*, 1904, pp. 114–123. *Science of Man*, xi., 1910, p. 192. Bunya-Bunya gatherings.

life. If we consider their modes of procuring food,
we find that the women had to go in search of roots,
grubs, etc., in short do purely collecting work. It is
obvious that this kind of work is never done well in big
bands. On the other hand it is probable that one
woman alone would be afraid to go on remote wanderings.
The most favourable unit would be a group of two to
three women with their children. The men hunted their
game also in rather small groups. There do not seem to
be any collective methods of hunting. The kangaroo was
perhaps tired out by the common effort of several men.
For the hunting of the smaller game, which was practically
also a kind of searching, it would be rather unfavourable
to go out in big parties. Considerations of an economic order, therefore, give no reason for discarding our
assumption; on the contrary it is corroborated by them.
To the question whether for security's sake the aborigines
would not be compelled to aggregate, we must also return
a negative answer. War was not the normal condition of
the Australian blacks.[1] And I have not been able to
find any statement of collective methods of organized
defence.

To sum up our results in a few words : the territorial
division points only exceptionally and problematically,
even in these exceptional cases, to possession of land by
single families. The territorial unit, called by us Local
Group, although varying in its extent according to the
locality, appears to consist usually of several families.
But these families in their turn live usually either in
one smaller group, numbering two or three families or,
exceptionally, one only. In more fertile tracts, near
big rivers and fertile coastal districts, the number of
families living in permanent contact appears to be
greater; in the extensive arid areas the number of
families grouped together seems to be rather small.

[1] Compare G. C. Wheeler, *loc. cit.*, p. 161, and chap. ix. on
War, pp. 148 *sqq.*

II

The second part of our problem must now be faced :
whenever there is a certain number of families aggregated
(permanently or temporarily), what are the features
of their social contact in daily life ? What are their
dwellings ? Do they belong to several families or only
to one ? Are there any rules of camping, or do they camp
quite promiscuously ? And if there are any customary
rules, of what status are they the expression ? Besides
the answers to these questions, we shall find also that
there are rules for occupying the huts, for eating, etc.
In general, all our questions will tend to elucidate
whether there is a quite unlimited, promiscuous social
contact among the members of an aggregate, or whether
there are facts pointing to the isolation and separation of
the individual families. Undoubtedly there is a difference
between aggregation which is merely temporary and that
which is permanent ; we shall try to find traces of this
difference indicated in the statements. These latter are
not very rich in information. The facts themselves
seemed perhaps to the majority of our informants much
too commonplace and unimportant. But we owe to some
of the deeper and more conscientious observers highly
interesting details in this connection. More especially this
remark applies to Howitt and some of his correspondents.
We begin with these statements.

Statements.—We have a clear and detailed description of the
mode in which a camp was disposed amongst the Kurnai as well
as of the mode in which a hut was inhabited in this tribe.[1]
As a rule each hut was inhabited by a man and his
wife. Even if some families [2] were closely related,[3] a certain distance was kept between their camps, which in-

---

[1] Howitt, *Kam. and Kurn.*, pp. 208–210, and *Nat. Tr.*, pp.
773–776.
[2] I use the word family only in the sense of a man, his wife or
wives, and their offspring before reaching puberty.
[3] As in the example, *Kam. and Kurn.*, p. 209.

creased as the consanguinity diminished.[1] A man's parents
could occasionally sleep with him and his wife in the same
hut.   But his sister-in-law or his brother would not sleep in
the same hut.[2]   We see, therefore, that each married couple
occupied a separate hut, and that even near relatives would
not be admitted, especially if sexual jealousy were possible.
In the hut " custom regulates the position of the individual.
The husband and wife would sleep on the left-hand side of the
fire, the latter behind it, and close behind her the children;
nearest to them the little boy, if any, next to him the little
girl ";[3] bigger children camped separately.   We shall find
this statement confirmed by another set of facts.   Similar
rules and customs applied as well to the Maneroo aborigines
of New South Wales (Murring)[4] as to the Wurunjerri[5] of East
Victoria.

Amongst the Gournditsh-Mara Tribe (Lake Condah, West
Victoria) " each family camped by itself."   During the meals
" each wife was . . . obliged to sit beside her own husband,"
and not " near any other man unless her husband sat between
them."[6]   It is a statement pointing to isolation of females
from sex jealousy.   We shall meet in the future with a few
statements referring to the way in which meals are taken.

Customs pointing to the isolation of families, on the ground of
sex jealousy are referred to by Curr.[7]   " A woman never sat in
a mia-mia (hut) in which there was a man, save her husband;
she never conversed nor exchanged words with any man
except in the absence of her husband and in reply to some
necessary question," and only from a distance.   Women had
" no communication with persons of the opposite sex except
little boys."   From the paternal hut, where they lived, " their
brothers of eight or ten years of age were excluded at night."
And again, " among the Bangerang and other tribes I have
known, each married couple had their own mia-mia, or hut."[8]
These statements are quite clear.   They coincide with the
majority of our information.   What is important and will interest us further in detail is the fact that boys at the age of
about ten were excluded from the paternal hut.   Females
were given away about the same age, so that we may say that

---

[1] See this example and diagram in *Nat. Tr.*, p. 774.
[2] *Kam. and Kurn.*, pp. 209, 210, and *Nat. Tr.*, p. 774.
[3] *Idem, Nat. Tr.*, pp. 774, 775. Compare *Kam. and Kurn.*,
p. 209.
[4] *Kam. and Kurn.*, p. 210.   [5] *Nat. Tr.*, p. 775.
[6] Rev. Stähle in *Kam. and Kurn.*, pp. 277, 278.
[7] *Recollections*, p. 250, refers to the Bangerang tribe.   Compare
also *ibid.*, p. 256 and *A.R.*, i. pp. 65, 98, 100.
[8] *Recollections*, p. 259.

only small children remained with their parents. " The bachelors had one (hut) in common." [1]

Describing the laying of a camp Curr says—

" As they arrived they formed their camps, each family having a fire of its own some half-dozen yards from its neighbour's." [2]

From Dawson's description of the aboriginal habitations,[3] we get a good glimpse into their mode of dwelling. Dawson says they have either a permanent or temporary habitation, and describes both. The former *wuurn* is bigger, and may accommodate about a dozen persons. But it serves only for the use of one family. " When several families live together each builds its *wuurn*, facing one central fire." But even the family, if the children are grown up, does not live in one party; " the *wuurn* is partitioned off into compartments. One of these is appropriated to the parents and children, one to the young unmarried women and widows, and one to the bachelors and widowers." Here we see that husband and wife sleep also quite apart, with their small children. Grown-up but unmarried male or female children have compartments of their own. And if they were married they must have had their own separate camp. The isolation seems to have been amongst these tribes much less accentuated than amongst the East Victorians, for instance. Although separated, grown-up children lived in the same habitation, and even the *wuurns* of separate families were situated round a common fire, so that it " appears to be one dwelling." In their temporary huts the isolation is more pronounced. " While travelling or occupying temporary habitations each of these parties (parent, male and female children) must erect separate *wuurns*." Moreover each family must camp separately. A certain communism of living is expressed also by the common cooking,[4] although each family has its basket in which it cooks food.[5]

Eyre's information about the Lower Murray River blacks agrees to a certain degree with Dawson's statements. " Sometimes each married man will have a hut for himself, his wives and family, including, perhaps, occasionally his mother or some other near relative. At other times, large long huts are constructed, in which from five to ten families reside, each having their own separate fire." [6] Of course, here the communism is much greater, although the separation of the fire circles is still kept. These natives, as well as the tribes

---

[1] Compare *A.R.*, i. pp. 109, 110. [2] *Recollections*, p. 133.
[3] *Loc. cit.*, pp. 10, 11. [4] *Loc. cit.*, pp. 17, 20.
[5] *Ibid.* [6] Eyre, ii. p. 302.

described by Dawson, were in better economic conditions, and therefore able to adopt sedentary life; they were also more skilful in the building of huts. The general type of a hut was a rude shelter of boughs only affording protection against rain.[1]

Brough Smyth affirms also perfect order and method in the arrangement of a camp. " The aborigines do not herd together promiscuously." If the whole tribe is present the natives are divided into groups each composed of about six dwellings. "Each mia-mia (hut) is five or six yards distant from its neighbours." If there are several "tribes" (groups), each camps in a separate place, in a position marking whence it came. Each hut has its separate fire (in opposition to Dawson's statement).[2]

Complete isolation and strict camp rules are stated by J. Moore-Davis. " Married men each with his family occupying the centre " of the camp.[3]

A statement quite contrary to nearly all others is given by Beveridge. He speaks of " the promiscuous manner they have of huddling together in their loondthals." [4] We need not, however, take this statement very seriously, as it is given in immediate connection with another doubtful one, viz. of absolute, even incestuous, sexual promiscuity.[5] Perhaps the observations were made on natives who were quite corrupted by contact with white men. At any rate this statement is directly opposed to all we know about these two features of Australian aborigines in their natural state of life. We may therefore discard them as unreliable.[6]

Collins writes : " In their huts and in their caves they lie down indiscriminately mixed, men, women and children together." [7] This statement is not quite clear, as we do not know whether these " men, women and children " form one family, or are related, or whether there is a great number of them, etc. It is also opposed to what we learnt from Howitt and many others of the customary order observed in occupying a hut. Besides, Collins had under his immediate observation blacks hanging round the town of Port Phillip, demoralized

---

[1] Compare Curr, *A.R.*, i. p. 97, and Prof. Frazer, *Tot. and Exog.*, i. pp. 321, 322.

[2] *Loc. cit.*, p. 124.

[3] Br. Smyth, ii. 318, refers to New South Wales.

[4] *Loc. cit.*, p. 24.   [5] *Loc. cit.*, p. 23.

[6] Beveridge seems to have been in long contact with the aborigines, but he never says in what state of social decomposition they were. In all he writes, although there is some interesting information, there may be seen a lack of accuracy of observation and expression.

[7] *Loc. cit.*, i. p. 555.

and degenerate; their females seem to have been already addicted to prostitution.[1] They were no longer in their primitive state; and all observations, especially relating to their mode of living, which changes immediately with the conditions of life, must be accepted with caution. I do not consider this statement any more reliable than that of Beveridge which I discarded. From other passages where he speaks of the small inland huts " affording shelter to only one miserable tenant," [2] and the larger huts on the sea-coast, " large enough to hold six or eight persons," we might infer that there was room only for one family in each hut. Here also we read that the coastal tribes, which probably had a better food supply and led a more sedentary life, had larger and better-built huts.

We read concerning the Turra tribe of South Australia [3] : " In camping, the place of the parents is to the right-hand side of their son's camp; the brother to the left side; sister-in-law to the right side or near his father's. In the camp the husband sleeps at the right hand of the fire, his wife behind him, and her young children behind her." This, less detailed than Howitt's statement, corroborates it to the full. We see that each camp is occupied exclusively by a married couple and their small children; and that inside the hut as well as in the configuration of the camp there is a strict customary order. It is important to notice that these statements, reporting strict camp rules and referring to tribes scattered over a great area (Victoria, New South Wales and South Australia) are given by very reliable authorities, and that Howitt at least gathered them by collecting information about the ancient customs of the Kurnai and Murring from old natives; using, therefore, the only correct method. They refer, therefore, to old customs, which probably were no longer observed in the tribes spoilt and demoralized by contact with settlers. Much weight is to be ascribed, therefore, in this matter to the information of Howitt and his correspondents.

Schürmann states shortly : " Each family occupies a separate hut; and, if there be any unmarried men, they sleep apart in a hut of their own." [4]

Henderson says about the New South Wales natives, " Each family has its own gunya and fire." [5]

George Barrington observes that among the Port Jackson natives each hut was occupied by one family. [6]

---

[1] *Loc. cit.*, i. p. 560 and *passim*.   [2] *Loc. cit.*, p. 555.
[3] Rev. W. J. Kühn in *Kam. and Kurn.*, p. 287.
[4] Woods, p. 222.   [5] *Loc. cit.*, p. 109.
[6] *Loc. cit.*, p. 82.

When the families who formed a " tribe"(=local group?) meet
" each family has its own fire and provides its own substance." [1]
In the description of his travels Dawson tells us that when
the native party was joined by a stranger with his wife
the latter did not approach the other men, but slept alone
by herself at a small fire.[2] This points to the fact that a
married woman normally never slept in the immediate neighbourhood of any other man but her own husband.

Spencer and Gillen affirm, again, the complete isolation of
families who, according to them,[3] normally roam scattered
on the territory of the local group. " Each family, consisting of a man and one or more wives and children, occupies
always a mia-mia, which is merely a lean-to of shrubs,
so placed as to shield the occupants from the prevailing
wind." This statement is perfectly clear, and we may fit
it into the general picture we drew from all the other
evidence.

Among the natives of Central Australia (probably of the
Arunta nation) a married woman " may speak to any but the
young men." [4] Thus she is practically excluded from any
intercourse with them.

Among the natives of Moreton Bay the conjugal relation
is maintained by them "with great decency and propriety,
every family having its separate hut and fire." [5]

A very clear and concise statement is given on this point
by the Rev. J. Mathew, referring to the Kabi and Wakka
tribes. " The family, consisting of husband and wife, or wives,
with their children, constituted a distinct social unit. They
occupied the same gunya (dwelling), they ate together,
they travelled together." [6] After having described the construction of the hut he adds: " This sufficed for a family.
The dwellings were placed a little distance apart, facing
in the same direction, and each had its own small fire in
front." [7]

Roth says about the tribes of North-West Central Queensland : " The husband sleeps in the same gundi as his wives." [8]
The way of taking meals is not quite uniform among all tribes
observed by this writer. At Cape Bedford " members of one
family take their meals together, except the single young men
(above puberty), who dine apart." In another tribe (Tully

---

[1] R. Dawson, p. 327.   Port Stephens Blacks.
[2] *Loc. cit.*, p. 249.   [3] *Nat. Tr.*, p. 18.
[4] *J.A.I.*, xxiv. p. 183 (W. H. Willshire in Prof. Frazer's
Questions).
[5] J. D. Lang, *loc. cit.*, p. 337
[6] *Loc. cit.*, p. 153.   [7] *Loc. cit.*, p. 84.
[8] *Eth. Stud.*, p. 182, § 327.

River) "each family dines by itself." On the contrary, "on the Bloomfield River men, boys and girls (up to four or five years of age) dine together; all the other females . . . mess apart."[1] Among the natives of Koombana Bay, "in the family, the man, women and children dined together."[2] There are three kinds of huts among the North Queensland tribes: the simple shelter of boughs; a hut built somewhat more carefully against rain; and a hut built for protection against cold, this hut, being of course, the most elaborate.[3] From the description of these huts we may infer that they were occupied each by one family only.

The isolation of families caused by the jealousy of the husband is plainly stated by Grey: "He cannot, from the roving nature of their mode of life, surround his wives with the walls of a seraglio, but custom and etiquette have drawn about them barriers nearly as impassable. When a certain number of families are collected together, they encamp at a common spot, and each family has a separate hut or perhaps two. At these huts sleep the father of the family, his wives, the female children who have not yet joined their husbands, very young boys[4] and occasionally female relatives; but no males over ten years of age may sleep in family huts. They have got their own separate encampment."[5] If any strangers are present with their wives, they sleep in their own huts, placed amongst the married people. If they are unmarried or without wives "they sleep at the fire of the young men."[6] "Under no circumstances is a strange native allowed to approach the fire of a married man."[7] Their huts being so scattered over a rather large area, their conversation is held by means of a loud chant.[8] It must be remembered that Grey asserts in several places the great and vigilant jealousy of the natives.[9]

Bishop Salvado, who speaks also of the great jealousy of the males and the fidelity exacted from the females,[10] gives us the following account of their mode of camping: "Lorsqu' une famille se dispose à dormir, les garçons qui ont passé l'âge de sept ans dorment seuls, autour du feu commun, les plus petits avec le père, et les enfants à la mamelle, aussi bien que les filles, quel que soit leur âge, avec la mère. Les femmes jouissent du droit d'ancienneté, la première dort plus près du mari, ainsi de suite."[11] Another passage[12] testifies also

---

[1] Bull. iii. p. 7. [2] Proc. R.S.Q., p. 48.
[3] Eth. Stud., §§ 159, 160, 161, pp. 105–107.
[4] Loc. cit., ii. p. 252. [5] Ibid. [6] Ibid.
[7] Loc. cit., pp. 252, 253. [8] Loc. cit., p. 253.
[9] Loc. cit., pp. 242, 253, 255. [10] Loc. cit., p. 279.
[11] Loc. cit., p. 280. [12] Salvado, loc. cit., p. 317.

that they roam in single families; the reason alleged is easier food supply.

We read in Browne that one hut holds only two or three persons.[1]

The general inference to be drawn from these twenty-four statements is, roughly speaking, that the general features of native camp arrangements were orderliness, fixed rules, isolation of families, settled and restricted social contact, and by no means social communism and unregulated social promiscuity.

Five instances give strict rules which obtain in arranging camps. These were probably much more widespread than might be supposed from these few instances. But, as mentioned above, these camp rules would probably fall into abeyance at once when the natives came in contact with civilization. It was only by attentive inquiries that Howitt extracted them from the natives. Besides these we read in fifteen statements that each family camped separately. So that twenty of twenty-four statements assert that there was in this respect complete isolation of the families. Sexual motives played undoubtedly an important part·in this isolation. We are told so expressly in several places (Curr, Grey, Salvado, J. D. Lang). In the case of even friendly strangers a certain amount of mistrust—of evil magic as well as of actual bad intentions—may have operated. There are indications of it in statements of Br. Smyth and Grey. But in the detailed examples given by Howitt, where all the camping families are closely related and usually consist of more than one generation (father and sons, etc.), we can hardly conceive that either of the above-mentioned motives would come into play. At any rate this regulated camp order shows how important this question was in the native social life and how strong the idea must have been that each family had its own place apart from the others, and the more remotely related people were, the less intimate contact would be.

---

[1] *Loc. cit.*, p. 448.

The aborigines possess different kinds of huts. Of interest for us is the fact that the majority of them are made to hold only one family. Fourteen statements assert it explicitly or implicitly. In three instances we are told of the existence of larger huts (Eyre, Dawson, Collins). In two of them the separation of families is maintained in spite of the larger dwellings. Only Collins' information is doubtful in this respect.

Within these huts the family camped according to fixed rules. We have five instances given by Howitt and his correspondents, and Bishop Salvado. These rules show clearly that each hut, each fire-place, was reserved for one family, and that this *status* had its customary form and sanction. There were three instances of separation during meals (Gournditsh-Mara, some of the North-West Central Queensland tribes, and the Kabi and Wakka). In three statements we are told that both sexes separated during meals (Curr, Angas, Roth). What Curr tells us of the marked social separation of families is remarkable; especially in respect to the isolation of the women.[1]

Two statements were rather in contradiction with our general results: Beveridge's statement of promiscuous huddling and Collins' vague information. We stated our reasons for not giving them much weight, and they cannot outweigh the sum-total of reliable information which is fairly unanimous on this point. It is also in general agreement with the information we gathered on sexual matters as well as with our conclusion as to territorial distribution, and it corroborates our results on both these points. For on the one hand it was found that in normal life there exists individuality of sexual relations; on the other hand the usual scattered mode of living would

[1] It is well to notice here that the isolation of families was closely connected with the isolation of both sexes. The men were in contact only with their wives and perhaps with their near female relatives. That this isolation cannot be due to motives of sexual jealousy is certain; it is in great part due to the dread of evil magic. But to work out this question would lead us too far. Compare Howitt, *Nat. Tr.*, pp. 776, 777.

correspond to a fairly complete isolation in cases of tribal assembly.

Our last considerations have clearly demonstrated how the individuality of the family unit shows itself in the aboriginal mode of living. A single family is normally in contact with a few other families only; sometimes it roams alone over its own area. But even when there are several families living together, the camp rules keep them apart from each other in nearly every function of daily life. The children, who live in intimate contact with their parents in the same hut, must necessarily set them apart from all their (the children's) other relatives. We must assume, therefore, that the individuality of the relation of each child to its actual parents is deeply impressed by all the circumstances of daily life on the child's mind. This assumption is in accord with the information we can gather on this point. But before we begin to look it through, let us discuss the theoretical side of the kinship (or relationship) problem.

CHAPTER VI

I

THEORETICAL ANALYSIS OF THIS CONCEPT

IT is undoubtedly one of the most valuable discoveries arrived at by modern sociological science that each institution varies in accordance with the social environment in which it is found. A given institution or social form (like the family, the state, the nation, the church) appears under various forms in different societies, and among peoples with a very low culture only rudiments thereof may be expected. This point of view, applied to marriage and the family, has led some writers to the assumption of forms as much opposed to those usual in our societies, as promiscuity and group marriage is opposed to individual marriage and the family. Nevertheless, although the variability and multiplicity of forms of marriage and family were acknowledged, the concepts applied to them were still the old ones, directly borrowed from our own society and formed upon the facts found amongst ourselves. In particular the sociologically untrained ethnographers comprehended the phenomena of kinship only under our own social concepts, judged them according to our own moral standard, and described them with words the meaning of which ought to have been defined when applied to a new case; nevertheless these terms have been nearly always used by ethnographers in the same sense in which we use them amongst ourselves, *i. e.* as expressing ideas of community of blood through

168

procreation.[1] That this is quite erroneous will be shown below. How far the idea of kinship changes from society to society, what are its essential invariable features, and what are the variable elements—these are the problems that must be set forth.

The inadequacy of our ideas of kinship as applied to lower societies has been often felt by those ethnographers who wished to enter deeper into the problems of kinship among a given people. They have found the greatest difficulty in conveying to a European reader the meaning of different terms of relationship. While warning the reader to put aside our (the modern European) ideas of kinship, they have hardly succeeded in giving any definite and clear concept instead. The reasons for this failure are simple : our ideas of kinship are defined by certain facts which are not to be found in the given primitive society. In order to define kinship so as to fit the latter, the author ought to bring forward a series of facts, playing a part analogous in the given society to that played by the essential defining elements amongst us. But it is by no means easy to know among which facts to look for such analogous, defining elements. And here again arises the necessity of a general definition of kinship, one which would afford indications in what direction to search for social facts giving a right idea of kinship in any given society. Such a general definition would be like an algebraic formula, having its constant and its variable terms; if for the latter special data be inserted (in this instance the special conditions proper to the given society), the special value for any given case is obtained (namely the special concept of kinship proper to the given society). And it should also be indicated within what range the variables should be taken; in other words, in what facts the elements which specifically determine kinship in the

[1] Compare, for instance, Morgan, *Systems*, pp. 108 *sqq*. For other examples see below, pp. 199 *sqq*. Sir Laurence Gomme writes : "One of our greatest difficulties, indeed, is the indiscriminate use of kinship terms by our descriptive authorities." —*Loc. cit.*, p. 235.

given society must be looked for. The practical value of such a general definition of kinship is obvious. On the one hand it indicates the constant elements in kinship common to all societies; on the other hand it indicates the general character of the variable elements, and the way in which they must be looked for and worked into the general formula.

By the word kinship, roughly speaking, is denoted a series of family relationships (those of parents to children, brothers to sisters, etc.), all of which consist of a set of extremely complex phenomena. They are made up of the most heterogeneous elements : physiological (birth, procreation, suckling, etc.), social (community of living, of interests, social norms, etc.), and psychological (different ways in which these relations are conceived, different moral ideas, and different types of feelings). Special care must be taken to select in all these elements the essential ones, as an omission would be just as fatal for the investigations as an overburdening with secondary elements. Moreover, it would be specially valuable to look at all these heterogeneous determining elements from the same point of view, and view them all under one and the same aspect. Leaving on one side the purely physiological problem of kinship,[1] it appears necessary to give a sociological view of kinship, *i. e.* to show the social bearing of physiological facts as well as of psychological elements. But it appears also necessary to view the whole of the phenomena of kinship from the psychological point of view; that is, to show how the sociological and physiological facts of kinship are reflected in the " collective mind " of the given society.

Besides for other reasons (adduced below) this appears

---

[1] This would be the place to point out the biological meaning of the social aspects of kinship and family; whether, *e. g.* the different social regulations of sexual intercourse, which in higher societies afford the basis to kinship, the different forms of family and kinship are the expression of biological laws. How far such would be possible could only be decided on the basis of a biological knowledge which the present writer does not possess.

necessary, because one of the most important scientific uses that has been made of the different human systems of kinship is one that presupposes a certain definite meaning, as given to the terms of kinship in very low societies. In Morgan's deductions a very important part is played by the assumption that kinship is always understood in terms of consanguinity; in particular that it was understood thus by primitive man; that in all (even the lowest) societies all ideas of kinship were essentially based upon the community of blood, established in the case of the mother by her share in bearing, in that of the father by his part in procreation. Only by assuming that these facts were known to the lowest, prehistoric savages, could Morgan draw inferences from systems of kinship terms about the forms of sexual intercourse. If, on the other hand, the relation between sexual intercourse and birth escaped the knowledge of primitive men, they could not have based their idea of kinship upon community of blood between father and offspring; hence there could be no connection between forms of sexual intercourse and forms of kinship as conceived by primitive man. Whether there could be connection between marriage, defined sociologically, and kinship is another and more complicated problem. In any case Morgan uses throughout his book the word consanguinity, and he defines it as the tie of common blood arising from the sexual act. In other words he sets forth the problem in a simplified and incorrect form. The question how kinship may be conceived in a given society, especially in a low one, naturally presents itself as a very important point of investigation.

As in the following pages there will be question more or less exclusively of the individual relation between parents and children, the present discussion may be fittingly restricted to the individual parental kinship in Australia. In the second part of this chapter facts giving some insight into the aboriginal collective ideas of kinship are set forth; and in the following chapter other different facts will be brought forward in order to complete the definition of *individual parental kinship*. But in accordance with what has been just said, it is needful to have some guiding principle in collecting this material, and this will now be looked for. This discussion, being only concerned with the Australian facts, does not pretend to be complete, but perhaps if the results are worked out so as to suit our modern European concept of kinship as well as the Australian one, it might, should it be correct, be applicable also to other societies.[1] Let us now proceed to give the general definition of kinship and in the first place to indicate which are its constant, uniform factors found in all societies.

Amongst the heterogeneous factors which together make up parental kinship, the physiological facts appear to be the most constant, for the natural process of procreation is in all human societies the same. But the social consequences of this process vary very widely according to other variable elements, as will appear clearly below in our discussion of consanguinity. Part of them only, together with some social elements, may be taken as the uniform, constant basis of kinship, such as must serve for the first point of departure in an attempt to discuss more in detail the kinship in any society. It appears probable that this basis is given by the existence of a group formed by a woman, her husband, and the children whom she has borne, suckled and reared. The existence of such a group will be considered as the necessary and sufficient condition for *individual parental kinship*. Where such a group exists we are justified in affirming that individual parental kinship exists, although it is not yet completely defined thereby; further facts must be adduced in order to complete the definition. Those further facts are precisely the variable terms in the general formula of kinship; it remains still to indicate their general character. But a few words must be first said about the constant factors of kinship just mentioned.

[1] Of course by result is meant a general formula for kinship.

They consist in the existence of the individual family group as determined by individual marriage and by individual motherhood. Individual motherhood means that the same woman who gave birth to a child stands to it in a special close relation in its later life also : she suckles it and rears it, and she is bound to him or her by the manifold ties resulting from the community of life and community of interests. This woman is bound on the other hand to a man by individual marriage ; and thereby her children are bound to him also ; and the mother, her husband, and her children form the social unit called the individual family. The existence of such a unit is to be established by showing its different social functions, and the different ways in which its solidarity and individuality are marked in a given society. It is clear that the position of the father is in this way first established socially only, as the husband of the children's mother. Nevertheless it must be borne in mind that thus his relation to the children is clearly marked ; and that this is only a preliminary, so to say formal, determination of fatherhood, which in all societies appears to be much more materially defined by other factors, discussed hereafter.

The existence of the individual family as a social unit, based upon the physiological facts of maternity, the social factor of marriage and other social factors, are thus chosen as the basis upon which we may proceed to analyze more in detail the individual parental relation. Whether this basis exists in all human societies and forms what was called above the constant, invariable elements of parental kinship, may remain an open question. This could only be answered correctly *a posteriori*, on the basis of a series of special researches in many societies. The existence of individual motherhood, as this word is defined here, seems to obtain in the majority of human societies (or even in all of them). Nevertheless, as pointed out above,[1] even this point cannot be treated as self-evident. This applies in still higher degree to

[1] In reference to Dr. Rivers' article, compare pp. 6, 7.

individual marriage, which has often been denied as regards many societies.[1] In this place we have mainly to keep before our eyes the Australian society and our own society, the latter of which affords, so to say, the heuristic principle, the clue to the understanding of the former. As far as those two societies are concerned, our choice appears to be the right one, and the social-physiological basis mentioned above contains the essential common elements of kinship in both societies.

The existence of individual marriage and its legal, sexual and psychological aspects have been discussed and established in the preceding chapters, as far as Australia is concerned. A discussion on individual motherhood will be given below. The existence of the individual family group in Australia, based upon individual marriage and upon individual motherhood, is the subject of the remaining chapters of this study. So that the existence of this physiological and social basis of kinship may be taken as granted.

Bearing now in mind that what will be said hereafter applies in the first place to Australia, it may be said that in the physiological and social basis of kinship adopted above, the minimum of conditions necessary for the application of the idea of individual kinship was enumerated. But this minimum is not sufficient to determine this idea completely in any given society. By studying only the social facts which determine the individuality of family life within the society, we should not exhaust all the features and essential aspects of parental kinship in any society. The existence of the individual family merely indicates unambiguously that individual parental kinship exists in the

[1] In some cases, when the position of the father is very subordinate in the family and his relation to the mother and her children is a very loose one—it seems doubtful whether the existence of the individual family (in the sense here defined) can be accepted (compare, for examples of such peoples, Dr. Westermarck, *H.H.M.*, p. 109, and Sir Laurence Gomme, *loc. cit.*, pp. 231, 232). In these cases the necessary condition for individual *paternal* kinship according to our theory would be lacking.

given society.   For this social unit having a deep analogy
with our own individual family, the relation between the
members of both these social units must also have some
deep resemblance.   But to exaggerate this resemblance
would be as erroneous as to deny it.   Besides the features
common both to our parental kinship and to that of the
Australian, there are also those which differentiate these
two relationships.   They must be sought for in the differences in the *social conditions*, which may even modify
the physiological basis of kinship, as for instance when
physical fatherhood is in one society established beyond
doubt by exclusive sexual appropriation, while in the
other there can be no question of it, owing to sexual
communism.   The variations in the general social conditions obviously also affect the purely sociological side of
kinship.   To point this out clearly, it is enough to mention
that each relation is subject to the normative influences of
the society in the midst of which it exists, and these norms
and their sanction vary with the general social structure.

The variable elements in parental kinship must be also
looked for in the different elements of the *collective mind*,
connected with the parental relationship; in other words,
in the different *collective ideas* and *feelings* which have
parental kinship for their centre.   Moreover, as mentioned
above, there are reasons why the knowledge of the
collective idea of kinship is sociologically important.
It may be emphasized here that we should cripple and
curtail our knowledge if we arbitrarily abstained from
inquiring what influence the collective knowledge as to
procreation, consanguinity, affinity, etc., may have upon
the social aspect of the relation in question.

The same thing may be said of another domain of
collective mentality : that is, of the feelings involved in
parental kinship.   The type of feelings underlying this
relationship may vary with the society, in the same way
as these feelings vary with each individual case in any
given society.   And as these feelings essentially determine
the character of parental kinship in any given society, it

appears that the discussion of this point cannot be omitted. Thus into the general formula of kinship there must enter also the psychological elements : collective ideas, expressing in a given society what is kinship, what are its legal, moral and customary aspects; and the collective feelings prevailing in a given society. From the interaction of these psychological elements with different variable social elements arise the more special, peculiar factors which define kinship in any given society. In other words, the variable elements in the general formula of kinship are seen to arise chiefly from the collective psychological interpretation and valuation of some of the physiological and social facts underlying parental kinship.

To sum up, it may be said that parental kinship is the personal tie obtaining between members of the *parental group* or individual *family*, and like all other personalties it must be further determined in each society by the characteristic *collective feelings* and *collective ideas* which in the given society give it its specific meaning.[1] This is that general formula of kinship which will yield us what we have demanded of it—that is, an indication of the facts for which to look in any given society. As the facts referred to in the first part of the above definition (the establishment of the existence of the family unit) are dealt with in the remaining chapters, it is necessary to discuss only the second part of the definition.

The influence upon kinship of the beliefs and ideas as to procreation appears quite plainly upon an analysis of the concept of consanguinity, and to this we may devote a few words.

Parental kinship is in our society conceived invariably

---

[1] This definition may appear a commonplace and a truism, a mere formulation of what is obvious to every one at first sight. But it is liable to this objection only when taken formally, *i. e.* when only its *form* is considered, because it contains in the words *parental group* (individual family) the substance of all that has been said in the preceding pages about this social unit; and the other terms of the definition (*collective ideas* and *collective feelings*) will be determined more in detail in the following discussion.

and exclusively in terms of *consanguinity*,[1] or, speaking more explicitly, parental kinship is conceived as established by the tie of common blood, resulting from birth (maternal kinship) or procreation (paternal kinship). Of course the mere physiological fact does not establish kinship in its full extent, with all its personal, emotional, social and legal aspects. It is only when the physiological facts of procreation or birth are sanctioned by society, in other words when they are consummated in legal marriage, that the children are full kinsmen of both their parents. Society takes all facts which are of vital importance for itself under its own supervision; and consequently the important facts of propagation are subject to the control of society, which regulates them by a series of religious, legal, customary and conventional norms, all of which are also necessary conditions and essential features of full parental kinship. But this sanction once granted, the tie of common blood is conceived as the main source of all mutual duties and moral and legal obligations; and from this also outflow the feelings of love, attachment, reverence, and so forth, which are in our society the essential features of parental kinship. Once a man knows that a child, which he considered his own, is in reality not begotten by him, undoubtedly all his feelings for this child are affected, and, under certain conditions, its legal position may be modified. The two conditions for full parental kinship in our society are (1) that the child be the real physiological offspring of both presumed parents; (2) that it be legally begotten or its birth legalized.

In our society the line of distinction between physiological consanguinity and social consanguinity is quite clear; the one is a mere physiological fact,[2] the other the

---

[1] Legal adoption being set apart as a case which only partly establishes the kinship relations.

[2] It seems hardly necessary to emphasize that for physiological consanguinity *as such*, pure and simple, there is no room in sociological science.

social acknowledgment of this fact and all its consequences, subject to certain norms, laid down by society.

There are two separate sets of circumstances in which we may speak of consanguinity : (1) the existence of social institutions, which allow us to trace the physiological blood ties (*e. g.* monogamy or harem institutions), in which case we can speak of the existence of physiological consanguinity as obtaining between the members of the individual family. (2) The existence of a social acknowledgment of the facts of procreation as creating ties of individual personal kinship, in which case we may speak of social consanguinity. If neither of these conditions are fulfilled, then it would be quite meaningless to speak of consanguinity.[1]

Now let us see whether these conditions are to be found in all human societies. That both are found in the majority of the more highly developed societies appears beyond doubt. But this seems not to be the case in the lower societies. Even a superficial glance at them is sufficient to prove it. Whereas, in some of the lowest peoples known conjugal fidelity seems to be the rule,[2] and consequently the physiological tie of blood between

[1] Keeping to the definition of this word as given above. It is a question of mere convention whether we call the general relationship not necessarily based upon ideas of community of blood *kinship*, as is done here, or whether we call it *social* in opposition to *physical kinship*, as does M. A. van Gennep. What is essential is to point out that our peculiarly European idea of kinship, which necessarily involves consanguinity, cannot be applied to other societies without discussion, but that it is only a special case of a more general concept of kinship which may be made up of quite different elements. It would seem convenient to reserve the word consanguinity for relationship based upon community of blood, and to use the word kinship to denote the parental relationship in general.

[2] Dr. Westermarck writes : " There are numerous savage and barbarous peoples among whom sexual intercourse out of wedlock is of rare occurrence; unchastity at least on the part of the woman being looked upon as a disgrace and even as a crime " (Westermarck, *H.H.M.*, p. 61). In support of his opinion he adduces some forty cases where chastity is considered a virtue. Besides, the Veddas (according to Sarrazins and Seligmann) and the Andamanese (according to Man) may be quoted as peoples by whom absolute marital fidelity is required.

children and both their parents is secured, in other societies
of low culture the sexual laxity is so great that there is
no possibility at all of tracing the descent of a child from
any individual man.[1] This applies in the first place to
the majority of the Australian tribes, as is shown in the
chapter on sexual matters. In consequence, it may be
said that in many low societies, and especially in some of
the Australian tribes, there is no possibility of speaking
of physiological consanguinity as regards the father.

How does the case stand with the social importance
attributed to the facts of procreation ? Here the variation seems to be still greater. This can be very well
exemplified by the Australian material. Over the greater
part of the continent the father's share in procreation is
not known. There cannot be any social acknowledgment
of it. Consanguinity in its social sense does not exist. In
some tribes of South-East Australia, on the other hand,
the mother's share in procreation is under-rated; the
father is considered to be the only consanguineous relative;
the child is the father's offspring only, the mother being
merely its nurse. Here the consanguineous relation
between mother and child is considerably reduced in social
importance, and consanguinity as it appears to the social
mind is purely paternal. It may be said, therefore, that
paternal kinship in the Centre and the North of the continent and maternal kinship in the South-Eastern tribes
cannot be called consanguinity (in the social sense of this
word), although in both cases very close kinship exists,
as will appear from a detailed discussion hereafter.

These examples show clearly that it would be incorrect
to treat physiological consanguinity as a constant and
indispensable constituent of parental kinship.

Besides these Australian examples [2] there may be
adduced many cases from other societies in which the ties

[1] For various examples of various peoples besides the Australians, see Westermarck, pp. 71, 81. Compare also Post, *Ethnologische Jurisprudenz*, i. pp. 17 *sqq.*, and Dargun, *loc. cit.*, pp. 9 *sqq.*
[2] Which are dealt with at length in the second part of this
chapter.

of blood play no part in the collective ideas of kinship. The Naudowessies have the curious idea that their off-spring are indebted to their father for their souls, the invisible part of their essence, and to the mother for their corporeal and visible part.[1] Here the father's part in procreation was probably known, but the interpretation thereof was not the correct physiological one, but one that created, so to say, a spiritual connection as the bond of paternal kinship, whereas maternal kinship was conceived in terms of consanguinity. On the other hand, " accord-ing to Kafir ideas a child descends chiefly, though not exclusively, from the father " [2]—a belief analogous to that of the South-East Australians. The same belief was held in several higher societies (Egyptians, Hindoos, Greeks).[3] Dargun has made a list of peoples among whom the (social) father of the children is quite indifferent as to whether they are really begotten by him.[4] Among the Todas, where the determination of paternity is quite out of the question, owing to their polyandry, fatherhood is determined only by the performance of a conventional ceremony (the rite of *pursütpimi*, or handing over to the pregnant woman a miniature bow and arrow). This constitutes fatherhood; the man who has performed this ceremony is the (social) father of the child, even if it were certain that he had not begotten it.[5] Another interesting case was discovered by Dr. Rivers amongst the Banks Islanders. There fatherhood is determined by the fact of paying the midwife.

But the most noteworthy cases in regard to the present subject are those where fatherhood in its social sense is not consanguineous owing to the ignorance of the physio-logical laws of reproduction (a state of things mentioned already as obtaining in Central Australia). This ignor-ance is of general sociological importance, because there are well-founded reasons for believing that it was once

[1] Westermarck, *loc. cit.*, p. 105.   [2] *Ibid.*, p. 106.
[3] *Ibid.*   [4] *Loc. cit.*, pp. 9–18.
[5] Rivers, *The Todas*, pp. 517 *sqq.*

universal amongst primitive mankind, as may be held
to be proved by Mr. E. S. Hartland in his thorough
treatise on *Primitive Paternity*. For the detailed argument the reader must be referred to this fundamental
work.[1] Mr. Sidney Hartland has besides drawn sociological conclusions from those facts in their bearing upon
paternal kinship. In Chapter IV of the first volume he
gives numerous examples of peoples among whom there
is no tie of consanguinity between father and son.[2]

To ascertain the influence of physiological ties of blood
on this relation in a given society it is needful to know the
way in which they present themselves to the aboriginal
mind. That is, we must know the collective ideas of
a given society on the facts of procreation. Do they
know, or do they not know, the father's part in procreation ? But this is not sufficient. Even if they know
a certain physiological fact, they may not acknowledge
its bearing upon kinship, they may attach no importance
to its social aspect. So it is with the fact of physiological maternity in the South-East Australian tribes and
with paternity in the cases quoted by Dargun. And it
happens very often that in peoples where the causal con-

---

[1] Mr. Sidney Hartland has given an exceedingly exhaustive
collection of stories " of birth other than what we know as the
only natural cause "; of customs in which the " means to which
in these stories birth is attributed are or have been actually
adopted for the production of children "; and he has compared
this folkloristic material with the Australian beliefs. Besides
this weight of facts, the author adduces other important reasons
why it is extremely probable that " such ignorance was once
greater and more widespread than now." The book of Mr.
Sidney Hartland is undoubtedly the most thorough and most
scientific discussion of the present problem. The strength of his
arguments and the mass of evidence strongly support his conclusions. The contrary opinion, viz. that the Australian nescience
is an accidental result of some animistic beliefs, an opinion chiefly
represented by Mr. A. Lang, seems to be based more on speculation than on facts. The view that the ignorance of paternity
was widespread in primitive mankind is shared by Prof. Frazer,
M. A. van Gennep, and Frhr. von Reitzenstein. (For references,
see below, p. 208, footnote 1.)

[2] How far Mr. Hartland's results appear incomplete on the
sociological side will be discussed hereafter.

nection between copulation and pregnancy is well known, fatherhood is by no means determined by its physiological aspect. Not only the collective knowledge of the physiological facts, but also the collective attitude towards them, must therefore be taken into consideration.[1] In short, it may be said that *physiological* consanguinity has no direct bearing upon social facts.

To define consanguinity in its social meaning, the collective ideas held by a given society on the facts of procreation must be considered. Consanguinity, therefore, is the set of relations involved by the collective ideas under which the facts of procreation are viewed in a given society. And it must be borne in mind that these ideas express not only the purely theoretical views of the social mind on the facts of procreation; they also involve different emotional elements, and especially the social importance given to these facts by society. Consanguinity (as a sociological concept) is therefore not the physiological bond of common blood; it is the social acknowledgment and interpretation of it.

It may be said, therefore, that consanguinity is not always considered as the essence of kinship. If now we wish to determine what are the common features of the different ideas which in different societies define kinship, the only answer is that the said ideas affirm in one way or another a very close, intimate tie between offspring and parents. These ideas may refer kinship to physiological facts (consanguinity as found in the major part of human societies); or they may base kinship on the performance of a quite conventional ceremony (Todas, Banks Islanders); or they may affirm a very close tie between parent and child, on the base of some religious or magic belief (spiritual

[1] Sir Laurence Gomme writes : " There is a wide difference between the mere physical fact of having a mother and father, and the political fact of using this kinship for social organization. Savages who have not learned the political significance have but the scantiest appreciation of the physical fact.   The Australians, for instance, have no term to express the relationship between mother and child.   This is because the physical fact is of no significance. . . " (*loc. cit.*, p. 232).

tie, transmission of soul : the Naudoweissies and some
Australian tribes, as will be seen below). It is evident,
therefore, that the general idea of kinship cannot be
construed in terms of any of these special sets of ideas.
The essential features that must be claimed for these ideas
(*i. e.* those ranged in the class of kinship ideas) are :
(1) that they must refer to the relation between child and
father or mother;[1] and (2) that they must affirm an
intimate bond of union of some kind between the parties
involved. As may be easily conceived, it will be difficult
in very low societies to get hold of these ideas, that is, to
obtain the exact answer to the question, " What is kinship ? " It is now impossible even to measure exactly
the difficulty of getting a precise answer to this question,
as ethnographers have never paid special attention to this
point. Nevertheless, in Australia we shall be able to get
at least some glimpses, which are of the highest theoretical
interest. And even the negative result—that the idea of
consanguinity must be considered wanting in the majority
of Australian tribes—is of considerable theoretical value.

Besides the general question, " What is considered as
the source of parental (maternal and paternal) kinship ? "
we may ask questions about the various other ideas connected with kinship. Here come in the legal, moral, and
customary ideas, by which society exercises its normative
power in reference to the said relation. Some of these are
expressed in different social functions.[2] Others may be
reached by the study of beliefs, traditions, customs and
other forms of folk-lore. The well-known customs of the
couvade are one of the typical functions of the father, in
which there is an expression of a deep connection of a
magical kind between the father and his offspring. What-

---

[1] The terms *child, father* and *mother* being defined first broadly
as explained above, pp. 172 *sqq.*

[2] As an example may be quoted the " functions of kinship "
described by Dr. Rivers for the Torres Straits Islanders. *Cam-
bridge Exp. to Torres Straits,* v. pp. 144 *sqq.*, and vi. pp. 100, 101.
Also by Dr. Seligmann for the Melanesians of New Guinea,
see passage under this heading in chap. iii. and chap. xxxvii.
op. cit.

ever explanation of these customs may be given,[1] it cannot be denied that they are based upon the idea of a very intimate tie between the two individuals involved, and that this tie is conceived as being of a mystical character.

There is also a series of social rules which regulate the social position of the offspring according to that of its parents. This group of rules might appropriately be called *descent* in the social sense of this word.[2] In the Australian societies, *e. g.* the membership of different social groups—as the local group, the totemic clan, the phratry, the class—is determined by the membership of one of the parents of the given individual. And many authors speak of tribes with paternal and maternal descent. It must be borne in mind, nevertheless, that in order to use the word descent in a definite sense it is always necessary to add what social group is meant. For it is possible that membership in the local group is determined by the father, membership of the phratry by the mother, and membership in the clan by neither of them. The facts of descent do not seem to play a very important rôle and are not suitable to be chosen as the most important feature of kinship. The facts of inheritance also have not very much influence upon kinship (compare below, pp. 290, 291).

As it is easy to see, looking at our own ideas on parental kinship, all the normative ideas, whether religious, moral or legal, are in close connection with the central, basic idea, *i. e.* in the case of our society, the idea of consanguinity. And these normative ideas are brought by the collective mind into causal connection with the central idea of community of blood.[3] It would be the ideal of

---

[1] Perhaps the best one is given by Dargun, *loc. cit.*, pp. 22 *sqq.*, where many other opinions are also quoted and criticized.

[2] The word descent is often used without any definition. Mr. E. S. Hartland, *op. cit.*, i. p. 258, uses it in a sense synonymous with kinship. Mr. Thomas, too, does not define the meaning of this word, but he uses it more or less in the same way as is done in the text. Compare Thomas, *loc. cit.*, pp. 11, 12 *sqq.*

[3] It is impossible to develop here this thought, which would require a volume if regard be had to the complexity of the fact. The references to higher societies are given by way of illustration only.

sociological research as regards our present subject if
we could bring in any given society all the normative ideas
into such a causal dependence upon the central idea, and
explain how they are conceived by the collective mind as
the outgrowth of this root idea; thus showing how all
the legal, moral and customary aspects converge on the
fundamental concept of kinship. Unhappily, in low
societies the imperfection of ethnographic material would
frustrate any attempt at such an enterprise. In Australia
our knowledge of these aspects—moral, legal and customary—is very scanty. Although they are all undoubtedly in quite a rudimentary state, careful investigation would possibly disclose many points of extreme
interest.

One other problem must be discussed here more in
detail, owing to its great theoretical importance, viz. the
legal aspect of parental kinship. We have defined above
the meaning of the word *legal*.[1] In connection with what
has been said, we may affirm that the *legal* is only one of
the many aspects of kinship; that legal ideas, as far as
known for any given society, must be taken into account
when defining kinship, but that the latter cannot possibly
be reduced to its legal aspect only. And it is still more
incorrect [2] to represent physiological consanguinity and
legal power over the child as two mutually exclusive sets
of facts beyond which there can be no determination of
parental kinship. We find the opinion expressed by many
authors, especially with regard to Australia, that where-
ever the tie binding parent and child was not constituted
by the acknowledgment of consanguinity, that there
always it was based on legal principles such as potestas,
authority, *Machtstellung*, or other similar ones.

The incorrectness of taking only these two alternatives is
shown by the three following considerations: (1) Such a
view overlooks the facts discussed below, which show that
there is actual kinship based on ideas neither physio-

[1] See above, p. 11.
[2] Comparing what we have said above on consanguinity.

logical nor legal. (2) This way of interpreting facts oper-
ates with very indeterminate concepts, for we nowhere
find any explanation of how to take the general term *legal*
in connection with a given aboriginal society, and still
less are we told how such legal concepts as *potestas*,
paternal authority, etc., are to be applied to a given
aboriginal society. (3) If a definition of *law* or *legal* be
given, it would plainly be seen that it is quite erroneous
to consider any of these concepts as defining parental
kinship. This is quite clear if we use the definition of
legal given above, p. 11. But even allowing a broad
margin for the variations which may result from a varying
definition of *legal*, it may be safely stated that in whatever
way we might try to define this word, our definition must
always involve factors of social pressure, stress and authority. In other words, the relation between two individuals
may be considered *legal only* when we imply that it is
wholly and exclusively determined by the outward regulating control of the society and by a potential direct action
of it. And in the case we are speaking of—that is, the
relation between parent and child in low societies—there
can be hardly any question of this. As will appear in the
Australian case, this relation is left quite to itself, and it
is regulated by the spontaneous emotional attitude of
the father towards his child. No factor of any outer
pressure or constraint enters into it, at least we are not
informed of any such by the ethnographical evidence
extant. The collection and analysis of the statements on
this point given below [1] will show that there cannot be
any question of potestas, authority, proprietorship, or
anything of the kind. Neither social pressure nor economic interest bind the parents to their children, nor does
any motive of this kind enter into this relation.

As this subject is very important, some examples of
the mode of reasoning just now criticized are set out here.
These passages are quoted from works of very distinguished
writers to show that the mistakes result from serious

[1] pp. 238 *sqq.*; and pp. 254-256.

defects in sociological knowledge, and not from any accidental causes. And they are taken from passages which either refer exclusively to the Australian aboriginal society, or are exemplified by Australian facts.

Mr. Thomas, at the end of a passage in which he discusses the relation between the concepts of kinship and consanguinity says that in Australia " some relation will almost certainly be found to exist between the father and child; but it by no means follows that it arises from any idea of consanguinity." So far we perfectly agree with the reasoning of the author. But when Mr. Thomas adds, " In other communities *potestas* [1] and not *consanguinity* [1] is held to determine the relations of the husband of a woman to her offspring; and it is a matter for careful inquiry how far the same holds good in Australia, when the fact of fatherhood is in some cases asserted to be unrecognized by the natives," [2] we see that he falls into the error of acknowledging only two possibilities : potestas or consanguinity. It is true that he speaks of consanguinity as being modified by native ideas, and that thus a social element is introduced into the physiological concept of consanguinity. But we are still left to guess how this social element is to be understood. And as pointed out above, the relation between father and child in the tribes in question cannot be considered as based upon consanguinity or community of blood, whatever meaning we give to these words. Erroneous in any case is the opposition of kinship and potestas, as if these two concepts were of the same order, and could be considered as two equivalent categories excluding each other. Whereas, as we saw, these two concepts are of quite different order and cannot be treated as excluding or replacing each other. Kinship is a very complicated social fact, very complex in its sociological and psychological aspects. *Potestas* is a legal category, expressing a set of attributes and rights of the father over his children. Potestas (or any analogous legal factor) may be a constituent element of kinship in

[1] The italics are mine.   [2] *Loc. cit.*, p. 5.

certain societies.   It cannot possibly replace kinship
entirely.

A similar unsatisfactory reasoning, it appears to me, is
to be found contained in a passage of the small but clearly
and deeply thought out work of the eminent sociologist,
the late Prof. Dargun.   He stipulates as the most important postulate of studies in family organization the
discrimination between authority and consanguinity :
" Strenges Auseinanderhalten der Gewaltverhältnisse von
den Verwandtschaftsverhältnissen," [1] And he defines
Verwandtschaft as a purely physiological fact : "die letztere,
(Verwandtschaft) ist durch das natürliche Blutband ge-
geben." [2] This is obviously an incorrect definition for
sociological use.[3]   Equally unsatisfactory is the definition
given of the *Gewalt* (potestas) : Gewalt vom natürlichen
Blutband unabhängig kann " auf sehr verschiedene his-
torische Wurzeln zurückführen." [4] This definition is both
negative and ambiguous, excluding elements of consanguinity from potestas and assigning to the latter " various
historic roots." We might, therefore, expect to find everything in this idea, but on the other hand such a definition
lacks precision and does not give either the direction in
which to look for the determining factors, or any criterion
for our recognition of the existence of personal kinship ties.
Now our definition of kinship responds to both these requirements when applied to the Australian facts.   Moreover we find in these phrases of Dargun the alternative
condemned above between authority and consanguinity,
the latter used here in the crude physiological sense.   It
may be noted that in some passages of the book in question
there are hints pointing to the fact that the author felt
the necessity of a psychological definition of paternal
kinship.   So when he says, speaking of the Australians :
" Vollkommenste Vaterherrschaft, ja *selbst ausgesprochene
Vaterliebe*—gehen mit ebenso unbedingter Verwandtschaft
—und Stammeszugehörigkeit in mütterlicher Linie, Hand

[1] *Loc. cit.*, p. 2.   [2] *Ibid.*
[3] See above, p. 182.   [4] *Loc. cit.*, p. 2.

in Hand," [1] we see that here the author speaks of paternal love and states that this is what determines the relation of father and child in Australia. When he speaks afterwards of the father as : " Beschützer und Fürsorger " [2] of his children, we see that he mentions purely personal factors of the relation of father to child, such as we lay stress upon in speaking of community of life and of interests. But still the author seems to be entangled in his alternative between consanguinity and potestas. So we read : " Wo zwischen dem Vater und seinen Kindern ein wirkliches Verwandtschaftsverhältniss bestehet, dort muss auf die faktische Zeugung durch den Hausvater entscheidendes Gewicht gelegt werden, und umgekehrt überall wo Gleichgültigkeit gegen dieses Zeugungsverhältniss an den Tag tritt, ist das Gewaltverhältniss des Vaters, noch nicht zur Blutsverwandtschaft herangereift." [3] In this phrase there is a complete oversight of the various actual ways in which an intimate relation between father and child may be established, and which have nothing to do either with consanguinity or with *patria potestas*.

In the new work of Prof. Frazer there are also some pages touching on this point. Although he distinguishes well between the *physiological* and *social consanguinity*, [4] still in another place he says, speaking of the Central Tribes : " Denying as they do explicitly that the child is begotten by the father, they can only regard him as the consort, and in a sense as the owner of the mother, and, therefore, as the owner of her progeny, just as a man who owns a cow owns also the calf she brings forth. In short, it seems probable that a man's children were viewed as his property long before they were recognized as his off-

---

[1] *Loc. cit.*, p. 7. [2] *Ibid.* [3] *Loc. cit.*, p. 8.
[4] " Fatherhood to a Central Australian savage is a very different thing from fatherhood to a civilized European. To the European father it means that he has begotten a child on a woman; to the Central Australian father it means that the child is the offspring of a woman with whom he has a right to cohabit, whether he has actually had intercourse with her or not. To the European mind the tie between a father and his child is physical; to the Central Australian it is social."—*Loc. cit.*, i. p. 236.

spring." It is impossible to agree with this opinion. The word " property " can in no strict sense be applied to the relation between father and child in Australia. Besides the author does not even clearly indicate in what sense he uses the word; and this word appears here only as a metaphor. Moreover, it is obvious that this opinion implies opposition between consanguinity and the legal category of "proprietorship," and contrasts the words " property " and " offspring."

In fact, as we hinted above, and as we shall have opportunity of discussing below [1] in connection with the evidence, there is little ground for speaking of *authority*, *patria potestas*, "*ownership*" or any similar attributes of the father as regards his children in Australia. It must not be forgotten that these words are nearly meaningless as long as they have not a legal sense. According to the definition of *legal* we should say that two people stand to each other in a purely legal relation when certain norms are laid down and actively sanctioned by society, which requires a definite mutual behaviour and attitude on the part of each. It was pointed out above that in Australia we have data allowing us to speak of the legal aspect of social institutions and relations; [2] it appears improbable, though, that there could be found any *purely* legal relation. At any rate, nothing of that sort determines or forms the substance of the relation between father and child in Australia. If a father should kill or abandon his child, he would, for all we know, be left quite undisturbed. Nobody compels him to provide for its subsistence, to protect it and care for it. [3] There are spontaneous elements that bind him

---

[1] pp. 186, 254.   [2] pp. 11 *sqq.*

[3] In our society, if parents wish to abandon their progeny while still dependent, they would be prevented by the law from doing it, and compelled to perform a series of duties and services, which usually spring from the natural parental love. Thus we see that in our society the relation between parents and children has much more of a legal character than in Australia. Nevertheless it would seem quite absurd to style this relation in our society as essentially a legal one. It has only its legal sides, which, comparatively, are seldom put into action, espe-

to it. And these spontaneous elements (to discover them will be our task) determine his relation to his child. Undoubtedly this kinship relation presents *some* legal features, such as, for instance, his right to dispose of his daughter in marriage (a right which in some tribes is reported to belong to the mother or mother's brother). But we know very little about it.[1] At any rate, there are only a few occasions on which the relation in question involves any possibility of social intervention.[2]

Nobody ever doubts, as far as I can see, the fact that all personal ties between two individuals consist not only of ideas, but also of feelings, and that they are influenced no less by the feelings the two individuals mutually inspire than by the ideas they form of each other. To ascertain, *e. g.*, if there be friendship between two people, one seeks to know their feelings towards each other, as well as what they think about each other. The relation between a parent and a child is in our society chiefly determined by their mutual feelings. And in a case where these feelings are absent, this relationship—in spite of all legal, moral, and other factors which tend to maintain its form—is deeply affected. It may be taken for granted that the sentimental side most essentially determines in a given society any kind of personal relationship. And in the same society the character of a given personal relation—be it parental kinship or anything else—varies with the intensity of the feeling and is essentially defined by the latter. It may be accepted also, that in different societies the types of feelings corresponding to given personal relations may vary according to the society, and

---

cially while the children are not yet grown up, *i. e.* just during the period when the relationship in question is the most important.

[1] Compare pp. 254 *sqq.*

[2] The legal norms are an essential object of study also from the standpoint that they may be the expression of some important ideas held about kinship. Especially the motivation of these norms, as given by the aborigines, may be of high value in this respect. But obviously this does not mean that kinship is a legal category.

may define in each one this given relation in its most essential character. In other words, the concept of collective feelings can be applied as well as the concept of collective ideas.[1] By this is to be understood certain types of feeling, which being dependent on corresponding collective ideas possess the same essential character as the latter : they exist in a certain society, and are transmitted from generation to generation; they impose themselves on the individual mind, and possess the character of necessity; they are deeply connected with certain social institutions; in fact they stand to them in the relation of functional dependence (in the mathematical sense). So, for instance, it is clear that in the hypothetical primitive promiscuous society, in which *ex hypothesi* there would be no individual relationship, the feelings of affection for the individual offspring could not exist. We could only speak of the " collective feeling " of *group affection*. So it seems to me that the relation of parents to children cannot be treated with any approach to completeness without seriously taking into account its emotional character.

But even if the foremost importance of emotional elements and the possibility of treating them as collective feelings were granted, there is another objection to be met. Granted that these elements are actually quite essential in determining family relations, it might be objected that they are too shapeless and indeterminate in themselves to be of any practical use in scientific research, especially if our theories have to be based upon ethnographic observations in which the more tangible and the more unambiguous the facts chosen, the less the risk of being misled. Now, are not feelings of the most indeterminate character, the most misleading, and the most difficult to ascertain ? In fact, the theory

[1] As is well known, we are indebted for the concept of *collective ideas* to the French school of Prof. Durkheim and his associates. Throughout this study, and especially in this chapter, I have done my best to avail myself of this valuable methodological standpoint.

of feelings and emotions seems to be the least developed
in individual as well as in social psychology. Especially
it might be suggested that to pursue the investigation on
double lines is useless; feelings always find adequate
expression in ideas, in fact crystallize in them.[1] Without trying to give a general answer to these objections,
they may be met as regards the special case under discussion. In Australia, as a matter of fact, they do not
hold good. For our knowledge of the sentimental side
of parental kinship is much better and much more determinate than our knowledge of any other aspect of this
relation.

It may be here indicated why our knowledge on this
point may be considered as a well-founded one. As stated
below (pp. 249, 250) the agreement between the statements as to parental feelings is quite an exceptional one.
Comparing it with the usual discrepancy between the
reports of different observers on many other points, which
would appear much less liable to any subjectivity, this
complete agreement and the relative exactness of our
information is highly remarkable.[2] It should be noted
that on this point there is no extrinsic reason, or secondary
motive, that would make us suspect an artificial cause
of agreement. The point in question forms no part of
any theory; it affects no moral or racial susceptibilities.
And there was no special reason why so many observers
should pay attention to it, and why they all should state
the same thing : viz. extreme love and fondness towards
the children on the part of the parents. This agreement

---

[1] It seems needless to add that the deep connection and mutual
dependence of both feelings and ideas is perfectly acknowledged.
This is not the place, of course, to pursue any detailed psychological investigations. I would like to remind the reader that
all that is said here must be judged by its application to the
Australian facts given below. In higher societies where art,
poetry and thought lend themselves much more to the expression of feelings, the former afford objective documents of
the latter. In low societies we must look for such objective
documents elsewhere, in different sets of facts.

[2] Compare below, p. 250.

shows that the facts which the ethnographers had under observation were so expressive of the underlying psychology, and they struck the writers so strongly that they simply felt compelled to notice them. And observing closely the facts through which those feelings of paternal affection found their expression, it becomes evident that these feelings are not so indeterminate as might *a priori* be supposed; that, on the contrary, they find quite an unequivocal expression in a series of facts. Let us look more closely at these facts.

In the first place consider the facts of daily life [1]—the behaviour of parents towards children in all the cases where the latter want help or merit punishment. We read that on all such occasions both parents exhibit great kindness and extreme leniency. The children are carefully looked after by the father as well as by the mother; and they are very seldom punished. In one place it is even stated that the father is more lenient than the mother. Now is it not in agreement with all our everyday experiences that in such facts and features of daily life prominent and characteristic feelings find their adequate expression? And is the accordance of opinion among all our Australian informants on this point not a proof that they were able to judge with great certainty from these facts concerning the underlying feelings? —that these outer signs were unmistakable expressions of the inner facts? Undoubtedly our information is too little detailed, and particulars referring to treatment of children and other features of the aboriginal daily life in this connection would be of the highest value. But considering that the attention of the observers was never specially drawn to these questions by any theoretical writer, and comparing our information on this point with other parts of our evidence, it must be acknowledged that it is exceptionally good. And this reliability is doubtless in the first place due to the fact that the subject of observation was clear, unambiguous and well determined.

[1] Conys. *Statements*, pp. 238 *sqq.*

We are, moreover, in possession of a few reports of actual occurrences in which the great love displayed by the parents for their children is shown in its full strength and under the stress of special circumstances.   In a battle that took place between some aborigines and settlers, the former were put to flight. They had to cross a river, but in doing so they left a child behind them.   It was seized by a Maori who was at the station, and it was shown to the blacks standing on the other bank of the river. The father of the child recognized it at once. He seemed almost frantic, held out his arms eagerly towards the child, making at the same time signs for it to be given to him. The Maori pretended to be willing to give it and made signs to the black to cross the river again. And the black swam across the river to rescue his child. Thus he did not hesitate to risk his life in order to save his child; in the end he was treacherously murdered by the Maori.[1] Another touching story is told by Rob. Dawson concerning a mother's grief after the loss of her son. He says that the woman was utterly transformed by the blow. " Before the catastrophe she was a remarkably fine woman, being tall and athletic beyond any other in the settlement; *now*, she was a truly wretched and forlorn spectacle, apparently wasted down by watching and sorrow. I have seen this poor creature often since our first meeting, at their different camps near us, and she has still the same wretched appearance." [2] These tales show that parental feelings could be as deep and pathetic among the Australian blacks as in any cultured society. We read another story in Howitt,[3] who tells us that when he was living one day in his camp in the Dieri country the father of a lad, who was visiting Howitt's camp the day before, came in a state of utmost alarm and terror. The lad, his son, was missing, and they could not find him. The father was terrified and, suspecting that the

[1] Br. Smyth, ii. p. 311.   [2] *Loc. cit.*, pp. 92, 93.
[3] *Kam. and Kurn.*, p. 189.

white men had concealed the lad and might carry him away, he looked through Howitt's luggage. It may be noted that this occurred among the Dieri, where it is said that individual paternity does not obtain. Nevertheless it was not a group of fathers that came worrying and striving to find the boy; neither was it a group of fathers that risked their lives for the child, nor a group of mothers that was grieving to death for their child. In the few anecdotes reported below with the other statements we see also how strongly paternal affection is marked. So in the story of the old man quite infatuated with his son and disconsolate after his death, and in the story of another man eager to rescue his boy, and the old man in Curr's story, who allowed his boy to do anything he liked.[1]

Such stories and anecdotes could be easily multiplied from the ethnographical material extant. They all corroborate our proposition, viz. that the sentimental side of the parental relation expresses itself quite clearly and tangibly in ever so many facts of different order, and that it would be easy for a well-informed observer to give a fairly exact account of the feelings in terms of facts. These facts, as said above, are in the first place the facts of daily life, which are quite unmistakable in their meaning and easily expressed in an accurate manner. The proof of it is that we have now relatively abundant data, although no methodical research was devoted to these facts. Then there are different occasions on which the limit of affection, the maximum and minimum of their range in a given society, is established. Such are the foregoing stories. I think we can safely conclude that the emotional side is on the one hand quite essential, and important enough to take the first place in our considerations.[2] On the other hand it can be accurately

---

[1] Compare pp. 248, 249; and 269 *sqq.*
[2] The importance of the emotional character of parental kinship has already been theoretically studied. Prof. K. Buecher (*loc. cit.*, p. 19) represents the primitive parents as selfish, heart-

described in terms of objective data for the purpose of being chosen as the chief characteristic of the parental relation.   It must be added that not a single other side or aspect of this relation appears to fulfil these conditions in the same degree.   As will subsequently appear, our knowledge about the aboriginal *ideas* on parental relationship are not so ample by far as our knowledge about their *feelings* in that connection.

The foregoing discussion has been mainly concerned with the collective ideas which define parental kinship, and the different sets of social facts in which these ideas find their expression have been enumerated.   It also dealt with collective feelings, and the different facts in which these are to be looked for were surveyed.   We must now emphasize the fact that just as we may say that the different ideas determining kinship converge towards one central concept, or rather flow out of one common central idea of kinship, so there is also an intimate connection between the ideas determining kinship and the feelings bound up with it.   This becomes obvious if our own social conditions be considered.   As mentioned above, a father in our society loves his child in a great measure because he knows that it is his own offspring. In societies in which the idea of consanguinity (in the social sense) does not exist, such a connection between feelings of paternal love and knowledge of a physiological procreation would be impossible.   And it would be of the highest sociological interest to trace what form such connections assume.   An attempt at such a study would be possible in our own society and in other higher

---

less, with no love or attachment for the child, and draws important conclusions from this.   Dr. Steinmetz has subjected this assumption to a thorough criticism; taking his stand on a rich collection of ethnological data, he shows that this assumption is without any ground; he fully acknowledges the importance in sociological researches of behaviour, treatment and emotional attitude in the parental relation.   Compare his important article in *Zeitschr. f. Sociologie*, i. pp. 608 *sqq.*, and *Ethnologische Studien*, ii. pp. 186 *sqq.*

societies, although there would be serious difficulties enough. But there would hardly be sufficient material to attempt it in any lower society, and there is absolutely no possibility of doing this for Australia.

A brief summary of the foregoing argument may now be given. It was stated at the beginning that parental kinship corresponds to a very complex and manifold set of phenomena; moreover in various societies this relationship is determined by various elements. The problem is to find in all this complexity the structural features, the really essential facts, the knowledge of which in any given society would enable us to give a scientifically valid description of kinship. In other words, the problem is to give a general formula defining kinship, which would state its constant elements and give heed to the essential varying elements therein; that formula being on the one hand not too narrow for application to the various human societies, it would be on the other hand not too vague to afford quite definite results when applied to any special case. A final solution of this problem cannot be arrived at *a priori*, but only by way of induction, after the facts in the different human societies have been studied. And in order to attempt such a preliminary study of the Australian facts, the foregoing remarks have been given; they aim at a general definition of the kind just described in the form of a tentative or preliminary sketch. Consequently in the first place the attempt was made to ascertain what could be taken as the constant elements in individual parental kinship. What appeared to be nearly universal in this connection is the fact that infants and small children are always specially attached, and stand in a specific close relation to a man and a woman.[1] The woman is invariably their own mother, who gave them birth; the man is the woman's husband. The existence of this group, which may be called the individual family, is the basis upon which kinship may be determined; it is

[1] Compare the footnote above, p. 174.

the condition under which it is possible to speak of individual parental kinship in any given society.

But it was shown that the knowledge of these facts is not sufficient to yield a precise idea of maternal and paternal kinship, and that many of its manifold aspects of foremost sociological interest would remain unknown if the inquiry were broken off at this point.   These latter aspects depend upon factors which are by no means constant in all societies, but have a very wide range of variation depending on the general social conditions.   A discussion of the concept of consanguinity has shown that the variations go so far as to affect the main question of paternal kinship : " Who is the father (in the social sense) of a child, and how is he determined ? "

In order to indicate in which direction the varying general conditions of society must be investigated so as to yield all that is essential for the sociological knowledge of kinship, it was found most convenient to range the facts in two main lines of inquiry :   (1) The different sets of facts which express the central collective idea of what fatherhood is; and the various other collective ideas—legal, customary, moral—of a normative character referring to the relation in question.   The social facts in which these ideas must be looked for are : Beliefs, traditions, customs referring to the relation in question (as for instance the couvade type), and functions of kindred such as legal duties and obligations between parent and child.   (2) The facts in which the expression of the collective feelings characteristic of the relation in question is to be found.   The facts of daily life, as well as the dramatic expression of feelings, come in here.   The emotional character of the parental kinship relation is of the highest importance in determining the social feature of this relation, and for the comprehension of its social working.

These points of view will be applied hereafter to the discussion of the Australian parental kinship.   But in order to illustrate here their theoretical bearing, a short

discussion will be given of some of the ways in which the
concept of kinship has been applied to low societies by
sociologists. Morgan's way of dealing with the meaning of kinship must be first mentioned.[1] He assumes
without further discussion that kinship was conceived
always and in all societies. even the lowest ones, in terms
of consanguinity.[2] Our discussion of consanguinity shows
how great a mistake it was on the part of Morgan
to impute to the primitive mind a whole series of ideas
which absolutely and necessarily must have been foreign
to it. As was said above, primitive mankind was certainly wholly ignorant of the process of procreation, and
the relation of the sexes cannot possibly have been the
source of kinship ideas. How great a part this assumption plays in Morgan's deductions it is easy to perceive.[3]
And he was led to it by omitting to discuss and analyze
the concept of kinship, and by applying to low societies
our own social concept of it.

J. F. MacLennan uses also the kinship concept as
identical with that of blood relationship.[4] But it must
be emphatically stated that MacLennan recognizes both

---

[1] Compare also above, p. 171.

[2] Compare especially *Systems, etc.*, chap. ii. pp. 10 *sqq.* " The
family relationships are as ancient as the *family*. They exist
in virtue of the law of derivation, which is expressed by the
perpetuation of the species through the marriage relations. A
system of *consanguinity*, which is *founded upon a community of
blood*, is but the formal expression and recognition of these relationships." (The italics are mine.) This is in other words the
assumption that kinship was always conceived as consanguinity,
or community of blood through procreation. Compare also
Ancient Society, pp. 393, 395.

[3] *Systems, etc.*, pp. 474 *sqq*:, where the only source of the classificatory system is attributed to different " customs " referring
to the sexual aspect of marriage. As we saw, precisely this
aspect is quite irrelevant to the formation of primitive kinship
ideas, consequently also of primitive kinship terms.

[4] See *loc. cit.*, pp. 83 *sqq.* It is difficult to pick out any one
clear statement to show that the author identifies kinship with
consanguinity. But a glance at the pages quoted is enough
to prove this. I quote a phrase from the table of contents :
" The most ancient system in which the *idea of blood relationship*
was embodied was a system of kinship through females only."
(The italics are mine.)

the importance of feelings in relation to kinship[1] and the fact that consanguinity was not known to primitive man,[2] although he unfortunately does not develop these two important ideas.

The same use of the concept of kinship (Verwandts- chaft) was pointed out above as a mistake of Dargun's. The ideas on kinship of Prof. Frazer and Mr. Thomas were also dealt with above, where it was found that they were not adapted to the complexity of the facts.

Mr. Sidney Hartland rightly sees that kinship is not necessarily identical with consanguinity in our sense. But he wrongly restricts kinship to a specific kind of ideas about community of blood. "Though kinship, however, is not equivalent to blood relationship in our sense of the term, it is founded on the idea of common blood which all within the kin possess, and to which all outside the kin are strangers. A feeling of solidarity runs through the entire kin, so that it may be said without hyperbole that the kin is regarded as one entire life, one body whereof each unit is more than metaphorically a member, a limb. The same blood runs through them all, and ' the blood is the life.' "[3] This definition, illustrated as it is by many examples, is one more instance showing that the idea underlying kinship may be different from the idea of consanguinity in our sense, *i. e.* consan- guinity of blood through procreation. But the affirma- tion that kinship is always based on some idea of common blood, seems to be not in accord with the facts. More- over this passage, which is the only one designed to define kinship, is quite inadequate to the importance of the

[1] Men are always "bound together by a feeling of kindred. The filial and paternal affections may be instinctive. They are obviously independent of any theory of kinship, its origin and consequences . . . they may have existed long before kinship became an object of thought," *op. cit.*, p. 83. From these remarks it is only one step to say that feelings ought to be con- sidered as determining elements, and that even if ideas corre- sponding to them did not exist, kinship could not be denied.

[2] "No advocate of innate ideas will maintain their existence on relationship by blood," *op. cit.*, p. 83.

[3] *Primitive Paternity*, i. pp. 257–258.

subject, especially in a treatise devoted to primitive paternity, and the result is that in this admirable work the purely sociological side presents some obscurities. The following remark : " Kindred with the father is first and foremost judical—a social convention "[1] is also incorrect in the light of the foregoing discussion of the legal aspect of kinship.

Dr. Rivers defines: " Kin and Kinship.—These terms should be limited to the relationship . . . which can be demonstrated genealogically." This is quite a formalistic definition and does not at all meet the full facts of the case. Moreover it seems that in this way we define the unknown by what is still more indeterminate. For to draw up a genealogy we must first know who are the individuals between whom the line of descent is to be drawn; in other words we must know how fatherhood is defined in a given society. Among the Todas, Dr. Rivers had to ascertain in what way the father of a given child is determined, before he could proceed to draw up the genealogies.[2] In any case the problem of kinship requires in the actual state of

---

[1] Sidney Hartland, ii. p. 99.

[2] Of course I insist here only upon the logical and methodological priority of the psychological determination of kinship over the genealogical. In reality, wherever individual paternal kinship exists, the genealogies may be drawn first, and they possess an independent value, even if we did not know what is the content of the aboriginal idea of kinship. There is a series of highly valuable sociological conclusions that may be drawn from a system of genealogies (compare Dr. Rivers' article on this subject in *Sociological Review*, 1910, pp. 1 *sqq.*).

I do not, therefore, agree with the following remark of Sir Laurence Gomme (*op. cit.*, p. 232): " It is of no use preparing a genealogical tree on the basis of civilized knowledge of genealogy if such a document is beyond the ken of the people to whom it relates. The information for it may be correctly collected, but if the whole structure is not within the compass of savage thought it is a misleading anthropological document." If it is possible at all to collect a genealogy, that means that individual kinship exists in such a community; in other words the " structure is within the compass of savage thought," only it is not apprehended by them in the same manner as by us. It is certainly true that in many cases the knowledge of this aboriginal apprehension is essentially needful for a sociologist. This has been argued in the text.

things not only a purely formal definition, but a detailed analysis. Much more important as regards the present problem is the way in which Dr. Rivers has described the kinship of the Torres Straits Islanders.[1] In introducing the study of the functions of kin he points to a series of important facts which determine some social aspect of kinship and afford an insight into some of the collective ideas concerning this relation. It must be borne in mind, however, that the set of functions described by Dr. Rivers gives us only a partial knowledge of the social aspect of kinship. The every-day functions corresponding to treatment, behaviour, feeding and so forth, which characterize the intimate or home aspect of the kinship relation, ought not to be omitted. They correspond, according to our analysis, to feelings which make an essential part of the relation in question. The social functions of kin collected by Dr. Rivers, expressing certain duties and privileges of the kinsmen involved, correspond to certain customary norms. A complete collection of all legal norms and all moral rules would be an essential addition. That such moral rules do exist among the Torres Straits Islanders appears certain from the precepts given at initiation to youths.[2]

Messrs. Fison and Howitt in their treatise on Australian kinship [3] do not give anywhere a clear definition of the concept in question. The only place where something like definition is given is page 121, where kinship is said to be " membership in the same tribal division," and where there is an acknowledgment that beyond " kinship" there still lies " personal relationship" between the parent and child. This is true, but this is only the first distinction upon which the actual discussion of the problem ought to be based. That the want of such a discussion is a serious defect in the book is obvious.

[1] *Camb. Univ. Exp.*, v. chap. iii. on Kinship, pp. 129 *sqq.* In particular, pp. 142–152, under the headings " The Functions of certain Kin," and " Kinship Taboos."
[2] Recorded by Dr. Haddon, *loc. cit.*, v. p. 210.
[3] *Kam. and Kurn.*

The important distinction between kinship (*parenté*) and consanguinity, which is one of the chief results of the foregoing pages, has been made already by Prof. Durkheim.[1] Nevertheless the exclusive stress that M. Durkheim lays upon the legal aspect of kinship would not seem adapted to the complexity of the facts. " La parenté est essentiellement constitué par des obligations juridiques et morales que la société impose à certains individus." This is not enough. There are certain ideas which affirm a strong bond between parent and child, and undoubtedly these ideas, although neither of legal nor moral character, exercise a strong influence on the relation in question. Possibly the difference could be reduced to the broader sense in which Prof. Durkheim uses the words *legal* and *moral ;* as his remarks are necessarily short, being contained in a review, it is difficult exactly to ascertain their sense. We have tried to show that, especially in reference to low societies, both these terms must be used with caution, and that a definite sense must be given to them. Besides, I do not share Prof. Durkheim's view that by substituting the word " kinship " for the word " consanguinity " all Morgan's deductions could be rectified.[2] The constitution of the family is something quite different from and much more complicated than the sexual aspect of marriage, and it cannot be at once seen whether the nomenclature of kinship (systems of kinship terms) could be shown to be rooted in the former with the same ease as it can be shown in the latter case. This would require a special study.

M. A. van Gennep also clearly establishes the distinction between *parenté sociale* and *parenté physique.*[3] According to our terminology the latter would correspond to physiological consanguinity, while the former would be identical with what we called parental kinship. We see that this distinction is quite in agreement with our theory. Only we called social consanguinity a special

---

[1] *A.S.*, i. p. 316.   [2] *Ibid.*, p. 318.
[3] *Loc. cit.*, p. lxiii. (of the Introduction).

case of kinship, where the collective ideas on procreation play the essential rôle. Obviously these ideas may be more or less physiologically correct or erroneous. But where they are completely absent (as in Australia) we prefer not to use the suggestive term *consanguinity*, and to distinguish these cases from the former we use the term *kinship*. M. A. van Gennep remarks further that the Central Australians do not know the real cause of procreation in spite of some illusory appearances (we shall deal with this question in detail below and solve it quite in agreement with the author in question); he shows the wide extension of this negative belief in the Australian continent, and speaking of the South Australian tribes, points out that the most important aspect is that they prove the independence of kinship and consanguinity.[1]

The same distinction between consanguinity and kinship is also made by Prof. Westermarck in his discussion of the classificatory system of relationship, and Prof. Westermarck has already brought the important objection against Morgan, viz. that the latter has " given no evidence for the truth of his assumption that the classificatory system " is a system of blood ties,[2] an objection which has appeared also to us as fundamental. Unfortunately, Prof. Westermarck has not given any exhaustive discussion of the concept of kinship.

Finally, I wish to mention a passage by Sir Laurence Gomme, which contains suggestive remarks nearly identical with some views set forth in this chapter. " It is of no use translating a native term as ' father,' if father did not mean to the savage what it means to us. It might mean something so very different. With us fatherhood connotes a definite individual with all sorts of social, economical and political associations, but what does it mean to the savage ? It may mean physical fatherhood and nothing more, and physical fatherhood may be a fact

[1] " L'indépéndance réciproque du point de vue biologique et du point de vue social chez les Australiens." (*Ibid.*, p. lxv.)
[2] *H.H.M.*, p. 89.

of the veriest insignificance.   It may mean social fatherhood . . . and thus becomes " (in some cases), " much
more than we can understand by the term father." [1]

It may also be pointed out for the sake of completeness
that in the great majority of human societies parental
kinship assumes the form of consanguinity; the ideas that
underlie kinship are generally gathered round the facts
of procreation.   These facts are connected with such deep
and powerful instincts and feelings that in the majority
of cases they naturally shape and influence the ideas of
maternity and paternity.   But the few exceptions to
this rule which we meet with in very primitive societies
are of the highest theoretical interest, both from the
evolutionist's and psychologist's point of view.   The final
remark I would like to make here is on the well-known
fact that physiological maternity is much more easily

[1] *Loc. cit.*, pp. 232, 233; compare also above p. 182, footnote.
Apart from the naturally somewhat loose terminology (the
passage about kinship is intended as an example only, and does
not aim at a full treatment of the subject)—the passages quoted
express the same ideas which served as a starting-point for
this chapter.

I came across the paragraph in question unfortunately only
after the MS. of the present chapter had been finished and
the foregoing chapters had been printed.   The opinion of Sir
Laurence Gomme would also have been of value in support of
the views expressed in the Introduction, pp. 6, 7, where I try
to show that it is meaningless to use the word " family " as
a rigidly determined concept of universal application.   " The
family as seen in savage society, and the family as it appears
among the antiquities of the Indo-European people, are totally
distinct in origin, in compass and in force " (Sir Laurence Gomme,
loc. cit., pp. 236, 237).   And the author applies his criticism to
the same two writers who have been the objects of my attacks
(Mr. A. Lang and Mr. N. W. Thomas, see *op. cit.*, p. 236, footnote 1).   And, again, Sir Laurence Gomme argues that the un-
qualified use of the term " family " is very harmful, " because
of the universal application of this term to the smallest social
unit of the civilized world, and because of the fundamental
difference of structure of the units which roughly answer to the
definition of family in various parts of the world " (*op. cit.*,
p. 235).   Certainly there is also a *fundamental analogy* of
structure between all forms of human family; but the problem
must be set forth and it must be acknowledged that this social
unit undergoes deep changes as other elements of social structure
change.

ascertainable than physiological paternity. Paternal kinship, therefore, will much more frequently differ from what we called consanguinity than maternal kinship. But some of the Australian examples and our previous general considerations should make us cautious in laying down *a priori* any assertion of the purely physiological character of maternity.

II

SOME EXAMPLES OF KINSHIP IDEAS SUGGESTED BY THE AUSTRALIAN FOLK-LORE

The foregoing remarks on kinship, and the sketch of a general definition of kinship given above, of course bear upon the whole of the present investigations, since parental kinship being one of the relationships involved in the individual family, all that refers to this latter unit relates more or less immediately to parental kinship. In the other chapters we attempt to discuss the existence of the individual family, and of those of its features which appear to be universal, and which have, therefore, been adopted as the basis of parental kinship. The general features of the Australian individual family are given in the concluding chapter, and a comparison of the results presented there with the foregoing general definition of kinship [1] will be sufficient to satisfy the first point of this definition, *i. e.* to prove the existence of individual parental kinship in Australia and to describe its constant elements.   In the following chapter (Chap. VII.) attention will be paid to the functions of kin, which correspond to the collective feelings of parents to children. Here we shall discuss the data taken from Australian folk-lore, which bear upon the parental kinship, and shall thus satisfy that part of our definition in which it was laid down that the ideas of kinship must be investigated.

The survey may commence with the Central tribes,

[1] pp. 198 *sqq.*

the folk-lore of which we know best, owing to the excellent information given by Messrs. Spencer and Gillen, subsequently confirmed in its main lines by the joint publication of Herr Strehlow and Frhr. von Leonhardi. In these works we possess a very detailed description of the aboriginal views on conception and birth, which are connected with their totemic beliefs. These views will not be reproduced here *in extenso*, and the reader is referred to the sources and the special works.[1]   The reader is therefore,

---

[1] Here in the first place must be mentioned the works of Spencer and Gillen, *Nat. Tr.*, pp. 123–127, 255; *Nor. Tr.*, pp. 144, 163 *sqq.*, 169 *sqq.*, 174–176, 150, 330, 331; Mrs. Parker, pp. 50 *sqq.*, 61, 98.

Strehlow, *loc. cit.*, i., on the second and third pages of the Preface by Frhr. von Leonhardi (there is no pagination), ii. pp. 51 *sqq.*, iii. pp. x.–xi. of the Preface by Frhr. von Leonhardi.   A short notice on totemic conception and on local distribution of spirit-children is communicated by Rev. L. Schultze, *Trans. and Proc. R.S.S.A.*, xiv. p. 237 (1891).   R. H. Mathews communicated in several places beliefs in reincarnation and totemic conception.   See *Jour. and Proc. R.S.N.S.W.*, xl. pp. 108 *sqq.*, *ibid.*, xli. p. 147.   And *Queensland Geographical Journal*, xx: p. 73, and xxii. pp. 75, 76.   *Am. Antr.*, xxviii. p. 144: *Bull. Soc. of Antr.*, Paris, vii. serie v. p. 171.   Herbert Basedow, *Trans. R.S.S.A.*, xxxi. (1907), p. 4.   (Short communication concerning the Larrekiya tribe of the Northern territory, South Australia.) Amongst the sources must be quoted the communications given by Prof. Frazer on the authority of Dr. Frodsham, Bishop of North Queensland, and the Rev. C. W. Morrison, which refer to the Northern and North-Eastern tribes in general.   Frazer, *Tot. and Exog.*, i., p. 577.

In fact, the theory of totemic conception is so closely connected with the whole of the aboriginal totemic beliefs that it is necessary to be acquainted with the latter in order to understand the former; and for this the perusal of both the works of Messrs. Spencer and Gillen and of Strehlow is necessary.

Among the theoretical works dealing with primitive views of conception and paternity (in Australia and in general), we must place first the treatise of Mr. E. S. Hartland, *Primitive Paternity*, which is the most extensive and thorough examination of all beliefs, referring to a supernatural cause of birth and all its social consequences.   The beliefs in question play an important rôle in Prof. Frazer's work on *Totemism and Exogamy*.   See especially vol. iv., on origins of Totemism.

We may mention also the works of van Gennep, *Mythes et Légendes d'Australie*, especially chaps. v. and vi. of the Introduction, pp. 44–67, in which the ignorance of the natives is illustrated by several interesting remarks and inferences from other facts (for example, the beliefs of the aborigines about the rôle and

supposed to be acquainted with the aboriginal views on conception, and only the ideas which in these theories refer directly to our subject, *i. e.* those underlying parental kinship, will be dealt with here.

Roughly speaking it may be said that these totemic beliefs and theories of conception prevent the aboriginal mind from forming the idea of physiological paternity and even probably weaken the social importance of maternity. For the only cause of pregnancy is that a " spirit-child " entered the body of a woman. " The natives one and all in these tribes believe that the child is the direct result of the entrance into the mother of an ancestral spirit individual. They have no idea of pro-creation as being directly associated with sexual inter-course, and firmly believe that children can be born without this taking place. There are, for example, in the Arunta country certain stones which are supposed to be charged with spirit children, who can, by magic, be made to enter the bodies of women, or will do so on their own accord." [1] Accordingly no tie of blood can be supposed to exist between the father and his child; there is no room for any ideas of physiological paternity; in other words, using our terminology, social consanguinity between father and child does not exist.[2] This is the

---

nature of the sexual organs, pp. 111 *sqq.*). Compare also the article of Frhr. v. Reitzenstein, *Z.f.E.*, xli., pp. 644 *sqq.* Mr. A. Lang's views (comp. above, p. 181, footnote 1) are expounded in *Anthrop. Essays*, pp. 203 *sqq.*, and in *The Secret of the Totem*, chap. xi.

[1] This refers to the whole Central and North Central area. Spencer and Gillen, *Nor. Tr.*, p. 330. In a short note of recent date (*Athenæum*, Nov. 4, 1911, p. 562), we read that Prof. B. Spencer has found the same absence of physiological knowledge in the tribes living North-West of the " Northern Tribes " (from Roper River to Port Darwin). According to his opinion this belief obtains from the South Coast of Australia over a broad belt right through the Centre to the North Coast. (*Ibid.*)

[2] It may be remembered here that this is not in contradiction with the passage in M. A. von Gennep's work, *Mythes and Légendes d'Australie*, p. lxiii, implying that there is social but not physiological consanguinity between father and child in the Central Australian tribes. The difference in terminology is

most general conclusion that can be drawn from the beliefs quoted. But in connection with this question there are still some details, some controversial points into which we must enter in order to dissipate any doubts as to the correctness of our general conclusions just mentioned, as well as of some subsequent reasonings.

(1) There seems to be some incertitude as to the complete absence among the natives of any knowledge regarding the physiology of procreation. We read in Strehlow,[1] " Ubrigens wissen die alten Männer, wie mir versichert wurde, dass die cohabitatio als Grund der Kinderkonzeption anzusehen sei, sagen aber davon den jüngeren Männern und Frauen nichts." This phrase might evoke some doubts as to whether we should attribute so much importance to the alleged ignorance.[2] But according to subsequent information in the same publication,[3] we must not attach to this phrase too much weight. Possibly the knowledge of the old men comes from alien sources; at any rate we see from the explanation given below by Frhr. von Leonhardi that this phrase does not rest on any concrete facts, or any well-founded information. From the point of view of collective ideas it must always be remembered that it is in the social institutions of a given people and in the whole of their beliefs that we must look for the foundation and confirmation of a given creed. It would be a superfluous digression to point out how deeply the totemic theory of conception is connected with all the other beliefs and the whole social life of the Australian aborigines—as this has been done by so many students

---

explained above, p. 178, footnote 1, and reasons are given explaining why I did not adopt M. A. von Gennep's terminology, although I completely share his views.

[1] Loc. cit., ii. p. 52, footnote 7.

[2] Attention was drawn to this phrase by P. W. Schmidt in his article in Zeitschrift für Ethnologie (1908), p. 866 sqq., where the theory of conception among the Arunta is discussed. He doubts: " Ob wirklich eine vollständige Unkenntniss des Zusammenhanges von Koitus und Konzeption in primitivem Zustande vorhanden ist."—Loc. cit., p. 883.

[3] Strehlow, iii. pp. x.; xi.

of the subject, and pre-eminently by Prof. Frazer in his
recent work on *Totemism and Exogamy*. Some doubts
might also arise from the fact that the natives apparently
know the real process of propagation in the case of the
animals. There is undoubtedly some difficulty here;
and additional information on this point would be most
valuable. Nevertheless the case is not quite hopeless :
if we assume that this correct physiological knowledge is
of a relatively late origin, it is quite natural that it would
arise first in relation to the animal world, because the
ideas about man, being the most important and elaborate,
would be the most conservative. Anyhow this point
requires further elucidation.[1]

(2) We must insist upon another point, which might at
first sight cast some shadow of suspicion even on the
foregoing one. We read in Spencer and Gillen [2] that
sexual intercourse " prepares the mother for the reception
and birth also of an already formed spirit-child who
inhabits one of the local totem centres." And this belief
of " preparation," although at first denied by Strehlow,[3]
was substantiated by him after a more careful investigation and emphatically affirmed.[4] Although there might
seem to be at first sight some room for doubt, whether
this belief does not create some connection between
copulation and pregnancy, and so a bridge for the formation of ideas of paternity, a moment's reflection dissipates
these doubts. For in this belief there is absolutely
nothing that would point to any *individual* male as the
father of the child. We do not know whether, according
to the native beliefs, there must be this preparation for
each incarnation, or whether it means only that a female
cannot conceive without being deflorated. Considering
the emphasis with which, according to Spencer and Gillen,

---

[1] Frhr. von Reitzenstein shares the view here accepted ; comp.
his review of Mr. Hartland's " Primitive Paternity " in *Zeitschr. f.
Ethnologie*, 43 Jhg. (1911), p. 175.

[2] *Nat. Tr.*, p. 265.

[3] *Loc. cit.*, ii. p. 52, footnote 7.

[4] *Loc. cit.*, iii. p. xi.

the natives deny any causal connection between copulation and birth, the second supposition seems to be the
more probable. But even if the first supposition were the
right one, it does not imply any knowledge that a given
man has contributed to the body or soul of the child.
The latter, already formed (although diminutive in form)
enters the womb of a woman. We see therefore that
our general conclusion of page 209 is by no means
contradicted by this detail in the aboriginal beliefs.

(3) In the third place I would like to deal with the
question whether the totemic beliefs concerning conception contain the idea of any reincarnation of ancestors,
as this point will be subsequently of importance to us.
And on this important question there is controversy too.
Spencer and Gillen emphatically state : " In the whole of
this wide area, the belief that every living member of the
tribe is the reincarnation of a spirit ancestor is universal.
This belief is just as firmly held by the Urabunna people,
who count descent in the female line, as in the Arunta
and Warramunga, who count descent in the male line." [1]

On the other hand, the belief in reincarnation is expressly and explicitly denied by Strehlow and Leon-

---

[1] *Nor. Tr.*, p. xi. Compare also pp. 145, 606. Spencer and
Gillen's statement is corroborated by various other independent
authors, some of them being even critically disposed. The reincarnation of ancestors is asserted by the missionaries Teichelmann and Schürmann, in reference to the Adelaide tribe (compare below, p. 217, note 4). Mr. Thomas has shown (*Man*, 1904,
§ 68, pp. 99, 100) that the belief in reincarnation is implied in
the Rev. L. Schultze's statement. Mrs. Parker quotes also beliefs
containing the idea of reincarnation (*loc. cit.*, pp. 50, 56, 73, 89;
quoted by Mr. E. S. Hartland, *loc.cit.*, i. p.243). Mr. R. H. Mathews
also emphatically affirms the existence of a belief in reincarnation
amongst the Central and even all the other Australian tribes
(*Trans. R.S.N.S.W.*, 1906, xi. pp. 110 *sqq.*). He says : " In all
aboriginal tribes there is a deeply-seated belief in the reincarnation of their ancestors." And he gives illustrations of this belief
among the Arunta. Mr. Mathews also draws attention to a
series of analogous statements from older authors (Taplin, *loc.
cit.*, p. 88, Schürmann, *loc. cit.*, p. 235). Prof. B. Spencer has
ascertained the existence of ideas about reincarnation in his
recent investigations among the natives of the extreme North
Roper River to Port Darwin). *Athenæum*, Nov. 4, 1911, p. 562.

hardi : " Den Glauben an eine immer wiederkehrende Reincarnation dieses altjirangamitjina (= alcheringa of Spencer and Gillen), den Spencer and Gillen gefunden haben wollen, hat Herr Strehlow nicht feststellen können." [1] In another passage of the same work the expression of Spencer and Gillen, " in every tribe without exception there exists a firm belief in the reincarnation of ancestors," is simply designated as misleading (" irreführend ") by the editor (Frhr. v. Leonhardi).[2]

We seem here to be again at a loss. For behind the mere assertions of both parties there is a considerable amount of fact which seems to corroborate each of them. Spencer and Gillen do not give us bare statements. Such concrete and detailed accounts of beliefs as those quoted below [3] are very cogent. We see by them that Spencer and Gillen's assertion concerning the existence of reincarnation is the general expression of a series of positive facts ; as there cannot be any doubt as to the authenticity of the latter, the general assertion of our authors is convincing ! But if we inquire more precisely into the nature of this reincarnation we find certain " contradictions " and " inconsistencies " in these beliefs, and we can quite safely agree with Frhr. von Leonhardi that if we " take the expression exactly to the letter " [4] we are compelled to deny the existence of any ideas of reincarnation. The only objection is that any attempt to give " strict " or " exact " sense to aboriginal ideas is completely misplaced. The aborigines are not able to think exactly, and their beliefs do not possess any " exact meaning." And if an attempt be made to interpret them in this way, we shall always fail to understand them and to trace their social bearing. We must accept those beliefs as they stand in their quaint concreteness, full of contradictions and inconsistencies, and endeavour

[1] Bn. Leonhardi in Strehlow, i. Introduction (third page ; there is no pagination).
[2] Strehlow, ii. p. 57, end of the long footnote.
[3] Compare p. 216.
[4] *Loc. cit.*, ii. p. 56.

to mould our ideas upon the given folkloristic material, of which an adequate knowledge is indispensable for sociological purposes and gives us a very deep insight into the mechanism of different social groups. So, for instance, the aboriginal beliefs of reincarnation will be found to be of some importance as regards the idea of kinship.

But let us return to our analysis of this aboriginal idea of reincarnation. To define the word *exactly* the expression of Baron Leonhardi may be accepted; reincarnation means " that the given totemic ancestor himself continually undergoes rebirth." In other words the belief in reincarnation logically defined consists in a strict identification of a given man with a given ancestor. From this it is obvious that one would look in vain for such a belief amongst the Australian savages, who do not know anything of logic, and can neither affirm identity nor perceive contradictions.[1] Instead of identifying two things, they feel only a strong but mystical bond of union between them. In this sense the new-born child is obviously a reincarnation of a given ancestor. For it is " identical " with the spirit-child or *ratapa* of which it is the incarnation, and this again is " identical " with a given Abheringa : obviously using the word " identity " in the sense indicated above, *i. e.* that there is some mystical tie between the Alcheringa and the spirit-child which has emanated from him or her.[2] That this tie exists, we know from the data,[3] from those given by Strehlow as

[1] M. Lévy-Bruhl writes : " En appelant la mentalité primitive ' prélogique,' je veux seulement dire qu'elle ne s'astreint pas avant tout comme notre pensée, à s'abstenir de la contradiction. Elle obéit d'abord a la loi de participation."—*Loc. cit.*, p. 79.

[2] In primitive thinking the identification is accomplished not according to logical categories, but according to the *loi de participation* introduced by M. Lévy-Bruhl. (Compare foregoing footnote.) To this work the reader must be referred for a deeper insight into the standpoint adopted in the present discussion.

[3] This assertion ought to be proved by a detailed analysis of the beliefs mentioned. As the problem is of no immediate importance, this discussion cannot be undertaken. The aboriginal ideas of reincarnation have been treated from the point of view of the *loi de participation* by M. Lévy-Bruhl.—*Loc. cit.*, pp. 396 *sqq.*

well as from those of Spencer and Gillen.[1]   And consequently it may be said that the Central Australians regard
each man as the reincarnation of a given ancestor; this
being, of course, understood with the restriction here laid
down.   Thus, any doubt as to this point—namely that
all human beings are reincarnations of *Alcheringa ancestors*—may easily be set at rest.

There still remains, however, the question, much
more important to us, whether there be amongst these
tribes the belief in the reincarnation of *human ancestors*.
Strehlow's information seems absolutely to deny any
idea of repeated reincarnation;[2] a man after death
goes to the *ltjarilkna-ala*, where after a certain time
his ghost undergoes perfect and final destruction.[3]   A
man who has lived his life never returns.   I confess that
to assume amongst savages the existence of such a neatly
defined and categorically-formulated belief in absolute
destruction or annihilation seems to me rather suspicious;
and there is perhaps some misunderstanding of a rather
theoretical character on the part of the Rev. C. Strehlow.
Moreover, we are informed by this latter author that
besides this belief in annihilation there are ideas according to which the souls of " good " men go to heaven to
Altjira,[4] and the souls of the " bad " people are eaten up
by the *atna ntjkantja*.[5]   Consequently not all souls perish
after death, and reincarnation is from this standpoint

---

[1] Spencer and Gillen themselves in many places make statements that stand in direct contradiction with a theory of reincarnation *literally* understood. Frhr. von Leonhardi takes
the trouble to adduce several instances of these contradictions (ii. p. 56, footnote 1). They might easily be multiplied,
but as argued in the text they do not affect in the least the value
of the information. The description of these beliefs given by
Strehlow (*loc. cit.*, ii. pp. 51 *sqq.*), does not differ radically from
what we know about them from Spencer and Gillen, although
Strehlow's account is more detailed.

[2] *Loc. cit.*, ii. p. 56.   [3] *Loc. cit.*, i. 16, ii. 7.
[4] The Altjira is the " good god (?) of the Aranda," i. p. 2.
[5] I cannot help feeling that this very belief in future rewards
(by the *good god*) and punishment appears somewhat tinged by
Christian teachings.

not impossible. And even if there were some belief as to this annihilation, it might perfectly well be connected by the natives with the ideas of reincarnation. The primitive mind, as has often been urged, does not perceive contradictions. It is not to negative instances that we must look for an answer, but always to positive ones : if we do find indications of a belief, we are then sure that it exists, even if it were in contradiction with ever so many others. If we do not find it, we can say nothing, and especially we are not justified in proving its absence by showing that it stands in contradiction with any of the beliefs ascertained.

Now Spencer and Gillen adduce in several places concrete instances of beliefs which prove beyond doubt that the idea of the reincarnation of human beings actually exists in the Central tribes. As this point is of some importance in our present study, these instances must be brought forward. One of them is the belief that infants, who either die or are killed, soon undergo reincarnation. Such a belief exists among the Arunta,[1] among the Kaitish and Unmatjera.[2] And again, in another place, such a belief is reported to exist in all the tribes examined by Messrs. Spencer and Gillen.[3] That this belief is deeply rooted is shown by the fact that it serves as an excuse for the practice of infanticide; for the natives believe that the same child will soon undergo rebirth from the same mother. It might, nevertheless, be objected that here rebirth is undergone only by persons who died in infancy; and that this has little connection with the reincarnation of ancestors dead long ago. But, first, this belief is the proof of the existence of reincarnation ideas in general, and moreover there are better instances still. There has been found amongst the Urabunna the belief that a person at each reincarnation changes sex, class and totem.[4] The same belief in the alternation of sexes at each succes-

---

[1] *Nat. Tr.*, p. 51.
[2] *Nor. Tr.*, p. 506.
[3] *Ibid.*, p. 609.
[4] *Ibid.*, p. 148.

sive reincarnation is held amongst the Warramunga.[1]
The knowledge of these concrete and detailed beliefs
enables us to affirm without hesitation that the general
idea of the reincarnation of human beings exists among the
Central Australian tribes.[2] A mere assertion on the part
of our informants might leave some doubts; but if they
adduce these beliefs in detail, the doubts can be only as
to their trustworthiness; and this is out of the question
in the present case.   There are yet other facts confirming
the assumption we are dealing with. Messrs. Spencer
and Gillen give a detailed account of the wanderings and
doings of the ghost after death.[3] They say expressly
that the ghost after a time goes to a certain place, where
it awaits reincarnation. A similar belief in a land where
the souls of the dead await reincarnation has been found
in the Adelaide tribes.[4] So that, dividing the problem
of reincarnation into two questions—Is there among the
Central Australians (1) a belief in a reincarnation of the
Alcheringa ancestors? (2) a belief in the reincarnation of
human ancestors?—both must be answered in the
affirmative.

To sum up our somewhat extensive discussion of the
totemic beliefs of conception, we may say that the collective ideas of the Central and North Central Australian [5]
aborigines ignore expressly and explicitly any connection
of blood between a father and his child, and probably
greatly reduce the importance of the maternal blood tie;
that even allowing for the greatest amount of physiological
knowledge amongst these aborigines, there cannot be
any question of paternal consanguinity. We have seen
further that in all these Central and North Central tribes

---

[1] *Nor. Tr.*, p. 358, footnote, and p. 530.
[2] And probably among the Australian tribes in general.
[3] *Nat. Tr.*, p. 515.
[4] Compare Mr. Thomas' article in *Man* (1904), p. 99, §68, where
he quotes Teichelman and Schürmann. The widespread belief
that white men are dead people returned to life is a proof of the
existence of beliefs in reincarnation.
[5] Including the tribes recently investigated by Prof. B. Spencer.

(and possibly in many others too) there is an idea of reincarnation, not only of the Alcheringa, but also of the human ancestors; the word reincarnation being used in the sense indicated above, page 214.

So far the results regarding parental, and especially paternal, kinship are purely negative; there is between father and child no *consanguinity*.[1] But is there no kinship? According to the theory of kinship sketched above, individual parental kinship must be accepted as existing in the Central no less than in all the other Australian tribes, for the reasons already specified. And, as was said above, and will be discussed again, it is even possible on the basis of the evidence extant to give an account of the emotional character of this relation. The greatest difficulty is to know what idea the aborigines themselves form concerning it; in other words, how is fatherhood determined in the collective psychology of the natives? Some indications at least of what we look for may be found.

If we examine the different items of the folk-lore, traditions, beliefs and customs of the Arunta, we can at first sight hardly discover any ideas that bear upon our subject. Fortunately, in the case of some of the Northern tribes, we are in possession of information which appears highly suggestive in regard to our problem. The Gnanji and Umbaia tribes of the Northern territory share the belief in totemic conception with all the more Southern tribes. But amongst them the child is always of the same totem as its father, wherever conception may have taken place. These tribes have a theory to reconcile these two beliefs that apparently are incompatible, viz. descent of totem in paternal line and birth by incarnation of a spirit-child.[2] They believe that spirits of the husband's totem follow the wife wherever the married couple may go, and that one of these spirit individuals enters the woman's body whenever it pleases; no spirit-

---

[1] Compare above, pp. 176 *sqq:*, for discussion of this term.
[2] *See* Spencer and Gillen, *Nor. Tr.*, pp. 169 *sqq.*

child of any other totem could enter her. The infant is therefore always of the husband's totem, and it is the *reincarnation of this individual spirit* which has chosen to follow the man and his wife on their wanderings. In this belief there are, undoubtedly, contained ideas of a strong tie of sympathy, affinity or kinship between the father and his future child. In the first place the spirit-child, which undergoes reincarnation, belongs to the totem of the husband; but that does not as yet create any individual relation between the father and the child, although it constitutes a bond of totemic kinship between them.

Nevertheless it must be remembered that the individual spirit-child, which sometimes has even to follow the married couple on their wanderings, chooses its mother on account of her husband and not in all probability on her own; for it is not of her totem, and it is improbable that the natives assume ties of preference between two beings of different clans, if there are at hand two members of the same clan—the father and the reincarnated child. Now this act of choosing, this special preference of a certain woman on account of her husband, clearly points to a very close tie between father and child. Unfortunately, the writers who report the beliefs in question have not investigated the side we have discussed, and as all hypothetical inferences are dangerous in sociology, we must consider this belief to be highly suggestive but nothing more. Nevertheless, setting one against another the two facts—the social existence of a close tie between father and child on the one hand (as we can affirm it on the ground of the emotional character of this relationship), and the existence of a belief that the reincarnated spirit-child is of the father's totem, and is, so to say, attached to him in his roaming life—it is difficult not to suspect some inner connection between them. Now, if our supposition is right, and if this belief has its social influence in defining fatherhood, it may be said that in the Gnanji and Umbaia tribes the essence of fatherhood is seen in the fact that a given man has determined a given spirit-child to take up its abode in his wife's body, and that the close tie of kinship lies in this mutual affinity or attraction exercised by the man on the spirit-child. This is hypothetical, but we may note another statement of Spencer and Gillen's which appears to bear upon our subject and corroborates our first hypothetical assumption.

We read that in the three coastal tribes of the Northern territory—Binbinga, Anula and Mara—the natives are very clear upon the point that the spirit-children know which are the right *lubra* for them respectively to enter, and each one deliberately chooses his or her own mother.[1] Now descent in these tribes is strictly paternal both as regards totems and classes.[2] This means that the father determines the class and totem of his child. We must assume, therefore, that the spirit-child chooses its mother chiefly in regard to her husband, *i. e.* its future father. It may, therefore, be once more repeated here that such an act of preference involves the idea of a very close tie between the spirit-child and the father; whether this idea is a real kinship idea, that is, whether it has its positive influence upon the different functions of the relationship in question, is not mentioned by our informants, and it would be quite vain to speculate upon the subject. But again, putting the two items—*i. e.* the belief in question and the existence of a close tie of kinship—side by side, it is difficult to deny that a connection between them appears very probable.

A similar social part appears also to be played by the most general belief connected with the question of birth—the belief in reincarnation. The question whether these beliefs may be assumed in the Arunta has been discussed at length, and an affirmative conclusion has been arrived

---

[1] *Nor. Tr.*, p. 174. The same is related in the recent note of Prof. B. Spencer (*Athenæum*, Nov. 4, 1911, p. 562). We read there : " The spirit-children know into what woman they must enter."

[2] *Nor. Tr.*, pp. 119, 172. Compare N. W. Thomas, *loc. cit.* Map No. 1, facing p. 40.

at. Moreover, it has been seen that this belief appears to be almost universal in Australia, and that it is reported by many writers. There seems to be some reason for assuming that this belief may possibly have some bearing on the aboriginal ideas of kinship. As the child is an incarnation not only of a spirit individual, and consequently of an Alcheringa ancestor, but also in the majority of cases of a series of human ancestors, it comes into this world with an already formed personality, and it stands in a definite relation to an Alcheringa ancestor; to a Nanja place and to a given Churinga; it has its place in a totemic group and in a class. We may, therefore, reasonably assume that among other attributes the child brings its individual kinship, derived from some vague ideas about a former life, with it into the world. In other words, the child is probably supposed already at its birth to stand in a definite kinship relation (dating from a mutual previous existence) towards its individual parents. In fact, if the child comes into the world as a member of other social groups, it may be taken as very probable that it comes as the individual kinsman of its father and mother. Father, mother and child have already lived in the past; they may already have stood in a very close relationship; perhaps they have even been members of the same individual family.

This supposition may appear at first sight highly hypothetical; plausible perhaps, but nothing more; yet there are other facts which in considerable measure support it. There is the belief that the spirit part of a child which is killed, or dies in infancy, comes to ife again by and by, and undergoes incarnation in the same woman.[1] In this belief we see that the ties of individual kinship, once established, do not give way after death, and that they determine the rebirth of the child. This belief may be a special case of a more general one, viz. that rebirth in all cases is determined by ties of individual kinship established in a former life. There is yet another

[1] Compare above, p. 216.

series of beliefs leading more directly to the same conclusion.   I mean the well-known fact that white men
were considered to be returned dead relatives, and
treated accordingly. We know that there were several
cases in which the life of a man was saved by this belief.
The best known is the case of Buckley, a run-away
convict, who lived about thirty years among the natives.
He was treated with the greatest kindness and tenderness
by his " relatives." [1] The same tokens of affection are
related to have been shown to a settler in the vicinity
of Perth by his " parents," who merely to see him
would travel more than sixty leagues through a country
which was in parts dangerous.[2]   In another place we are
informed that a white convict identified with a dead
relative was presented with a piece of land which
" belonged to him by right." Similar statements are
numerous.[3] In order to establish the relevancy of these
facts to our problem, it may be remarked that the most
important features of the beliefs in question are (1) that

[1] J. Morgan, *Life and Adventures of William Buckley* (Hobart,
1852).   The value of this book and especially of the ethnographic
information contained in it, has been disputed by Bonwick.   See
J. Bonwick, *William Buckley, the Wild White Man* (Melbourne,
1856), p. 7.   I have not used Morgan's book as a source.   The
life-story of Morgan told therein is admittedly authentic.

[2] Stokes, quoted by M. Lévy-Bruhl, *loc. cit.*, p. 400.

[3] Another instance where a white woman was received by a
man as his daughter and accepted into the tribe and into all her
rights and relationships, is told by Macgillivray, *loc. cit.*, i., p. 303.
She was shipwrecked, came into the power of the natives, and, of
course, lived in a very miserable condition.   Her only comfort
was derived from the man who imagined that she was his reborn
daughter.   Henderson says that among the blacks of New South
Wales the belief in white men being dead relatives who had
returned was quite general.   Such white men were accepted into
the tribe and cordially treated.   *Loc. cit.*, p. 161.

For other statements about white men being reincarnated dead
relatives see Wilhelmi, *Trans. R.S.V.*, v. p. 189. Br. Smyth, *Aborigines of Victoria*, ii. p. 224.   (Article by Chauncy) *ibid.*, p. 307
(article by Howitt).   R. H. Mathews, *Jour. and Proc. R.S.N.S.W.*,
xxxviii. (1905), p. 349.   W. E. Roth, Bull. 5th, p. 16.   R. H.
Mathews, *Jour. and Proc. R.S.N.S.W.*, xl. pp. 113, 114.   Earl,
loc. cit., p. 241. Howitt, *Nat. Tr.*, pp. 445, 446. The latter says
that the natives were " ready to do anything " for the white
people, once they recognized in them their relatives.

white men are identified with a given dead individual, (2) that they get then *ipso facto* a definite place in the tribe, in the local group, and—what is most important as regards the present question—in the individual family. The belief that people after death become white may account for the identification of white men with the dead. But the fact that in ever so many cases a white man was identified with a certain individual, and became thereby entitled to a social position, implies some additional beliefs. One of these beliefs is the idea of rebirth or reincarnation that we have established above in another way. The other collective idea, which must be assumed in order to explain the ease and readiness with which feelings of affection as well as worldly goods were bestowed upon these alleged relatives, is that in the ordinary form in which dead men return to this life, *i. e.* in reincarnation by birth, each individual brings with him, or her, full social position, including individual relationship. And this is the point at issue in the present discussion. The fact that white men were recognized as dead relatives compels us to assume that children—who were considered as reborn men—were also accepted as relatives. If the natives had not their mind turned that way, if they were not used to identify every new member of their society with some ancestor of their own, could they do it so easily in the case of white men, who were so different from them, and could not present any striking physical similarity ? Of course this inference is not a cogent one. But putting side by side all the facts we have gathered : the belief in reincarnation of the dead ; the easy recognition of dead relatives in white men ; and the promptitude with which, in some cases, the latter were given their places in society, their hunting-grounds, their parents, relatives, and so on—all this allows us to affirm with a high degree of probability that a new-born child was looked upon as a reincarnated member of the tribe, and that an intimate kinship between him and his parents was considered to be established

on the ground of kinship in a previous life. Is not
the parental affection which was bestowed on some
of the white men one of the most astonishing traits
in the evidence in question ? Of course white men
were considered to be immediate reincarnations, or
rather a return of the dead in ghost condition; whereas
rebirth was a much longer process, and was, perhaps,
considered as reincarnation of a long-dead ancestor.
Consequently the ties of kinship between a white man
and his "relatives" were the repetition of an actual
relation which had already existed for the native in his
life. Whereas if a reborn child is considered, as we here
assume, to be a "previous" kinsman, this kinship is
based upon a relation obtaining in some former existence.
But it may be urged that if we deal with aboriginal
collective psychology no very clear ideas can be expected. The only thing that we assumed here was that
the ideas of rebirth, combined with some other specific
Australian beliefs, suggest very strongly that children
might have been both held, and felt to be, kindred, on
the ground that they come with some sort of ready-made
personality; and on the ground that, as E. S. Hartland
argues, rebirth is the result of some spontaneous action
of the creature to be reborn. I think that if we ask
for the source of the widespread belief in white men being
returned ghosts, and especially for the readiness and
ease with which they were accepted into the family
and into the tribe—we must presuppose some beliefs
and institutions to account for it, and the explanation
proposed above seems to me very plausible.[1] But the

---

[1] Similar ideas have been enunciated by M. Lévy-Bruhl, *loc. cit.*,
pp. 388–402. Some of the Australian facts are quoted and
interpreted there in an analogous way. M. Lévy-Bruhl naturally
does not enter into as many particulars as has been necessary here,
but his conclusion, "l'enfant-esprit qui se réincarne est déjà dans
une relation déterminée avec le père et la mère qui lui donnent
naissance," is nearly identical with what we have endeavoured to
prove here. Perhaps the word "relation" does not quite coincide
with what we are especially concerned with in this place, *i. e.*
individual kinship, and has a wider, more general meaning.

best example of the ideas of kinship of the magic order is to be found among the tribes studied and described by W. E. Roth.

Before we proceed to the North Queensland tribes, there may be mentioned some customs of the *couvade* type, referring to the Central tribes. These customs, as has been said above, express an intimate connection of a mystic character between father and child. They also involve a considerable amount of paternal affection and care for the welfare of the offspring, as they expose the father to various inconveniences, privations and hardships for the benefit of the child. Thus we read that among the Central tribes the father has to observe certain taboos and restrictions during the pregnancy of his wife, otherwise she would have a difficult confinement.[1] This only shows a connection between the behaviour of the man and the act of birth. But we read in another place that the non-observance of certain hunting taboos by the man during the pregnancy of his wife would have baleful consequences for the offspring.[2] We are informed, also, of a few functions of parental kin expressed in different customs which accentuate the intimacy of this relation. Thus the mother plays some part in the initiation ceremonies,[3] as well as in mourning and funerals. Concerning the important social functions of the father, I may quote what Mr. R. H. Mathews writes about the Central tribes : " The privilege of working incantations, making rain, performing initiatory ceremonies, and other important functions, descends from the men of the tribe to the sons." [4] Moreover all the ceremonies in common with totems " are likewise handed down through the men." [5] We see from this that many important social functions descend from father to son. Messrs. Spencer and Gillen report that the position of the Alatunja is hereditary amongst the

[1] *Nat. Tr.*, pp. 466, 467.   [2] *Nor. Tr.*, pp. 344, 607.
[3] *Nat. Tr.*, p. 250.   [4] *Trans. R.S.N.S.W.* (1907), p. 75.
[5] *Ibid.*, p. 77.

Arunta.[1] And similarly the position of the headman is hereditary amongst the Northern tribes.[2] All these facts serve on the one hand socially to define individual kinship, and on the other to show that there exist certain ideas of a mystic bond between father and child. How far these ideas, as expressed in the customs of the *couvade* type, harmonize with the ideas dealt with above, it is quite impossible to know. It may be said that in both respects we have hints showing the existence of ideas on kinship, but that we can by no means go beyond mere supposition when we try to reconstruct these ideas and to find some mutual connection. Let us now pass to the other tribes.

The belief in a supernatural cause of pregnancy is spread not only all over the Central and North Central area, *i. e.* among all the tribes included in the researches of Spencer and Gillen.[3] The same ignorance of physiological fatherhood is found in the whole of the Northern territory, in Queensland, and probably in West Australia. We read that among the tribes of the North-West territory of South Australia (Port Darwin and Daly River) " conception is not regarded as a direct result of cohabitation."[4] And we read in Dr. Frazer's new work : " The view is shared by all the tribes of Central and Northern Australia. In point of fact, I am informed by the Bishop of North Queensland (Dr. Frodsham) that the opinion is held by all the tribes with which he is acquainted both in North Queensland and in Central Australia, including the Arunta; not only are the natives in their savage states ignorant of the true cause of conception, but they do not readily believe it even after their admission into mission stations, and their incredulity has to be reckoned with in the efforts of the clergy to introduce a higher standard of sexual morality among them." [5] This is a very strong

---

[1] *Nat. Tr.*, p. 10.   [2] *Nor. Tr.*, p. 23.   [3] *Ibid.*, p. 330.
[4] H. Basedow, in *Trans. R.S.S.A.*, xxxi. p. 4, of the reprint quoted by Prof. Frazer, *Tot. and Exog.*, i. p. 576. This has been recently verified by Prof. B. Spencer; compare above, p. 209, footnote 1.   [5] *Tot. and Exog.*, i. pp. 576, 577.

proof of the depth of these beliefs, and of the absolute ignorance of the natives on this point.[1] In the South-Eastern region this belief is to be found as far as the Northern part of New South Wales. We have statements of Mrs. Parker [2] which, although not very clear, seem at least to imply a great amount of magical beliefs as to procreation, if not complete ignorance of the physiological part borne by the father. With regard to the Western tribes, Mrs. Bates writes in a letter to Mr. Lang [3] : " They did not believe that procreation had anything to do with conception."

That in spite of this absence of any kind of consanguinity, especially in the father's case, there exists in the Queensland tribes an individual kinship relation between both parents and their children, is clear from the statements collected on page 245, and from the conclusion on page 249, to which the reader may be referred, as well as to the theoretical conclusion on page 198. Looking at the rich and interesting collection of folk-lore of these tribes given by Mr. W. E. Roth, it will be possible to find the way in which fatherhood is determined by the animistic ideas of the aborigines. As just said, among the North-West Central Queensland tribes, the causal nexus between conception and copulation is not known. We read in Roth that, according to aboriginal ideas, there are several ways in which a child may enter a woman's body : it may be inserted into her in a dream ; she may be told by a man that she will be pregnant and so on. But in whatever mode the child has come, " the recognized husband accepts it as his own without demur." [4] This phrase seems to point to the fact that a man has certain ways of recognizing a

[1] That the ignorance in question was complete is also the opinion of Mr. E. S. Hartland, *loc. cit.*, ii. pp. 275, 276. He adduces several reasons and statements in support of it. Compare also what we said above about the completeness of this ignorance among the Central tribes.

[2] *Loc. cit.*, pp. 50, 61, 98.   [3] See *Man* (1906), p. 180.

[4] Roth, *Bull.* V. p. 22, § 81.

child as his own, and ideas under which he conceives
this tie.

In fact we read that man possesses several " souls " or
vital principles.   One of them, *ngai*, leaves the body soon
after death; if the deceased was a male his *ngai* " passes
into his children, both boys and girls equally." The *ngai*
of a female goes to her sister or passes away.   Nobody
has a *ngai* before his father dies, but receives his father's
ngai after the latter's death.[1]   This is an important
connection, which by itself might very well serve to establish the most intimate tie of kinship.   The child is
supposed to be its father's spirit's heir.   It shares in his
most personal and individual element.   Is this spiritual
communion not something quite as strong and deep as
any community of blood ?

In another tribe of this area there is a similar belief
concerning the *choi* (another " soul ").   The aborigines of
Pennefather River believe that babies are made out of
swamp mud and then inserted into the wombs of women
by a being called Anjea.   Now it is particularly important
for us to note that Anjea animates the baby with a piece
of its father's spirit if it is a boy, and with a piece of its
father's sister's spirit if it is a girl.   For each new baby
Anjea provides a new piece of spirit.   But he does not
take these pieces from the spirit of the living father or
his sister.   He has a special source from which to take it;
he takes it from the father's or father's sister's afterbirth.
When a child is born a portion of its spirit stays in its
afterbirth.   Hence the grandmother takes the afterbirth
and buries it in the sand, and marks the place by thrust-
ing sticks into the ground.   So when Anjea comes along
and sees it, he knows where to look for the father's (or
father's sister's) spirit, which he wants in order to animate
the new baby.   And in this way all babies are animated
by a spiritual part of their father or paternal aunts.[2]

---

[1] Roth, *Bull.* V. p. 18, § 68.   This refers to the Pennefather
River tribes.
[2] *Ibid.*

Both these examples illustrate perfectly well the general definition of kinship ideas we have given above. Here the relation between father and child is established in the native ideas by a purely spiritual connection. But obviously this connection is a very important one. The deep tie between a man and his child is here explicitly indicated and not inferred by us, as in the foregoing cases, in which we could only state that the beliefs and facts point to such a tie. In the present case the father's spirit is the material from which the child's soul is to be built up. It is not his bodily germ that procreates the child, but his spiritual germ. What does it matter that the mother gives birth to the child? The latter is animated by the father's (or father's sister's) spirit, and this spiritual connection is of course as strong a bond of kinship as can possibly be imagined.

There is in the second of these examples a complication produced by the fact that a female child is not animated by her father's, but by her father's sister's, spirit. But this complication is more apparent than real. We must always remember that the aborigines do not think in clearly defined ideas, and that there is always a question rather of some broad emotional connection than of a tie logically apprehended. And here the connection between the female children and their father is broadly marked by the spiritual tie between his sister and the children. It may be said that " spiritual propagation " follows the male line exclusively, for all children are animated by a spirit taken from their father or his sister.

We have still a few examples to quote where there appears to be involved a tie between father and child established on other grounds than the sexual act. In some of the North Queensland tribes (Cairns district) " the acceptance of food from a man by a woman was not merely regarded as a marriage ceremony, but as the actual cause of conception." [1] A similar belief obtains

[1] J. G. Frazer, *Tot. and Exog.*, i. p. 577, on the authority of Bishop Frodsham.

among the Larrekiya and Wogait of Port Darwin. " The old men say that there is an evil spirit who takes babies from a big fire and places them in the wombs of women, who must then give birth to them. When in the ordinary course of events a man is out hunting and kills game or gathers vegetable food, he gives it to his wife, who must eat it, believing that the food will cause her to conceive and bring forth a child. When the child is born, it may on no account partake of the particular food which produced conception until it has got its first teeth." [1] In these cases we might look also for some material from which the ideas of individual paternity might have been evolved, but this is a supposition merely, which obviously is much less well founded than our inferences referring to the Central and North Central tribes.

Let us turn to another portion of the continent, to the South-Eastern tribes, where the natives have to a certain extent inverse ideas on procreation. They seem to know that conception is due to copulation. But they exaggerate the father's part. The children are begotten " by him exclusively; the mother receives only the germ and nurtures it; the aborigines . . . never for a moment feel any doubt . . . that the children originate solely from the male parent, and only owe their infantine nurture to their mother." [2] This theory is not a logical and consistent one, but none of the aboriginal views possess these qualities ! But this theory of procreation is quite clear and categorical in acknowledging exclusively what seems to the native mind important for the formation of consanguineous ties in the act of procreation. Let us adduce the examples in detail, as they are very instructive. The Wirdajuri nation [3] believe that the child " emanates from the father solely, being only nurtured by its mother." There is a strong tie of kinship between the child and the father; the latter nevertheless has not the right to dispose

---

[1] H. Basedow, *loc. cit.*, quoted by Frazer, *Tot. and Exog.*, i. p. 576.

[2] Howitt, *J.A.I.*, xii. p. 502.

[3] Cameron, *J.A.I.*, xiv. p. 351.

of his daughter in marriage; that is done by the mother
and the mother's brother. We see here that curiously
enough strong paternal consanguinity coincides with
weakening of the *patria potestas* (provided the information be accurate on both points). For disposal of the
daughter is one of the chief features of a parent's authority
over the child. Among the Wolgal the child belongs to
the father, and he only " gives it to his wife to take care
of for him." [1] This is probably an interpretation of the
facts of procreation. In this tribe the father disposes
of his daughter; in fact " he could do what he liked "
with her on the ground of his exclusive right to the child.
Here, apparently, the ideas on kinship enhance the
paternal authority. A strong proof of this unilateral
paternal consanguinity is given yet more in detail in the
case of the Kulin tribes. There, according to a native
expression, " the child comes from the man, the woman
only takes care of it." [2] And when once an old man
wished to emphasize his right and authority over his son
he said : " Listen to me ! I am here, and there you
stand with my body." [3] This is clearly a claim to
kinship on the basis of consanguinity. It is interesting
to note that in the examples just quoted this consanguineous kinship seems to give some claims to authority.
Analogously amongst the Yuin the child belonged to his
father " because his wife merely takes care of his children
for him." [4]

Withal this information leaves us in the dark about
the detailed working of these ideas. Especially we are
not quite clear whether the assertions of " being of the
same body," of " belonging to him," etc., do actually
refer to the act of procreation, whether they form an
interpretation of this act, or whether they have quite a
different basis; although it seems from the expressions
quoted above that the first alternative is the right one.
On the other hand, when we read that the mother only

---

[1] Aboriginal phrase quoted by Howitt, *Nat. Tr.*, p. 198.
[2] Howitt, *Nat. Tr.*, p. 255.
[3] *Ibid.*   [4] *Ibid.*, p. 263.

nurtures the child, that she merely takes care of it and so
on, does it mean that the aboriginal mind *decrees* or
interprets that during pregnancy the mother is a kind of
nurse only, that she is the soil in which the father has
deposited the seed ?   And as the relation between the
plant and the seed is closer than that between the plant
and the soil, so the relation between father and child is
nearer than that between mother and child ?   All this is
left to hypothesis, strongly supported by the statements,
but unfortunately not affirmed by them in a clear and
unambiguous way.   We are not at all sure whether all
these ideas, instead of being theories of the act of impreg-
nation, have not some mystic, legendary basis like the
beliefs of the Queenslander dealt with above.

A survey of different points of Australian folk-lore has
been made in order to find some kinship ideas corresponding to the definition given on page 183.   From all
the results obtained, the most certain and best founded
one is the negative fact that the majority of the Australian
tribes are wholly ignorant of the physiological process of
procreation.   This result, although at first sight a negative
one, leads, when viewed in the proper light, to sociological
conclusions of some importance.   In regard to the discussion on consanguinity (given pp. 176 *sqq.*), it follows from
this fact that we cannot speak of paternal consanguinity
among these tribes in the social sense of this word,[1] and
that the individual tie of kinship, which does nevertheless
exist between father and child, must be conceived of by the
natives in some different way.   This conclusion is also
very important, for it obviously tears asunder the intimate
connection between the sexual side of marriage and kinship, a connection that has often been assumed hitherto.
The lack of sexual exclusiveness found in Australia does
not affect the structure of the individual family, of which
kinship is the index.   Waiving the question whether
this holds good for primitive mankind in general, it may

---

[1] It has been already remarked above on page 179, that there
can be no question of physiological consanguinity for other
reasons.

be assumed as quite a final result for the majority of Australian tribes.

The positive ideas of kinship enumerated in this survey fulfil the two conditions set up on page 183; they refer to the individual relation between father and child,[1] and they affirm a close tie between the two. But in order to prove that such ideas are sociologically relevant ideas of kinship, it must yet be shown that they possess some social functions; that is to say, that they play an essential part in the collective formulation of the various norms regulating individual parental kinship. Now it was not possible to find any data on this point, so this gap remains unfilled, and therefore the results arrived at here must be considered as incomplete. It was necessary to introduce the conjectural assumption that all the facts known which give sociological evidence of individual parental kinship stand in close connection with the beliefs in question. Nevertheless, this assumption is neither arbitrary nor scientifically barren, as far as I see. It may first be remarked that the complete absence in our ethnographic information of any attempt to connect the data of folk-lore and the facts of sociology is not astonishing at all, as it is the consequence of one of the shortcomings in social science at the present day. This lack is due to reasons connected with the ethnographer and not with the material. The intimate relation which must exist between social beliefs and social functions was quite a sufficient justification for the introduction of this assumption. Moreover, this assumption, although hypothetical, lies quite within the limits of verification. A conjectural assumption referring to facts which lie necessarily outside the reach of observation, incurs much more the risk of scientific barrenness. But this cannot be the case with new points of view, the enunciation of which imposes itself as an inevitable logical inference, and which, being capable of verification, may serve as a fertile working hypothesis.

[1] Defined at first only as members of the same individual family.

CHAPTER VII

PARENTS AND CHILDREN

I

CONSIDERATION may first here be given to the cares and benefits a child receives from its mother during the first few years of its infancy. These facts constitute a very strong bond of union between the child and its nurse. Suckling is a physiological tie between the child and the mother, and next to the fact of birth it marks very strongly the individuality of this relation. Group motherhood has therefore never been a very popular idea and has never found a favourable reception amongst sociologists. We saw above, however, that it is very probable that the facts of birth may lack any social significance in the native mind. If it be further possible to imagine in the same tribe suckling performed, according to Dr. Rivers's suggestion,[1] not by the actual mother, but by a group of kindred women, group motherhood would be quite comprehensible in such tribes.

In Australia, however, suckling seems to be strictly individual. This might indeed be inferred in the first place from the aboriginal mode of living. Communism in suckling and rearing a small child would involve a complete communism in life; and we know that unless two women are wives of the same man, they are to a great extent isolated in daily life. It is also highly improbable that in the two or three families which are roaming together there would be always a woman at hand who could help the other in these cares.

There are several other reasons which still more strongly

_____
[1] Compare above, p. 6.

support our view. The best argument may be deduced
from the statements referring to infanticide. It is
practised amongst all Australian natives. One of the
chief reasons given for it is that the mother cannot possibly
suckle and carry two children at one time, especially as
children are not weaned before their third to fifth year.
If there were a custom of common suckling and nursing
a child, and another woman who would replace the mother
in her functions could be easily found, the practice of
infanticide could scarcely be attributed to the above-
mentioned reasons. Let us adduce a few statements.

Statements.—Infanticide is carried on among the Lower
Darling natives to prevent the toils and troubles of carrying
and caring for too many children. The mother's brother
decides if the child should be killed or not.[1]

Amongst the Encounter Bay natives " no mother will
venture to bring up more than two children, because she
considers that the attention which she would have to devote
to them would interfere with what she regards as the duty
to her husband in searching for roots, etc." [2]

Amongst the Adelaide tribes " female infants at birth are
not infrequently put to death for the sake of more valuable
boys who are still being suckled." [3]

As justification of infanticide " women plead that they
cannot suckle and carry two children together." [4] It is
clear from this statement that the impossibility of suckling
more than one child at a time is given as justification for
infanticide by the *natives themselves;* and that it is not only
an inference of the observer.

Infanticide was practised among the Port Lincoln tribes.
" In extenuation of this horrible practice the women allege
that they cannot suckle and carry two babies at once." [5] This
statement also quite unmistakably points to the fact that
children were suckled and attended by their own mother.

Bennett writes that among the New South Wales natives
women practice infanticide in order to avoid too much trouble
in carrying their infants about.[6]

---

[1] Bonney, *J.A.I.*, xiii. p. 125.
[2] Meyer in Woods, pp. 186, 187.
[3] Wyatt in Woods, p. 162.
[4] Chas. Wilhelmi, quoted by Br. Smyth, i. p. 51. (Port Lincoln
Tribes.)
[5] Schürmann in Woods, p. 224.
[6] *Loc. cit.*, i. pp. 123, 124.

Another statement, maintaining still more strongly the view
that only the mother suckled her child, is that of Collins.[1]
He says that he knew two instances in which infants were
killed by the father at their mother's grave, the reason alleged
being that as no one else could be found to suckle the child
and to rear it it must have died a worse death. Collins
supposes that this is a general custom.

Gason states that among the Dieri nearly thirty per cent.
of the children were destroyed by their mothers at birth to
avoid the cares and trouble of rearing.[2]

"The Arunta native does not hesitate to kill a child—
always directly it is born—if there be an older one still in
need of nourishment from the mother; and suckling is continued up to the age of three years and even older."[3] And
again: "The child is killed . . . when the mother is . . .
unable to rear it owing to there being a young child whom
she is still feeding."[4]

Among the Kabi and Wakka: "The motive for infanticide
with these tribes could not be to save food in times of dearth,
for the food supply was constant and plentiful. It would
be mainly, if not entirely, that mothers might escape the
irksomeness of nursing and caring for infants and of carrying
them on their frequent journeys."[5]

Mrs. D. M. Bates writes that when a mother died at childbirth the infant was put to death.[6] We are not informed
what reasons the natives gave for this practice; but most
probably they are the same as those mentioned by Collins.

All this evidence makes it nearly impossible to suppose
that suckling, carrying the baby and caring for it, was
the task of a group of women. For then it would not be
necessary to kill the infant at the death of its mother, or
to kill it when there was another one to be suckled, as the
toils could easily be shared by the other women of the
group. The assumption we are now able to draw,
namely that the mother always suckles and nurses her
own child, is of great importance.[7]

---

[1] Collins, i. pp. 607, 608.   [2] In Woods, p. 258.
[3] Spencer and Gillen, *Nat. Tr.*, p. 264.   [4] *Ibid.*, p. 51.
[5] Mathew, p. 166.   [6] *Loc. cit.*, p. 50.
[7] It is very important to note that this individual rearing is,
in all probability, deeply connected with the aboriginal mode
of life; viz. their scattered manner of living in small groups and
their roaming habits. Both these latter seem to be, on the other
hand, dependent upon the economic conditions of the stage of

Amongst the Australian aborigines suckling establishes undoubtedly much stronger bonds between mother and child than amongst civilized races, for it lasts much longer. As we saw and shall see in a few statements, the child is never weaned before its third year, and sometimes suckling lasts much longer.   Between a bigger child and its mother this constant dependence upon each other must necessarily create a strong bond of union.   The child must be continually with its mother.   During infancy it is carried by her in a pouch or bag on the shoulders.   Afterwards it accompanies her on all her wanderings and in all her work.   A great addition to her work is the continuous care she must display towards it.   This will be exemplified in our statements referring to the economic division of labour.   To sum up, we may say that natural necessities of nurture and of the earliest cares, combined with the aboriginal mode of living, make the child absolutely dependent on the personal, individual help it receives from its mother, and creates therefore an intimate relation between the two.

This is not so much in evidence as regards the relationship between the father and child.   But here it must be remembered that owing to the character of the native mode of living the man lives in close contact and to a great extent in isolation with his wife, and consequently also with his wife's children.   Some of our statements show that he shares to a certain extent in the cares and labours connected with carrying children, feeding them, etc.; he seems to have a great affection towards them and never to treat them with severity.   So that we may infer that the general character of his feelings is of the same description as that of the mother's, *i. e.* one of parental love and attachment.

---

primitive hunting and fishing, and it may be assumed that all lower races have passed through, broadly speaking, the same circumstances of life; it is, therefore, probable that the fact of common nursing can never have taken place in very low societies. I do not think, consequently, that Dr. Rivers's hypothesis, basing group motherhood on communism in suckling and rearing, can be accepted even in its general form.

II

An attempt will be made to illustrate by a series of statements all these characteristics of domestic life as far as they embrace the relations of parents to children. The chief points of inquiry will be : Is there between parents and children any kind of affection ? What is the general character of the treatment of children by parents ? Are rudiments of education given by father or mother to their offspring ? In what way does the position of the father differ from that of the mother—is there any special trait of severity ? In what consists the paternal authority and how does it show itself ? Is there any strong difference made between male and female children ?

Statements.—" In infancy the young Kurnai is an object of love and pride to its father and mother. From observation of various tribes in far distant parts of Australia, I can assert confidently that love for their children is a marked feature in the aboriginal character. I cannot recollect having ever seen a parent beat or cruelly use a child ; and a short road to the good-will of parents is, as amongst us, by noticing and admiring their children." The greatest grief is exhibited at the death of a child by all the relatives in a camp. These observations refer as well to the Kurnai and the other South-Eastern tribes, as to the Dieri, of whom the author gives an illustrative story.[1] The boy lives with his parents and "is very much under the control of his mother."—This statement is very valuable. It gives us the opinion of perhaps our best Australian observer on the psychology of parental feelings; it refers to all the tribes known to Howitt, *i. e.* to a very extensive area. And it states in plain terms that the feelings of love and affection for children which form the chief characteristic of parental relations are to be found with an intensity which is as strong as that prevailing in our society. In another place the same author quotes an instance " of a mother watching her sick child and refusing all food, and when it died she was inconsolable." [2]

Curr says that among the Bangerang the father had absolute authority over his children.[3] In another place he says that the father had to decide in case of infanticide and in every more important occasion of the child's life.[4] But we

---

[1] Howitt, *Kam. and Kurn.*, p. 189.
[2] Howitt, *Nat. Tr.*, p. 766.
[3] *Recollections*, p. 278.   [4] Curr, *A.R.*, i. p. 76.

read : " Parents were much attached to their children and rarely punished or corrected them." Not only did they not control them (although occasionally a child was beaten in a fit of anger),[1] but " they were habitually indulged in every way; and as a consequence, in case of the boys at least, grew up as self-willed, thorough little tyrants as can well be imagined." [2]

In his general book on Australia the same author gives us some more information on family life. The father makes small weapons as toys for his sons. The children are seldom chastised and they are very independent. The real training of the boys begins when they leave their parents' camp and undergo the series of initiations.[3] These statements point also unmistakably to feelings of attachment and love, which are, as we tried to prove above, the very essence of family ties. The father seems to care as much as the mother for his children's education, and he is very kind and lenient to them.

As a crude and pathetic example of maternal love there is the case reported by Angas, of a mother carrying for ten years the corpse of her dead child.[4] Similar cases are reported by Howitt about the Kurnai.[5]

We find many statements referring to this subject in the compilation of Br. Smyth. I mention them only shortly, as the author was never directly acquainted with the aboriginal life, and we value him only when he quotes some little-known authorities, or gives actual facts gathered for him by his correspondents. He speaks of the heavy task of a woman having to carry her babe, besides all the other work and trouble of a journey.[6] The father occasionally nurses the baby too and is very fond of it.[7] The child is suckled for three years; it is carried in an opossum rug during infancy and attended to solely by its mother.[8] A description of the way in which an opossum rug is dried is given.[9] In another passage the same author speaks again of the general kindness, affection and indulgence of parents to children, as of a well-known fact. He adds besides that the parents were very judicious in the treatment of their children.[10]

---

[1] A similar statement is given by Spencer and Gillen, *Nat. Tr.*, p. 51.

[2] *Recollections*, p. 252.   [3] *A.R.*, i. p. 71.

[4] *Loc. cit.*, p. 75.   [5] *Kam. and Kurn.*, p. 244.

[6] *Loc. cit.*, i. p. 47.   [7] *Ibid.*

[8] Mr. John Green (superintendent of a station, see vol. i. p. vi.), quoted by Br. Smyth, i. p. 78.

[9] *Ibid.*, p. 48. Another description of the mode of child-carrying is given by Basedow, *Jour. and Proc. R.S.S.A.* (1907), xxxi.   [10] Br. Smyth, i. p. 51.

"As a general rule, both fathers and mothers are very kind to their children and very rarely indeed strike them; and I have been often amused at seeing a rebellious urchin, of perhaps eight or nine years of age, take up his mimic spears, run a few yards away and then hurl them with all his force at his mother." "They are very fond of their children, and will at any time venture their lives for them."[1]   And the author tells of an occurrence in corroboration.[2] Here, again, we hear of kindness, leniency and real affection. The instance of a native losing his life in trying to save his child is very convincing.

The children that escape infanticide enjoy great affection from their parents.[3]

Of the Lower Darling River tribes it is stated that the children are not only very leniently treated by their parents, but that they are not spoilt at all. "One word from the parent generally is sufficient to check a child when doing wrong, and the greatest respect is shown to parents by their children."[4] The loss of a child would be lamented by the whole camp; the mother and near relatives would especially mourn.[5] A description of the mode of carrying children by their mother is also given by the same author.[6]   In this statement we may remark that the children are said not to be spoilt; this does not agree quite with some of our other statements. But this information agrees with all others in respect of the affection and lenient treatment the children enjoy.

According to Mitchell children are carried by the mother in skin bags on the shoulder. She carries also toys for her children.[7] As we have said above, the close connection in life between child and mother must have been of importance in making the tie between them especially close. The existence of toys, mentioned already in J. M. Davis' statement, characterizes the tender care bestowed on the young folk by their parents.

"The child is brought up with great care. . . . Should it cry, it is passed from one person to another and caressed and soothed, and the father will frequently nurse it for several hours together. When the child commences to walk, the father gives it a name."[8]   They are long suckled—sometimes

---

[1] J. Moore Davis in Br. Smyth, ii. p. 311. He speaks in this article indiscriminately of South Australians.

[2] Referring to natives of Victoria.

[3] Br. Smyth, ii. p. 290. Note on Australians, by A. Le Souëf. It refers, probably, to the Victorian blacks.

[4] Bonney, *J.A.I.*, xiii. p. 126.   [5] *Ibid.*

[6] *Ibid.*   [7] Vol. i. pp. 332, 333.

[8] Encounter Bay tribes (Narrinyeri), Meyer, *loc. cit.*, pp.186,187.

up to five or six years of age. A boy " when weaned, accompanies his father upon short excursions, upon which
occasion the father takes every opportunity to instruct his
son. For instance, if they arrive at a place concerning which
they have any tradition, it is told to the child if old enough
to understand it. Or he shows him how to procure this or
that animal, or other article of food, in the easiest way." [1]
We see here that the tie between father and child is a very
close one. The father nurses the child when it is small, and
educates it when it is bigger. Affection, care and kind treatment are stated here as everywhere else. And again we
read : " If the father dies before a child is born, the child
is put to death by the mother." [2] This marks again how
important is the father's part in bringing up a child.

Wyatt says of the Adelaide tribe that " they display strong
affection towards each other," which is shown especially in
a " great fondness for children." [3]

We read about the Port Lincoln tribes : " Both sexes are
very fond of their children." [4]

Howitt, speaking of infanticide among the Murring tribe,
adds : " Yet they are very fond of their offspring, and very
indulgent to those they keep, rarely striking them, and a
mother would give all the food she had to her children, going
hungry herself." [5]   In several statements on infanticide
it is said that no difference was made between boys and girls.[6]
Here again we have a strong assertion of parental love, and
of the kind treatment the children enjoy.

Among the Murrumbidgee tribes " it is well known that as
their children become older they [the parents] evince much
attachment towards them." [7]   A well-known tragic instance of
parental love is reported about the New South Wales natives by
the same author. " They display an extraordinary degree of
affection for their dead offspring, evidenced by an act that
almost exceeds credibility, had it not so often been witnessed
among the tribes in the interior of the colony. I allude to
the fact of deceased children, from the earliest age to even
six or seven years, being placed in a bag made of kangaroo
skin, and slung upon the back of the mother. . . . They
carry them thus for ten or twelve months, sleeping upon the
mass of mortal remains, which serves them for a pillow,
apparently unmindful of the horrid fœtor which emanates
from such a putrefying substance." [8]

---

[1] Encounter Bay tribes (Narrinyeri), Meyer, *loc. cit.*, p. 187.
[2] *Ibid.*, p. 186.   [3] *Loc. cit.*, p. 162.   [4] Chas. Wilhelmi, p. 181.
[5] *Nat. Tr.*, p. 748; informant : H. Williams.
[6] *Ibid.*, pp. 748–750.   [7] Bennett, i. p. 123.
[8] *Ibid.*, pp. 125, 126.

G. S. Lang in his account of the Australian blacks speaks of great leniency of treatment, and quotes several examples.[1]

An exceptional statement is given by a member of the United States expedition. " As far as our observation went, the women appear to take little care of their children."[2] But we gather from the whole account that the authors had no good opportunities of making observations on the natives, if they had any at all. Probably the natives they saw were in a state of deterioration, hanging round towns, etc.

We read in the old account of J. Turnbull about the natives of New South Wales, that all children who escape infanticide are " nursed with an anxious affection, very creditable to these savages. The infant no sooner begins to use his limbs than he is instructed in throwing the spear ; a bulrush or other reed being put into his hand for this purpose."[3]

In his memoirs, Hodgson says that aboriginal children are very kindly and tenderly treated by their parents.[4]

The following statements, referring to New South Wales blacks, give a good testimonial to their parental feelings. " An old *mammy*, who was much about the farm of another of my friends, was a perfect picture of maternal sorrow," after the death of her son. " If you spoke of her son, she was dissolved in tears, and answered in whispers." " The women appear to be always kind to their children, carrying the young ones on their backs."[5]

" They are remarkably fond of their children," says R. Dawson. In another place the author speaks of a great liberality towards children, displayed in distributing food. He speaks also of the adoption of orphans. " When the parents die, the children are adopted by the unmarried men and women and taken the greatest care of " ; and " children of both sexes who had lost their parents were uniformly adopted by those who had no families, and sometimes by those who had."[6]

As a matter of illustration I may adduce what Dr. J. Fraser says on that subject in his compilation on the New South Wales tribes. The aborigines love their children and treat them very kindly. The father makes for the boy a toy spear to practise throwing it and the girl gets a small stick to learn how to dig with it. The parents teach them to do all these things, and they " take as much delight in this business as we do in teaching our children their alphabet. The son is soon

---

[1] p. 33. The author knew personally some tribes of New South Wales and Queensland.
[2] Chas. Wilkes (smaller ed.), i. p. 225.   [3] p. 100.
[4] p. 244 (N. S. Wales).   [5] Henderson, p. 121.
[6] pp. 239, 268.   Port Stephens blacks.

able to go out with his father on hunting expeditions," imbibes all sorts of woodcraft and learns to know his tauri (hunting district).[1] We may add that the book of Dr. Fraser, although only a compilation, seems to be a very reliable one, and he probably had much personal information from settlers, missionaries, etc.

We have already seen from the first statement of Howitt that parental love obtained among the Dieri. Gason affirms that parental love for children and the love of these for their parents is one of their greatest virtues.[2] We read also that " the children are never beaten, and should any woman violate this law she is in turn beaten by her husband."[3] This statement would astonish us at first sight, as we usually expect severity from the father. But when we remember that the mother had probably all the drudgery and work with the children we can understand that she might easily lose her temper, and then the father took the children's part. It is characteristic that the father's authority was directed rather to protect the children from a probably merited punishment than to punish and correct them.

Amongst the Urabunna, where, as we are informed, " individual marriage does not exist either in name or in practice,"[4] all children of " men who are at the same level in the generation and belong to the same class and totem are *regarded* as the common children of these men." Still there exists " a closer tie between a man and the children of the woman who habitually live in camp with him."[5] This statement is the only one which tries to deny individual fatherhood and states the existence of group fatherhood. But as we do not know what sense should be given to the words " closer tie" and to the phrase " are re-garded as the common children" we must drop this statement as quite meaningless. We know already that the relations of a father to his child have several very characteristic features; the father fondles his child; is especially attached to it; he often carries it on the march (as these same authors state in another place, see below); he has certain economic duties towards his family; he lives in the same wurley with his children. Not a single word is said about any of these things, and only quite general assertions are made. We may repeat here, with Mr. Thomas, that if the authors knew more concrete facts about this question they ought to have communicated them. If they told us everything they knew about the subject, then their inferences are false. This statement

---

[1] pp. 4, 5, 60.   [2] *Loc. cit.*, p. 258.   [3] *Ibid.*
[4] Spencer and Gillen, *Nat. Tr.*, p. 63; repeated *Nor. Tr.*, p. 73.
[5] Spencer and Gillen, *Nat. Tr.*, p. 64.

loses its force for the reason especially that we know how close the personal tie between the Dieri parents and their children was, and that it was quite individual. And the Dieri had the same Pirrauru institution which induces Messrs. Spencer and Gillen to inform us that there was no individual fatherhood or marriage, amongst the Urabunna. There is, therefore, much reason to mistrust this statement.[1]

Children are treated with extreme leniency among the Central Australian tribes. " If the children are unruly the mothers try to quiet them with fair words, or may scold them a little, or even slap them gently, but never take any extreme means." Mothers often quarrel and even fight with each other defending their own offspring. " When a child sickens, the mother takes it in her lap, and does not leave the spot, the father sitting by."[2] All this shows a deep parental affection towards the children. And that it is limited to individual parents is confirmed by the following phrase : " Orphans fare the worst, and usually the nearest relative looks after them, but does not assume a parent's position. Such children receive blows and have to provide for themselves as best they can."[3] Although I avoid the problem of relationship terms, as lying outside the narrow limits of the present study, that deals exclusively with facts of family life, I quote the following statement of the same author as especially instructive. " *Kata* signifies father of the class; *Kata iltja* sexual father." The affix *iltja* indicates the individual relationship and the affix *lirra* class reference. " Ordinarily they leave out the words *iltja* and *lirra* and do not use them, because they all know, among themselves, who is personally related, and who is not. They are only used casually when conversing with strangers, to whom they wish to explain their family relationship."[4]

We read of the Arunta : " To their children they are, we may say uniformly, with very rare exceptions, kind and considerate, carrying them, the men as well as the women taking part in this, when they get tired on the march, and always seeing that they get a good share of any food."[5] Here it is stated explicitly that the cares are shared by father and mother. In another place the authors, speaking of the burial ceremonies, say that the display of grief and sorrow is not so much due to real feeling, as to tribal custom and fear

---

[1] Compare what has been said about the Pirrauru and Piraungaru above, pp. 108 *sqq.;* especially p. 117, under 7.

[2] L. Schultze, *loc. cit.,* p. 238 (Finke River natives).

[3] *Ibid.,* p. 240.   [4] *Ibid.,* p. 237.

[5] Spencer and Gillen, *Nat. Tr.,* pp. 50, 51.

of offending the dead one's spirit. And they add, "At the same time, he (the native) is certainly capable of genuine grief and of real affection for his children." [1] The foregoing statement appears to be very emphatic. Parental love is apparently quoted as a genuine feeling conspicuous *par excellence* and therefore to be opposed to any other more or less fictitious display. The intimate connection between the mother and her child appears also from some details in the initiation ceremonies. [2]

In the Kabi and Wakka tribes, "the wife was the regular nurse of the infants, but the husband occasionally took a turn." [3] "Children were over-indulged." [4]

" The mother is always fond of her child, and I have often admired her patience with it. She constantly carries it with her, at first in a basket, but later on . . . on her shoulder. Thus she carries it with her till it is several years old. If the child cries she may perhaps get angry, but she will never allow herself to strike it. The children are never chastised either by the father or the mother." But they are nevertheless as a rule " obliging and kind." " The black children are not . . . as bad as one might suppose, considering their education, in which their wills are never resisted." [5] " The woman is often obliged to carry her little child on her shoulders during the whole day, only setting it down when she has to dig in the ground or climb trees." [6] The mother, in one instance, was much excited when a white·man struck her naughty child. The same author says that the tie between mother and child is closer than that between father and child. The children " are fonder of their mother than of their father." (This seems quite "natural" to us as we observe it as a rule in our society.) Sometimes the father cares much for his child too; " he frequently carries it, takes it in his lap, searches . . . its hair, plays with it, and makes little boomerangs, which he teaches it to throw. He . . . prefers boys to girls." " Boys are not permitted to go hunting with their fathers before they are nine years old." [7]

Amongst the Georgina blacks the child's education is carried on chiefly by the mother. She teaches the boys respect for the tribal elders. [8]

The way of carrying a child among the Queensland blacks is described by E. Palmer. [9]

[1] *Nat. Tr.*, p. 511.   [2] *Ibid.*, pp. 227, 250.
[3] Mathew, *loc. cit.*, p. 153.   [4] *Ibid.*, p. 153.
[5] Lumholtz, on the Herbert River Natives, *loc. cit.*, pp. 192, 193.
[6] *Ibid.*, p. 160.   [7] *Ibid.*, p. 193.
[8] Purcell in *R.G.S.*, Victorian Branch, xi. pp. 19, 20.
     Loc. cit., p. 280.

Among the North Central Queensland aborigines the mother carries her child in a koolamon or on a sheet of bark, slung to her side; later on her shoulders.[1] She is accustomed to lullaby it to sleep by a sort of droning humming sound.[2] She suckles it until it reaches the age of three to five years.[3] "A father could do what he pleased with his children, but neither parent would ever strike a boy; if beaten the latter was supposed to lose courage." The mother taught the girls, and could beat them if necessary.[4] The father taught the boys climbing trees and making arms and implements.[5]

In North-West Australia (Pilbarra district) children are reared affectionately and never chastised. They often listen to stories on native traditions.[6]

Ph. Chauncy, speaking of the West Australian blacks, says that love between children and parents was very strong, and that it was one of the principal virtues of the aborigines. He gives an example of a native who after five years, seeing again his son, a grown-up lad, displayed a good deal of affection and tenderness.[7]

The mode in which women carry their children in West Australia is described by Moore.[8]

Oldfield says: "Sometimes the love of their offspring (male) is excessive." As an example he describes an old man "who had a son, a lad of about nine years of age, of whom he was excessively fond, always tenderly embracing him and recommending him to the care of others when he went on any expedition." When he returned from the chase "he invariably first of all fondly kissed the boy before proceeding to cook," and all the best parts of the meal "were bestowed on the child." The child was consequently quite spoilt and tyrannized over his father, who was quite obedient to him.[9]

"Elles aiment d'ailleurs éperdument leurs fils et aussi celles de leurs filles qui ont échappé à la mort. S'il arrive que quelqu'un de leurs enfants s'éveille en sursaut ou se fasse du mal, ses gémissements sont couverts par ceux de la mère, qui ne se donne aucun repos jusqu'à ce qu'elle ait trouvé le moyen de guérison, quelque fatigue qu'il doive lui en couter. Elles nourrissent avec soin leurs petits enfants et les veulent toujours propres et bien tenus, autant que leur permet leur position. Elles les allaitent pendant plus de quatre ans; aussi n'est-il pas rare de voir de petits garçons jouer et faire

---

[1] Roth, *Eth. Stud.*, p. 183, § 330.   See also figs. 436–438.
[2] *Ibid.*   [3] *Ibid.*
[4] Roth, *Proc. R.S.Q.*, p. 51.   [5] *Ibid.*, p. 60.
[6] Withnell, pp. 8, 9.   [7] Br. Smyth, ii. p. 275.
[8] *Loc. cit.*, p. 32.   [9] *Loc. cit.*, pp. 224, 225.

des armes avec leurs petits *ghicis*, et puis courir se restaurer au sein de leur mère, qui souvent allaite ainsi deux enfants à la fois. J'ai vu des enfants de six ans prendre encore le sein, et les mères non seulement s'y prêter, mais les caresser et se priver des meilleurs morceaux pour les leur donner." [1] I quote this statement *in extenso*, as it includes a good deal of what we know in general of this subject. We see that a mother might suckle two children at a time, but if it were too difficult for her, the child is killed. Salvado speaks also of adoption by another woman as an alternative (comp. above, Dawson's and Shultze's statements; but adoption seems rather to be an exceptional escape from infanticide.[2] In another place, the same author speaks of a " véritable tendresse maternelle" showing itself towards a child recently dead. Often did he observe that a mother who had just lost a child would rise in the night and go for miles through the woods, calling her child by its name, speaking to it, and giving many tokens of her tender feelings.[3] This instance gives us a good insight into a class of feelings that the general, popular mind would hardly ascribe to savages.[4] Salvado says that they make a great difference between a boy and girl, in the joy which they display at a child's birth. Not only the mothers (as we saw above), but also the fathers show great fondness for their children. Salvado blames the " déférence des pères pour les enfants." Whatever a child might do, it is never chastised. If a small boy wishes to obtain something from his parents, he cries, bites and beats them, until he succeeds in his purpose. The only punishment ever inflicted on their children is " une fâcherie plus ou moins remarquée par eux, et cela encore après leur avoir accordé tout ce qu'ils demandent." The father prepares for his son small arms and teaches him how to use them. He displays the greatest tenderness towards him and is extremely fond of him.[5] And the author gives as the reason why the aborigines would not send their children to white men for education, the parental attachment to their offspring.[6] The father disposes of his daughters in marriage.[7]

Among the natives of King George Sound the mothers display a great love for their children, often crying after the death of one of them.[8]

---

[1] Salvado about the natives of Swan District, West Australia, pp. 275, 276.
[2] *Ibid.*, p. 275.
[3] *Ibid.*, p. 250.
[4] *Ibid.*, p. 274.
[5] *Ibid.*, p. 276.
[6] *Ibid.*, pp. 276, 277.
[7] *Ibid.*, p. 278.
[8] Browne, *loc. cit.*, p. 450.

About the same tribes it is recorded : " Of their children they appear to be fond, and rarely chastise them ; but their treatment of the women is not always gentle." [1] Here the difference between the usual good treatment that children uniformly enjoy from their parents, and the unsettled character of marital treatment is clearly expressed.

Our best information on many points comes rather from anecdotes and reports of real occurrences than from bare statements. Some stories illustrate very well the present question. So, for instance, the following, which proves beyond any doubt that paternal affection among the Australian aborigines might amount to a passion.[2] Old Davie was a native of great personal strength and skill, strong will, and great courage. He was not especially clever, but was apparently kind to children and to his wives. His inoffensive exterior, however, hid a truly demoniac character ; he was quite egotistical, " he had never had any strong liking for anything else," but had only one peculiar passion : " his special craving was for murder." He had ever so many lives on his conscience. When he grew old, he became the father of a rather nice boy. He got deeply and passionately attached to his son, called the Jumbuk-man. " To watch the gradual expansion of Jumbuk-man's faculties ; to see him balance himself with his feet astride and throw his spear at his sister's back ; to observe him tomahawk the sleeping dogs, maltreat any birds or insects he could lay hands on, bite his mother ; to hear him lisp foul words, and give himself up to the charming ways of savage infancy, became henceforth the chief delight of his father." Here we see a neat, condensed picture of what might be called educational training under the father's eyes. After a few years of life the boy died ; the death of the boy was a terrible blow " to Old Davie. He had been his special delight . . . and (he) bore his loss in a very unstoical way. He sat on the ground, streams of tears welling from his eyes." The end of the story (Old Davie's murder of a young woman in revenge for " sorcery " done by her tribe) does not touch our subject.

As an interesting and good illustration of parental authority may be adduced the story of how a Bangerang girl was made to join her promised husband. She was, apparently, quite unwilling to do it ; consequently her father tried to persuade her. After his patience had been exhausted he tried to compel her ; having at last resource to his club. This and the unanimous and rather strong persuasions of both

---

[1] Scott Nind, *loc. cit.*, p. 37.
[2] Told by Curr, *Recollections*, ch. xxviii. " Old Davie."

parents made her follow the prescribed course.[1] This story
shows that the father had not a great amount of authority
over his daughter. He had to persuade her for several
hours and she brought him by her stubbornness to a fit of
anger, which finally settled the matter.

Another story clearly exemplifying paternal affection, is
told by Grey.[2] For some small trespass Capt. Grey got hold
of a young boy, the son of an influential native. The father
tried to liberate him. " The natives are always ardently
attached to their children, and this the boy's father now
evinced in the strongest manner." He tried by persuasion,
begging and even threats to induce the white man to give
him back his child. He fairly wept upon his child's neck."
When this had no result, and the boy was imprisoned, he
made all possible efforts to plead for him. The paternal
love is clearly conspicuous in the whole tale.

Our forty-one statements agree fairly well on many
points, but especially on the principal question, namely
on the existence of very close personal and individual
bonds of union between parents and children.[3] As so
much stress has been laid on the emotional element in
these bonds, it may be shown now how far the evidence
confirms the views expressed above.[4] Speaking in concrete terms, the evidence affirms beyond any doubt the
existence of strong feelings of affection and attachment
between parents and children. Thirty-five of our forty-
one statements explicitly affirm the existence of such
feelings. In many places this is expressed in a very clear
and emphatic manner. We read that the children are the
" pride and love " of their parents; that affection for

[1] Curr, *Recollections*, pp. 141–145.

[2] *Loc. cit.*, ii. pp. 350–361 (refers to natives of King George's
Sound).

[3] An exception may be seen in the statement of Spencer and
Gillen on the Urabunna, as far as it seems to point to a group
relationship, but there are reasons for not attaching too much
importance to this statement. We dealt also above (p. 117)
with the question whether there is group relationship between
parents and children in the tribes where the Pirrauru custom
prevails, and it was found that the assumption of its existence must
be absolutely discarded, and that everywhere there is individual
relationship between parents and children.

[4] pp. 191 *sqq.*

their children is a "marked feature" of the aboriginal character (Howitt). Deep affection is quoted as their chief virtue (Gason); and as the most sincere and strongest feeling (Spencer and Gillen); and so forth. Instances might easily be multiplied. The only negative instance is the completely unreliable statement of Wilkes. This exceptional agreement of all authors and the uniform emphasis that they lay upon their statements is in itself a very strong proof not only that this assertion is true, but that these facts strongly impressed themselves upon the observers.[1]   On this point our best authorities entirely agree with the remaining observers. Such an agreement on the point of a general judgment, which is necessarily an induction from a considerable number of observations, can only mean that the latter were not liable to misinterpretation; that they plainly expressed their deeper psychological meaning. These observations seem at first sight very difficult to be made correctly, for they are of a rather subtle character, referring to impalpable psychological facts. And yet all authors interpreted them correctly, of which fact such an agreement is the best proof. The expression of the feelings in question amongst savages must obviously differ very little from our ways of showing feelings. The complete agreement of the statements points, therefore, to the unmistakable clearness and strength in which the native feelings show themselves, in all the details of family life as well as in some more important facts.[2]

But even if unwilling to trust to the emphasis of our informants' general affirmations and to the agreement between them, we find many concrete details and examples, mentioned by the authors, which convince us that the conclusions they have drawn from observation were correct. Howitt says that to secure the good-will of the parents the most direct way is to admire their children; a fact which is characteristic of parental infatuation in our

---

[1] Compare above, pp. 193, 194.
[2] Compare the passages above, pp. 195, 196.

own society. When the children are ill the parents watch over and look after them most carefully (Schultze, Salvado, Meyer, Howitt); they make toys for their children (Mitchell, Curr, Fraser); and they look very carefully after their food (Spencer and Gillen, Dawson). On the death of a child the parents display great sorrow (Browne, Henderson, Curr in the story of old Davie).[1] And the horrid custom of carrying a dead babe on their wanderings is also a token of deep affection (Angas, Bennett, Howitt). After long absence the parents display great joy and tenderness (Chauncy). And although adoption is reported in some tribes (R. Dawson, Schultze, Salvado), nevertheless there is not always the same degree of love and affection towards adopted children as towards the offspring. And the former are often illtreated (Schultze). Such examples could easily be multiplied. And they show in how many quite unmistakable facts the main features of the parental feelings for children found their expression. These feelings as a rule consisted of love, pride, affection and attachment.

All this seems to hold good for the father, as well as for the mother. In the majority of statements both the parents are mentioned indiscriminately. Some of them say expressly that they refer to the father also (Meyer, Wilhelmi, Moore Davis, Br. Smyth, Fraser, Gason, Mathew, Spencer and Gillen, Mrs. Parker, Salvado). Nevertheless we must assume that owing to the closer tie in daily life the relationship between mother and child was a yet more intimate one (Lumholtz, Salvado). There seems to have been but little difference made between male and female children. We read in a few places (Schürmann, Spencer and Gillen) that boys were more welcome than girls, and that infanticide was more frequently carried out amongst the latter. But this is contradicted elsewhere,[2] where we read that in several tribes no difference in infanticide was made between boys and girls.

[1] Compare also the examples referred to in foregoing footnote.
[2] Howitt, *Nat. Tr.*, pp. 748–750.

Parallel with great affection towards the children ran considerable leniency of treatment. In about eighteen of our statements (*i. e.* in all of those in which there is anything said about treatment besides affection) we read that the natives treat their children with kindness, absolute leniency and indulgence, never chastise them, and give them their own way in everything. It is well to notice that these two things—real love on the one hand and leniency of treatment on the other—must be treated as two independent phenomena. Affection may be perfectly well combined with severity and rigour; and a want of punishment need not be necessarily based upon love; it may result just as well from carelessness. But this latter does not seem to be the case; we know that the parents are not careless about their children; that on the contrary they take the greatest trouble about them and look carefully after all the necessities of their life. Here the leniency of treatment seems to be exclusively due to excessive fondness for their children and the resulting weakness shown towards them. In other societies the reason of the same phenomenon is often (especially in the case of male children) the wish not to frighten the boy and not to make him a coward, in which belief magical elements may also play a rôle. (Compare Steinmetz, article in *Z. f. S.* i.) A suggestion of such a reason is contained in only one of our statements (Roth in *Trans. R.S.Q.*) In general it may be said that the way in which the aborigines treat their children is a symptom of their great parental love.[1] Only in two places (Spencer and Gillen, Lumholtz) is it said that in fits of anger and impatience the natives chastise their children, and even this seems to be quite exceptional. Very interesting is Gason's statement, according to which it seems that the father was even more lenient than the mother; and this seems quite natural, for the mother had much more opportunity to get angry with the child.

[1] Compare also the general reason given by Steinmetz for the prevalence of this indulgence among savage peoples. *Zeitschr. für Socialwissenschaft*, Band i. pp. 254–285.

It is characteristic that even those authors who write in strong terms of the bad treatment which the husband shows towards his wife (compare the statements above) say nothing of the kind as to the treatment of the children by their fathers. On the contrary, we read in several places of the tyranny of the young boy, under which often his mother and sisters and sometimes even his father had to suffer (Curr in several places, especially in the story of Old Davie; J. Moore Davies, Oldfield, Salvado). But two other writers (Lumholtz and Bonney) inform us that in spite of the entire lack of severity the children are not naughty at all, as might have been expected.

It may be safely concluded that the evidence gives a quite true picture of the parental feelings. The latter may be considered as elements which essentially characterize the relation of parents to children. And it may be said that in Australia the parents are most devoted and loving to their children. The importance of this conclusion in regard to our ideas of parental kinship in Australia has been argued sufficiently above.[1]

The facts stated in this conclusion seem to have an important bearing upon the relation between husband and wife. This point is completely ignored by the first-hand observers, who never troubled to inquire deeper into the mutual dependence of such most important sociological facts, viz. of the relationship between parents and children on the one hand and between husband and wife on the other. There are no statements on this point, and consequently one is obliged to draw the inference for oneself. But the bearing of the parental relationship upon the conjugal relations is so obvious and the mutual dependence of marriage and family so clear, that the following inference seems not at all hypothetical and arbitrary. If both parents are strongly attached to their children, if their feelings are so outspoken, these must constitute a strong binding tie between them. It is hardly possible to think that a man could be

---

[1] See pp. 191 *sqq*.

merely a brutal master and tyrant to his wife if they both had the same feelings for the same object. But it is still less possible to admit that a man and a woman would on the first occasion, or even without any reason, part and form new unions if they were both attached so strongly to the same person—an attachment which, as in so many examples, sometimes amounted to a real passion.

Turning to the other question, to be answered from our evidence—the question of paternal authority or *potestas*—let us first fix the meaning of the word. To the word authority (*potestas*) a legal sense can be given. Then it expresses the sum of the rights that legally are allotted to the father over his children. So in Rome *potestas* meant the absolute power of life, death and liberty that the father legally possessed over the persons of his children.[1] Every legal relation presupposes a possibility of interference or enforcement on the part of some social authority, and it assumes a set of fixed norms sanctioned in some way by society. Now we do not possess any knowledge of any such possibility in the case of the parental relationship, or of any norms that are laid down in any form by the Australian aboriginal society for the said relationship. The terms *authority* or *potestas*, therefore, cannot be used in their strict sense or indeed in any sense at all if we imply a *legal meaning* to them. We are more justified in applying them to the Australian natives, if we use them as an expression of the mere fact that the father could do anything he liked with his children, that he had an absolute power over them. But even here we should be careful in ascribing the exclusive power to the father. In the only cases where the question of a decision as to the child's lot arises, *i. e.* in the cases of infanticide and giving the girl away in marriage, there are contradictory instances ascribing the power of decision to some one else. So, for instance, in the Mukjarawaint tribe the father was not allowed to decide whether his child was to be killed or not at birth; it was

---

[1] Compare also the discussions above, pp. 185 *sqq.*

the grandparents' affair.   Curr affirms, on the other hand, that infanticide depended exclusively upon the father. In some tribes it was not the father's privilege to give his daughter in marriage.   Nevertheless, as was shown above in Chapter II, as a rule it was the father who disposed of his daughter.

Although our information on these points is scanty, these few hints seem to prove that there were some infringements of the father's liberty from outside.   How far they were *legal* is difficult to ascertain.   At any rate we see that the father's authority was rather limited by legal factors than enhanced.   But even if this be an exceptional instance, and if as a rule nobody could interfere with the father in whatever he was pleased to do with his children—a supposition which seems fairly to agree with the general authority of the husband and the isolation of families—it must still be remembered that the father as a matter of fact never made use of his unrestricted authority.   In the first place, as will be plainly shown below, the father's contact with and exclusive influence over his children ceased at the moment they reached puberty.   Our question is therefore limited to the period before reaching puberty (in the boys perhaps even sooner, from about seven to ten years; see below), and *eo ipso* loses a great deal of its contents.   A small child living with its parents alone in the wilderness is naturally entirely in their hands and at their mercy.   But it would be a fallacy to lay any stress on that point.   As our statements show, the child is protected against any illtreatment, or even against any severity from either of its parents, by their own feelings much better than it could be by any legal measures.   And the fact remains that the father's *potestas* or authority (or whatever any kind of coercive power may be called) is by no means a characteristic feature of his relation to his children, for according to aboriginal custom and psychology, any element of that kind is absolutely absent from their family life.

In other words we may say that our information on the

regulation of paternal authority in the few cases where it can come into play is very scanty. Probably there are no rules, or only a few,[1] and the father is more or less free to dispose of his child. But I mentioned some contradictory instances, and I would not lay any stress on that assertion. What appears to be quite clear is that paternal authority does not play any important part in family life; for the parental relation is a *régime* of love, and not of coercion. And considering that we know very little about the father's authority and only feel sure that it is insignificant, it cannot be reasonably chosen as a determining factor of the paternal relation.

From the lack of any chastisement we may infer that the education given by the parents to their children was a very insignificant one, for it is impossible to conceive of any serious education without coercive treatment, especially at that low stage of culture. But as the children are continually with their mother and very often with their father, the parental influence must be of great importance in the questions of the arts of life and of all the knowledge necessary in tribal affairs. We read in several places of the control and educative influence exercised by the mother on her children (Kurnai, Euahlayi, Georgina Blacks, Herbert River tribes, North-West Australian tribes according to Withnell, Salvado). The father makes toys for his children and teaches the boys how to throw the spear, use the boomerang, and so on (Curr on Australians in general; Encounter Bay; Turnbull; Salvado; compare also Dr. Fraser's statement).

Here it must be remembered that education depends still more on another set of facts, namely on the facts of initiation and the secret society formed by all initiated men. The boy's education begins with the moment when he leaves his parents, joins the young men's camp, and begins to undergo a series of initiations. At any rate he begins then to be educated in quite a new order of

[1] As mentioned above it is impossible to say how far such rules are legal, *i. e.* laid down and *enforced* by society.

ideas, initiated into the tribal mysteries, etc. And apparently he has then to submit to a severe *régime*, besides going through the ordeal of initiation itself. It seems, therefore, that the education received by the children in their parents' camp, where they are probably more under the influence of their mother and perhaps of other women who happen to be in the same encampment, that this education is definitive only for the females, who can learn from their mothers all they will want in their future life. For the boys this first education is of secondary importance. All they have learned of the tribal traditions and beliefs—their whole knowledge of the world— is destroyed at the initiation and replaced by a new one. We see, therefore, that the relations between parents and children are limited to a relatively short period; for the girls marry at about ten years of age, and the boys at the same age leave their parental camp and begin a new life. These facts are so important, as characterizing the aboriginal family life, that we must dwell upon them more in detail.

III

The relation of children to their parents undergoes an essential change at the time when the former arrive at puberty. At this time they are removed from their parents' immediate presence and control. The girls marry very early, that is they are very early removed from their parents' camp to that of their husband. Boys have to undergo the initiation ceremonies at about the age when the girls marry, and according to all we know never return any more to their parents' camp. The fact of the early marriage of Australian aboriginal females is well known. The age at which it takes place is stated to be from eight to fourteen years of age; but generally the age of about ten to twelve is alleged.[1]

[1] Curr states it to vary from eight to fourteen, at various places : *Recollections*, pp. 50, 129, *A.R.*, i. p. 107; Meyer in Woods, p. 190, states it to be from ten to twelve; Schürmann in

Very important is also the point which Curr emphasizes, viz. that no girl above about sixteen or widow under about forty-five is left unmarried.[1] So that, according to this statement, practically all women who are marriageable would be married. But this is perhaps in contradiction to a couple of statements we shall meet below, which affirm the existence of a camp of unmarried females. So that this point seems to present some ambiguity. At any rate it seems quite certain that unmarried females are not left long in this state.

We know very little as to how far the relations between a girl and her parents cease when she leaves them. Marriage seems to be as a general rule patrilocal; the wife leaves her parents' camp and removes to her husband's. The only exception to this rule will be quoted below (see p. 266). With that, a great part of the parents' influence and contact seem to be necessarily interrupted; for we saw in the discussion on the mode of living that the families camp either separately or in very small groups. And therefore a wife living in her husband's camp would probably not live in the same local group with her parents. And in some cases, where as in the Bangerang the local divisions seem to have been more numerous, or as in the Kurnai the population seems to have been more dense (the local groups living nearer each other), local exogamy prevailed and the girl naturally went away.[2]

Moreover, the mother-in-law taboo obtained well-nigh in all tribes, so that the husband was cut off from contact

---

Woods, p. 222, at arriving at puberty; Fraser, p. 2, at a very young age; Eyre, ii. p. 319, at about twelve years of age; Br. Smyth, i. p. 77, very early; Spencer and Gillen at from fourteen to fifteen years of age (*Nat. Tr.*, p. 92 and *Nor. Tr.*, p. 134); Withnell, p. 8, at about twelve years of age; Parkhouse, *A.A.A.S.*, vi. p. 641, at arriving at puberty; Grey, ii. pp. 229, 231, very early.

[1] Curr, *Recollections*, p. 129.

[2] Such local exogamy prevailed also in some of the North Central tribes, viz. in the Warramunga nation, owing to the local segregation of the two moieties. There the girl must always marry far away from her natal place. Compare *Nor. Tr.*, pp. 28-30.

with his parents-in-law; therefore his wife was to some extent also handicapped in her relations with them. That when the married couple were in the same local group with the wife's parents there were some binding elements and forms of close intercourse between both parties appears in the description given below of the economics of the household. But in all probability the authority of the parents over the girl and the real intimacy of their relations ceased at the moment she was given over to her husband.[1]

There is another point connected with marriage and age. We saw that girls marry very early, at the age of about twelve years. The men on the other side do not marry so early. We do not possess very copious information on this point. It is certain that boys were not allowed to marry before they passed the initiation ceremonies. Now these began at puberty, and were extended probably over several years. So it appears, at least, from all the more exact and detailed descriptions we possess of these ceremonies.[2] And it seems that the males had to pass through a whole series of ceremonies before they were allowed to marry. We read in Salvado (p. 277) that it was a crime, severely punished, often by death, for a man to marry below the age of thirty. And he adds that they had a marvellous skill in ascertaining age by means of a series of ceremonies through which every male had to pass. The same is stated by Curr (*A.R.*, i. p. 107), viz. that the men seldom marry under thirty. According to some statements from the South-Eastern area boys appear to be allowed to marry younger.

From these few data it appears that males married much later and that consequently there must have been some disparity of age. But this disparity was much greater, owing to the circumstance that the young girls were as a rule allotted to old men, and the boys whenever they were

[1] Grey, ii. pp. 229, 231, and Parkhouse, *A.A.A.S.*, vi. p. 641.
[2] Compare the description of initiation ceremonies in the works of Spencer and Gillen, Howitt, Roth, and Mathew.

allowed to marry got old *lubras* as wives. We have a whole series of statements affirming this and reporting the difference of age to be usually about thirty years, if the female was younger; and at any rate stating that there was seldom a couple in which both partners were young. These statements refer to tribes scattered all over the continent, so that disparity of age in marriage seems to be quite a universal feature in Australia.

We may point to the circumstance that this disparity of age stands in connection with the very prevalent form of betrothal, viz. the promising of a girl in infancy usually to a mature man. Other modes of obtaining wives, as exchange of a daughter for a wife, and levirate, stand also in connection with the disparity of age.

Statements.—We read in Curr: "The Australian male almost invariably obtains his wife or wives either as a survivor of a married brother, or in exchange for his sisters, or later on in life for his daughters." An old widow often falls to the lot of some young bachelor.[1] On the other hand young girls are allotted to old men. "One often sees a child of eight the wife of a man of fifty." And we read further: "The marriage rules of the blacks result in very ill-assorted unions as regards age; for it is usual to see old men with mere girls as wives and men in the prime of life married to old widows. As a rule women are not obtained by the men unless they are at least thirty years of age. Women have very frequently two husbands during their lifetime, the first older and the second younger than themselves."[2] "I never heard of a female over sixteen years of age, who, prior to the breakdown of aboriginal customs after the coming of the Whites, had not a husband."[3]

Speaking again on marriage among the Bangerang, Curr says: "As a rule, girls would be about twelve or fourteen years of age, and their husbands-elect some five-and-thirty years older, and already the lords of one or two spouses." "In this way it happened that one seldom saw a couple in which both the parties were young."[4] And further on we read, "Few men under thirty have lubras." But in the age

[1] Curr, *A.R.*, i. p. 107. This is said about the Australians in general.   [2] *Ibid.*, p. 110.
[3] *Ibid.*   [4] *Recollections*, p. 129.

between fifty and sixty men usually possess two or three wives. The difference between the spouses is usually twenty years; sometimes much more.[1]

We find the disparity of age in marriage mentioned by Howitt in several places. So we learn that old men were often betrothed to young girls among the Wolgal.[2] We read that in Australia old men secure the young females for themselves.[3] And that young men obtain for wives some old repudiated wife of one of the old men.[4] Among the Geawe Gal "girls were affianced to men much older than themselves." [5] Speaking of the Dieri and other South Central tribes he says that old wives of old men are handed over to young boys.[6]

Howitt informs us also that no man might marry before duly initiated; and then the old men of the tribe had to give their consent.[7] Obviously, therefore, the age at which men could get married was much later than that in which females were given away.

Eyre found in the tribes with which he was in contact that women of between thirty and forty years of age were often cast off and given to young boys.[8] Young girls were often allotted to old men.[9]

Disparity of age is stated also by Angas. Old men get often the youngest and comeliest women; whilst the old and haggard females were left for the young men.[10]

Among the Encounter Bay tribes the girls "are given in marriage at a very early age (ten or twelve years)." And as it is very often the father who exchanges his daughter for a wife, it is evident that a great disparity of age must prevail.[11]

Mrs. Parker says that among the Euahlayi baby girls were often betrothed to " some old chap " who might have even already as many as two or three wives.[12] Whereas quite a young man was often allotted to an old woman. Age is not a disqualification for a woman to marry.[13]

In the Central tribes, owing to the Tualcha Mura institution,[14] " men very frequently have wives much younger than themselves, as the husband and the mother of a wife obtained in this way are usually of approximately the same age." [15] And

---

[1] *Recollections*, p. 171.   [2] *Nat. Tr.*, p. 197.
[3] *Kam. and Kurn.*, p. 354.   [4] *Trans. R.S.V.* (1888), p. 126.
[5] *Kam. and Kurn.*, p. 280.   [6] *J.A.I.*, xx. p. 55.
[7] *Trans. R.S.V.*, p. 116.   [8] *Loc. cit.*, ii. p. 322.
[9] *Ibid.*, p. 319.   [10] *Loc. cit.*, i. p. 82 (Murray River tribes).
[11] Meyer in Woods, p. 190.   [12] *Loc. cit.*, p. 55.
[13] *Ibid.*, p. 56.   [14] See above, p. 41.
[15] Spencer and Gillen, *Nat. Tr.*, p. 558.

it may be remembered that this is the " most usual method
of obtaining a wife." [1]

We are informed that among the tribes near Victoria
River Downs [2] a man may marry at about thirty years of
age, and the older he grows the younger girls he gets.   Girls
are married on reaching puberty; and usually to old men;
whereas young men often receive old women.

In the Kabi and Wakka tribes " the elder men had sometimes a plurality of wives, while the young men had for a
long time after reaching manhood to remain, perforce, single.
I never knew a man to have more than two wives at the one
time, and generally one sufficed.   There was no minimum of
age for the marriage of girls, and so it occasionally happened
that a child of twelve became the wife of a man of sixty.
I knew a case in point." [3]

" Il est défendu a un Australien . . . de se marier avant
au moins vingt-huit à trente ans, et la mort est le châtiment
de tout infracteur de la loi." [4]

In the tribes of King George Sound the old men seem
partly to monopolize the young females.[5]

As we have mentioned above, boys leave their parents'
camp to undergo the initiation ceremonies.   These latter
seem to obtain in all tribes, with a few insignificant exceptions such as the Bidwelli mentioned by Howitt.
This is a quite well-known fact.   But what is their mode
of living during this, in some tribes, rather prolonged period
and afterwards, before they marry ?   They do not live
in their parents' camp; and they have not yet their
individual settlement.   They appear in the great majority
of cases to club together, have their own encampment,
roam and hunt on their own account, and in general to
live a life apart.

Statements.—Howitt, speaking of the camping rules among
the Kurnai, says that a " ' brogan ' (a man initiated at the
same time, a comrade, or tribal brother, see *Nat. Tr.*, p. 737),
although calling the man's wife ' wife ' and she calling him

---

[1] *Nat. Tr.*, p. 558.
[2] Northern Territory, South Australia, *J.A.I.*, xxiv. p. 181.
In the answers to the *Questions* of Prof. Frazer.
[3] Mathew, p. 162.   Compare also Lumholtz, *loc. cit.*, p. 192.
[4] Salvado, p. 277; natives of South West Australia.
[5] Scott Nind, *loc. cit.*, pp. 38, 39.

' husband,' would have to camp with the young men, if any were there, or else by himself." [1] And again : " The young men (brewit) and the married men who have not their wives with them, always encamp together at some distance from the camps of the married men." [2] " The young man, or brewit, after his initiation, may be said to have commenced a life independent, to some extent, of his parents." [3] " He lived with the other young men, and with those who were initiated with him, and accordingly his brothers." [4]

We read of the Wolgal tribe : " A married man would never stay in the young men's camp when travelling, unless he were without his wife, when he would be considered as being single. The married people and the single young men camp entirely apart." [5] Howitt mentions further the young men's camp in connection with animal food division amongst the Ngarigo (Maneroo blacks).[6] That the bachelors' camp was a rule is confirmed by Howitt's statement that amongst the Mukjarawaint there was no young men's camp.[7] The unmarried men seem to have lived with their grand-parents.[8]

Curr, speaking of the laying out of a native camp in the Bangerang tribe, says : " the fire of the bachelors . . ." is " rather further off and somewhat isolated from the rest." [9] The same author says : " Over the girls his (the father's) authority ceased when they became wives, and after his twelfth year or so the boy was very little subject to the father." [10] " When eight or ten years of age he was sent to sleep in the bachelors' camp, when there was one at hand, with the young men and boys of various ages, his parents still supplying him with food. In his new home, though no violence was used, its inmates being all his relatives, the child gradually became to some extent the fag " of all older and stronger. In short this was the real school he had to pass through, the most important moment of which formed the initiation, when he became *kogomoolga*.[11] " The bachelors, in their camp, cooked each for himself " [12] (at least the older ones ; as for the quite young, the family provided, according to what we were told above). " The bachelors had one (hut) in common." [13] Curr also emphasizes

[1] *Kam. and Kurn.*, p. 210.   [2] *J.A.I.*, xiv. p. 318.
[3] *Kam. and Kurn.*, p. 199, and *Nat. Tr.*, p. 737.
[4] *Ibid.*, and *Nat. Tr.*, p. 737.   [5] Howitt, *Nat. Tr.*, p. 776.
[6] *Ibid.*, pp. 759, 760.   [7] *Ibid.*, p. 764.
[8] *Ibid.* Compare Roth, *Eth. Stud.*, p. 183.
[9] *Recollections*, p. 133.   [10] *Ibid.*, p. 248.
[11] *Ibid.*, pp. 250, 253.   [12] *Ibid.*, p. 256.
[13] *Ibid.*, p. 259.

the importance of the training enjoyed by the youths in the bachelors' camp for the general tribal order.[1]

J. Dawson says that one partition of a big wuurn "is appropriated to the parents and children, one to the young unmarried women and widows, and one to the bachelors and widowers. While travelling or occupying temporary habitations, each of these parties must erect separate wuurns."[2] Here the young boys and young unmarried girls lived with their family, but in separate compartments of the hut. We are not informed if, when travelling, they formed a separate group in the encampment.

"Young, unmarried men frequently muster in parties of six or eight, and make a hut for themselves."[3] In cases when a larger number of natives are assembled it is required by custom that "all boys and uninitiated young men sleep at some distance from the huts of adults."[4]

"Until his fourteenth or fifteenth year he (the boy) is mostly engaged in catching fish and birds, because already, for some years, he has been obliged to seek for food on his own account. Thus he early becomes, in a great measure, independent; and there is nobody who can control him, the authority of his parents depending only upon the superstitions which they have instilled into him from infancy."[5]

A vague but suggestive piece of information as regards our point is given on the Turra tribe, by the Rev. J. Kühn: Two or three months after initiation the lad is allowed to marry. But some of the married men undergo a further operation and become "Willeru"; "after this they are not permitted to go to their wives for two years."[6] Do they live in a separate camp during these two years? It is probable, but the statement is not clear enough to be useful for us.

We read about the Port Lincoln tribes: "If there be any young unmarried men, they sleep apart in a hut of their own."[7] This statement throws some light on the preceding one: there we had no mention of any separate camp. But as both these tribes lived quite close and must have had similar institutions, we may safely assume that the seclusion from wives which is reported in the foregoing passage was combined with an independent mode of living, i.e. with a bachelors' camp.

---

[1] Recollections, p. 252.
[2] Loc. cit., p. 10; this refers to the West Victorian tribes.
[3] Eyre, ii. p. 302 (Murray River tribes).
[4] Ibid., p. 304.
[5] Encounter Bay tribes, Meyer, loc. cit., p. 187.
[6] Kam. and Kurn., p. 286.
[7] Schürmann, loc. cit., p. 222.

Teichelmann and Schürmann report that there was a separate hut in which women dwelt during their period.[1]

We read in the description of the United States expedition to New South Wales that the youths have to avoid women from initiation till marriage and that they have their separate encampment.[2]

In the Euahlayi tribe boys go after their seventh year to the Weedeghal, bachelors' camp.[3]

Among the Central tribes (Krichauff Ranges) there is a separate men's camp and a camp for women, where these latter are confined during certain periods of their life.[4]

We read that among the natives of Finke River (Central Australia) "separate places are assigned for the unmarried men and for the single females respectively."[5] The same author reports that the natives are fond of visits. "The meeting-place is usually the Tmara-nkanja for the men, *i. e.* the bachelors' camp."[6]

In the Arunta tribe the boys "go out with the women as they searched for vegetable food and the smaller animals," up to the first initiation ceremony. Afterwards "they begin to accompany the men in their search for larger" game. At this first initiation they change also their mode of living; "in the future they must not play with the women and girls, nor must they camp with them as they have hitherto done, but henceforth they must go to the camp of the men, which is known as the Ungunja."[7] Among the Arunta there is a "special part of the main camp where the men assemble and near to which the women may not go."[8] It must exist only when a greater number of natives are assembled,[9] for normally the people roam scattered over the country. But during these latter periods the unmarried men lead probably an existence of their own, as they cannot live with families (compare above mode of living). This information about the bachelors' camp in the Arunta is not quite clear, as we see. But all we read points to its existence.

We find the bachelors' camp (Lagerplatz der jungen Männer; tmarankintja) mentioned by the Rev. E. Strehlow, in connection with the totemic ceremonies amongst the Arunta.[10]

---

[1] In Waitz Gerland, p. 778. That refers probably to South Australian aborigines in general.

[2] Chas. Wilkes, smaller ed., i. p. 225; larger ed., ii. p. 205.

[3] Mrs. Parker, *loc. cit.*, p. 61.   [4] Krichauff, *loc. cit.*, p. 78.

[5] Schultze, *loc. cit.*, p. 230.   [6] *Ibid.*, p. 234.

[7] Spencer and Gillen, *Nat. Tr.*, pp. 215, 216.

[8] See index, p. 656; the Ungunja is mentioned several times in the text, p. 557 and *passim*.   [9] See Chap. V.

[10] Part iii. p. 7 and *passim*.

We read about the tribes near Port Darwin : " Children live with their parents until puberty, when girls become members of their husband's households, residing sometimes with him, and at other times at the parental camp." [1] I may add here, that this is the only example where matri-local marriage is mentioned in Australia. Everywhere else we find it stated that the girl removes to her husband's camp.[2] We read farther that the boys are taken, after their initiation, "in charge by those whose duty it is to train " them. " They lived in a large wurley, which would accommodate all the boys. As a fact . . . no boys between seventeen and nineteen are seen at Port Darwin." [3] Here we are told that there was one big hut in which all the boys lived ; but this seems rather to be an exception.

Roth says that children of about seven years of age leave their parents' camp and go to stay with their grandparents.[4] We are not informed whether there exists a bachelors' camp in the North-West Central Queensland tribes ; but this statement does not deny it, for boys are apparently not at once initiated after leaving their parental camp. Another statement of the same author about the natives of Koombana Bay (Queensland), affirms it explicitly : " The younger single males at a certain stage (puberty and onwards) always had a fire to themselves." [5] And again : " The grown-up lads sleep together, apart from the others." [6]

Grey says that strangers visiting a tribe, if unmarried or without their wives, " sleep at the fire of the young men." [7]

Bishop Salvado, according to whose information the South-West Australian natives live in small tribes of six to nine persons, says that when a family disposes itself to sleep " les garçons qui ont passé l'âge de sept ans dorment seuls autour du feu commun." [8]

It is stated in two statements above (Dawson and Schultze), that there were camps of unmarried females as well as of single men. We may add here two other statements about such camps.[9] In the Maryborough tribes there were camps of unmarried girls, in connection with which there was some sexual licence. Similarly in the North-West Central Queens-land tribes,[10] studied by Roth, single girls lived in groups, under the control of an old man. Such phenomena would account for the licence of unmarried females, which we

[1] T. A. Parkhouse, *loc. cit.*, p. 641.
[2] Compare N. W. Thomas, *loc. cit.*, p. 16.
[3] *Ibid.*, p. 643.   [4] *Eth. Stud.*, p. 183.
[5] *Proc. R.S.Q.*, p. 48.   [6] *Ibid.*, p. 51.
[7] Grey, ii. p. 252.   [8] p. 280.
[9] Howitt, *Nat. Tr.*, pp. 232, 233.   [10] *N. Q. Eth. Bull.* 8, p. 6.

find sometimes reported. But they do not seem to have a very large extension in the Australian aboriginal society.

We see in the first place from this evidence [1] that boys were actually removed from their parents' care and that they acquired a complete independence of their parents on reaching puberty. This is especially mentioned in several of our statements (Kurnai, Bangerang, Lower Murray River tribes, Encounter Bay tribes, Port Darwin tribes). It appears also to result *ipso facto* from the circumstance that the boys lived in quite a different part of the encampment, and so could not be under the control of their parents. It appears from Curr's and Parkhouse's statements that they even lived in a separate locality. And confronting our evidence concerning the bachelors' camp with what we know about the aboriginal mode of living, it appears also highly probable that if the boys' camp numbered from six to eight inmates (compare Eyre's statement) they must have roamed about in a separate group. We read that in two cases the boys joined their grandparents (Howitt about the Mukjara-waint tribe and Roth). Only the statement of Dawson suggests that boys remained with their parents, and even that, as we saw, does not follow very clearly from this statement.

We are informed in several places about the mode of living of the lads in their separate camp. They seem to have partly provided their own food and cooked it (Curr). They slept in one big hut (Parkhouse) or round a common fire (Salvado and others). In general they seem to have formed a distinct, separate social unit. This time, spent in the bachelors' camp, was the real time of training (see Curr's statement. Compare Hutton Webster, *loc. cit.*, chap. iv. pp. 49–51). They came under the influence of a new authority—the authority of the tribal elders. And, especially during the actual time of initiation, all the

[1] We have collected here twenty-two statements in which there are many more tribes included.

wisdom and morality they had to learn was imparted to the young people by the old men of the tribe. Probably there also they formed new acquaintances and relationships besides the family ones in which they were brought up. The institution of bachelors' camp is general among all the Australian tribes. Our evidence is not detailed enough to allow us to trace geographical differences in any particular feature. We may mention here, by the way, that the bachelors' camp of Australia was a form of the widespread institution of the men's-house.[1]

In sum, all these factors give great weight to the facts here discussed; viz. to those of the early marriage of girls and the initiation of boys. We see that these facts take away from the Australian family its patriarchal character. The father's authority is exercised over his children merely during their early childhood, *i. e.* during a period when there is in a general way very little room for the display of any serious authority. Still more, as there was no serious and real training during this time, all education, as far as it was given at all by the father. assumed more the form of play, as we saw above (p. 256) ; and, as we saw, during that period great leniency towards the offspring was the chief feature of the father's behaviour.[2] When a serious and often harsh training took place, it was not the father's individual authority that enforced it, but the tribal elders'. So we see that our former result is hereby confirmed, viz. that there is no foundation for designing the father's relation to his child as based upon authority or any idea of proprietorship. That applies to a girl as well as to a boy. But in the case of the former we might attribute some meaning to the

[1] In this connection the bachelors' camp in Australia is mentioned by Hutton Webster (amongst the Kurnai, Euahlayi, Arunta and Port Darwin tribes). The author speaks of it as a symptom of the general principle of separation of sexes. *Primitive Secret Societies*, pp. 1, 3.

[2] On these connections in general compare the interesting article of Steinmetz, *Zeitschrift f. Socialw.*, II, pp. 613, 614.

word property, although it would be rather straining the sense of the word.

IV

It was seen that on reaching a certain age the children leave their parents' camp and are removed from their control; still the personal, individual bond of kinship is not broken.   And although it does not find its expression in facts of daily life, for the children and the parents live apart, yet there are some facts which unmistakably reveal the existence of a strong lifelong affection and attachment between parents and children.

These facts are: real sorrow displayed at the death or funeral of a near relative, and especially that displayed by parents at the death of their children; joy and tenderness shown to children whenever met for the first time after a long absence.   Here also must be placed the numerous occurrences in which love was displayed for white men who were recognized as dead relatives. In these cases their supposed parents always displayed the greatest amount of tenderness towards them, and often underwent considerable sacrifices for the sake of helping or even seeing their " children."   The close connection between grandchildren and grandparents shows also that there was a near individual tie between the parents of the children and their parents.   Let us adduce some statements.

Statements.—Curr remarks shortly but clearly: " Parental affection always endured," after the children left their parents and became practically independent of them.[1]

A story showing strong filial attachment is told by R. Dawson. Relating an anecdote, he concludes: " The manner in which Youee told the story was exceedingly interesting; his lamentations, that ' white pellow ' should treat his father so, and the mild complaining tone in which they were made, thoroughly portrayed his filial attachment to his father, of

---

[1] *Recollections*, p. 248.

whom he said several times, turning to him with a tone and manner that could not be mistaken, ' *Murry* good wool man ! *Murry* good wool man, massa.' " [1]

A characteristic story, proving paternal affection, is told by Bonney. An old man was once cut with a tomahawk by his son, a big, strong man who had fits of madness. " The old man returned to the camp and with tears in his eyes told me what had happened, and begged me to assist him to bring back his mad son before he had perished in the bush." [2]

We have also a few statements about the relations between grandparents and grandchildren. We are informed that among the Mukjarawaint the grandparents had the exclusive right to decide whether the child should be killed directly after birth or allowed to live. In the former case the grandparents had the privilege of eating the child. [3] We read of the important rôle the grandmother played in the North Queensland tribes at the naming of the child, [4] and amongst the Euahlayi at the Betrothal Ceremony. [5] Amongst the Kurnai also " the name is given by the paternal grandfather or grandmother, or in default by the mother's parents." [6]

A series of interesting instances is told by Fraser. He says, " Their natural affections are keen; in proof of this I need only refer to their grief over a dead relative, even though it be a very young child; they utter loud lamentations and cut and burn the flesh of their bodies in grief. This expression of grief is not all artificial or professional like the hired ' ululatus ' of the Romans or the ' keening ' of the Irish. That it is genuine on the part of the near relatives of the deceased I can prove by examples. Jackey, the ' king ' of the Gresford blacks, died and was buried; his mother could not be induced to leave the spot; she sat there night and day, refusing food, until one morning she was found dead on his grave. She was buried beside her son." [7]—" A woman of the Dungog tribule had a child which was hunch-backed and otherwise deformed ; she carried it on her back for eighteen or nineteen years; it seemed always no bigger than a child of six or seven years. Her husband also carried about, for two or three years, a son whose feet from the ankles had been destroyed by frostbite." [8]—" At Durham Downs (Queensland), ' king ' Brady had a little boy, two years old, who became

[1] R. Dawson, *loc. cit.*, p. 312. Pt. Stephens tribes.
[2] Bonney, *J.A.I.*, xiii. p. 135. Riv. Darling tribe.
[3] Howitt, *Nat. Tr.*, pp. 243, 749.
[4] Roth, *Bull.* V. p. 8.
[5] Mrs. Parker, *loc. cit.*, p. 51. Comp. above, p. 40.
[6] Howitt, *Kam. and Kurn.*, pp. 190, 191.
[7] J. Fraser, *loc. cit.*, p. 44.   [8] *Ibid.*

helpless from disease; the mother carried him about with
her for many years." [1]—" Then again, the transport of delight
with which Buckley was received by a woman of a local tribe
who believed that this white man was her deceased son come
to life again, is a proof of the strength of natural affection
among them." [2]

To this last might be added several other instances where
white people were received with the greatest love and affection
by their " black parents," who believed them to be their dead
children. As we mentioned these examples above (p. 222)
in another connection we merely refer the reader to that
place.

Salvado says : " Reprenant la suite de mon récit, je dirai
que les fils adultes payent de retour l'affection de leurs parents.
S'ils sont vieux, ils réservent pour eux les meilleures pièces de
gibier, ou de tout autre mets, et se chargent de venger leurs
offenses. Enfin ils leurs témoignent leur amour au delà de la
tombe, en tuant un ou deux sauvages quand leur père vient
à mourir." [3]

In the description of mourning and burial it appears in
several places that the " immediate relations," probably in
the first place their own parents and children, have special
duties and obligations. " In the Tongaranka tribe, when a
death occurs, the immediate relations smear themselves with
Kopai (gypsum)." [4]

" When one of the . . . Wiim-baio tribe died . . . the relations used to lie with their heads on the body, and even
stretched at length on the corpse." [5] In the same tribe
after a man's death " his immediate relations cut off their
hair and applied to their heads a paste." [6]

In the Chepara tribe " the relations of a dead person for
several months after wore emu feathers, dyed red." " The
mother of the deceased had her nose and all her body painted
with stripes of white pipeclay, and wore red feathers over the
whole of her head. A sister had also her head covered with
red feathers, but was not painted white. After a few weeks
the painting was changed to red, and then was worn by
father, mother and sisters for a long time." [7]

At Port Stephens " an old couple had an only daughter of
whom they were very fond. She died, and her parents built
their hut over her grave close to the shore of the harbour,
and lived there many months, crying for her every evening
at sunset." [8]

---

[1] J. Fraser, *loc. cit.*, p. 44.   [2] *Ibid.*
[3] Salvado, *loc. cit.*, p. 277.   [4] Howitt, *Nat. Tr.*, p. 451.
[5] *Ibid.*   [6] *Ibid.*, p. 452.
[7] *Ibid.*, p. 469.   [8] *Ibid.*, p. 465.

In the description of mourning ceremonies given by Spencer and Gillen it appears plainly that the rôle of the individual mother was quite singular and the most important. " The actual mother of the deceased was painted deeply all over with pipeclay." [1] " On the way to the grave the actual mother often threw herself heavily on the ground and attempted to cut her head with a digging stick." [2]

Also the blood brother plays, apparently, a part different from that of the tribal ones. " After going a short distance they were met by a man who was a blood brother of the dead woman, and was accompanied by a number of his tribal brothers." [3]

All this evidence, although relatively scanty, shows clearly that the individual relations between parents and children continued to be strong and intimate. This fact also throws light on the character of these relations during early childhood. In this period the bonds were formed, and they must have been formed in a very strong and thorough manner indeed if they lasted so long. This conclusion is of such a general and fundamental character, and the evidence is so scanty, that it would be futile to attempt tracing any geographical distinctions between the different tribes. Like the other general conclusions arrived at in this chapter, it has features common to all the aboriginal tribes of Australia.

We have extremely scanty information concerning the relation between brothers and sisters; and the few hints we possess are very contradictory. Thus Gason says that a brother and sister " would sacrifice their lives for one another if called upon." [4] And Fraser informs us that when a man is sick it is his brother's duty to tend him and carry him about. And the author gives an example in support of this statement.[5] And again we read in Oldfield that a girl, if her mother is dead, " is bound to supply them (her brothers) with food for a certain period; indeed, brothers in general retain the privilege of maltreating their sisters long after these

[1] Spencer and Gillen, *Nat. Tr.*, p. 508.   [2] *Ibid.*, p. 509.
[3] *Ibid.*, p. 508.   [4] *J.A.I.*, xxiv. p. 170.   [5] *Loc. cit.*, p. 44.

latter became the property of another."[1] On the other hand, Grey states that no " common bond of union " exists between brothers and sisters of the same father.[2] And according to Spencer and Gillen a man may never speak from a near to his younger sister, although he may speak freely to his older one.[3] Among the natives of Yorke's Peninsula brothers and sisters were not allowed to converse.[4] In some West Australian tribes the boy was never allowed to speak to his sisters after the initiation ceremony. He had to say farewell to his sisters before he went to the initiation. The " own " brothers and sisters keep apart from each other. And even boys or girls of the same class cannot speak or play together.[5] The first three statements appear to indicate a close individual relationship between brother and sister; the four following seem to deny it again. Recalling to mind what we learned about the relation in question in other connections, we hardly get much help therefrom. The exchange of sisters would point to some ties; but, it is too uncertain a hint. The facts that children are suckled for a long time, and that owing to that and to the practice of infanticide connected with it, the children succeed each other at long intervals, reduce the possibility of close ties between the children of the same parents; especially as they so soon leave the parental camp, and as probably afterwards the intercourse between the sisters and brothers is interrupted (compare statements of Curr and Spencer and Gillen). On the whole we know very little about the relation in question; and we may only conjecture, although with a high degree of probability, that the tie is not a very strong one and does not play an important part in family life; if it were otherwise we probably would know more about it.

---

[1] Oldfield, p. 249.   [2] *Loc. cit.*, ii. p. 230.
[3] Spencer and Gillen, *Nat. Tr.*, p. 89.
[4] Sutton, *loc. cit.*, p. 19.
[5] Mrs. D. M. Bates, *loc. cit.*, p. 5. The same is reported by A. L. P. Cameron of the natives of Cooper's Creek. *Science of Man.* July 1904.

CHAPTER VIII

ECONOMICS

Now we proceed to pass in survey the economic facts connected with family life in Australia. As we are dealing with the individual family, the first question that naturally presents itself is: How far in Australia is the individual family an economic unit? In other words, in what way is the individuality of the single family determined by the economic facts?

To answer this general question we are led to examine various sets of facts. In the first place, we know that in primitive societies there is already a rudimentary division of labour, or rather a division of economic functions, within the household. It is usually called the sexual division of labour; obviously it makes the household an economic unit; for it is just the division of labour which establishes the unity of a social group from the economic point of view. We must ask, therefore: Which, respectively, are the chief functions of the husband and of the wife? Who provides the food and performs the labours of the camp?

The economic unity of the family may also be constituted by other facts. It is necessary in this connection to say a few words again of individual land ownership, discussed above in connection with the mode of living; several statements must be adduced referring to the well-known features of communism and general liberality among the Australian blacks. These features throw considerable light upon native economics with reference to the constitution of the family. Let us begin by examining the evidence on the sexual division of labour.

Statements.—The question of the economic side of family life is quite correctly set forth and answered by Howitt[1]: Amongst the Kurnai, as " the pairing family is strictly established," we might expect " that the domestic life, the arrangements of the family circle, and the division of labour should conform, more or less perfectly, to that condition. . . . The man has to provide for his family with the assistance of his wife. His share is to hunt for their support and to fight for their protection." The woman has to build the hut, to fish, to gather fruit seeds and all vegetable food, and to weave rush bags or nets. " The supply of vegetable food procured by the woman is all devoted to her husband, her children and herself." [2] The man's contribution goes only in part to supply the wants of his own family, the rest being divided between other relatives (see below). Fishing belonged to both sexes.[3]

Dawson reports the existence of permanent and temporary dwellings in his tribes. " The men share the labour of making the permanent dwelling, but the women are compelled to erect the smaller one." [4] The women carry in bags on their back all domestic utensils, as sticks, tinder for producing fire, gum for cement, shells, tools, charms and food. The custom of carrying burning fire-sticks is also reported by Dawson.[5] And in another place we read : " After marriage the women are compelled to do all the hard work of erecting habitations, collecting fuel and water, carrying burdens, procuring roots and delicacies of various kinds, making baskets for cooking roots and other purposes, preparing food, and attending to the children. The only work the men do in time of peace is to hunt for opossums and large animals of various kinds, and to make rugs and weapons." [6]

A still clearer picture of the division of labour between the sexes is drawn by Curr in his Memoirs. On the march the men carried the arms and their personal effects; the women had to carry all the other implements as well as the small children. The supply of vegetable food belonged to them.[7] When several families camped together the women went in parties to procure roots, small animals and other food, carrying babies on their backs and followed by other children.

---

[1] *Kam. and Kurn.*, pp. 206, 207.

[2] *Ibid.*, p. 263.

[3] *Nat. Tr.*, p. 761.

[4] It is probable that these are innovations since the advent of white men. See Howitt, *Kam and Kurn.*, p. 206.

[5] J. Dawson, p. 11.

[6] *Ibid.*, pp. 36, 37.

[7] *Recollections*, p. 251.

The men, in parties of three or four, went out hunting. After returning to camp, each party cooked its food. The men, however, gave to their wives only the remainder of their food, sharing it first with the children; it seems, therefore, that the food supply provided by the female was much more regular and reliable, and therefore of greater importance to the family, than the man's share.[1] And again we read : " At the family fires the father generally cooked the animals which he brought home, and the woman the roots which were her contribution." [2]

Speaking of all the Australian tribes in general, Curr says : " Among the Australian blacks the common occupations of the men are the manufacture of arms and implements for hunting, fishing and occasionally war. The women generally procure and cook vegetables and fish, collect wood for fire, manufacture nets and bags. On the march the woman carries child, household effects, fire-stick, and digs for roots and vegetables.[3] " Wives have to undergo all the drudgery of the camp and the march, have the poorest food and the hardest work." [4] This statement gives quite clearly the division of labour, the greater share falling on the wife.

Amongst the Mount Gambier tribes (West Victoria) the females have to construct the lodge, to collect firewood, and to make the fire.[5] They always carry the fire-stick when travelling.[6] They fetch water and collect all vegetable food, roots, and mushrooms, with their digging-stick.[7] The men's task is hunting; they do it generally in company.[8] Men make arms and prepare skins; women, objects of use and adornment.[9]

We read in Angas that carrying all the things, digging of roots, and making the huts is woman's work.[10]

Eyre says that the women had to dress the huts.[11]

We read in Br. Smyth that women had to carry all the " worldly goods " of their husbands, even part of their arms.[12]

The men hunt and women collect food during their march according to Protector Thomas. There exists a customary communism among them.[13]

Mitchell says that because of their great skill in manufacturing all the things of daily use as "nets, cloaks, mussel-fishing, rooting, etc.; and their patient submission to labour,

---

[1] *Recollections*, p. 256.   [2] *Ibid.*
[3] Curr, *A.R.*, i. p. 99.   [4] *Ibid.*, p. 110.
[5] Stanbridge, *loc. cit.*, p. 290.   [6] *Ibid.*, p. 291.
[7] *Ibid.*   [8] *Ibid.*, p. 293.   [9] *Ibid.*, p. 295.
[10] *Loc. cit.*, pp. 82, 84, 87.   [11] *Loc. cit.*, ii. p. 302.
[12] *Loc. cit.*, p. 85.   This is a quotation on the authority of an observer (Jardine).   [13] Howitt, *Nat. Tr.*, p. 767.

always carrying bags containing the whole property of the family while they follow their masters, the great value of a gin to one of these lazy fellows may be easily imagined." [1] They are, therefore, the chief objects of all their fights.

Meyer states about the Encounter Bay tribes that the man regarded his wife as a slave and let her do all the hard work, employing her in all ways to his advantage.[2] He even prostituted her for objects of use.[3] But he states also the typical division of labour : " the men employ themselves . . . either in fishing or hunting emus, opossums, kangaroos, etc., while the women and children search for roots and plants." It is also the women's task to arrange the encampments.[4]

In the Port Lincoln tribes men provided animal and women vegetable food.[5]

We read in another author, about the same tribes, that women have to collect vegetable food, while the men are hunting.[6] There is also some kind of division of consumption; men eat male, women female animals, and children the small ones.[7]

Among the Wiradjuri (New South Wales) : " The wife always looks after the camping arrangements." [8]

Speaking of the Port Jackson tribes, Tench says that they derive their principal food supply from fishing. Both men and women take part in this; the men spearing the fish and the women catching them from land and sea. Both husband and wife bring their shares to the common household.[9]

Both men and women take part in procuring the fish supply among the natives of Botany Bay.[10]

According to Henderson, among some of the New South Wales tribes the women have to carry children and all burdens; they procure also roots and shellfish.[11]

Gribble says : " The women always look after camp arrangements." [12]

Fishing was the chief support of the aborigines of Port Jackson described by D. Collins. In procuring this food, men, women and children were employed.[13]

In the compilation of Dr. Fraser, on the New South Wales tribes, we have a detailed account of the sexual division of labour. The woman has to put up the wurley; to light and

---

[1] Quoted by Br. Smyth, i. p. 85.   [2] *Loc. cit.*, p. 191.
[3] This may be the influence of culture, as Europeans are mentioned in connection therewith.
[4] pp. 191, 192.   [5] Schürmann, *loc. cit.*, p. 221.
[6] Chas. Wilhelmi, pp. 174, 175, 177.   [7] *Ibid.*, p. 176.
[8] Howitt, *Nat. Tr.*, p. 776.   [9] *Loc. cit.*, pp. 193–196.
[10] Phillip, p. 31.   [11] *Loc. cit.*, p. 122.
[12] *Loc. cit.*, p. 117.   [13] Collins, i. p. 556.

keep the fire, to carry the fire-stick, to cook the food. On the march she carries the bag containing the whole property of the family, the children and the yam-stick. Her duty is to provide fish and vegetable food.[1] The man has only to hunt.[2]

All the drudgery of the camp and all the hard work was the lot of the women. They made nets and bags and they carried, on the marches, all the domestic implements as well as the children.[3]

In the Arunta tribe the women have " to do a considerable part, but by no means all, of the work of the camp." [4] From a detailed description we see that the women have to procure vegetable food and small animals, marsupials, etc., which they do with their digging-sticks. The man's task is hunting.[5]

In the Port Essington tribes, the digging of roots and collecting of shellfish was the woman's task.[6]

" I have observed that upon the northern coasts of Australia the amount of the population upon a certain tract of country is great or small in proportion to the quantity of *vegetable* food it produces. However abundant animal food may be, a toilsome search for edible roots gives almost constant occupation to a portion of every tribe. Women and children labour for hours together, with no other implement than a pointed stick, in following up the creeping stem of the wild yam through the earth until the root is arrived at, often at a depth of six or eight feet below the surface. A certain proportion of vegetable food appears, indeed, to be absolutely necessary to their existence, and they willingly forego the use of the animal food, if this more grateful diet can be obtained in sufficient abundance." [7]

We are informed that among the Bunya-Bunya people (Turrubul and kindred tribes, South East Queensland) the woman had all the heavy work to do.[8]

Among the aborigines of Moreton Bay, women have to erect the huts and provide vegetable food for the whole party, as the men only have to supply fish and game.[9]

We owe a good description of the division of labour on the march to Mathew : " When shifting from one camping-ground to another they usually moved slowly through the bush, the families separating and gathering their food on the way—opossums, bandicoots, honey, grubs, birds, and so forth. At other times they marched along singly, the lords

---

[1] *Loc. cit.*, p. 2.
[2] *Loc. cit.*, p. 60.
[3] Port Stephens tribes. R. Dawson, p. 67.
[4] Spencer and Gillen, *Nat. Tr.*, p. 50.
[5] *Ibid.*, p. 19.
[6] Macgillivray, i. p. 148.
[7] Earl, p. 251.
[8] Petrie, p. 61.
[9] B. Field, p. 75.

of creation stepping out with elastic tread and graceful bearing, carrying their light weapons with perhaps some game, the weaker vessel loaded with the chattels and possibly a baby on the back in a loop of a rug or sitting stride-leg on a shoulder. Some would carry live fire-sticks to save the trouble of producing fire by friction. Arrived at the familiar, well-chosen rendezvous, it was the duty of the women to cut the bark of the humpies (dwellings) and prepare the fires." [1] Further on we read : " The women were skilled in the manufacture of nets and of dillie-bags made of grass or twine." [2] " The man's chief home duties consisted in cooking and eating. He would also spend much time in fashioning his weapons." [3]

Lumholtz speaks of the woman as the slave of her husband. " He does only what pleases himself, and leaves all work to his wives; therefore the more wives he has the richer he is." [4] We see here again the economic value of a wife directly stated. In another place : " It is the women who daily provide food," often making long excursions for this purpose, and collecting fruits, digging roots and chopping larvæ out of the tree-stems. "She must do all the hard work," carry the baby, make the fire, cook, provide water and fuel, dress the hut. She carries all the baggage on the march, as well as the children. The man carries only his arms. " The husband's contribution to the household is chiefly honey, but occasionally he provides eggs, game, lizards, and the like. He very often, however, keeps the animal food for himself, while the woman has to depend principally upon vegetables for herself and her child. Upon the whole he feels no responsibility as the father of a family." [5] It is interesting to find that the men make not only weapons but also, exclusively, baskets.[6]

Among the North-West Queensland tribes : " It is the husband's business, in the main, to supply the animal food for the family, and although a particular dietary may be forbidden him he has no compunction in hunting or killing it for his kith and kin." [7] It is necessary to add that according to Roth's information each member of a given family has some special food forbidden to him; because each class has its special food taboos, and in a family the father, the mother and the children, each belong to a different class.[8] Roth sees in this institution the chief aim of the class system.[9] Vegetable food and fish seem to be supplied by women

---

[1] *Loc. cit.*, p. 83. [2] *Ibid.*, p. 82. [3] *Ibid.*, p. 86.
[4] *Loc. cit.*, p. 100. [5] *Loc. cit.*, p. 160, 161.
[6] *Ibid.*, p. 193. [7] *Eth. Stud.*, p. 184.
[8] *Ibid.*, p. 57. [9] *Ibid.*, p. 69.

chiefly.[1]   The same general principle of sexual division of labour is reported in another place by the same author. We read there that the father's duty was to supply his family with animal food, whereas the mother had to provide the vegetable food. On the wanderings the wife follows her husband at a considerable distance, carrying all the implements and often the children.[2]

Among the natives of Cape York the woman has to procure practically all food for herself and her husband.[3]

Moore describes the women in West Australia as being almost the slaves of their husbands. They have to attend upon the men and to carry all their property. They construct the hut, kindle the fire, and have to provide all the vegetable food.[4]   The digging of the yams is a very laborious task.[5]   In return they often do not get even their share of game.[6]

John Forrest writes in his account : " The women are nearly slaves, having to do most of the hard work, such as making huts, carrying wood, and also carrying all the baggage, which includes many weapons, grease, ' wilgie,' and a host of articles, wooden dishes, etc., besides often a child. The man does not generally carry much except his spears, etc." [7]

Among some of the West Australian blacks, a female, before she is married, has under certain circumstances to provide " individuals of a certain degree of relationship to herself with a certain amount of vegetable food." [8]   After her marriage her husband is entitled " to the chief part of her services. While she has to supply him with unlimited quantities of yams and other roots, he does very little towards providing for her wants, merely giving her the offal of game." The woman is thus the chief caterer of the family. She is " a slave in the strictest sense of the word, being a beast of burden, a provider of food." [9]

In South-West Australia the woman carries all the domestic implements on her back. " Pendant que la femme chemine avec toute cette charge, l'homme marche devant sa famille, portant seulement ses armes de la main gauche." He looks for animals,[10] the chase is his task.[11]   The woman has to light the fire, carry the fire-stick,[12] fetch the water [13]; she has also to construct the hut.[14]

---

[1] Eth. Stud., ch. v. passim, especially pp. 91, 94, 95.
[2] N.Q. Eth. Bull. 8, p. 9, § 2.
[3] Macgillivray, loc. cit., ii. p. 9.   [4] Loc. cit., p. 80.
[5] Ibid., p. 74.   [6] Ibid., p. 80.
[7] Loc. cit., p. 319.   [8] Murchison District, Oldfield, p. 249.
[9] Ibid., p. 250.   [10] Swan District, Salvado, p. 295.
[11] Ibid., see ch. viii. passim.   [12] p. 317.
[13] Ibid., p. 315.   [14] Ibid., p. 321.

We are informed by Browne that all the hard work, the carrying of heavy burdens, camp arrangements, etc., is done by the women among the natives of King George's Sound.[1]

The economic division of labour, based upon the co-operation of both sexes, is stated by Scott Nind. The women and men go out in search of food, or hunting, in separate parties. The women chiefly collect roots and small animals; men go out hunting. Each sex reserves a part of its share for the family. " The women are very useful for them (their husbands), not only in procuring food, but also in preparing their cloaks, building their huts and other menial offices." [2]

We see that our thirty-five statements agree pretty well as to the general features of the division of labour. Certain of the economic functions, like hunting, making of weapons and, undoubtedly, the important function of protecting the family, are allotted to the men. Other work—the providing of roots, bulbs and other vegetable food, camp work and carrying heavy burdens, manufacturing nets and usually fishing—all this is the duty of the woman. Our statements more or less agree upon this division of labour. The more detailed ones (Howitt on the Kurnai, Dawson, Curr, Stanbridge, Mathew, B. Field, Oldfield, Moore) depict to us the occupations of the man and of his wife in nearly the same words. Only in the statements of Collins, Tench and Phillips is fishing mentioned as a common occupation of men and women. But these statements (probably not independent of each other) are not so explicit and reliable as to lead us to make exceptions of the Port Jackson tribes. We may, therefore, affirm the existence of a very marked sexual division of labour, which seems to present everywhere the same features and to be nearly identical over the whole continent. *Prima facie* this division of labour consists only in each sex having its different occupations prescribed by custom. But more careful analysis shows that there are other features which more deeply differentiate the economic activities of the sexes.

[1] *Loc. cit.*, p. 450.
[2] *Loc. cit.*, pp. 36, 37. Refers to the tribes of King George's Sound.

It is easy to see that the amount of work allotted to women is *considerably greater* and that their labour is much *harder* than the men's work. This is directly affirmed by a series of statements (Curr, Dawson, Stanbridge, Tom Petrie, Mathew, Lumholtz, Forrest, Salvado, Scott Nind, Moore). This is also undoubtedly a reason why so many authors designate the wife's position as that of a slave and drudge. But it also results directly from a comparison of the occupations allotted to women with those allotted to men. A woman had to carry all the heavy things, all the objects of domestic use, her own as well as her husband's; for the man carried only his weapons (Dawson, Curr, Stanbridge, Angas, Br. Smyth, Thomas, Phillips, Fraser, Lumholtz, Salvado). The woman had to construct huts and look after camping arrangements (Howitt on the Kurnai, Dawson, Stanbridge, Meyer, Schürmann, Angas, Howitt on the Wiradjuri, Gribble, Henderson, Fraser, Field, Mathew, Lumholtz, Forrest, Salvado, Browne). All this was rather hard work, especially when compared with the man's share of work, which was mainly hunting and fashioning weapons. It must not be forgotten that women were often encumbered in their work by suckling, carrying their children, and by the various cares demanded by the latter. The digging for roots is also exceedingly hard work (Moore, Earl).

More regular and *systematic* kind of labour is also called for by the nature of the woman's tasks. These are intimately connected with the wandering mode of life of the aborigines. Obviously in a people which was forced by natural conditions to lead a roaming life, such tasks must necessarily have required regular labour. The other chief female occupation—collecting roots and small animals—required also a regular kind of labour. All these occupations—being, as just said, harder and more systematic than men's work, clearly appear also to be much more wearing and tiresome; compared with the men's occupations they appear much less in the light of

sport and amusement. The man makes his weapons and
hunts, and this is a natural and pleasant sport for him.
There are no elements of excitement or variety in the
women's work; it is just this element of system and of
regularity which makes work repulsive and hard to man,
and especially to primitive man. Work of this kind is
usually done only under a strong compulsion; and
woman's work in Australia appears also to be compulsory.
This is directly stated in several places (Dawson, Curr,
Mitchell, Forrest, Moore, Oldfield). This compulsory
character is undoubtedly another reason why the women's
position is described in other statements as that of a
slave and drudge.

A very important point is that the woman's share in
labour was of much more *vital importance* to the maintenance of the household than man's work. This is quite
obvious, seeing that the general occupations of camp life
were of essential necessity for a roving people. But even
the food supply, contributed by the women, was far more
important than the man's share. We read that the chief
resource of the natives, especially in bad seasons, is
vegetable food (Oldfield). And the interesting statement
of Earl confirms this in a still stronger manner. So that
it appears fairly probable that, on the whole, food collected
by women was the staple food of the natives. But not
only does the kind of food supplied by the man appear on
the whole to be less important than that contributed by
the woman, but it seems as if the man's contribution,
which in the main was reduced to his hunting products,
was devoted much less exclusively to his family's benefit.
In order to understand this, let us adduce some statements
relating to communism of food, and giving besides some
interesting details about aboriginal economics.

Statements.—Among the Kurnai [1] the hunter who killed a
big piece of game gave some of it to the men who assisted
him in killing, cooking or carving. The chief parts were

[1] Howitt, *Kam. and Kurn.*, App. D, p. 261. Compare *Idem*,
Nat. Tr., pp. 756–759.

divided among his wives' parents and his own parents. These in return supplied their son and son-in-law respectively with meat the next day. Similar rules, varying according to the game and tribe, obtained also among the Murring tribes of New South Wales.¹ Important for us is the general feature of communism; the preponderancy given to the parents of a man and his wife. If the man be unmarried he provides chiefly his parents and his brother and sister.² The grandparents cared especially for their grandchildren.³

In the Wurrunjeri tribe a kangaroo was distributed among those present in camp and the hunter's family. The man had (even in case of a limited food supply) to provide for his own and his wife's parents. They cared in turn for him.⁴ Communism obtained among the Kulin tribes.⁵

A communism, similar to that of the Kurnai, prevailed among the Narran-ga.⁶ The same is related about the tribes of the Karamundi⁷; the Wolgal tribe,⁸ amongst whom the woman was provided for with food by her parents; the Wiradjuri; Wotjobaluk; Mukjarawaint.⁹ Among the Gournditch-Mara game was divided amongst all present in camp.¹⁰

J. Dawson states that food brought by a hunter to the camp was distributed so that he and even his brother gets the worst part of it. "The best pieces of birds and quadrupeds and the finest eels" were given away. An anecdote is told in support of this statement which appears trustworthy.¹¹ It may be pointed out that this apparently refers only to food brought by men; and that this statement only says that the shares of the individual and his brother were neglected; but it does not make clear how the shares of the other relations (family, wife, parents) were regulated, if they were favoured or the reverse.

In the Chepara tribe, the men, women and children went out every morning to hunt and search for food. It was a man's duty to provide food. This food was divided equally amongst all those present by the old men. A man had special duties towards his wife's parents if they were sick and unable to hunt.¹² Here we see a communism which gives no preference to any relation, and apparently treats equally all the members of the local group.

---

¹ *Kam. and Kurn.*, pp. 264–267, and *Nat. Tr.*, pp. 759–760 (refers to the Ngarigo tribe of the Murring nation).
² *Kam. and Kurn.*, pp. 259.   ³ *Ibid.*, pp. 262, 263.
⁴ Howitt, *Nat. Tr.*, p. 765.   ⁵ *Ibid.*, p. 767.
⁶ Of South Australia, Howitt, *Nat. Tr.*, p. 762.
⁷ *Ibid.*   ⁸ *Ibid.*, p. 764.   ⁹ *Ibid.*
¹⁰ *Kam. and Kurn.*, p. 277 and *Nat. Tr.*, p. 765.
¹¹ Dawson, p. 22.   ¹² Howitt, *Nat. Tr.*, p. 768.

Curious customs obtained among the Narrinyeri, when an emu was killed. It was first divided by an old man with some ceremonies, apart from the camp, and then carried to the camp and eaten by men, women and children alike.[1] This shows, by the way, that big game like emu, or kangaroo, must be rather an exceptional feast; and as all the communistic customs in this connection refer to bigger game, they do not affect, perhaps, so much the everyday food supply, which is due chiefly to females.

Among the Port Lincoln tribes " the custom of dividing their food amongst each other is so common that he who fails to observe this rule is branded as a sort of miser." [2]

Among the Yerkla-Mining tribe, all present in camp shared equally the animal killed. The slayer had to distribute it. Women and children had also their equal share.[3]

In his book about the New South Wales aborigines, the Rev. J. B. Gribble writes : " Food is distributed on the principle of community of goods." [4]

Amongst the Port Stephens blacks each family provided for its own subsistence, "except in a general kangaroo hunt, where the game is impounded and taken in large quantities, when it is fairly distributed." [5]

Game was divided according to customary rules among the Euahlayi.[6] We are informed also of some other interesting details in this tribe : stones, used to grind seed, are kept in family possession.[7] There seems also to be a kind of harvest, and the storing up of some kinds of food is known.[8]

A series of interesting regulations as to how game is distributed among several New South Wales tribes is given by Mr. R. H. Mathews.[9]

We read in Spencer and Gillen [10] that a man shares his food with his father-in-law and other relatives. It is there explicitly stated that he shares it not only with his actual but also with his tribal relations; in another place, however, the same subject is treated as if the father-in-law in question were the actual one, not a group of them. So we read [11] that if the man or boy neglected his father-in-law the latter would take revenge at the initiation ceremony ; and that the giving of food may be considered as a form of payment for his wife.[12]

Among the Bunya people (Turrubul tribe, near Brisbane),

---

[1] Howitt, *Nat. Tr.*, p. 763.   [2] Chas. Wilhelmi, p. 192.
[3] Howitt, *Nat. Tr.*, p. 762.   [4] *Loc. cit.*, p. 117.
[5] R. Dawson, p. 327.   [6] Mrs. Parker, *loc. cit.*, p. 117.
[7] *Ibid.*   [8] *Ibid.*, p. 118.
[9] *J.R.S.N.S.W.* (1904), p. 258.   [10] *Nat. Tr.*, p. 469.
[11] *Nor. Tr.*, pp. 610, 611.   [12] Compare above, ch. ii.

the trees belonged to the people of the place. Visitors might be invited to the feast; but they " purchased bags of the seeds when they returned home." [1]

Exact rules of division of game are followed among some Queensland blacks (North-West Central), " the best part going to the father's camp, the next to the father's brother." [2] The man himself goes often very short, being with his gin quite neglected.

Among some of the West Australian tribes (Murchison District, Watchandee tribe) a very high degree of communism in food is reached among the men. If a man was unlucky at the chase he was sure to receive food in the evening at camp from all the other hunters. Was a man pre-eminently successful, he divided his booty with all his friends.[3] We find also another testimonial to the high liberality of the natives and their sense of communism, in a passage of the same writer,[4] where we are informed that a native supplied a party of white settlers with game for many days, being told that they were short of food.

Let us apply these statements in the first place to the question of the division of labour. We see that in all this evidence, the question is merely one of communism in game. With the exception, perhaps, of the summary statements of Mrs. Parker, J. B. Gribble and Wilhelmi, all the others speak clearly of communism in game only. And, on the other hand, we can conclude, as so many statements report the customary division of any large hunting products, that game was practically always divided more or less equally among those present in camp, the relatives of the hunter receiving the major part, but he himself and his wife being probably neglected.[5] The valuable statement of R. Dawson expresses this directly : in other respects each family provided for its own subsistence, but if big game were killed it became the property of the whole group. We

[1] Petrie, Howitt's *Nat. Tr.*, p. 768.
[2] Palmer, *J.A.I.*, xiii. p. 285.
[3] Oldfield, p. 271.   [4] *Ibid.*, p. 226.
[5] This communism and liberality stand in close connection with the fact that the natives did not lay in provisions. They have to partake with their neighbours of any large booty, since otherwise it would perish.

see that in all probability the results of the man's labour—the big game—did not go to the exclusive use of his family. This is stated emphatically by some authors, who say that the woman did not get even her share of the results of the man's work (Moore, Curr, Lumholtz, Oldfield). But some say, on the other hand, that both husband and wife shared equally in providing food. From several statements of the authors (Roth, Spencer and Gillen, Howitt) it must probably be assumed that the husband also gave in his share to the common household. But on summing up all the data here brought forward, it may be considered positively certain that the woman's part is of vital importance for the mainten-ance of the family, while the husband's share is quite secondary.

To sum up, it may be said that the sexual division of labour consists not only in different occupations being laid upon the man and the woman by custom. This division of labour is much deeper rooted, viz. in the fact that man's and woman's work is of quite different kind. The woman's work is on the whole much heavier than that done by the man; her work is much more regular; it is compulsory, and it forms the chief support of the household. These features of the division of labour are of great sociological importance.

1. It appears that the sexual division of labour is based only partly on differences in the natural capacities of the sexes. Heavier work ought naturally to be per-formed by men; here the contrary obtains. Only so far as the hunting is allotted to men and collecting to women, do natural gifts appear to be taken into account. But even here the woman's work appears to be much more exacting, inasmuch as it requires a steady strain, patience and regularity. Such work is the most repulsive; it differs most essentially from sport, and it is carried on only under strong compulsion. Compulsion is therefore, as we saw, the chief basis of this division of labour, and it may be said that in the Australian aboriginal society the

economic fact of division of labour is rooted in a sociological status—viz. the compulsion of the weaker sex by
the "brutal" half of society. This fact gains a deeper
and more general aspect if brought into connection
with the "terrorism produced upon women"[1] by the
members of the tribal secret society, i. e. by all the
initiated men.

2. From its compulsory character it follows that the
distribution of economic functions does not correspond
to true co-operation, but that the relation of a husband to his wife is, in its economic aspect, that of a
master to his slave.[2] And this throws also some light
on the value of a wife to a man. (Compare the statements
of Mitchell, Br. Smyth, Lumholtz.)

3. The woman's work appears as the chief basis
of the economy of the Australian household. Her work
goes exclusively towards the benefit of the individual
family, and this latter economically is entirely dependent
upon woman's work. It is her work which, taking to
itself the most considerable share in the sexual division
of labour, plays the main part in giving to the individual
family its economic unity.

There is still to be noted the statement of Roth,
who reports the existence of class taboos which establish
what we would call a division of consumption between
the father, mother and children; each of these three parties
belonging to a different class. That this statement is a
result of careful and frequent and not merely casual observation, further, that this division of consumption plays an
important part in the native family life, may be accepted
as very probable. For the author, who is undoubtedly
among our best, most exact and conscientious ethnographers, builds upon the rule in question a theory of the
origin of classes. The whole class system has been
devised by a process of natural selection, to regulate
the proper distribution of the total quantity of food

---

[1] Hutton Webster, loc. cit., pp. 99, 100 (ch. vi.).
[2] Compare Niboer, loc. cit., p. 23.

available.[1] And although we cannot enter here into the
discussion whether this view be right or not, it may serve
us as a guarantee that Roth had ascertained the great
importance of the class taboo he describes and its prevalence over a wide area. For otherwise he would not have
based such an important theory about one of the most
crucial problems of ethnology on a single fact. Besides
Roth's statement there is further the information of
Wilhelmi about division of consumption within the family.

At all events, although the evidence upon the division
of consumption is rather scanty, the evidence about the
division of labour is plentiful, and this latter may be
regarded as one of the well-established features of Australian sociology.[2] The features of communism show us
also that individual property in land has little economic
meaning. If there is game, the privilege of hunting it is
not an important one, since all members of the friendly
group will partake of the results. To what was said

[1] In a paper read before the Royal Society of Queensland,
December 11, 1897, *Proc.*, p. 10. Quoted by Frazer, *Tot. and
Exog.*, i. p. 137. Also in *Eth. Stud.*, p. 69.

[2] Prof. Durkheim has pointed out (*D. Tr. S.*, pp. 19 *sqq.*) that
the division of social functions has a most important share in
creating the unity of a given group, and amongst other things
in creating the solidarity of marriage : " C'est la division du
travail sexuel qui est la source de la solidarité conjugal " (*loc. cit.*,
p. 19). This view is fully appreciated in the present study where
the sexual division of functions is represented as being of foremost importance in defining individual family and marriage in
Australia. But Prof. Durkheim says that in low or primitive
societies division of sexual labour and conjugal solidarity are
both quite rudimentary : " plus nous remontons dans le passé,
plus elle se réduit à peu de chose " (*loc. cit.*, p. 20). The same
applies to the persistence of marriage—" la solidarité conjugale y
est même très faible " (*loc. cit.*, p. 22). If Prof. Durkheim applies
both his assertions to hypothetical prehistoric societies, then this is
not the place to discuss his views. But if he has had before his
mind actually existing primitive societies, then the evidence here
collected, on both these points, might possibly compel him to
discuss his views more in detail, as far as the Australian society
is concerned. Prof. Durkheim lays the stress of his argument
on the small sexual differentiation in respect to physiology and
anatomy of primitive and prehistoric men and women. But
sexual division of labour may have as well *social* as *physiological* sources, as shown above.

regarding the unity of the family as an exclusive land owner (above, pp. 150 *sqq.*), there is, therefore, nothing to be added.

The custom of a communistic division of game points also to the acknowledgment of family ties beyond the narrow circle of the individual family.[1] For the duty of a man in distributing the game, according to the majority of our statements (about eight in thirteen), is governed in the first place by the degree of relationship in which he stands to different people. And it is the individual, not the group relationship that is to be taken into account here. In Howitt's statements (which are the best) we see that the parents-in-law stand always in the first place. This agrees with what we read in Spencer and Gillen; and from both these statements we may conclude that these duties are a sort of continuation or equivalent of the bride-price, of which we find traces in Australia.

Let us say a few words about inheritance. As inheritance implies the existence of private property, we may look for it only where there is private property in Australia. In the first place there is " private landed property." We saw that " property " must be understood in the cases of individuals much more in a mystic, magical sense than otherwise.[2] Moreover, in the few cases where there is any mention of individual property in land, we found very little information about the principles according to which it is inherited. According to Roth, whose statement on individual proprietorship is the clearest one, we know that this individual right to land is not hereditary, but determined for magical and mystical reasons. In the other cases we are not informed at all how the individual or family comes into possession, or are informed in such an inexact way [3] that we cannot

---

[1] It will be remembered that individual family means throughout this book : husband, wife and their young children living with them.

[2] Compare above, pp. 150, 153.

[3] Compare Eyre's and Grey's statements, where heredity appears to be in the male line. Also Salvado, p. 265.

attach much value to the information.   From our best
sources (Spencer and Gillen and Roth) we know that the
ties binding an individual to a given locality are of mystical, magico-religious character, and were determined not
by heredity, but by a special principle connected with
their beliefs, and we may suppose that this was the rule,
especially as individual land ownership seems to be on the
whole more of a magico-religious than of a purely economic
order.   As to the inheritance of other property, there is
little to say about it, unimportant as it was itself.[1]
According to some writers, it passes from father to son
(*e. g.* Fraser).   Elsewhere we read that it is inherited
by certain groups of men from their common relations.[2]
On the whole, inheritance does not seem to form any
important binding element between parents and children,
either in the male or in the female line.[3]

[1] Compare Wheeler, *loc. cit.*, p. 36.
[2] Spencer and Gillen, *Nor. Tr.*, pp. 615–617.
[3] Compare also the statements collected by Wheeler on this
point, *loc. cit.*, pp. 36 *sqq.*

CHAPTER IX

SUMMARY AND CONCLUSIONS

THE aim of the foregoing pages was to give a correct description of the Australian individual family.[1] The chief practical difficulties lay in the methodological treatment of the evidence; in other words, in making the fullest possible use of the material, without inadvertently introducing conjectural elements. We established the necessity of our task by pointing out the following facts: (1) The contradictions, incompleteness and lack of precision in the descriptions of the individual family, given by field ethnographers, who sometimes even go so far as to deny the existence of this institution, such denials being based not upon observation, but upon speculative inference. (2) The discussion of the problem in question or of parts of it (marriage, relationship, descent, etc.), as usually found in ethnographical and sociological works, relates chiefly to the earlier stages of this institution, and as a rule leaves out of sight a series of important points, concerning its actual working, to draw attention to which was in part the aim of the present investigations. Now, considering that ethnological material, especially that from the Australian continent, plays a very important rôle in all general speculations on the history of marriage and the family—Australia being the best-known and the most extensive country inhabited by a very primitive race—it seemed that a careful examination of the facts of family life in Australia would be useful. (3) In the third place it appeared that a minute investigation in this direction might be interesting as an example of a correct sociological definition of the individual family in a given society. To give it, there had to

[1] *See* p. 290, note 1.

be made a careful collection and classification of material in order to show which facts play an important part in the structure and functions of this institution.

An over-hasty comparative survey of social phenomena, especially if the writer is disposed to see everywhere analogies or even identities without due criticism, too often exaggerates irrelevant features and under-rates the most essential ones in a given area. To obtain an adequate picture of any social institution, even if so well marked by many physiological facts as is the individual family, it is necessary to set forth those of its features which are characteristic in a given society. Further, it appeared necessary to point out some facts, which show that the institution of the individual family is deeply connected with a whole series of customs, beliefs and fundamental phenomena of Australian society; and that it thus appears deeply rooted in its social conditions. In other words, that the individual family is the object of a set of well-determined, categorical, collective ideas. This modest task of a correct and detailed description, made on the basis of sufficient ethnographical material, was the chief aim of the present study.

A few words may be said in the first place about the practical difficulties met with in dealing with the evidence, as foreseen and discussed in the chapter on methodology. The views there set out were, briefly, that it is impossible to use the statements in their crude form, and that consequently they must be submitted to criticism; and that it is necessary also to use caution and method in drawing inferences from the evidence. The results seem to confirm these views. So, for example, we often met with a great deal of inaccuracy—e. g. in expressions like tribe, tribal, community, group, family—and we had always to be cautious and to ascertain carefully their meaning when dealing with the aboriginal mode of living. Sometimes we were able to ascertain this real meaning; sometimes the statement was quite or nearly useless owing to complete confusion. Furthermore, all qualifying expressions referring to the treatment and behaviour of husband and wife, expressions referring to sexual morality, etc., were in the highest degree inexact. Throughout the whole study there was constant necessity for dealing critically with the text of the evidence.

In the second place we had always to analyze the information and to ask a series of definite questions of it. So, for example, in the sexual side of family life we divided our problem into three main questions, and these again into sub-headings. Again the relations between husband and wife were viewed from the legal point (authority of husband), from the psychological point (affection), and in their functional aspect (behaviour and treatment). The relations between parents and children were divided into several headings (affection, treatment, education, etc.), and so forth. On some of such particular points it has been possible to obtain quite definite answers. Where there was a hopeless contradiction, it was carefully pointed out. In the same manner a reliable but apparently singular statement was carefully noted, even if it differed from all the rest of the information. In general the chief methodic rule in utilizing the evidence was to arrange the whole argument and inferences in the clearest possible manner. To this end the number of the statements for and against any opinion was always given; the compatibility of a given inference with the well-established facts of Australian sociology was investigated; and the *experimentum crucis*, so much recommended by Steinmetz, was applied wherever possible. Attention also has been paid to the geographical point of view. Wherever it has been possible to ascertain local differences in customs, beliefs or institutions, or to show that such differences are localized in more extensive areas, care was taken to point it out. It is obviously an error to take " the Australian Aborigines " as an ethnic unit. Nevertheless many general, fundamental features of family life are undoubtedly common to all the tribes.

The individual family involves both the individual relations between husband and wife, and between parents and children.[1] These two relationships are obviously so intimately connected that the individuality of one of them has as its consequence the individuality of the other; each characteristic feature of one of them stands in a functional relation to some characteristic feature of the other. Both these relationships were studied and their mutual dependence in several respects was indicated.

A series of facts was adduced in order to prove that the individual relationship between husband and wife is unquestionably affirmed in the collective ideas of the natives. These facts, chiefly connected with the modes of obtaining wives (also with burial and mourning), implied even more detailed ideas : the affirmation that the husband has a series of individual rights and duties in regard to his wife; in other words that there is a mutual personal appropriation of husband and wife.

From some of the details as to the modes of obtaining wives the idea of individual appropriation can be clearly gathered. The family disposes of the female and benefits thereby; the disposal is effected in infancy, so it appears that the majority of females are always allotted. The individual appropriation is, so to say, a permanent status, extending not only to the married women, but to all females in the tribe. Only a man deeply in love, or impelled by some other desperate reason, attempts to elope with a female or to capture one. This always constitutes a crime, and is either punished or atoned for. Nevertheless, elopement occurs pretty often and has its fixed forms of legalization. This state of things obviously expresses the idea of individual appropriation in the strongest and most certain manner. Individual appropriation is further expressed in a whole system of ties binding the families of the two contracting parties, and especially binding the man to his (future or actual)

---

[1] In the more restricted sense used throughout this book. Extended family, *Grossfamilie*, involves more remote relationship.

parents-in-law. In this latter case the ties consist in the
first place of obligations, chiefly gifts and the duty of
supplying game. These obligations and the widespread
custom of exchange of females appear to be a rudimentary
form of marriage by purchase. Hence, again, a confirmation that individual marital rights are well known and
acknowledged. Marriage by purchase implies a fair
knowledge of individual appropriation, and shows that
it is highly valued in a given society. In Australia the
" bride money " is paid by an individual, not by a group.
We find evidence of a number of betrothal and marriage
ceremonies which carry in themselves binding powers.
Such ceremonies mean that the underlying ideas are deeply
rooted in the society where the ceremonies are found. In
this case, the underlying ideas are that man and wife
are firmly bound to each other by the ceremony. All
these facts appear very important. Not only do they
indicate that the ideas of the legality or illegality of the
marriage contract—those of personal individual appropriation and of a high value attaching to marriage rights—
exist in Australia. But it is difficult to reconcile with
them the view that individual marriage is in Australia
something new, a kind of innovation ; that it is considered
by the natives as something immoral, illicit, an encroachment of the individual on the rights of the group ; and as
something unimportant, secondary, merely temporary.
On the contrary, as we find it existing, it bears the
character of a deeply-rooted institution. All these conclusions have also been drawn independently from the
general character and several details of the mourning
customs. So that the discussion of these customs afforded
another proof that marriage ties are considered very
strong, and that the institution of marriage is the object
of definite collective ideas, consequently is firmly established in the social organization. It has a social sanction
and appears fairly permanent.

These facts suffice formally to define the individual
marriage and individual rights of the husband to his wife.

To give full context to this definition, and to characterize it more in detail, we must, on the one hand, investigate the general character of the behaviour of the consorts towards each other, and the feelings to which this behaviour points. On the other hand, an attempt must be made to determine the collective ideas expressing this relationship in its legal aspect. There have been, however, considerable difficulties in determining the emotional side of the relation between husband and wife. The results were rather negative; it appeared that we cannot accept either the extreme view of absolute bad treatment and want of affection, or the contrary opinion that the relations are of idyllic character. In general—allowing for a natural variety of feelings—the preponderance of feelings of attachment appears to be the rule. Much clearer are the results reached concerning the husband's actual rights over his wife. His authority is limited in some extreme cases only; and it is difficult to say who would interfere with it and what would be the legal form of such an interference. It may be said, therefore, that the treatment of females in Australia is determined much more by personal feelings than by legal norms, and that the latter only afford protection to the woman in cases of extreme illtreatment. In accordance with what has just been said as to personal feelings, it appears also that the treatment of women was not so exceedingly rough as is usually assumed.

The sexual rights of the husband must rather be understood in the sense that the husband is a proprietor of his wife, who may and occasionally must dispose of her; not in the sense of an inviolable exclusiveness of sexual access. The idea of chastity is absent. And consequently jealousy is not in existence in the sense in which we use that word in our society. But it exists in the form of ideas and feelings affirming the husband's definite right of control over his wife. And the natives highly disapprove of any transgression without the husband's consent and the sanction of custom. All sexual licence is regulated and subject to strict rules. Consequently the ideas on what is right or wrong in sexual matters are fairly well defined. In other words, there is a more or less defined code of sexual morality, which has also its legal aspect, as crimes against it are punished by society in a regulated manner.

In reference to the problems of individual marriage and the individual family, it may be said, however, that the individualistic character of these institutions is not accentuated in the first place by the exclusiveness of sexual rights. In connection with sexual problems an excursus on the Pirrauru customs was made, in order to prove that the relationship involved does not possess the character of marriage. For it completely differs from marriage in nearly all the essential points by which marriage in Australia is defined. And above all the Pirrauru relation does not seem to involve the facts of family life in its true sense.

In order to investigate the latter in detail on a broader basis, that is including both the relations between parents and children and between husband and wife, we entered into a discussion of the relation of the family unit to the territorial distribution of the natives. It was found that the mode of living points to a very complete isolation of each family; some of the tribes live scattered in very small groups—one to three families on an average. Other tribes live in much larger groups, but these are by no means promiscuous and undivided hordes. There are camp rules, which point to the isolation of the family within the local group; and customary rules for the arrangement of individuals within the family, round camp fires and at meals, etc. These rules and the isolation of families are reported especially from the South-Eastern tribes, where we may perhaps assume that the local groups are more numerous. So that over the whole continent the lowest unit of the tribal structure appears to be the individual family.

After a long digression on the concept of family

kinship,[1] the facts illustrating the relation between children and parents were surveyed. It was found that the characteristic features of this relationship are parental love and attachment of both father and mother to their children. The close tie between mother and child is set up by the fact of the first cares, suckling and carrying the child. The father is, as a rule, also extremely fond of his children; his relation to them is by no means characterized by any legal authority or tyrannical power, but by his affection. The father as well as the mother treat children of both sexes with extreme leniency, and give them some rudiments of education. Attention was drawn to the fact that the common attachment and extreme fondness of both parents for their children must constitute a strong bond of union between husband and wife. The family unit is nevertheless restricted to parents and children under the age of puberty. For although the ties between parents and children last throughout life, still after reaching puberty the children enter into new relationships, which superimpose themselves on the former ones. These new bonds result for the girl from marriage, for the boy from his entering into the tribal secret society (initiation and life in the bachelors' camp).

The discussion of the economic facts shows that the sexual division of labour is considerably developed; that the man's and the woman's share in the maintenance of the household is quite well defined and diverse. Further we find that the woman's work is of first-rate importance for the economic unity and subsistence of the household.

The careful survey of the facts has led to some conclusions which may be pointed out. Thus, for example, we have been driven to the conclusion that, in considering marriage, the importance of the sexual facts ought not to be exaggerated. In the majority of tribes sexual facts do not seem to play any part in the formation of bonds

---

[1] As this chapter is of a more theoretical character, it is omitted in this summary, where, on the whole, only actual facts and results are dealt with. The reader is referred to the conclusions and summaries of the said chapter (pp. 198 and 232).

of kinship. Ideas of consanguinity are absent in these tribes,[1] and herewith the sexual relations between husband and wife lose their chief influence upon the unity of the family. On the other hand, the sexual rights of the husband, although very well determined, are so often crossed by other customs that *exclusive* access to a woman must not be made a part of the sociological definition of marriage. The importance of the economic features of family life, and of the common affection for children, is much more in the foreground.

Stress has been laid throughout the investigation on the importance of bearing in mind the connection of our special problem with the general structure of society. As said above, each conclusion has been submitted to a kind of test as to whether it stands in agreement or in contradiction with well-established general facts. The main points in which the dependence of the individual family upon social facts has been traced were the connection of the individual family with the territorial and tribal structure, the mode in which land ownership in some cases distinguishes the family as a unit, the influence of economic communism upon the economics of the individual family, etc. But the manner in which society most directly influences any institution lies in the various norms, moral, customary or legal, by which society regulates different aspects of the given institution. The importance of such social rules is emphatically affirmed by Prof. Durkheim : " Une communauté de fait entre des consanguins qui se sont arrangés pour vivre ensemble, mais sans qu'aucun d'eux soit tenu à des obligations déterminées envers les autres et d'où chacun peut se retirer à volonté, ne constitue pas une famille. . . . Pour qu'il y ait famille, il n'est pas nécessaire qu'il y ait cohabitation et il n'est pas suffisant qu'il y ait consanguinité. Mais il faut de plus . . . qu'il y ait des droits et des devoirs, sanctionnés par la société, et qui unissent les members dont la famille est composée. . . . La famille

[1] Compare above, Chap. VI., esp. pp. 182, 209 *sqq.* and 226.

n'existe qu'autant qu'elle est une institution sociale, à la fois juridique et morale, placée sous la sauvegarde de la collectivité ambiante."[1] Although this opinion is certainly exaggerated,[2] it quite rightly lays stress on the importance of the social regulation of the individual family.[3]

[1] *A.S.*, i. pp. 329, 330.

[2] Because "*cohabitation*," community of life, is one of the *essential* constituents of the family. Besides, there cannot exist a " communauté de fait "; a social group cannot exist without the sanction of the surrounding society, and this creates obligations between the members of the group.

[3] We obviously cannot agree with Prof. Durkheim when he says further (*loc. cit.*, p. 331), speaking of the Australian family : " Ce sont des associations de fait, non de droit. Elles dépendent du gré des particuliers, se forment comme elles veulent, sans être tenues de s'astreindre à aucune norme préalable." The Australian family is not a casual but a legal association, for it does not depend upon the whim of individuals; neither is it formed when and how they choose. There are norms governing its formation, duties and obligations while it lasts, and even afterwards when it has been dissolved by a natural cause, such as the death of the husband. All these norms, duties and obligations are legal (compare the definition of legal, p. 11), for non-compliance with them leads to the interference of society; and they directly show that society approves of this institution. The reasoning of Prof. Durkheim—who enumerates four domestic rights and obligations (vendette, law of inheritance, name and cult), and says that those four functions are attached to the *clan*—is open to very serious objections. In the first place it is dubious whether those four duties constitute the main body of primitive domestic law. The economic functions, the duties and rules of cohabitation, the various duties towards children, the mourning duties of religious character—all these legal functions, which are domestic rights and obligations even in our society, were shown to exist in Australia. They belong to the family and not to the clan. On the other hand, when revenge is to be taken on members of another local group, then it is the local group offended which carries it out. The cases of inter-group justice are very few, for evil magic is always looked for at a distance, and we have hardly any information about justice within the local group. (For all particulars compare Wheeler, chap. viii. pp. 116 *sqq*.) It is not the clan, but the local group about which we know most in this respect. Inheritance, owing to the unimportance of private property (compare Wheeler, p. 36) plays a very subordinate rôle. From the six instances collected by Wheeler (pp. 37, 38), three point to inheritance according to class, three to inheritance according to family. Land was not a clan property, as we saw. There remains of Prof. Durkheim's legal customs the name and the cult. Cult may be obviously as well a public as a domestic institution; the name is not enough to show that the clan was the only legal form of family.

The importance of such norms, and especially of the legal ones, clearly appeared in the foregoing investigation. In order adequately to discuss this matter, the exact sense in which the concepts of *law* and *legal* may be used was defined, and the legal organization in Australia was sketched. Furthermore, in all the questions discussed we have tried to ascertain whether there are any norms sanctioned by society, and what form this social enforcement assumes in any given case. And here it appears that nearly all sides of family life, far from being left to follow their own course, are more or less subject to definite norms of moral, customary or legal character. It was possible to establish beyond doubt the legal aspect of marriage by analyzing the modes of contracting marriage, and the duties of the widow, as shown in the mourning ceremonies. The relation between husband and wife, although characterized by a very extensive authority of the former, has nevertheless its legal basis. For the husband's authority is limited to a certain extent by exterior factors (tribal government, woman's kin) and must conform to certain norms (he has the right to punish her for certain crimes in a definite way); and he acquires his authority in a legal way (by a legal marriage contract). Sexual matters in general, and the sexual rights of the husband are well defined and regulated. Customary (or legal) rules govern the mode of living of a family, the distribution of food within the family, the sexual division of labour. The relation between parents and children, and especially the paternal authority, hardly presented any legal aspect. But on the whole it appears perfectly legitimate and necessary to define the individual family in Australia as a legal one, inasmuch as very many aspects of this institution are subject to legal norms. And, it would be completely erroneous to call, with Prof. Durkheim, these units " agrégat de fait, sans liens de droit, désapprouvé même le plus souvent par la loi et par l'opinion." [1]

There is yet another point in Australian sociology most

_____
[1] *A.S.*, i. p. 330.

intimately connected with the individual family. I mean the other forms of kinship organization : the exogamy class, the totemic clan, possibly also the other divisions reported by Mr. R. H. Mathews and Mrs. Parker (" blood " and " shed " divisions, etc.). And on this point the present study is obviously incomplete, as it neither clearly fixes the line of demarcation between the individual and the group kinship, nor solves any of the difficulties and contradictions indicated at the outset. A few words must be said here in order to avoid misunderstandings. If in any society there exist two institutions of very close resemblance, as in Australia, the individual family creating individual relationship and the various kinship organizations creating group relationship, the only way to understand their working is by describing minutely the social functions of each of them. This has been done for the individual family in the foregoing pages ; it remains to be done for the kinship groups.[1]

Social institutions should in the first place be defined by their social functions; if the functions—religious, magical, legal, economic, etc.—of the totemic class, the exogamous class, and other divisions be known and compared with the functions of the individual family, each of these institutions will appear as occupying a definite place in the social organization, and playing a determinate part in the life of the community. And such a knowledge would afford a firm basis for further speculations.

In the foregoing investigations we have omitted this side of the problem partly in order to avoid increasing the bulk of the monograph, but above all, that we might develop more clearly the features of the institution described.

The individual family was shown to be a unit playing an important part in the social life of the natives

[1] The writer hopes to return to this subject on another occasion. The material for the description of *social functions* of the exogamous class and totemic clan is comparatively scanty, although so much has been written on this subject.

and well defined by a number of moral, customary and legal norms; it is further determined by the sexual division of labour, the aboriginal mode of living, and especially by the intimate relation between the parents and children. The individual relation between husband and wife (marriage) is rooted in the unity of the family. Moreover, it is expressed by a series of facts connected with the modes in which marriage is brought about and in the well-defined, although not always exclusive, sexual right the husband acquires over his wife.

ADDENDA

Several points omitted in the body of this book, as well as a few works and passages of special importance, which I noted whilst reading the proofs, may be mentioned shortly in this place. I read the book of Mr. Crawley (*Mystic Rose*) unfortunately after the foregoing pages were in type; my study would have been more complete had I known it before. Mr. Crawley analyzes the psychology underlying human relations (those of sex in particular) from their religious side. Primitive man is full of apprehension of the mutual danger inherent in social and especially in sexual contact. Hence the different systems of *taboo;* the sexual taboo being one of the most important. To establish harmless relations between people of different sexes requires a system of *breaking the taboo*.

The ceremonies and rites of marriage are treated in the *Mystic Rose* from this point of view (removal of taboo). In my opinion this book is of great sociological importance chiefly because it shows that the sexual act must be treated in its bearing upon social forms, not as a simple physiological fact, but as a phenomenon complex both in its sociological and psychological aspects. For " savages " in particular it is surrounded by a network of magico-religious ideas, apprehensions and emotions, resulting in a system of rites, customs and institutions, which never can be comprehended without reference to the underlying psychology. It follows as an important consequence that everything connected with matters of sex is an object of well-defined rules and laws (compare the passage above, p. 123, where the same has been pointed out with reference to the Australians).

Another important result of Mr. Crawley's work is the establishment of the principle that marriage rites, being the breaking of a dangerous taboo, are an essential part of marriage, and therefore their study is essential for the understanding of this institution. The rites, being exclusively intended to break the taboo between two individuals and not between two groups, lead to individual marriage and family, and not to " group marriage " and " group family."

Mr. Crawley's book is full of valuable remarks, some of which must be quoted in the following paragraphs. I complete also the information on several points by the addition of statements from Mr. Roth's *North Queensland Ethnography* (*Bull.* 9 *sqq.*), which I have only recently been able to peruse.

Pp. 27–29. *Methodic presentation of evidence.* As in summing up the evidence the number of statements supporting one view or another has been adduced sometimes by way of illustration, it is necessary to say explicitly what is considered to be a *unit of information* (or an *individual statement*). I consider as independent statements : (1) Observations of different ethnographers. (2) Observations of the same author made on different tribes, provided that the author has pointed out the differences and that they are substantial enough. It seems hardly necessary to emphasize that the numeric treatment of statements has no pretentions to be a " statistic method of presenting evidence." It is meant only as a convenient and clear way of summarizing evidence.

P. 35 and Chap. VII. *passim. Mystic.* By this word I understand belonging to the category of magico-religious ideas.

P. 42. *The marriage ceremonies of the Central and Northern tribes, religious and magical.* Compare Crawley (*M.R.*, p. 347).

P. 48. *Betrothal* is prevalent all over the tribes of North Queensland (Roth, *Bull.* 10, pp. 3–7, §§ 6–14). Among the tribes of Pennefather River (§ 6) it is effected during the infancy of the female and it is invariably adhered to. In the hinterland of Princess Charlotte Bay the bridegroom has to visit his fiancée before marriage for several weeks (§ 7). Infant betrothal is rare among the natives of Cape Bedford (§ 8). On the Bloomfield River female children are betrothed at birth (§ 10). Infant betrothal obtains also among the Cape Grafton and Tully River natives (§§ 11, 12). A betrothal ceremony (recalling that of the Euahlayi tribe, see above, p. 40) held when a girl is about three years old is described with reference to the Torilla and Pine Mountain Blacks (§ 13). There are an elaborate ceremonial, taboos and duties connected with betrothal in all these tribes. In the North-West tribes betrothal is generally known (§ 14).

Pp. 50–52. *Marriage gifts.* In the Pennefather River tribes a man is bound to supply his fiancée's parents with gifts (food, arms, etc.) (*Bull.* 10, § 6). Presents form an important feature of the marriage contract among the natives of Princess Charlotte Bay (*ibid.*, § 7). The same is reported about the tribes of Normanby River (§ 9), Bloomfield River (§ 10), Torilla and Pine Mountain (§ 12).

P. 52. *Publicity of marriage and betrothal* is mentioned by Roth among the natives of Pennefather River (*Bull.* 10, § 6) and Bloomfield River (§ 10). There is a public ceremonial sign for marriage (" building of a hut and lighting of a fire " by the girl) common to all tribes (§ 5).

P. 52. *Marriage ceremonies more prevalent than appears from evidence.* To corroborate my supposition that marriage ceremonies are much more frequent in Australia than stated by the authorities I may quote Mr. Crawley's view. He says that " as to those (peoples) who are said to possess no marriage ceremony, it will generally be found that there is some act performed which is too slight or too practical to be marked by an observer as a ' ceremony,' but which when analyzed turns out to be a real marriage rite." And as an example the author quotes two forms of marriage ceremony among the tribes of Central Australia (*Mystic Rose*, p. 318).

Pp. 52, 53. *Marriage ceremonies* are reported by Roth with

reference to all tribes of Northern Queensland (*Bull.* 10, "Marriage Ceremonies," etc., especially §§ 1–19). In § 5 a public ceremonial sign of marriage common to all these tribes is described; in §§ 9, 13 and 15, such ceremonies in different tribes are given with details. Ceremonial sexual intercourse with other men before marriage is mentioned in § 20.

Pp. 56–58. *Legal aspect of marriage.* The different social conditions enumerated by Roth (*Bull.* 10, §§ 1, 2 and 3) are a valuable addition to our knowledge of the legal aspect of marriage. "Essentials of marriage before it can be publicly recognized" are : membership in suitable exogamous groups, absence of intimate consanguinity and a suitable social status. If these conditions are not fulfilled the community either violently break the match, or by ridicule, plots, etc., will take an action "usually quite sufficient to cause a separation " (§ 1, p. 2).

P. 61. *Ideas embodied in marriage ceremonies.* In the survey of various marriage ceremonies Mr. Crawley first enumerates those in which the aspect of *breaking the taboo,* of securing immunity from danger, dominates (*M.R.*, pp. 322–370); then come those in which the magical and religious elements " actually and materially uniting the man and woman" are prominent (*loc. cit.*, pp. 370–390). This aspect corresponds to what I have expressed above emphasizing that marriage is a "sacrament" (p. 61). Very important is the analogy between marriage rites and love charms which Mr. Crawley points out; the same has been said above (p. 41), where it was pointed out that the Arunta love charm has its legal (=binding) aspect. Mr. Crawley lays emphasis on the fact that all marriage ceremonies and rites possess an *individualistic* character (*loc. cit.*, pp. 320 *sqq.*). They refer always to individuals and not to groups, and all their magical, religious (I would add *legal*) consequences refer to the two individuals concerned and not to two groups.

P. 63. *Polygyny.* Although this fact had no special theoretical bearing in any of my arguments, still it seems advisable to state it here explicitly and with references for the sake of completeness. Polygyny seems to be restricted to the old and influential men, and to be rather an exception, although it seems to be found in all tribes. *Cf.* Curr, *A.R.*, i. pp. 106, 107, 110 *sqq.*; Br. Smyth, ii. p. 291; Howitt, *T.R.S.V.*, p. 115; Woods, p. 191 (Meyer), and p. 222 (Schürmann); Angas, ii. p. 222; Curr, *Recollections*, p. 129; Wilson, p. 143; Macgillivray, i. p. 151. *Idem*, ii. p. 8; Hodgkinson, p. 230; Bennett, p. 173; Henderson, p. 110; Roth, *Bull.* 10, p. 12; Tom Petrie, p. 61; Brown, p. 450; Salvado, p. 278. Compare besides Westermarck, *H.H.M.*, p. 440, and the references given there.

Pp. 63, 64: *Levirate. Cf.* Westermarck, *H.H.M.*, p. 510, for Australian references and for the exposition and criticism of different theories concerning this custom.

Pp. 64–66. *Divorce* is mentioned by Roth (*Bull.* 10, pp. 11, 12). Usually the man repudiates or gives away his wife.

Pp. 82–84. *Marital affection.* Mutual attachment and love between man and wife is stated explicitly by Roth (*Bull.* 10, § 17). It plays an important part in marriage arrangements (marriage by elopement). That love must be prevalent among the Australian savages is shown also by the different love charms they possess. (Compare, for instance, above, p. 41, footnote 9).—Compare Westermarck, *H.H.M.*, p. 359, where Australian references are given, and Chap. XVI. pp. 356 *sqq.*, where the problem in general is discussed.

Pp. 84–88. *Mourning and burial.* In Roth, *Bull.* 9, pp. 366, 367, we read that only after the elaborate mourning and burial ceremonies have been finished and the dead man's spirit appeased and got rid of, is the widow allowed to remarry. On pp. 394, 396 and 402, we read that the widow and widower have the greatest share in these ceremonies. P. 381 recounts the severe ordeals that a widow and widower have to undergo. Unfortunately it it impossible to enter here into the many details given by Roth which strongly confirm the views expressed above, in Chap. III. From the description of mourning and burial customs among some tribes of New South Wales, given by Mr. R. H. Mathews, it appears that the widow has long and toilsome mourning duties; she is specially adorned, she may not go out hunting, and has to chant customary lamentation for several months (*Eth. Notes*, pp. 71, 72).

P. 93, footnote 4 and p. 107. *Incest.* Roth affirms that incest is absolutely never perpetrated in the North Queensland tribes (*Bull.* 10, pp. 2, 3).

Pp. 108–123. *Pirrauru not a group marriage.* Mr. A. Lang gives an excellent criticism of the view that *Pirrauru* is a survival of ancient promiscuity. Still less tenable, of course, is the view that it is actual group marriage. Lang, *The Secret of the Totem*, Chap. III.—A similar view has been expounded by Mr. Crawley, *loc. cit.*, pp. 475–483.

Pp. 168 *sqq. Necessity of adapting sociological concepts to the social and psychological conditions of the given society.* "It is only in early modes of thought that we can find the explanation of ceremonies and systems which originated in primitive society; and, if ceremony and system are the concrete forms in which human relations are expressed, an examination, ethnological and psychological, of human relations is indispensable for inquiry into human institutions." And, speaking of some previous inquiries into human kinship, the same author adds : "They have interpreted primitive custom by ideas which are far from primitive, which, in fact, are relatively late and belong to the legal stage of human culture. The attribution of legal conceptions to primitive thought has had the usual effect of *a priori* theory, and has checked inquiry " (Crawley, *loc. cit.*, p. 1). The second phrase covers in particular the views expounded above, pp.185 *sqq.*

P. 170. *Social factors of kinship.* "Habitual proximity and contact is the strongest and most ordinary tie, and is earlier in thought than the tie of blood " (Crawley, *loc. cit.*, p. 452).

P. 175. *Collective mind.* This expression does not postulate the existence of any metaphysical entity—any mysterious spiritual medium, independent of any human brains. Of course every psychological process takes place in an individual mind. This term is an abbreviation for denoting the *ensemble* of " collective

ideas " and " collective feelings." And by these are expressed
such mental facts as are peculiar to a certain society, and at the
same time embodied in and expressed by its institutions. For
sociological purposes psychological facts must be treated from a
special point of view, and, to emphasize *that*, the adjective " collective " seems appropriate. Compare p. 192, footnote 1.

Pp. 179–182. *Absence of social consanguinity in primitive
societies.* " The strong conception of the tie of blood, best seen in
feudal and semi-civilized societies, is by no means so strong in
primitive culture " (Crawley, *loc. cit.*, p. 451).

P. 183. *The meaning of " kinship " ought not to be restricted
to any special set of ideas.* " ' Kinship ' in primitive thought is
a vaguer term than in later culture . . . because the tie of
blood had not attained prominence over looser ties of contact "
(Crawley, *loc. cit.*, p. 451).

Pp. 183, 184. *Couvade.* An extensive bibliography on this
subject is forthcoming in *Zeitschr f. Ethnol.* Band 43. Heft iii.
and iv., pp. 560–63. Berlin, 1911.

Pp. 260–262. *Young females monopolized by old men.* Besides
the statements set forth in the text, I find three more collected
by Prof. Webster referring to the Queenslanders (Lumholtz),
to the West Australians (Frogatt), and to the Australians in
general (J. Matthew) (*loc. cit.*, pp. 70, 71). Among the tribes of
Northern Queensland infant betrothal widely prevails; " the old
men usually getting the pick " (Roth, *Bull.* 10, pp. 3–7).

Pp. 262 *sqq.* The *bachelors' camp* is mentioned by Roth
(*Bull.* 10, p. 4).

Pp. 272, 273. *Relations between brothers and sisters.* Mr. Crawley
has shown that avoidance between brother and sister, rooted in
apprehensions of mutual danger is the rule among savages.
This is corrobated by the scanty Australian evidence we possess.
(See *M.R., passim ;* for references see Index under " Brother and
Sister ").

Pp. 283–286. *Communism in food.* An interesting statement
of an old explorer concerning the aboriginal communism in food
may be adduced here. It refers to the North-Western blacks.
" Be it little or much that they get, every one has his part, as well
the young and tender as the old and feeble, who are not able to
go abroad, as the strong and lusty " (Dampier, *loc. cit.*, p. 103).

References and Reading List

BARNES, J. A. 1961. "Physical and Social Kinship." *Philosophy of Science* 28 : 296-298.

BERNDT, R. M. 1957. "In Reply to Radcliffe-Brown on Australian Local Organization." *American Anthropologist* 59 : 346-351.

—— 1959. "The Concept of 'The Tribe' in the Western Desert of Australia." *Oceania* 30 : 81-107.

BERNDT, R. M., and BERNDT, C. H. 1942-1945. "A Preliminary Report of Field-work in the Ooldea Region, Western South Australia." *Oceania* (reprinted). 343 pp.

—— 1951. "Sexual Behavior in Western Arnhem Land." New York; Viking Fund. 247 pp. *Viking Fund Publications in Anthropology* 16.

BOAS, F. 1896. "The Limitations of the Comparative Method of Anthropology." Reprinted in 1940. *Race, Language and Culture.* New York; Macmillan. Pp. 270-280.

DURKHEIM, EMILE. 1947. *The Division of Labor in Society.* G. Simpson, trans. Glencoe, Ill.; Free Press. [1st ed., 1893].

—— 1915. *The Elementary Forms of the Religious Life.* J. W. Swain, trans. London; Allen and Unwin. [1st ed., 1912].

ELKIN, A. P. 1951. "Reaction and Interaction: a Food Gathering People and European Settlement in Australia." *American Anthropologist* 53 : 164-186.

—— 1954. *The Australian Aborigines: How to Understand Them.* 3rd ed. Sydney; Angus and Robertson.

FALKENBERG, J. 1962. *Kin and Totem: Group Relations of Australian Aborigines in the Port Keats District.* Oslo; Oslo University Press.

FIRTH, R., ed. 1957. *Man and Culture: An Evaluation of the Work of Bronislaw Malinowski.* London; Routledge and Kegan Paul.

FORTES, M. 1957. "Malinowski and the Study of Kinship." In Firth, R., ed. *Man and Culture.* Pp. 157-188.

FRAZER, J. G. 1911-1915. *The Golden Bough.* 3rd ed. London; Macmillan. 12 vols. [1st ed., 1890].

FREUD, S. 1938. *Totem and Taboo.* London; Penguin Books. [1st ed., 1913].

GLUCKMAN, M. 1949. "An Analysis of the Sociological Theories of Bronislaw Malinowski." Cape Town; Oxford University Press. 28 pp. *Rhodes-Livingstone Papers* 16.

HART, C. W. M. 1955. "Contrasts Between Prepubertal and Postpubertal Education." In Spindler, G. D., ed. *Education and Anthropology.* Stanford; Stanford University Press. Pp. 127-145.

HART, C.W. M., and PILLING, A. R. 1960. *The Tiwi of North Austra-lia.* New York; Holt.

HIATT, L. R. 1959. "Social Control in Central Arnhem Land." *South Pacific* 10 : 182-192.

—— 1962. "Local Organization in Australia." *Oceania* 32.

KABERRY, P. M. 1939. *Aboriginal Woman, Sacred and Profane.* London; Routledge.

LASSWELL, H. 1931. "A Hypothesis Rooted in the Preconceptions of a Single Civilization Tested by Bronislaw Malinowski." In Rice, Stuart A., ed. *Methods in Social Science.* Chicago; Chicago University Press. Pp. 480-488.

LEACH, E. R. 1961. *Rethinking Anthropology.* London; Athlone Press. *London School of Economics Monographs on Social Anthropology* 22.

LÉVI-STRAUSS, C. 1949. *Les structures élémentaires de la parenté.* Paris; Presses Universitaires de France.

McCARTHY, F. D., and McARTHUR, M. 1960. "The Food Quest and the Time Factor in Aboriginal Economic Life." In *American-Australian Scientific Expedition to Arnhem Land.* Records. Vol. 2. Mountford, C. P., ed. Melbourne; Melbourne University Press. Pp. 145-194.

McCONNEL, U. 1957. *Myths of the Munkan.* Melbourne; Melbourne University Press.

MALINOWSKI, B. 1912. "The Economic Aspect of the Intichiuma Ceremonies." In *Festskrift Tillegnad Edvard Westermarck.* Helsingfors. Pp. 81-108.

—— 1913. Review. Durkheim. *Les Formes Elémentaires de la Vie Religieuse.* Folklore 24 : 525-531.

—— 1930. "Kinship." *Man* 30 : 19-29. Art. 17.

—— 1937. Foreword. In Montagu, M. F., Ashley-, *Coming into Being among the Australian Aborigines.* Pp. xix-xxxv.

MEGGITT, M. J. In press. *Desert People.* Sydney; Angus and Robertson.

MORGAN, L. H. *Ancient Society.* Chicago; Kerr. [1st ed., 1877].

MONTAGU, M. F. Ashley-. 1937. *Coming into Being among the Australian Aborigines: A Study of the Procreative Beliefs of the Native Tribes of Australia.* London; Routledge.

RADCLIFFE-BROWN, A. R. 1914. Review: Malinowski, *The Family among the Australian Aborigines.* Man 14 : 31-32. Art. 16.

—— 1930-1931. "The Social Organization of Australian Tribes." *Oceania* 1 : 34-63, 206-246, 322-341, 426-456.

ROSE, F. G. G. 1960. "The Australian Aboriginal Family: Some Theoretical Considerations." In *Forschen und Wirken:* Festschrift zur 150-Jahr-Feier der Humboldt-Universität zu Berlin. Berlin; VEB Deutscher Verlag der Wissenschaften. Band III. Pp. 415-437.

—— 1960. *Classification of Kin, Age Structure and Marriage amongst the Groote Eylandt Aborigines: A Study in Method and a Theory of Australian Kinship.* Berlin; Akademie-Verlag. Deutsche Akademie der Wissenschaften zu Berlin, Völkerkundliche Forschungen, Band 3.

SCHAPERA, I. 1957. "Malinowski's Theories of Law." In Firth, R., ed. *Man and Culture.* Pp. 139-155.

STANNER, W. E. H. 1956. "The Dreaming." In Hungerford, T. G., ed. *Australian Signpost*. Melbourne; Cheshire. Pp. 51-65.

—— 1959-1962. "On Aboriginal Religion." *Oceania* 30-32.

—— 1960. "Durmugam, a Nangiomeri." In Casagrande, J. E., ed. *In the Company of Man*. New York; Harper. Pp. 63-100.

STEWARD, J. H. 1955. *Theory of Culture Change: The Methodology of Multilinear Evolution*. Urbana; University of Illinois Press.

THOMSON, D. F. 1949. *Economic Structure and the Ceremonial Exchange Cycle in Arnhem Land*. Melbourne; Macmillan.

WARNER, W. L. 1958. *A Black Civilization: A Social Study of an Australian Tribe*. Rev. ed. New York; Harper.

WESTERMARCK, E. 1921. *The History of Human Marriage*. London; Macmillan. 3 vols. [1st ed., 1891].

INDEX